kare kano

his and her circumstances

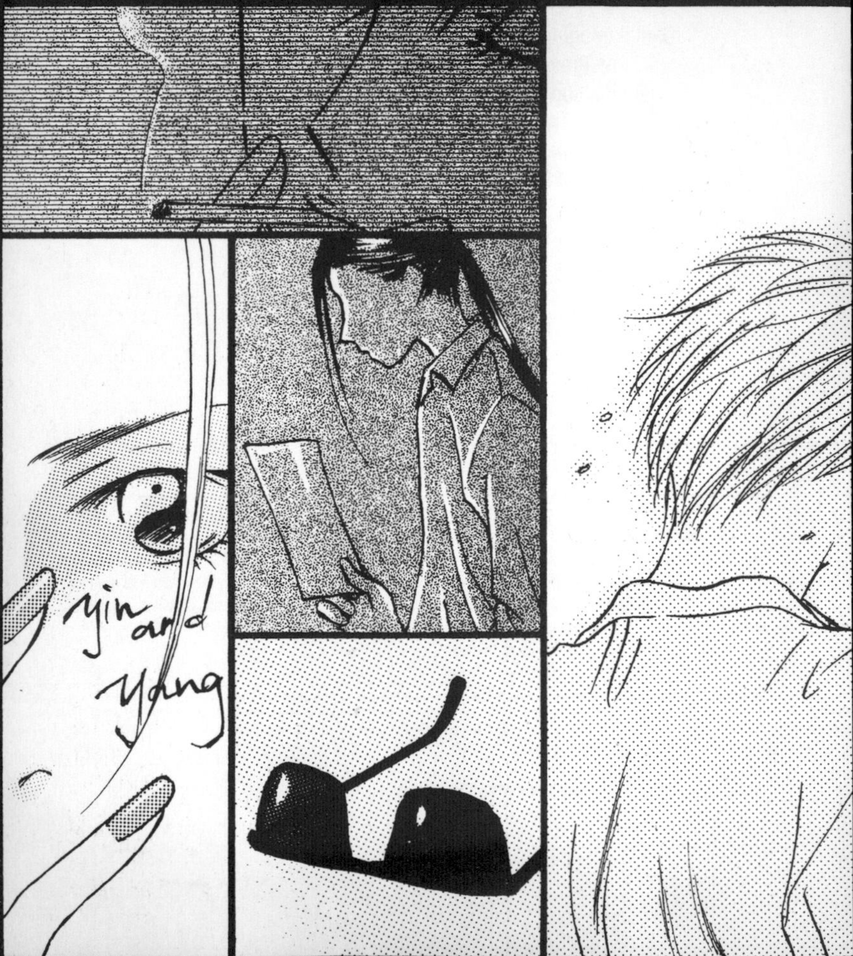
Yin and Yang

Kare Kano Vol. 12
Created by Masami Tsuda

Translation - Michelle Kobayashi
Additional Translation - Chrissy Schilling
Retouch and Lettering - Norine Lukaczyk
Graphic Designer - Vicente Rivera, Jr.
Cover Design - Gary Shum

Editor - Jake Forbes
Digital Imaging Manager - Chris Buford
Pre-Press Manager - Antonio DePietro
Production Managers - Jennifer Miller and Mutsumi Miyazaki
Art Director - Matt Alford
Managing Editor - Jill Freshney
VP of Production - Ron Klamert
President and C.O.O. - John Parker
Publisher and C.E.O. - Stuart Levy

A  Manga

TOKYOPOP Inc.
5900 Wilshire Blvd. Suite 2000
Los Angeles, CA 90036

E-mail: info@TOKYOPOP.com
Come visit us online at www.TOKYOPOP.com

ISBN: 1-59182-477-x

First TOKYOPOP printing: November 2004
10 9 8 7 6 5 4 3 2 1
Printed in the USA

kare kano

his and her circumstances

volume twelve

by Masami Tsuda

HAMBURG // LONDON // LOS ANGELES // TOKYO

Exclusive interview with the new sibling of Yin and Yang's vocalist!

Kare Kano Beat: What did you think when you found out you were going to get a new brother?

Tsubasa Shibahime: I was so mad! I couldn't believe dad was going to remarry. I guess I was a little jealous.

KB: What was your first impression of Kazuma?

TS: When I first heard he was in a band, I totally thought he'd be this jerky rock star wannabe. After I saw his bleached hair and jewelry, I thought, "Who does this guy think he is?!" But then once I got to know him, I realized how wrong my first impression was. He's so sweet! I love him to death! He's SO much cooler than Arima-kun (and that's saying a lot).

KB: You seem to really like your new brother. Is there something going on between you two?

TS: Hey, mind your own business!

Yin and Yang's Original Fab Four

© Masami Tsuda

MARTIN *(Drums)*
Once on stage, this dumpy four-eyes becomes a drop-dead gorgeous drummer in a style reminiscent of his "Visual Kei" days. He's #1 with the fans.

© Masami Tsuda

JOKER *(Keyboard)*
The keyboardist in Yin and Yang. He also works as a bartender at the establishment where Kazuma is a waiter.

© Masami Tsuda

ATSUYA *(Guitar)*
The beer-happy guitarist of Yin and Yang. He can be a goof but he's very dedicated to the band.

© Masami Tsuda

USHIO *(Bass Guitar)*
The band's leader, it was Ushio who first suggested Kazuma join.

Yukino and Arima: Where are they Now?

Regular readers of *Kare Kano* are probably wondering what happened to the over-achieving stars of the series, Yukino and Arima. In volumes 11 and 12, Tsuda-sensei will be giving the leads some well-deserved time out of the spotlight, but fear not—they'll be back in full force (with some shocking new developments in their relationship) in *Kare Kano* 13.

Kare Kano Beat Profile
Yin and Yang's Kazum

By Jake Forbes
TOKYOPOP Editor

Darlings of the Indie Rock scene **Yin and Yang** are breaking out in a big way! Fans love them for their infectious lyrics and catchy rhythms, but the band members themselves are shrouded in mystery. Just who are Yin and Yang? *Kare Kano Beat* got the scoop on these elusive pop stars in the making.

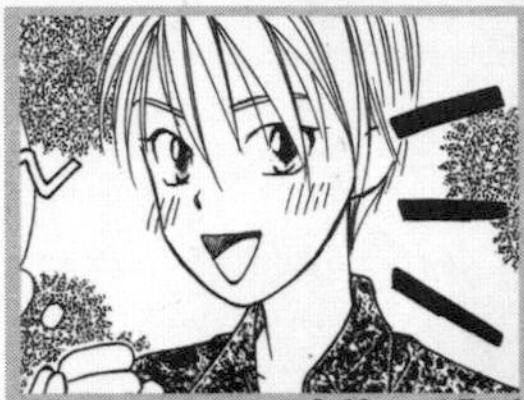

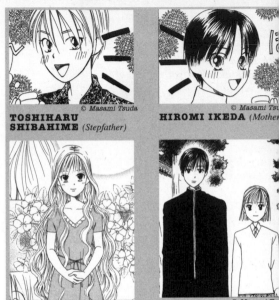

© Masami Tsuda

TOSHIHARU SHIBAHIME *(Stepfather)*

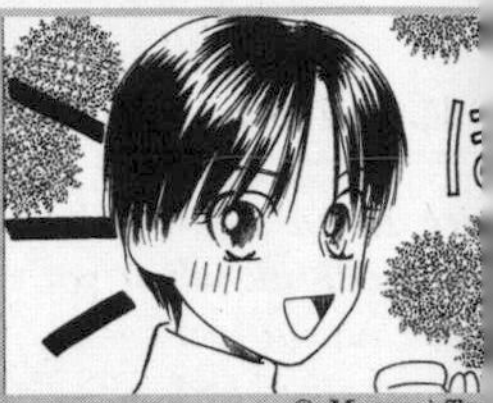

© Masami Tsu

HIROMI IKEDA *(Mother*

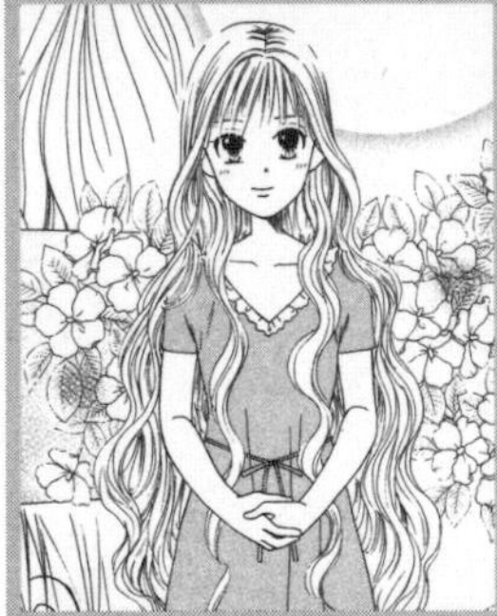

© Masami Tsuda

TSUBASA SHIBAHIME *(Stepsister)*

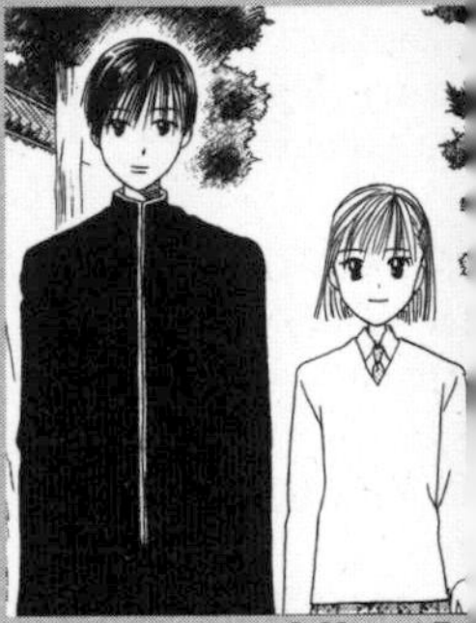

© Masami Ts

SOICHIRO ARIMA *(Classmate)*

YUKINO MIYAZA *(Classmate)*

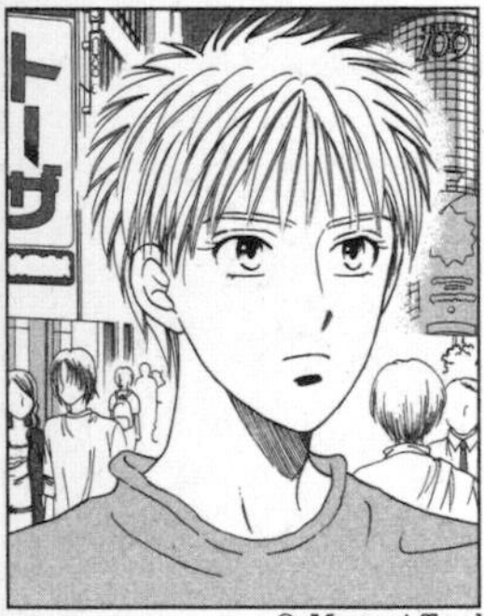

© Masami Tsuda

KAZUMA SHIBAHIME
(Vocals)

This bleach blond *bishi* is Yin and Yang's newest member, but he's also the most controversial. Not everyone was happy when the group started having a high school student fill in for the former front man, but the 16-year-old Kazuma persevered. Now he has almost as many female fans as Martin!

Kazuma's home life has been going through a lot of changes, too. Back in volume 5, his mother, a nurse, married noted youth fashion designer Toshiharu Shibahime. As an added bonus, Kazuma also scored a *kawaii* new sister. But don't let Tsubasa-chan's petite stature fool you—this cutie is actually a little *older* than Kazuma!

In volume 8, Kazu transferred to his stepsiste school. At first, sources s the siblings' classmates w worried that Soichiro Ari who always conside Tsubasa as something a little sister, would animosity toward the n guy. But when the s spoken Arima first laid e on Kazuma, he positiv melted. (If only Tsub could have shown s maturity when she fo out that Arima was dat Yukino Miyazawa...)

kare kano
volume twelve

TABLE OF CONTENTS

....

....

kare kano

his and her circumstances

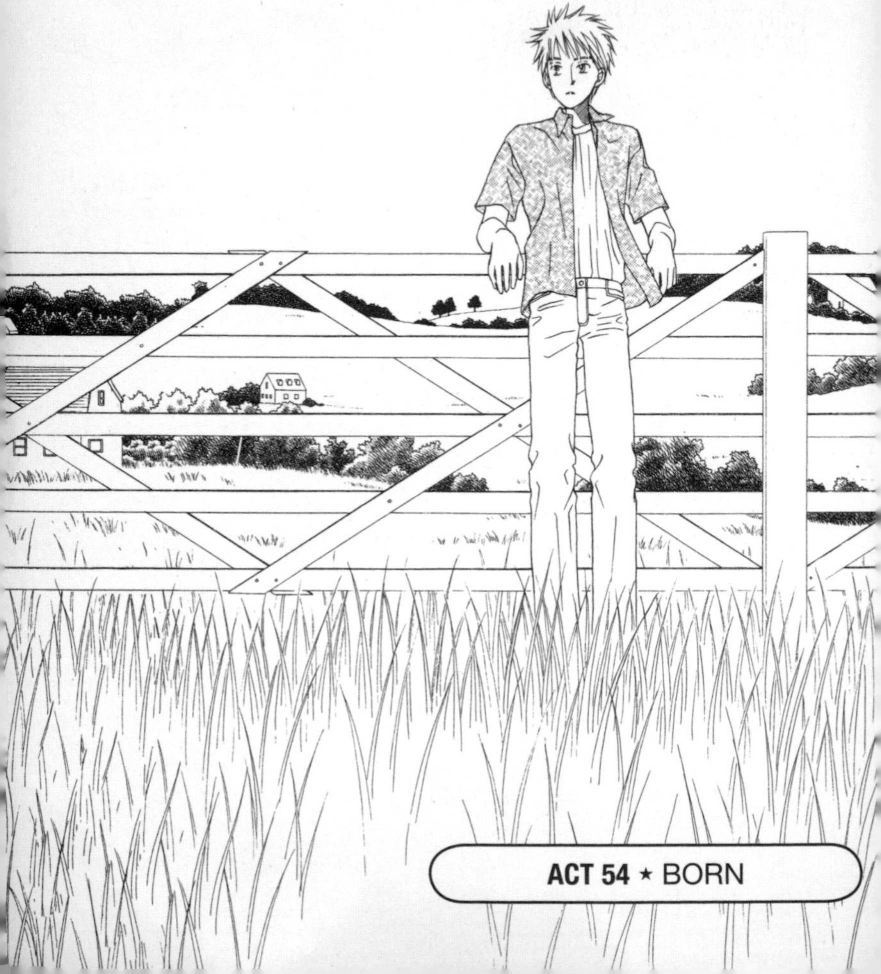
ACT 54 ★ BORN

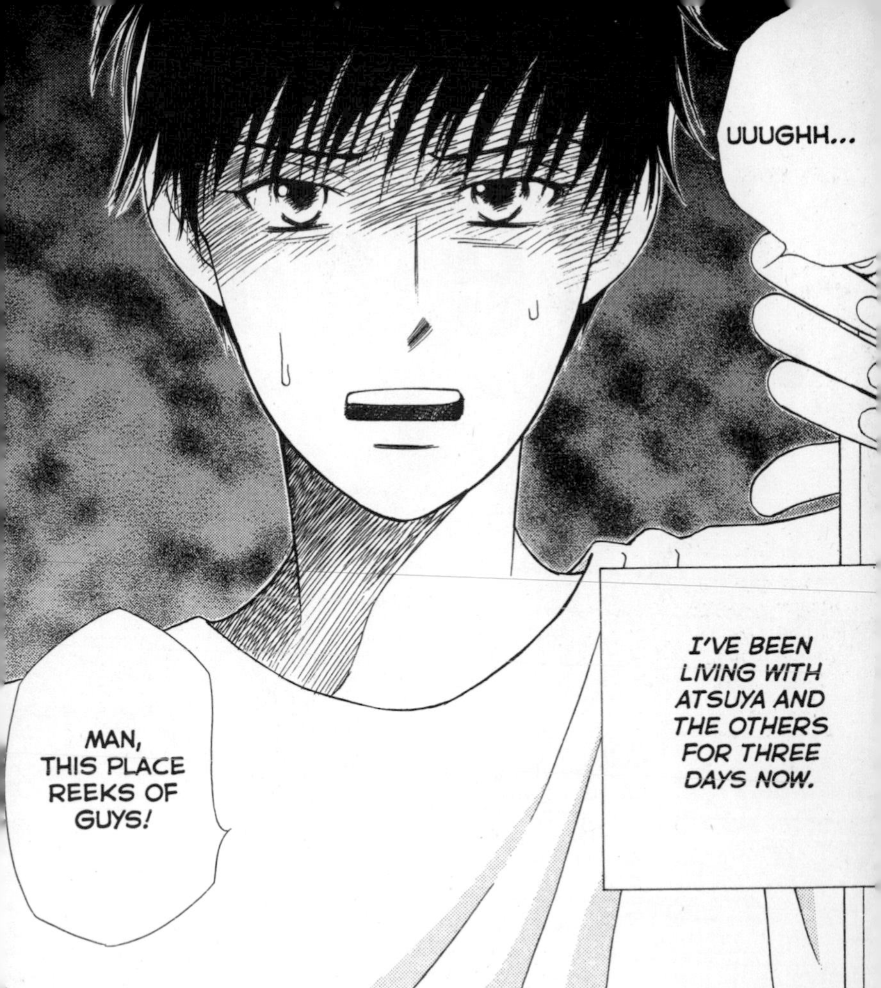
UUUGHH...
I'VE BEEN LIVING WITH ATSUYA AND THE OTHERS FOR THREE DAYS NOW.
MAN, THIS PLACE REEKS OF GUYS!

I love sweets that are lightly fried, like financiers—those French cakes. The treat I got from a fan at the autograph session in Taiwan was REALLY good! I'm going to buy some more the next time I go there!

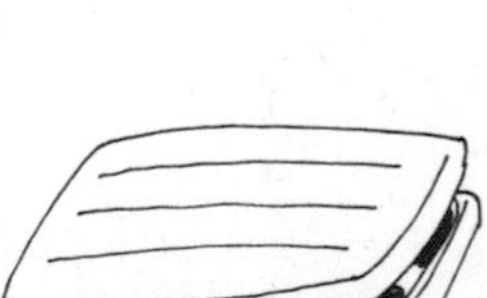

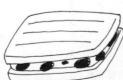

Raisinwich

This is my favorite treat.

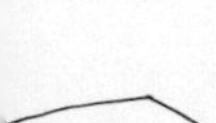

here was pineapple inside a cookie.

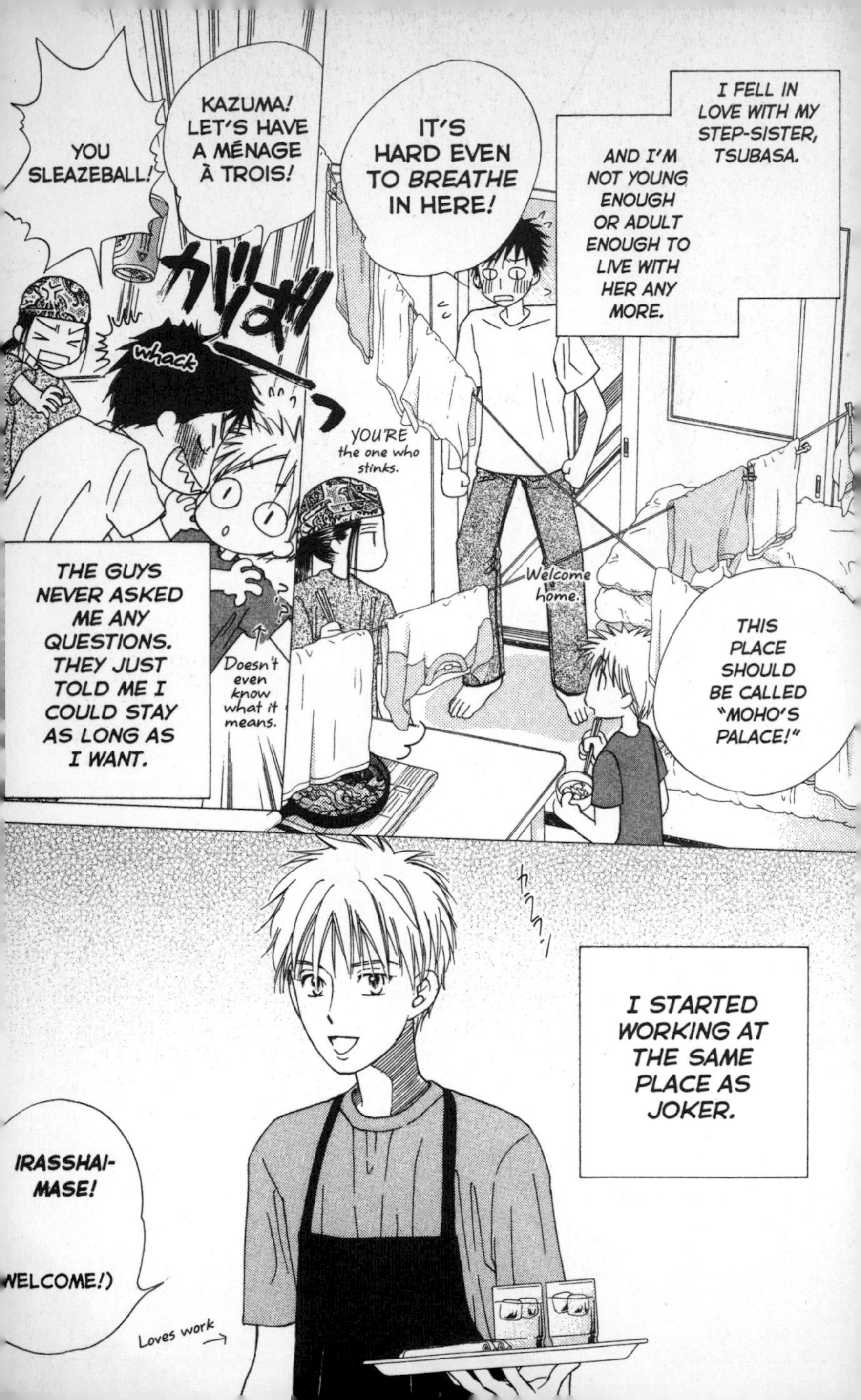
I FELL IN LOVE WITH MY STEP-SISTER, TSUBASA.
AND I'M NOT YOUNG ENOUGH OR ADULT ENOUGH TO LIVE WITH HER ANY MORE.
IT'S HARD EVEN TO *BREATHE* IN HERE!
KAZUMA! LET'S HAVE A MÉNAGE À TROIS!
YOU SLEAZEBALL!
whack
YOU'RE the one who stinks.
Welcome home.
THIS PLACE SHOULD BE CALLED "MOHO'S PALACE!"
Doesn't even know what it means.
THE GUYS NEVER ASKED ME ANY QUESTIONS. THEY JUST TOLD ME I COULD STAY AS LONG AS I WANT.
I STARTED WORKING AT THE SAME PLACE AS JOKER.
IRASSHAI-MASE!
WELCOME!)
Loves work

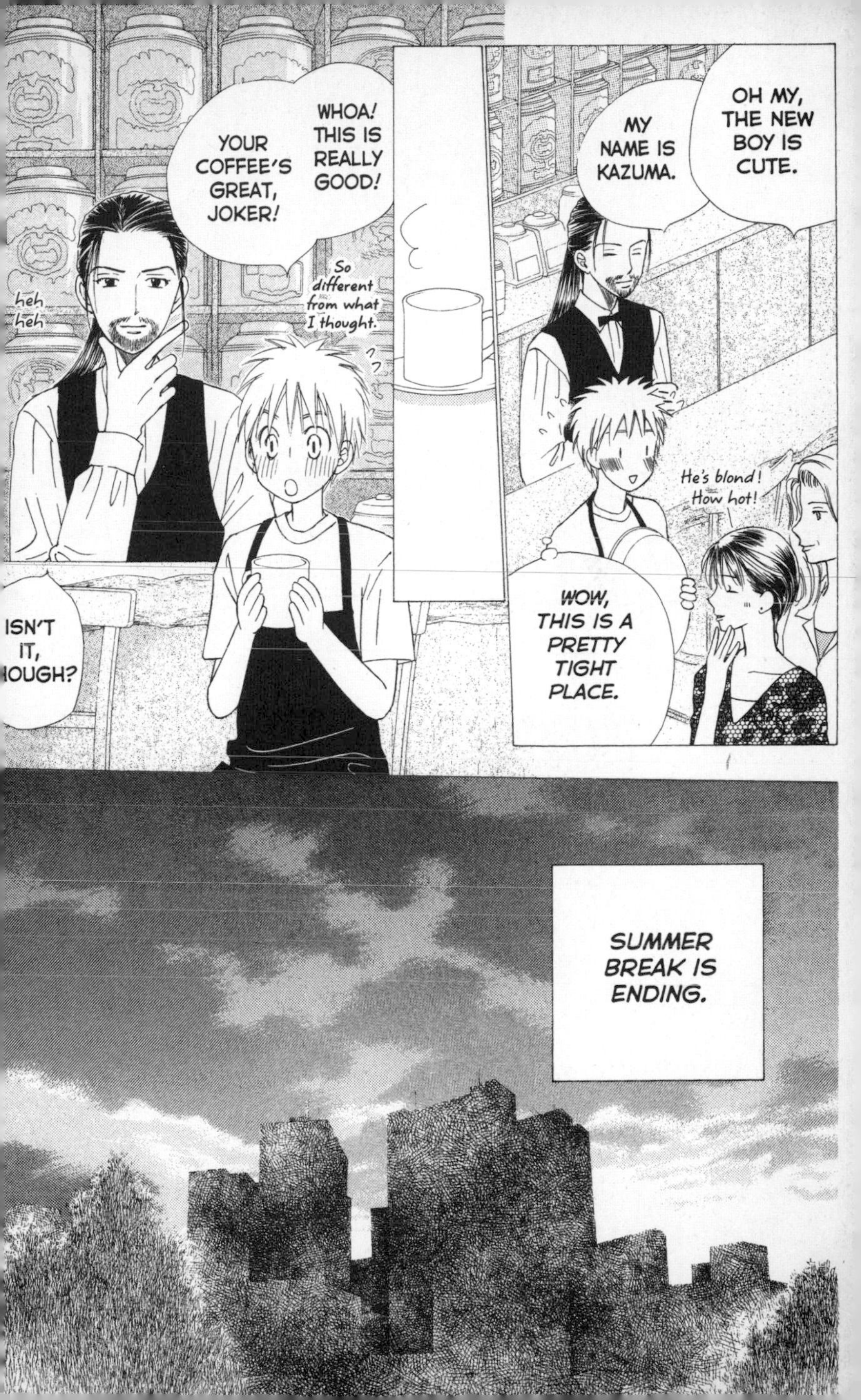
OH MY, THE NEW BOY IS CUTE.
MY NAME IS KAZUMA.
He's blond! How hot!
WOW, THIS IS A PRETTY TIGHT PLACE.
WHOA! THIS IS REALLY GOOD!
YOUR COFFEE'S GREAT, JOKER!
So different from what I thought.
heh heh
ISN'T IT, HOUGH?
SUMMER BREAK IS ENDING.

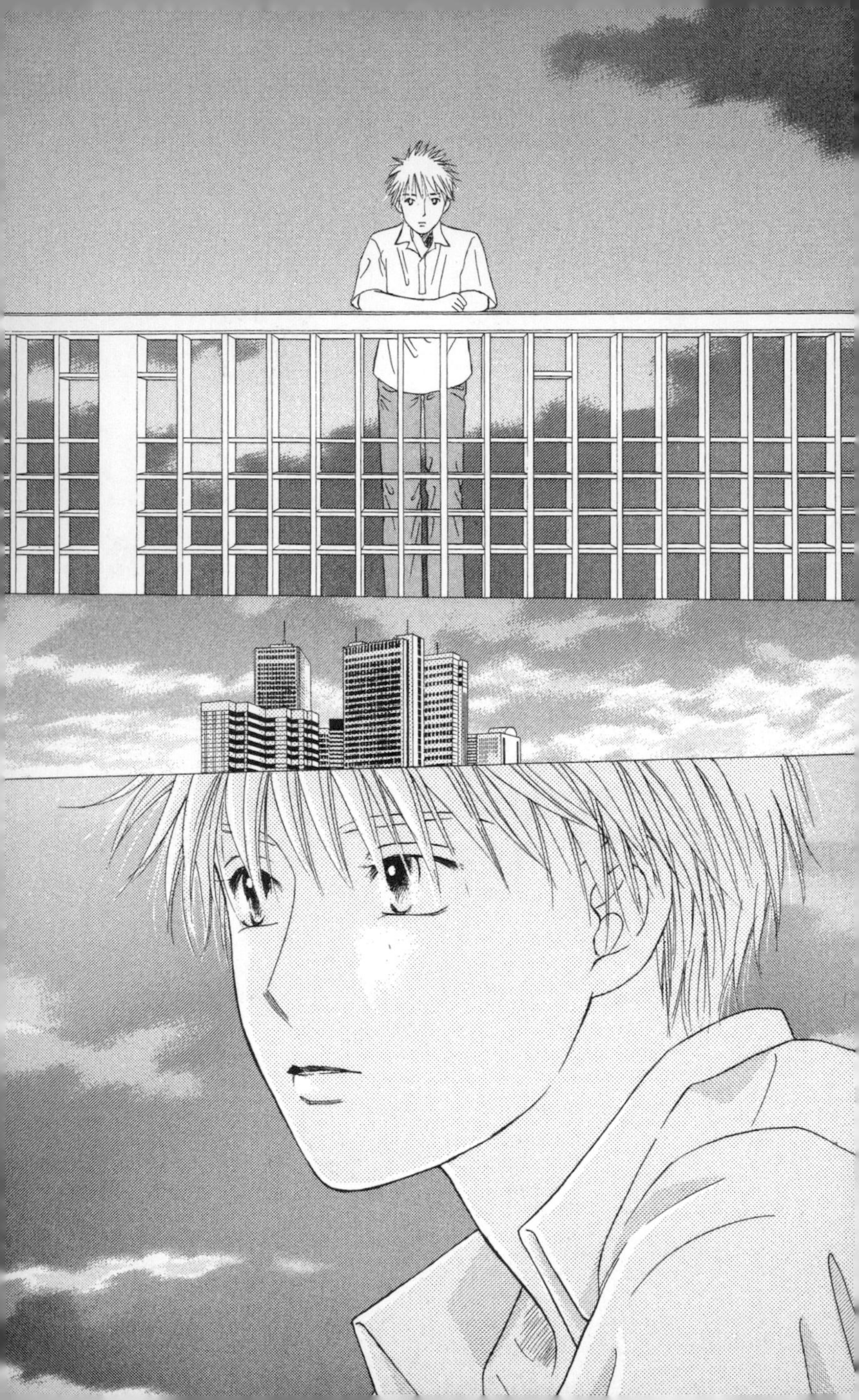

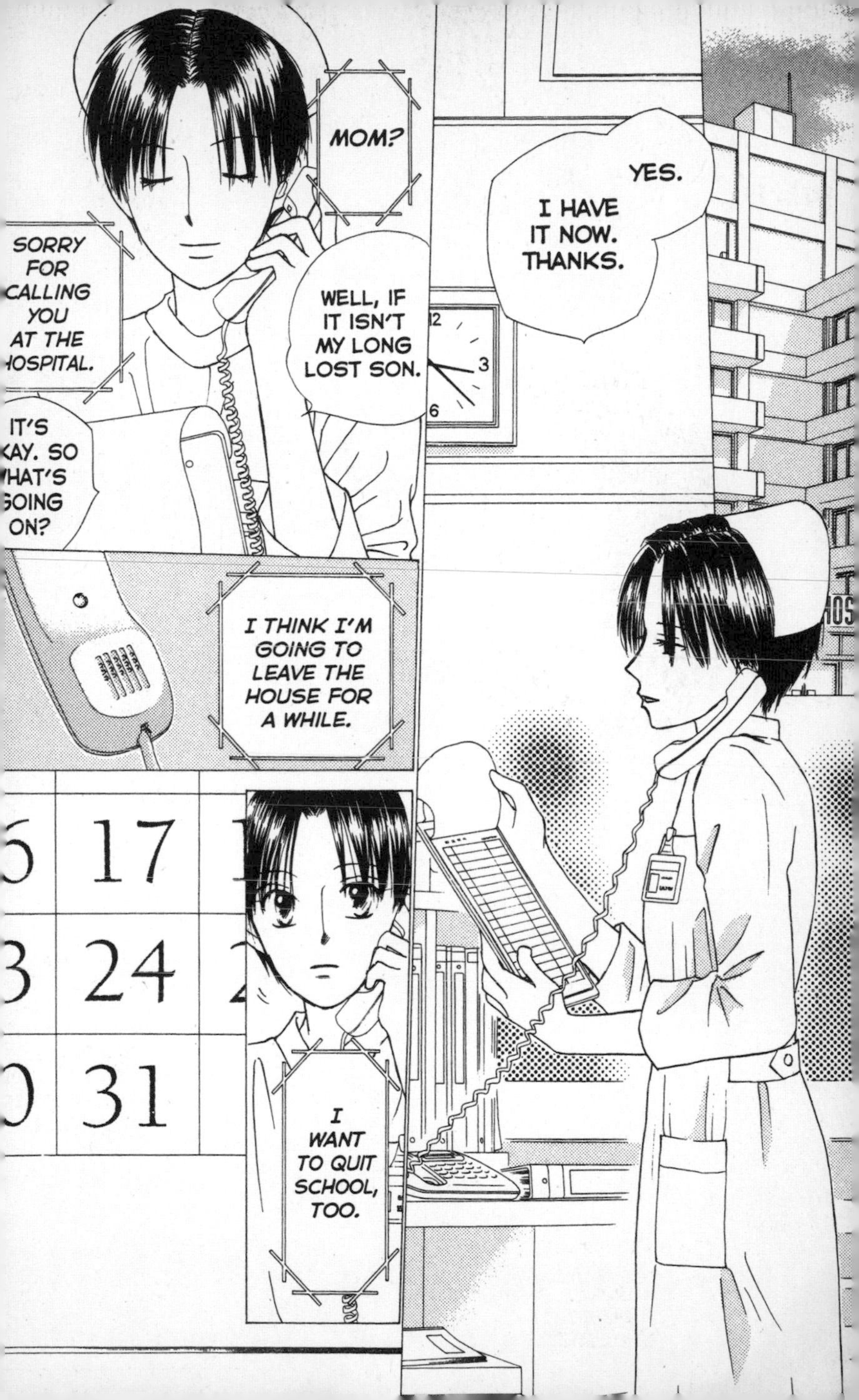
YES. I HAVE IT NOW. THANKS.
MOM?
WELL, IF IT ISN'T MY LONG LOST SON.
SORRY FOR CALLING YOU AT THE HOSPITAL.
IT'S KAY. SO HAT'S OING ON?
I THINK I'M GOING TO LEAVE THE HOUSE FOR A WHILE.
I WANT TO QUIT SCHOOL, TOO.

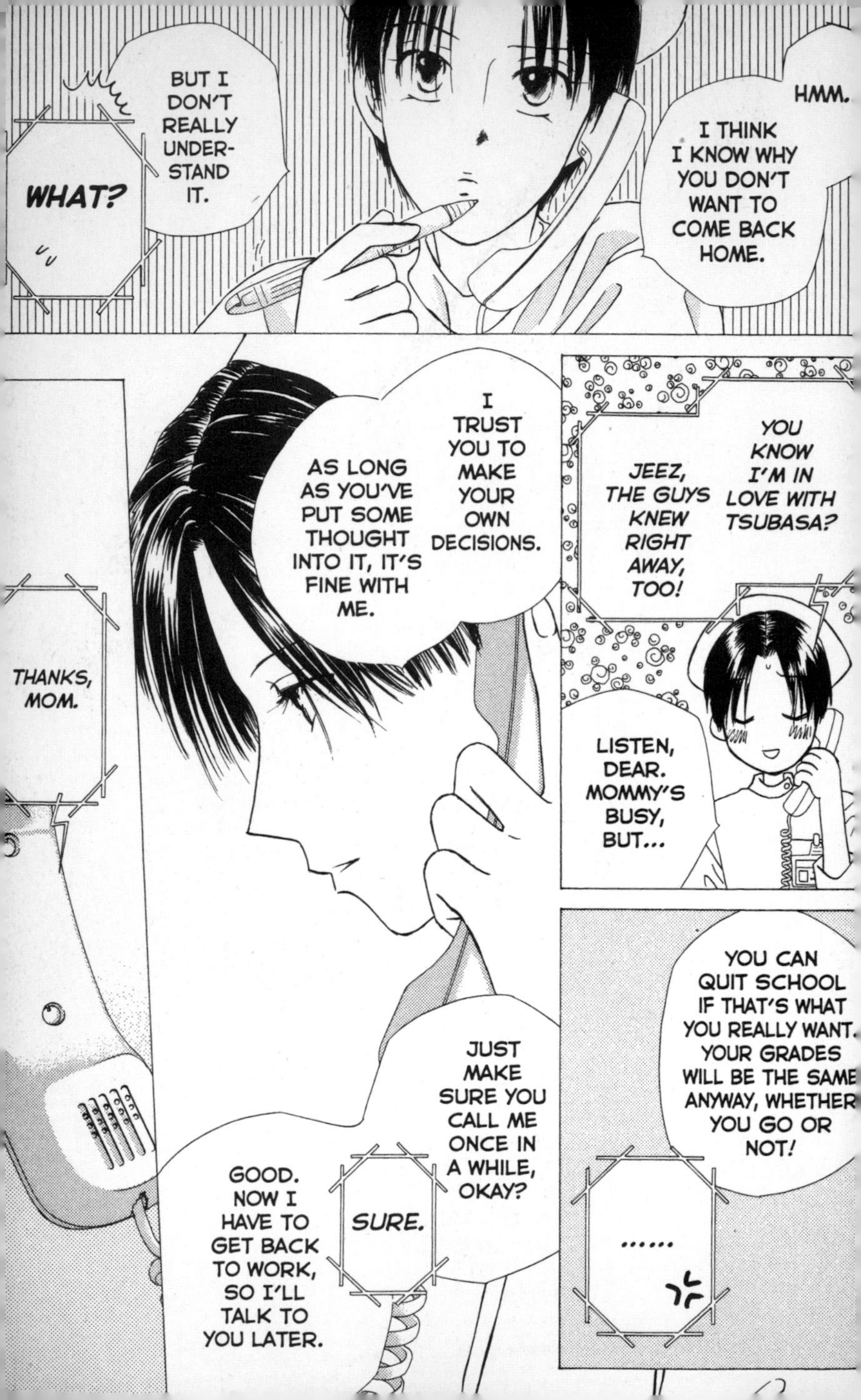
HMM.
I THINK I KNOW WHY YOU DON'T WANT TO COME BACK HOME.
BUT I DON'T REALLY UNDERSTAND IT.
WHAT?
YOU KNOW I'M IN LOVE WITH TSUBASA?
JEEZ, THE GUYS KNEW RIGHT AWAY, TOO!
LISTEN, DEAR. MOMMY'S BUSY, BUT...
YOU CAN QUIT SCHOOL IF THAT'S WHAT YOU REALLY WANT. YOUR GRADES WILL BE THE SAME ANYWAY, WHETHER YOU GO OR NOT!
......
I TRUST YOU TO MAKE YOUR OWN DECISIONS.
AS LONG AS YOU'VE PUT SOME THOUGHT INTO IT, IT'S FINE WITH ME.
THANKS, MOM.
JUST MAKE SURE YOU CALL ME ONCE IN A WHILE, OKAY?
SURE.
GOOD. NOW I HAVE TO GET BACK TO WORK, SO I'LL TALK TO YOU LATER.

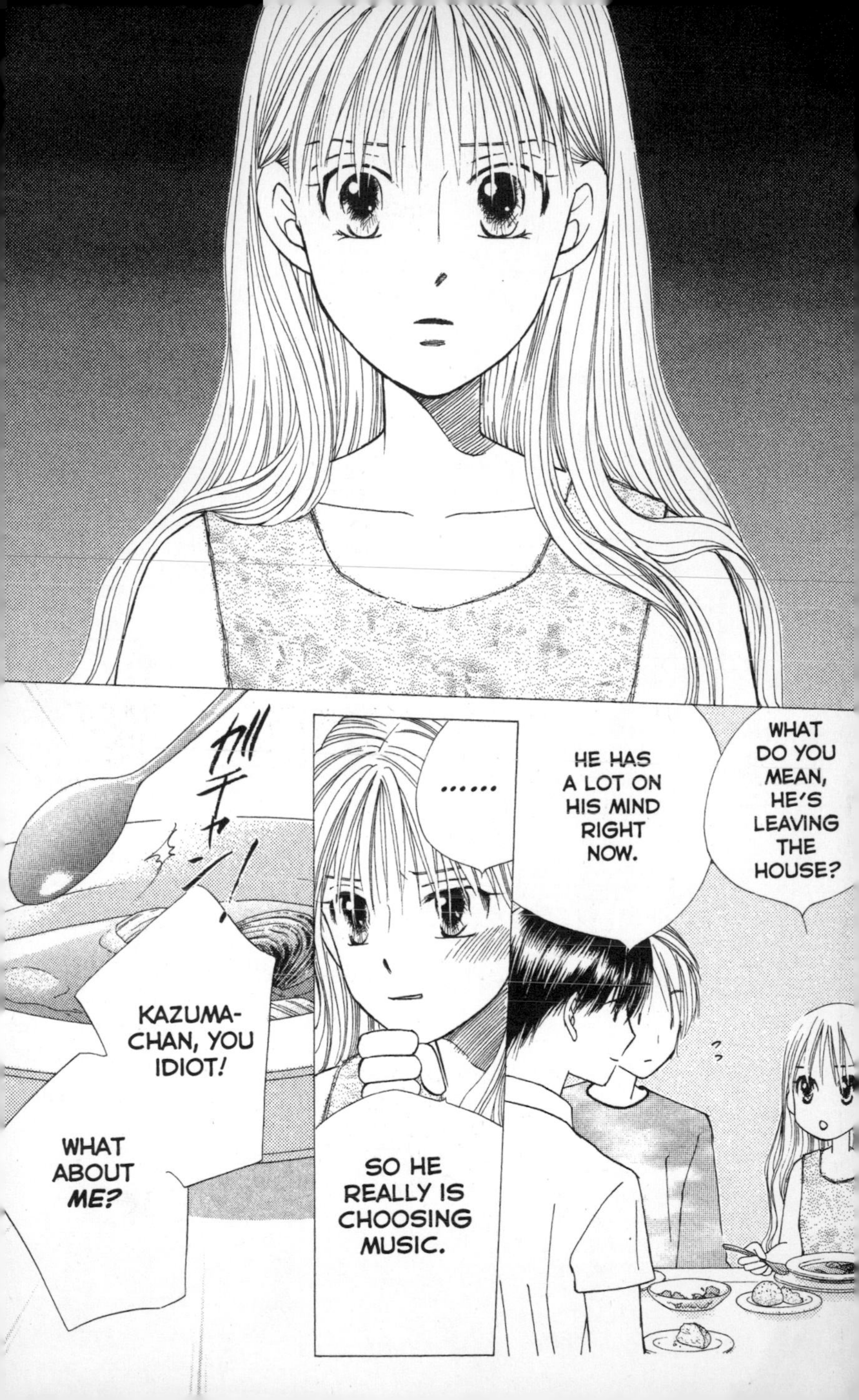
WHAT DO YOU MEAN, HE'S LEAVING THE HOUSE?
HE HAS A LOT ON HIS MIND RIGHT NOW.
......
SO HE REALLY IS CHOOSING MUSIC.
ガチャン!
KAZUMA-CHAN, YOU IDIOT!
WHAT ABOUT *ME?*

1

Hello! This is Kare Kano 12! As I promised, I got it published in 3 months. That's almost as fast as if it was running in a weekly magazine! I'm so happy!

Yay!

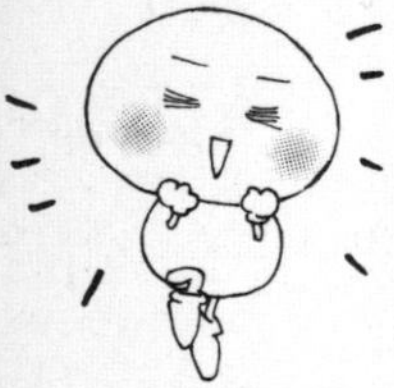

Volumes 11 and 12 are best read together anyway, so I'm glad 12 was published so quickly!

Phew!

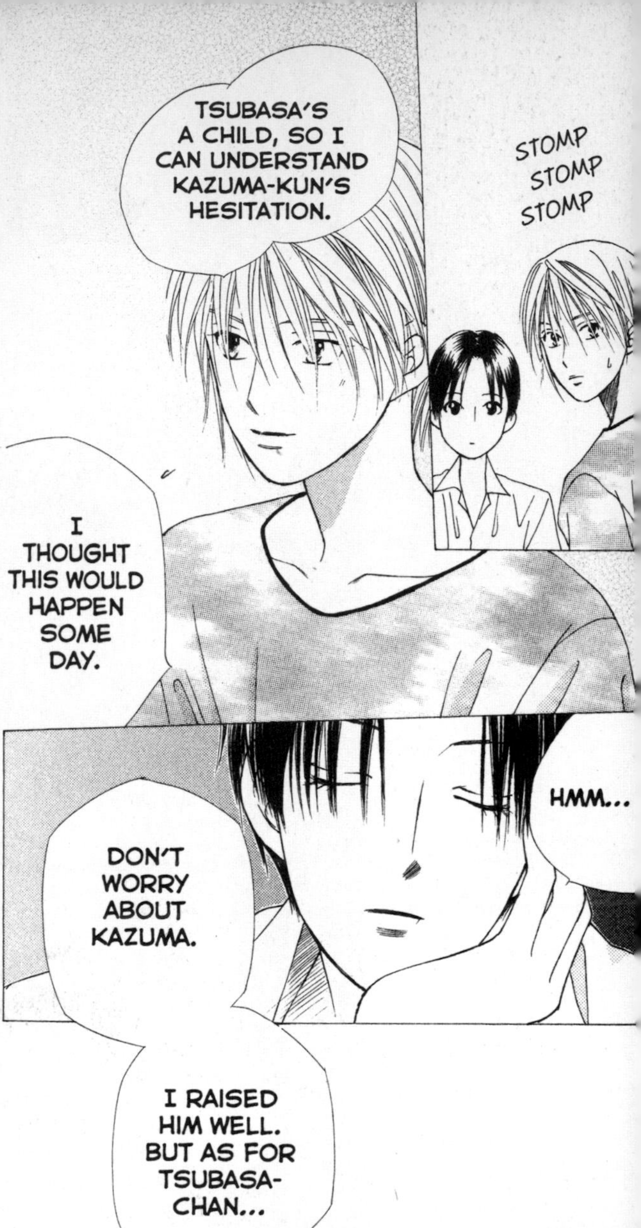
STOMP STOMP STOMP
TSUBASA'S A CHILD, SO I CAN UNDERSTAND KAZUMA-KUN'S HESITATION.
I THOUGHT THIS WOULD HAPPEN SOME DAY.
HMM...
DON'T WORRY ABOUT KAZUMA.
I RAISED HIM WELL. BUT AS FOR TSUBASA-CHAN...

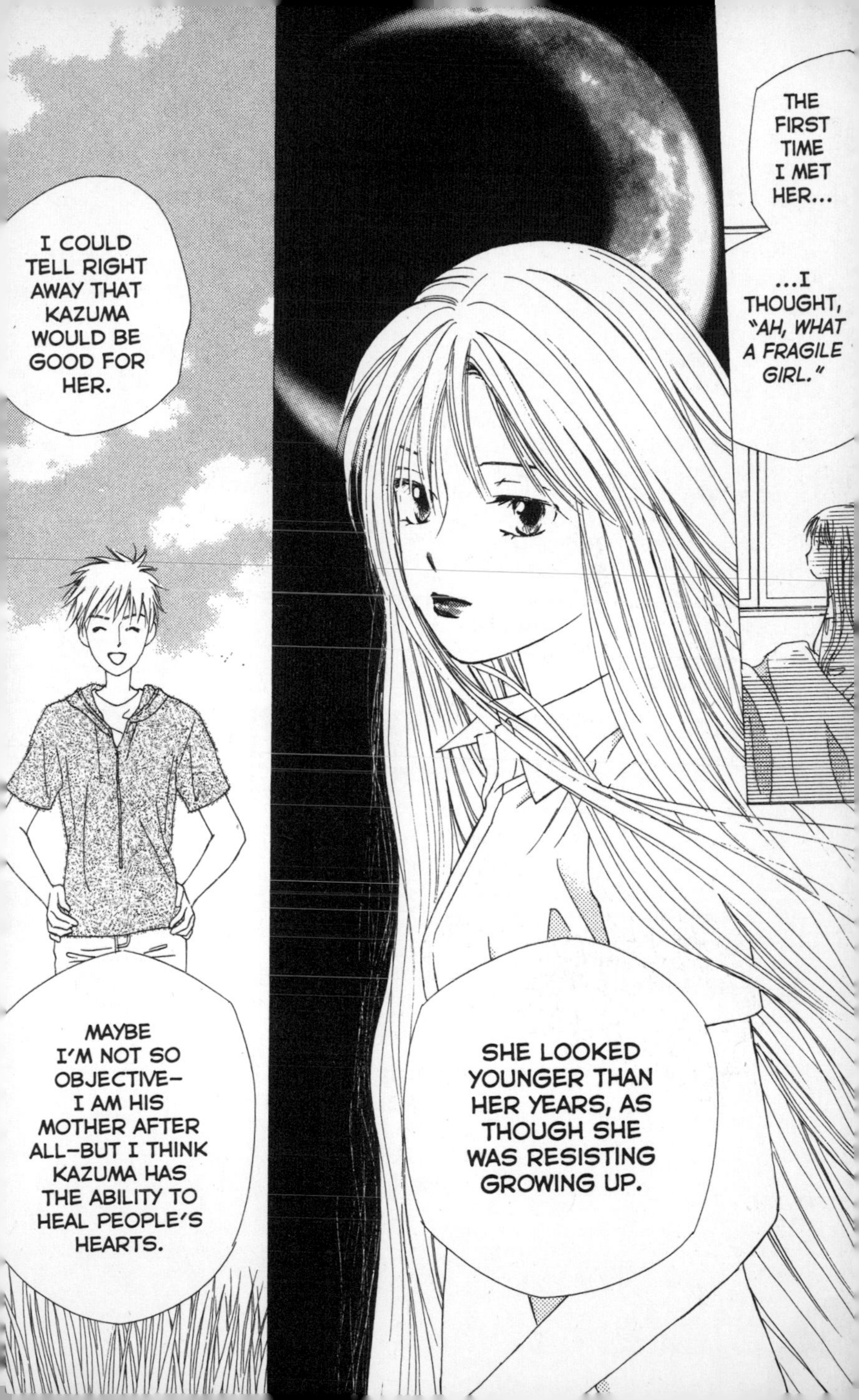
THE FIRST TIME I MET HER...
...I THOUGHT, "AH, WHAT A FRAGILE GIRL."
SHE LOOKED YOUNGER THAN HER YEARS, AS THOUGH SHE WAS RESISTING GROWING UP.
I COULD TELL RIGHT AWAY THAT KAZUMA WOULD BE GOOD FOR HER.
MAYBE I'M NOT SO OBJECTIVE–I AM HIS MOTHER AFTER ALL–BUT I THINK KAZUMA HAS THE ABILITY TO HEAL PEOPLE'S HEARTS.

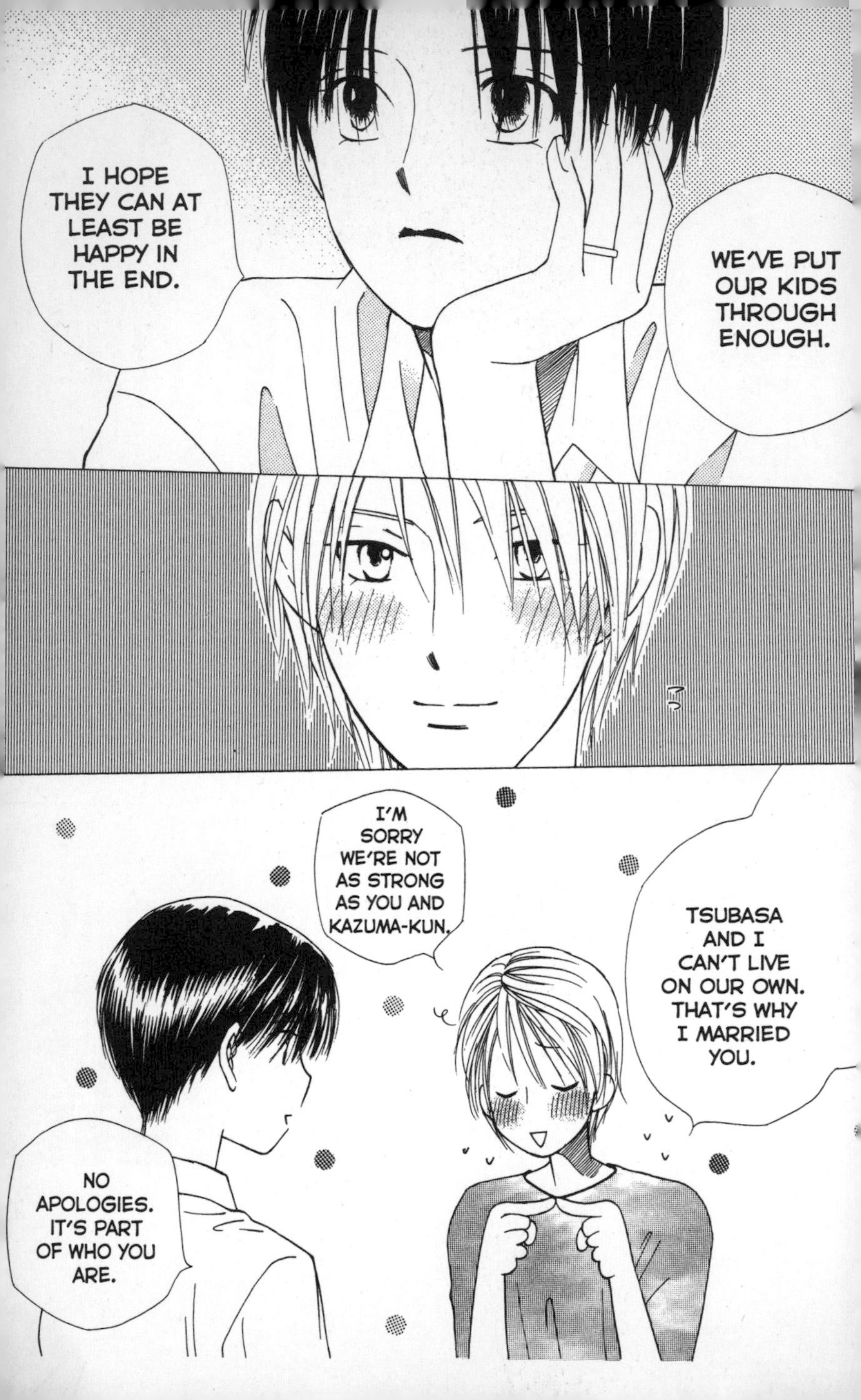
WE'VE PUT OUR KIDS THROUGH ENOUGH.
I HOPE THEY CAN AT LEAST BE HAPPY IN THE END.
TSUBASA AND I CAN'T LIVE ON OUR OWN. THAT'S WHY I MARRIED YOU.
I'M SORRY WE'RE NOT AS STRONG AS YOU AND KAZUMA-KUN.
NO APOLOGIES. IT'S PART OF WHO YOU ARE.

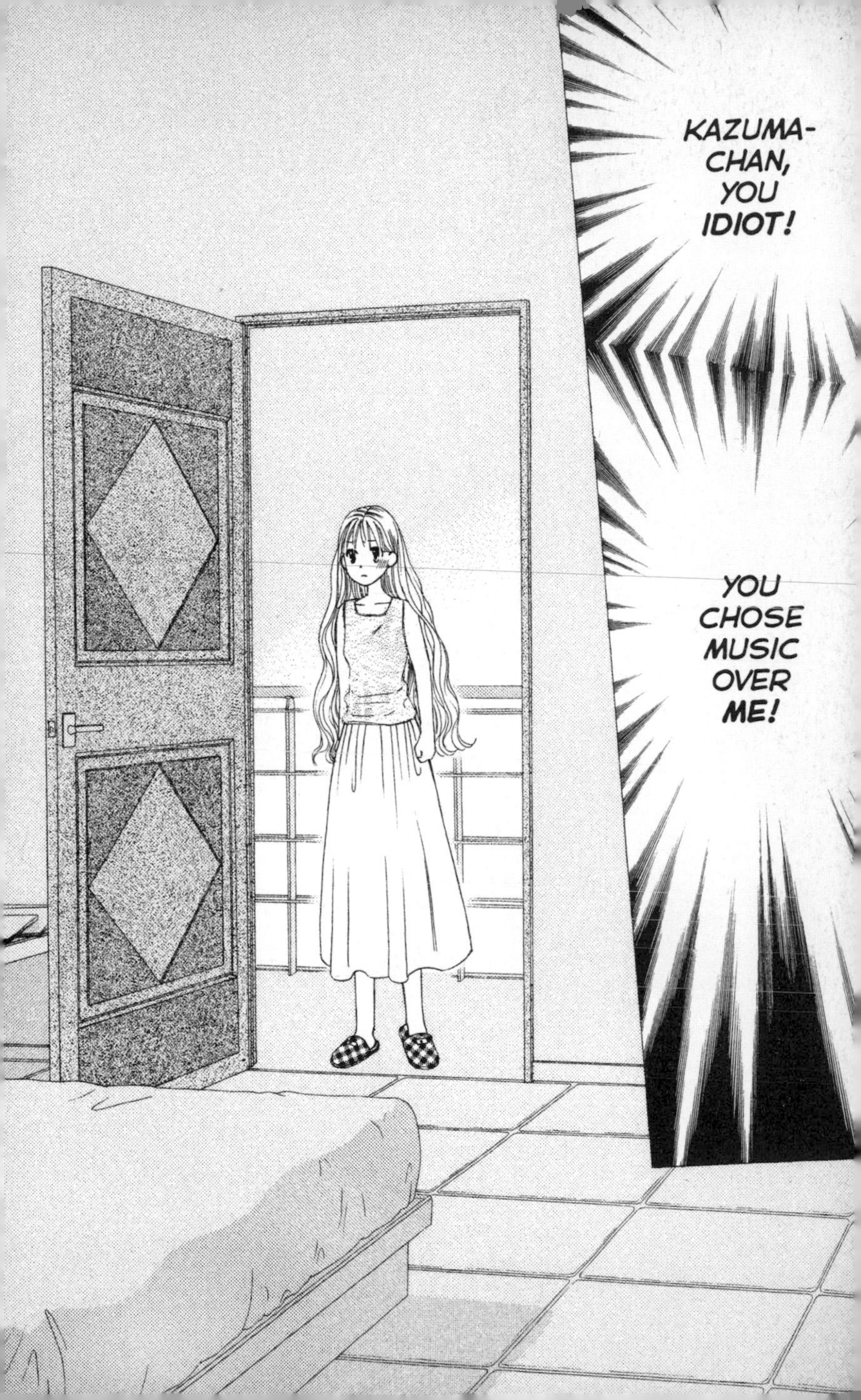
KAZUMA-CHAN, YOU IDIOT!
YOU CHOSE MUSIC OVER ME!

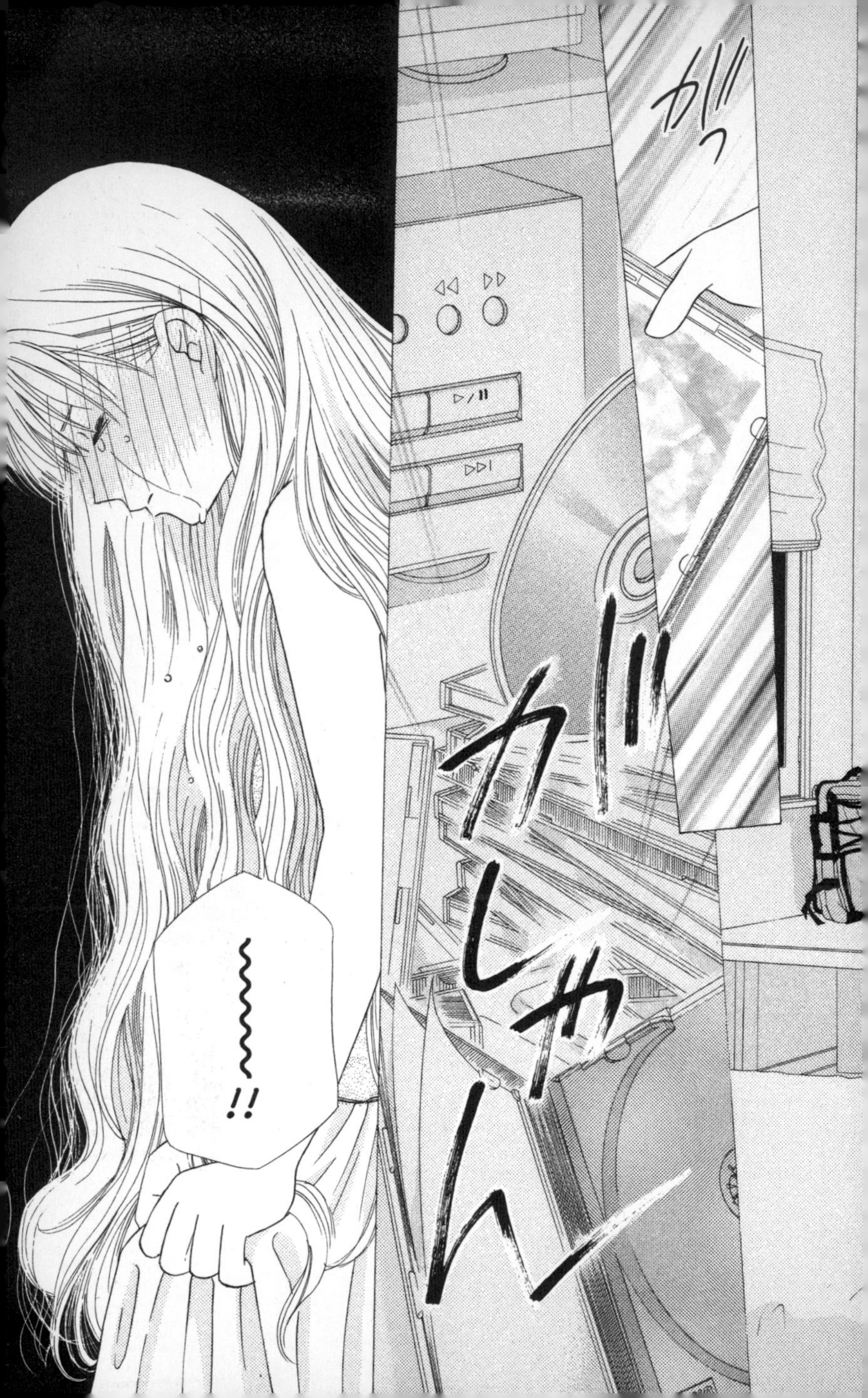
がっ
がしゃん
〜〜!!

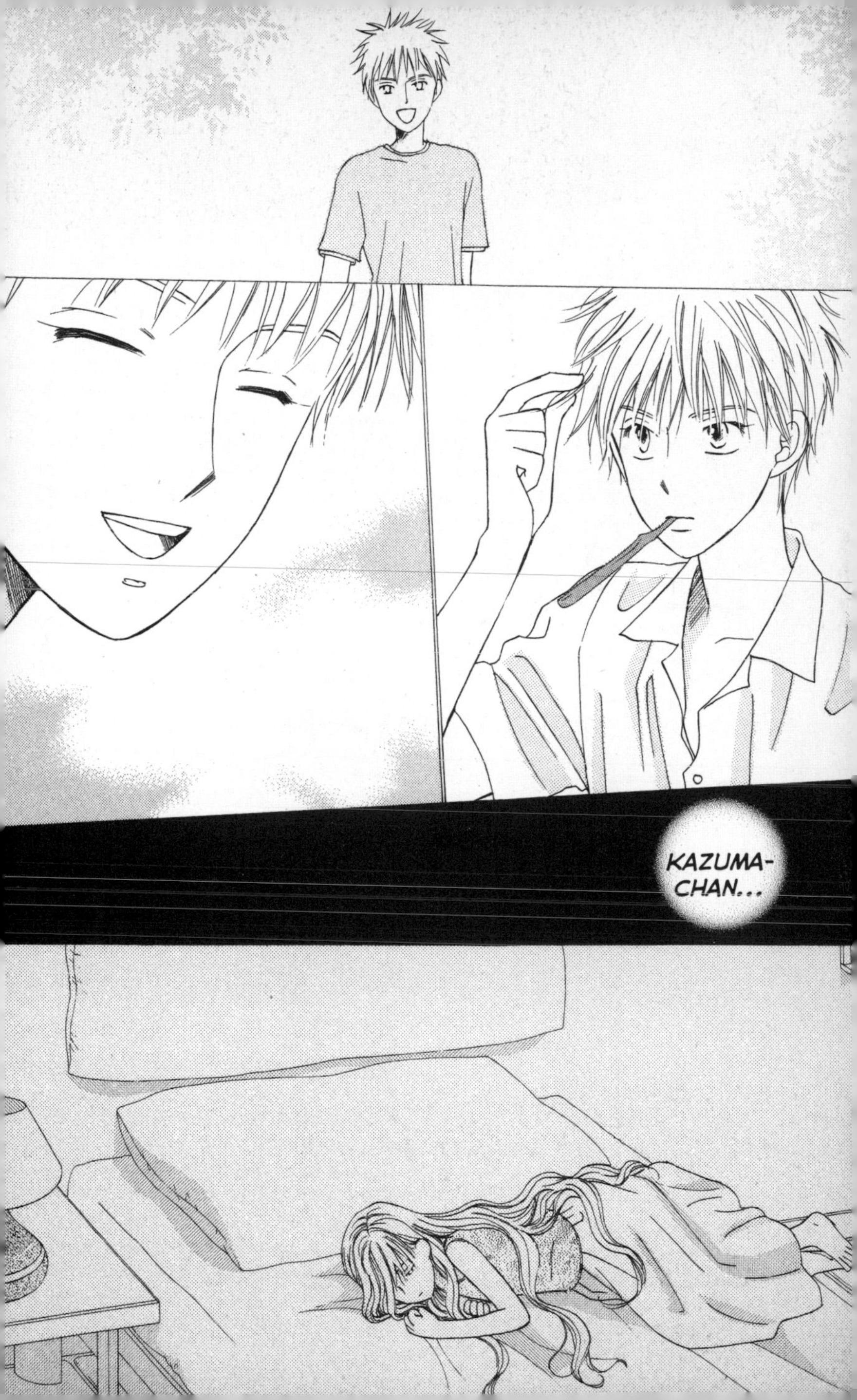
KAZUMA-
CHAN...

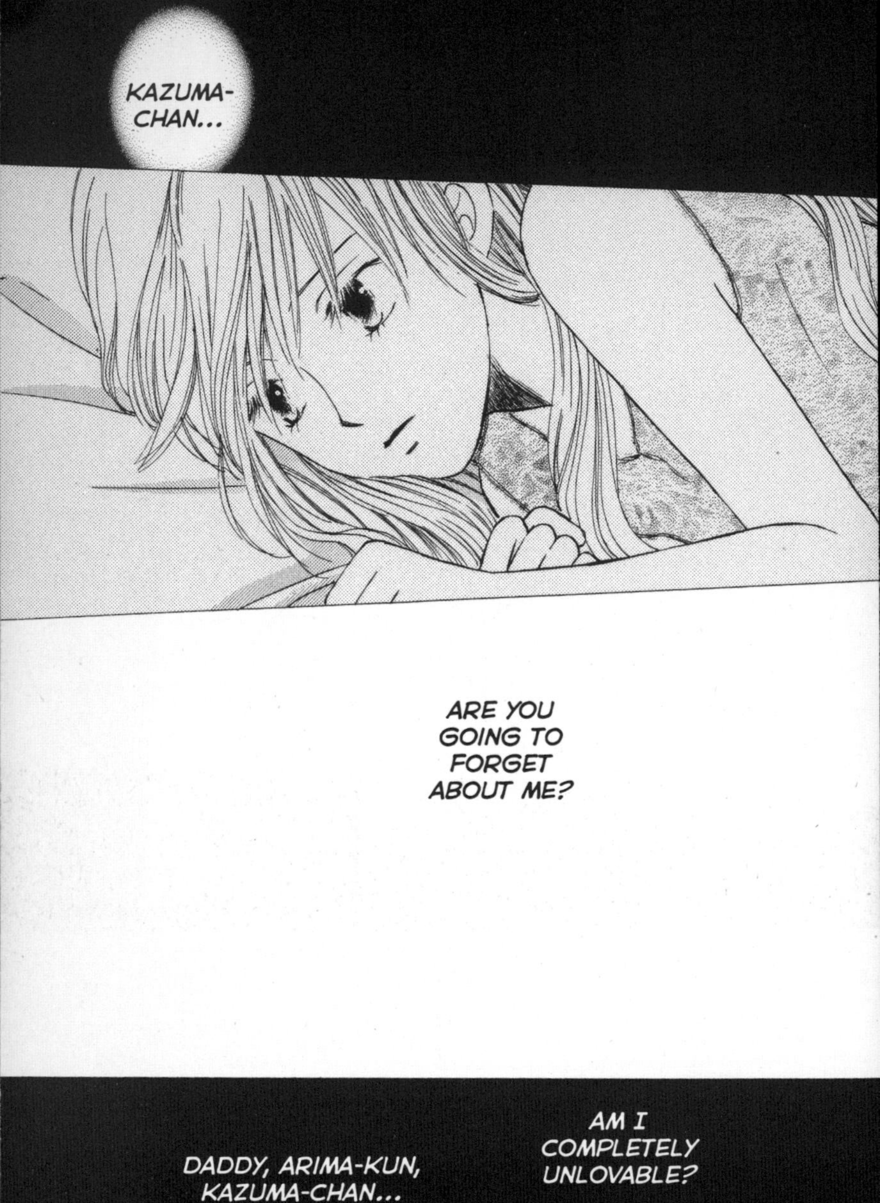
KAZUMA-CHAN...
ARE YOU GOING TO FORGET ABOUT ME?
AM I COMPLETELY UNLOVABLE?
DADDY, ARIMA-KUN, KAZUMA-CHAN...

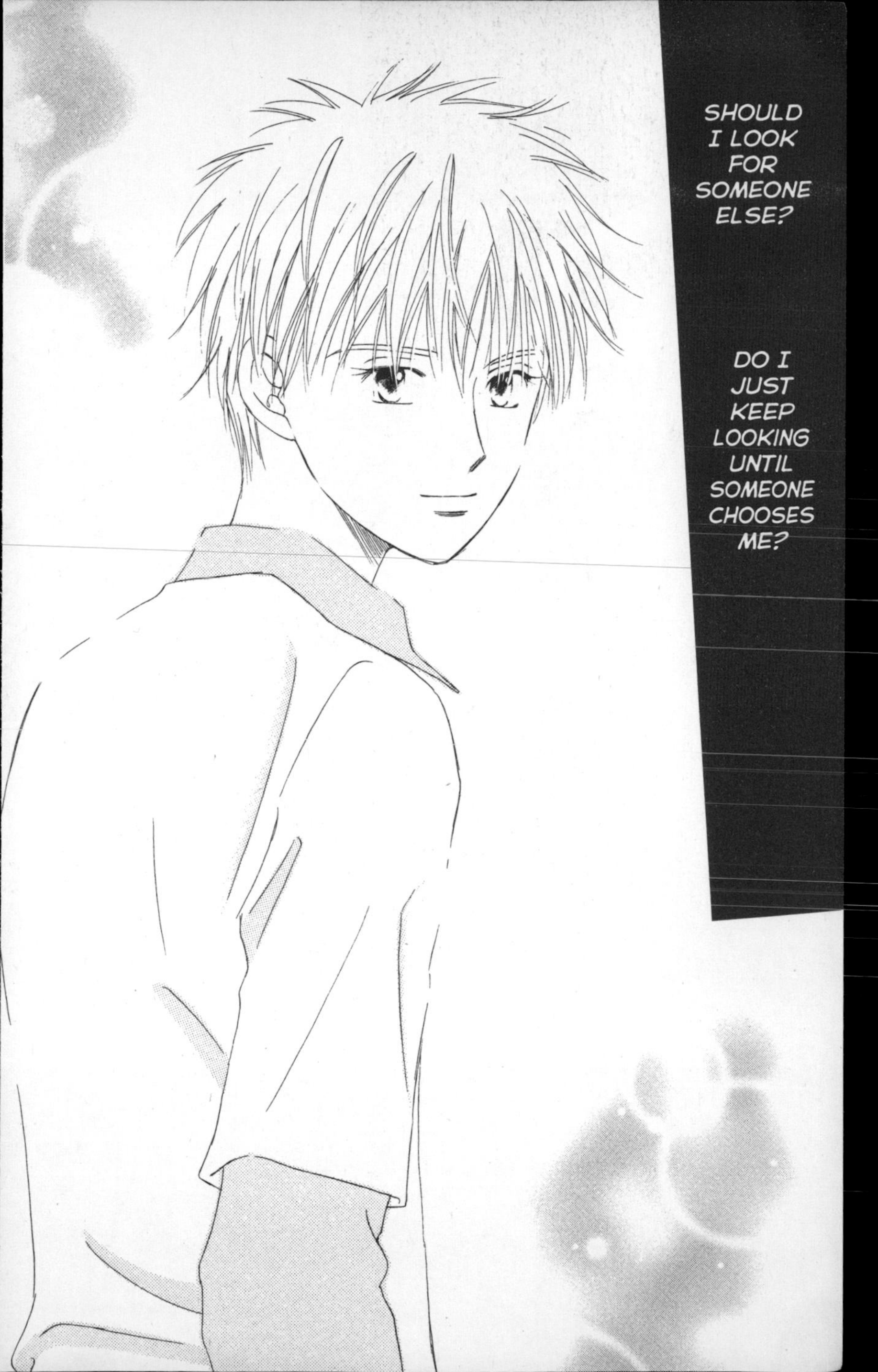
SHOULD I LOOK FOR SOMEONE ELSE?
DO I JUST KEEP LOOKING UNTIL SOMEONE CHOOSES ME?

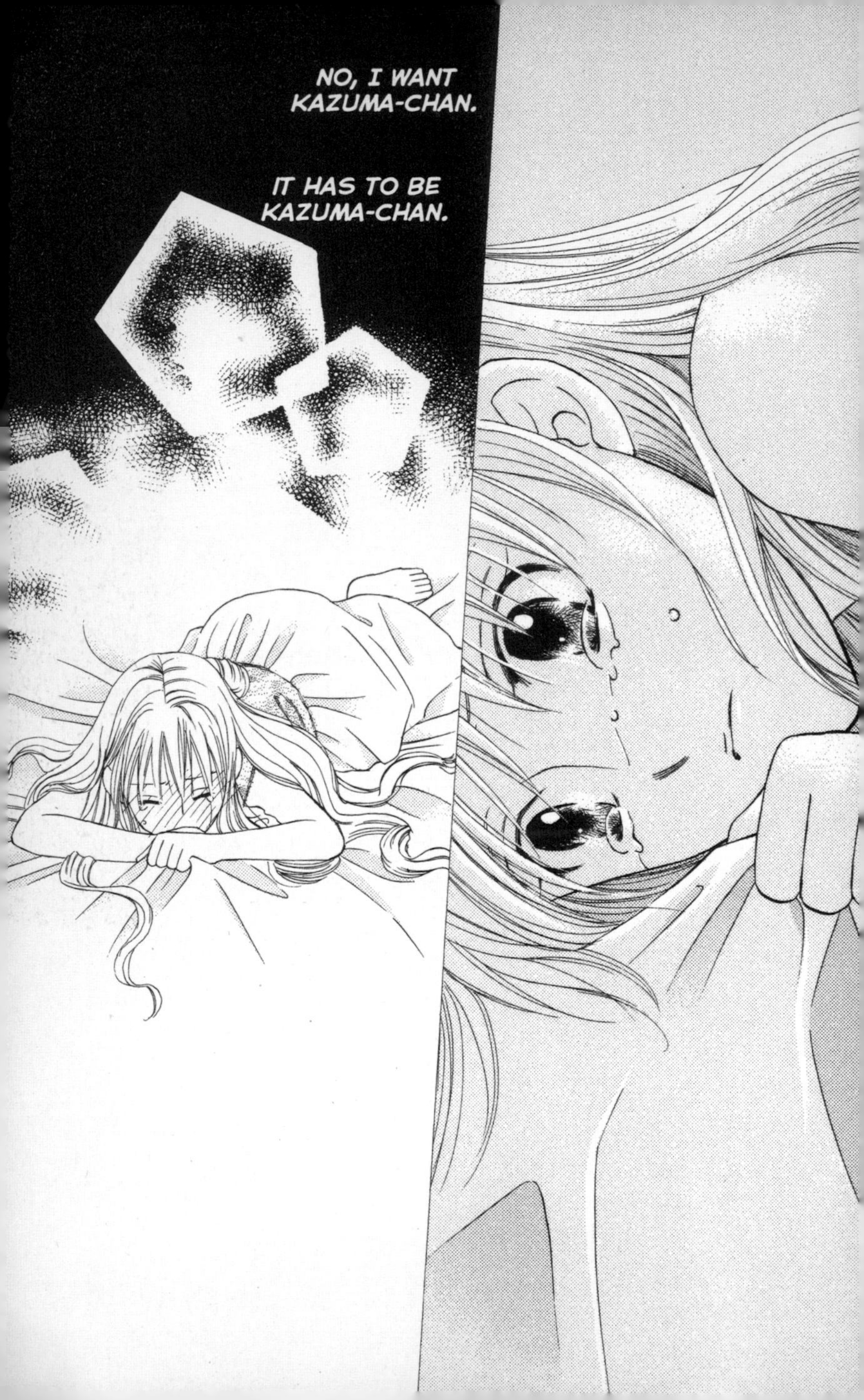
NO, I WANT KAZUMA-CHAN.
IT HAS TO BE KAZUMA-CHAN.

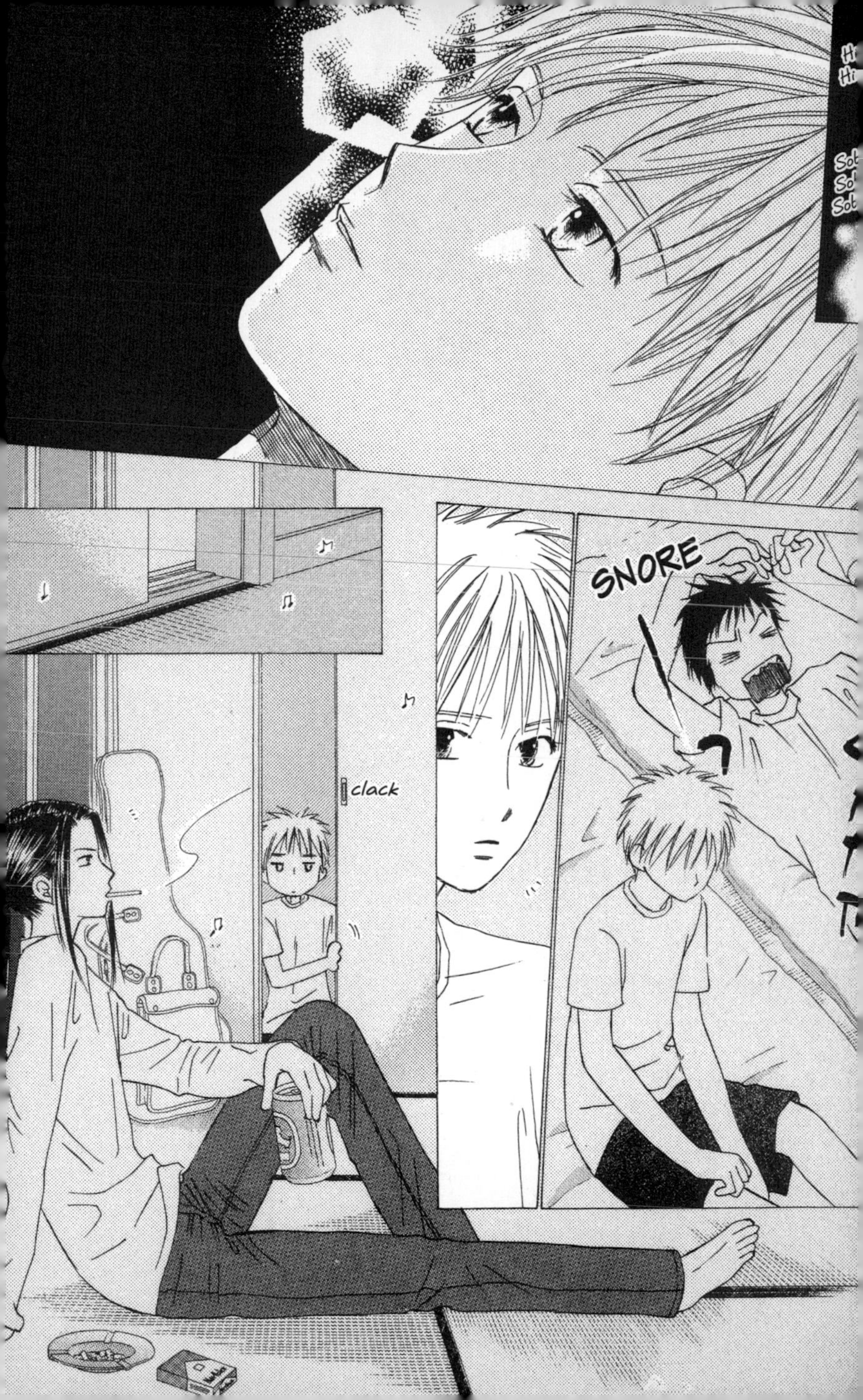
SNORE
clack

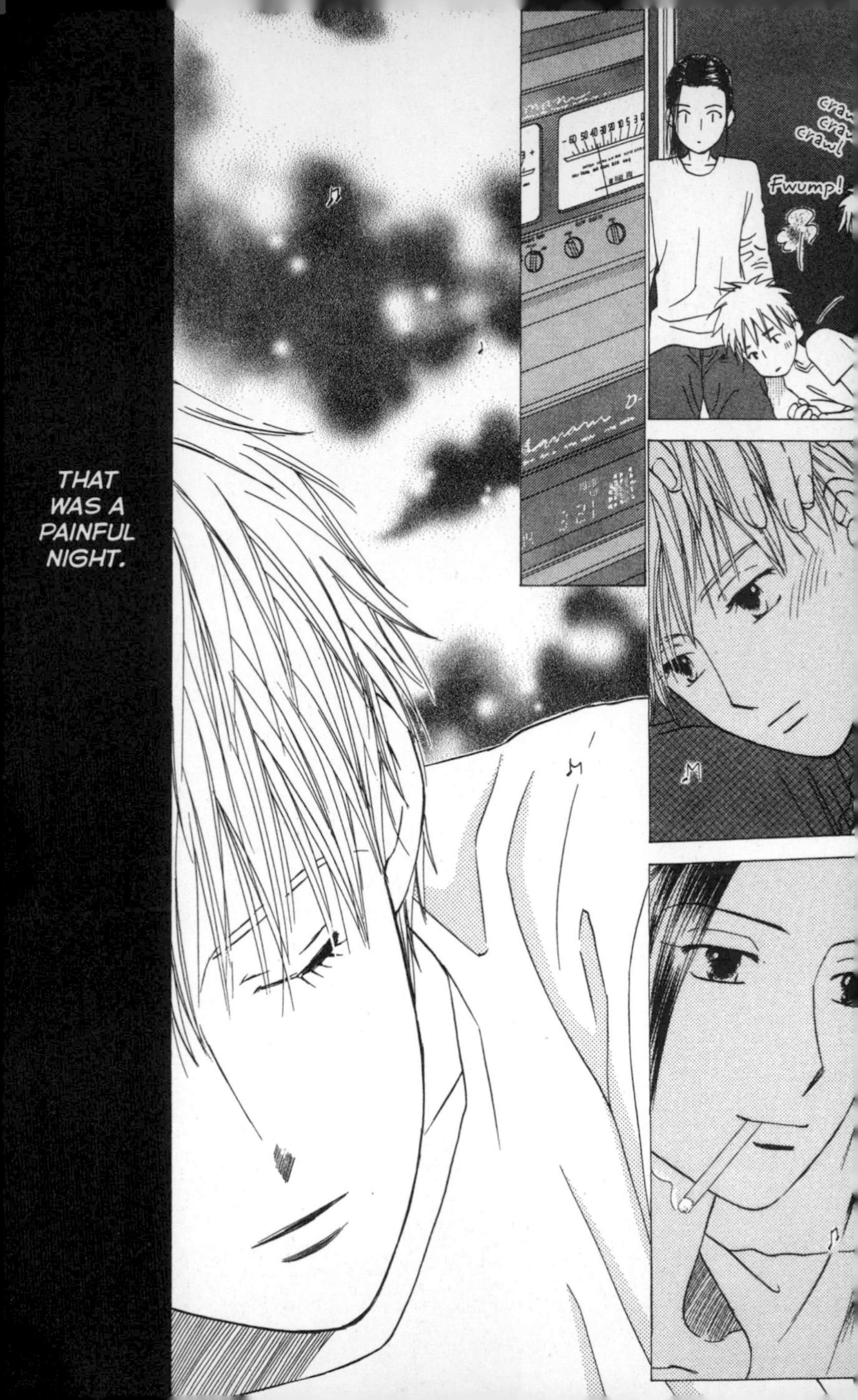
crawl
Fwump!
THAT WAS A PAINFUL NIGHT.

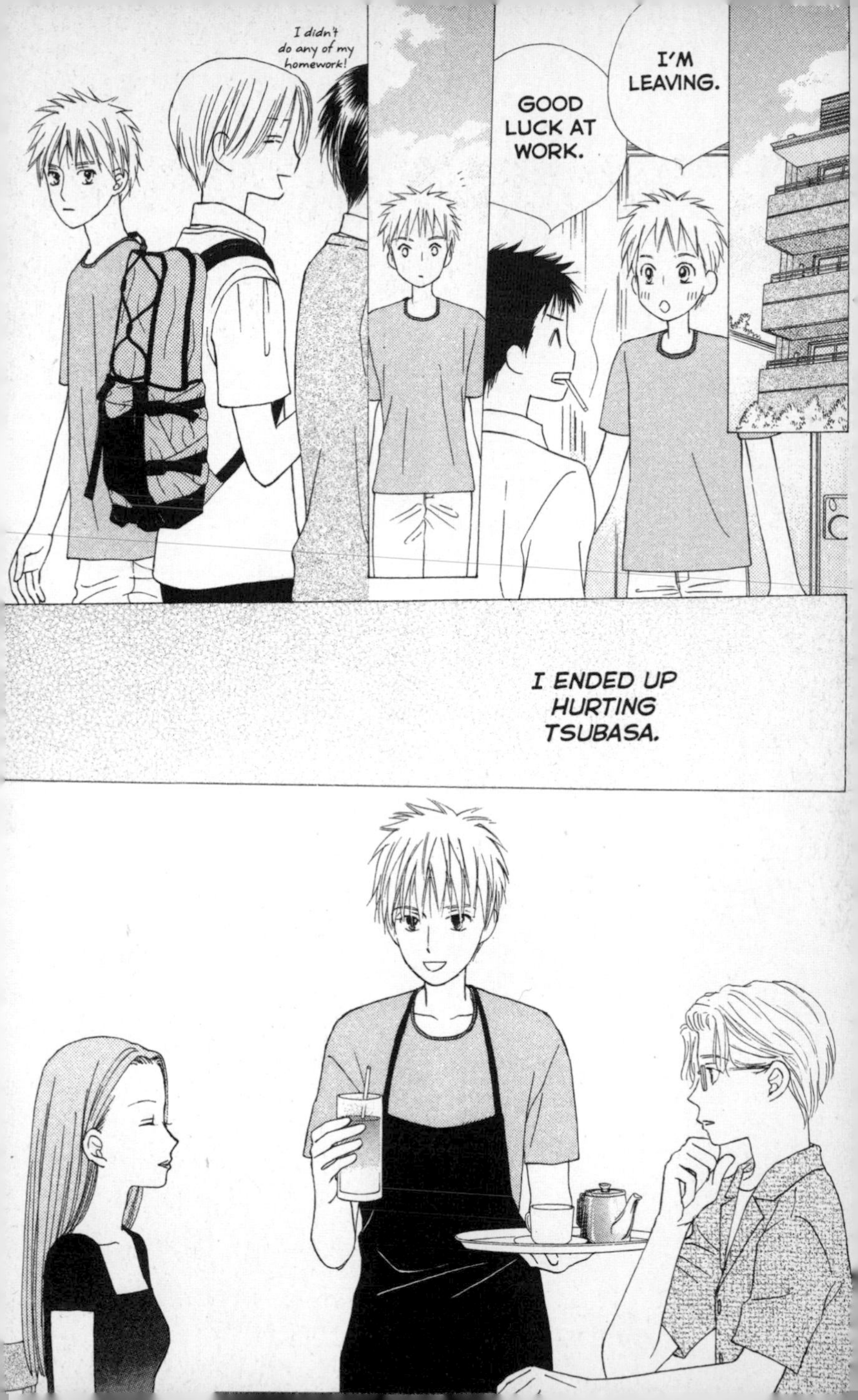
I'M LEAVING.
GOOD LUCK AT WORK.
I didn't do any of my homework!
I ENDED UP HURTING TSUBASA.

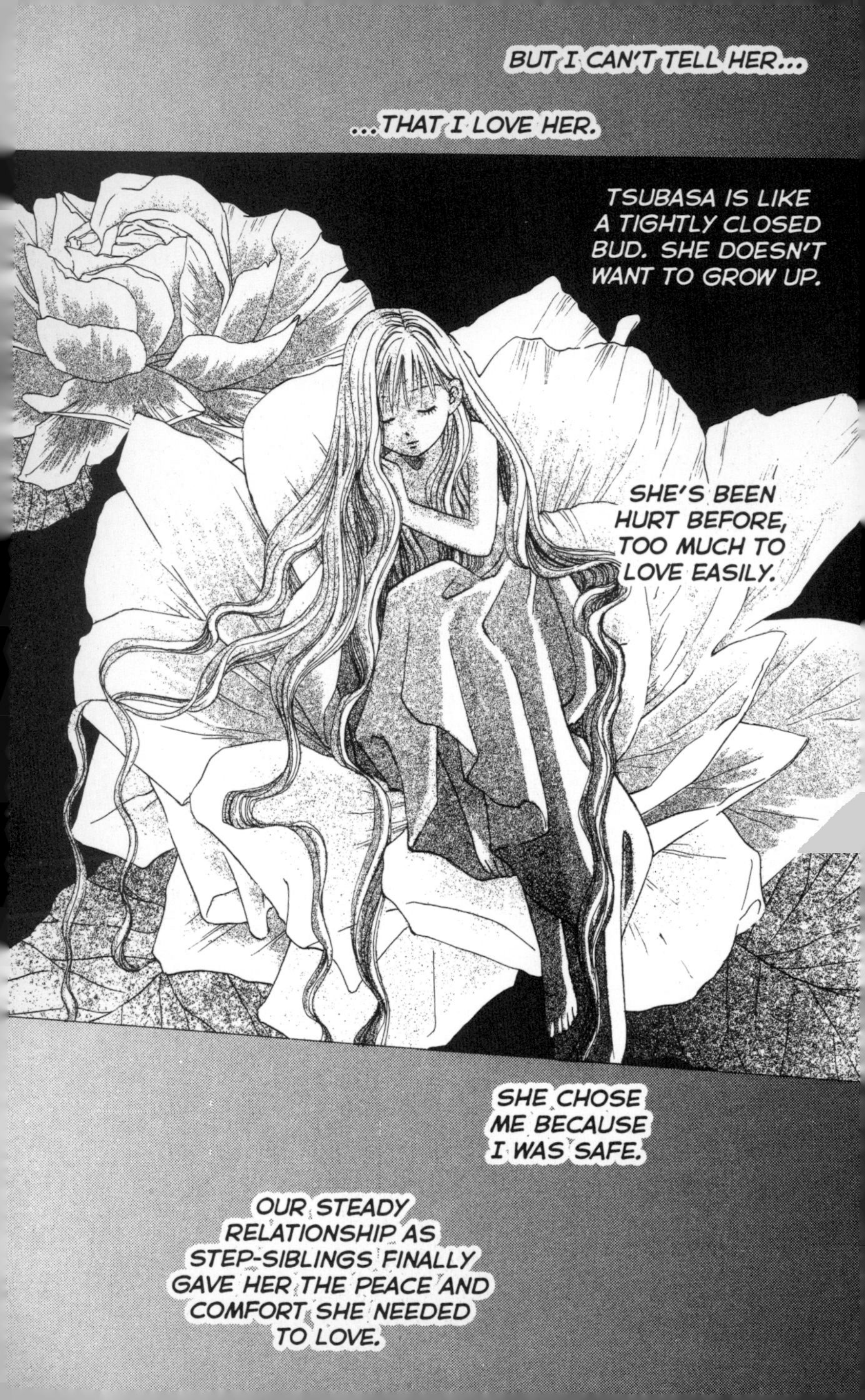
BUT I CAN'T TELL HER...
...THAT I LOVE HER.
TSUBASA IS LIKE A TIGHTLY CLOSED BUD. SHE DOESN'T WANT TO GROW UP.
SHE'S BEEN HURT BEFORE, TOO MUCH TO LOVE EASILY.
SHE CHOSE ME BECAUSE I WAS SAFE.
OUR STEADY RELATIONSHIP AS STEP-SIBLINGS FINALLY GAVE HER THE PEACE AND COMFORT SHE NEEDED TO LOVE.

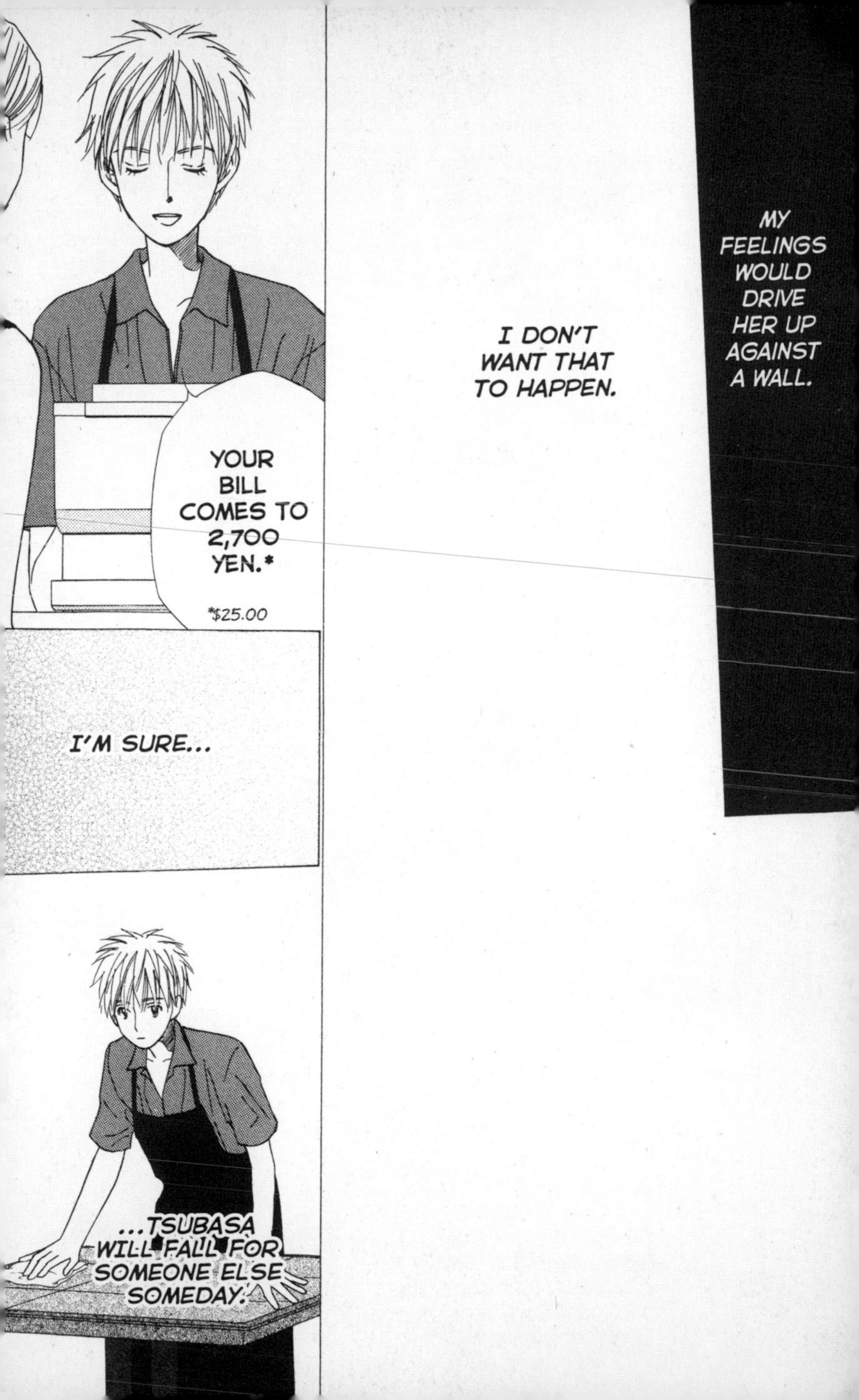
MY FEELINGS WOULD DRIVE HER UP AGAINST A WALL.
I DON'T WANT THAT TO HAPPEN.
YOUR BILL COMES TO 2,700 YEN.*
*$25.00
I'M SURE...
...TSUBASA WILL FALL FOR SOMEONE ELSE SOMEDAY.

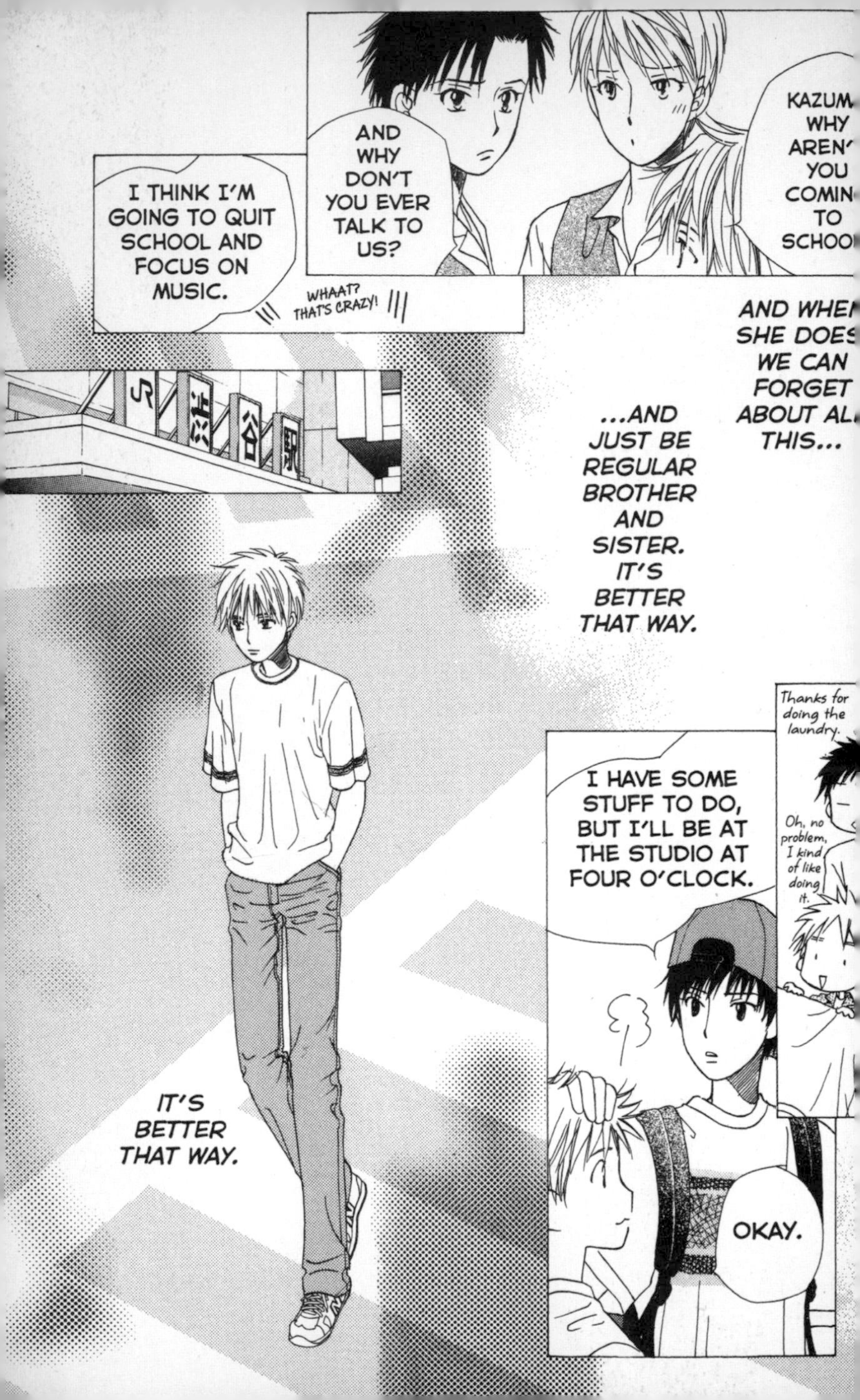
KAZUM WHY AREN' YOU COMIN TO SCHOO
AND WHY DON'T YOU EVER TALK TO US?
I THINK I'M GOING TO QUIT SCHOOL AND FOCUS ON MUSIC.
WHAAT? THAT'S CRAZY!
AND WHE SHE DOE WE CAN FORGET ABOUT AL THIS...
...AND JUST BE REGULAR BROTHER AND SISTER. IT'S BETTER THAT WAY.
渋谷駅
Thanks for doing the laundry.
Oh, no problem, I kind of like doing it.
I HAVE SOME STUFF TO DO, BUT I'LL BE AT THE STUDIO AT FOUR O'CLOCK.
OKAY.
IT'S BETTER THAT WAY.

Beep

Beep

d you
ear
 new
ng?

Yeah, at
Aoyama.

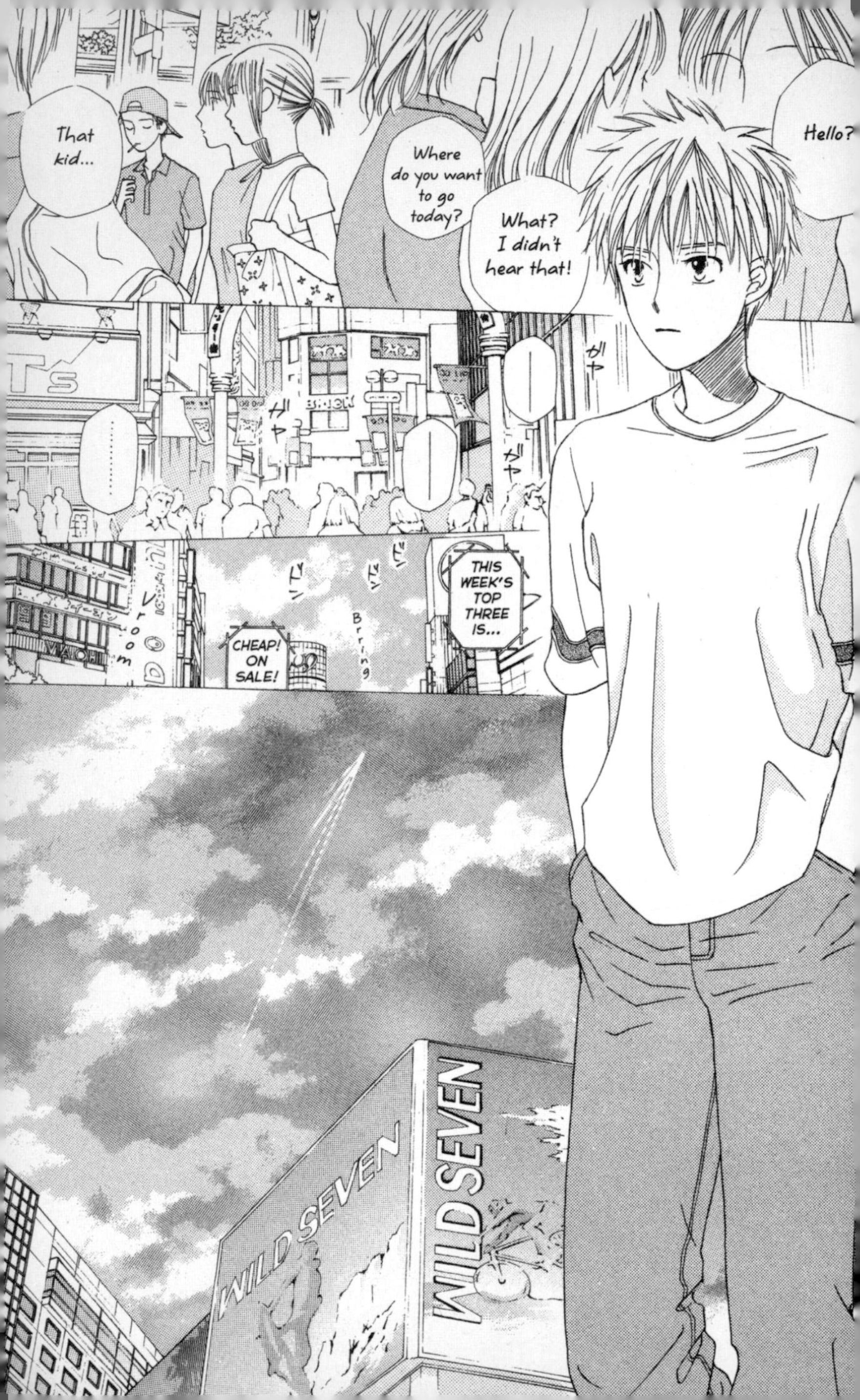

Hello?
What? I didn't hear that!
Where do you want to go today?
That kid...
......
THIS WEEK'S TOP THREE IS...
Brring
CHEAP! ON SALE!
Vroom
WILD SEVEN
WILD SEVEN

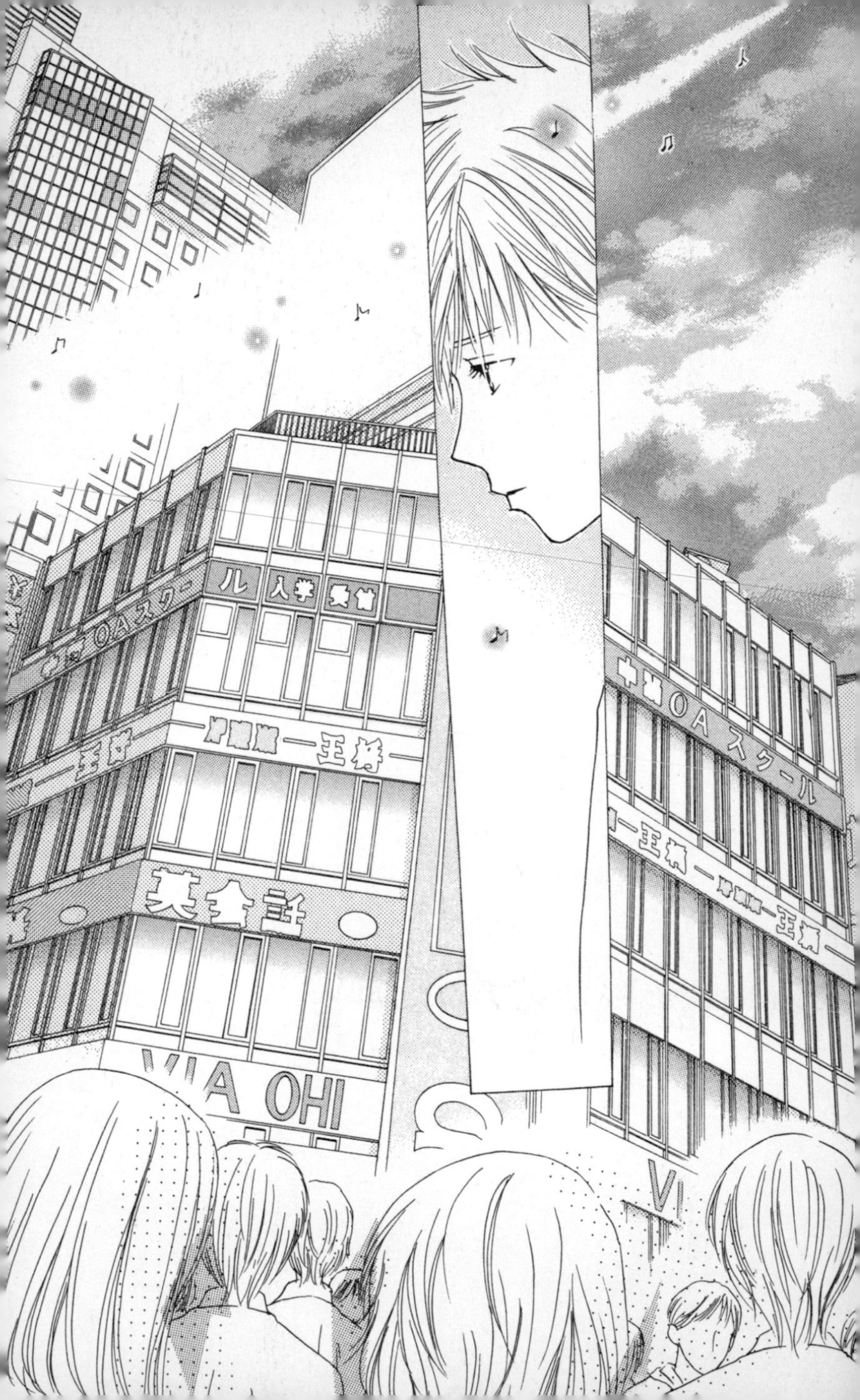
入学受付
OA スクール
王将
VIA OHI

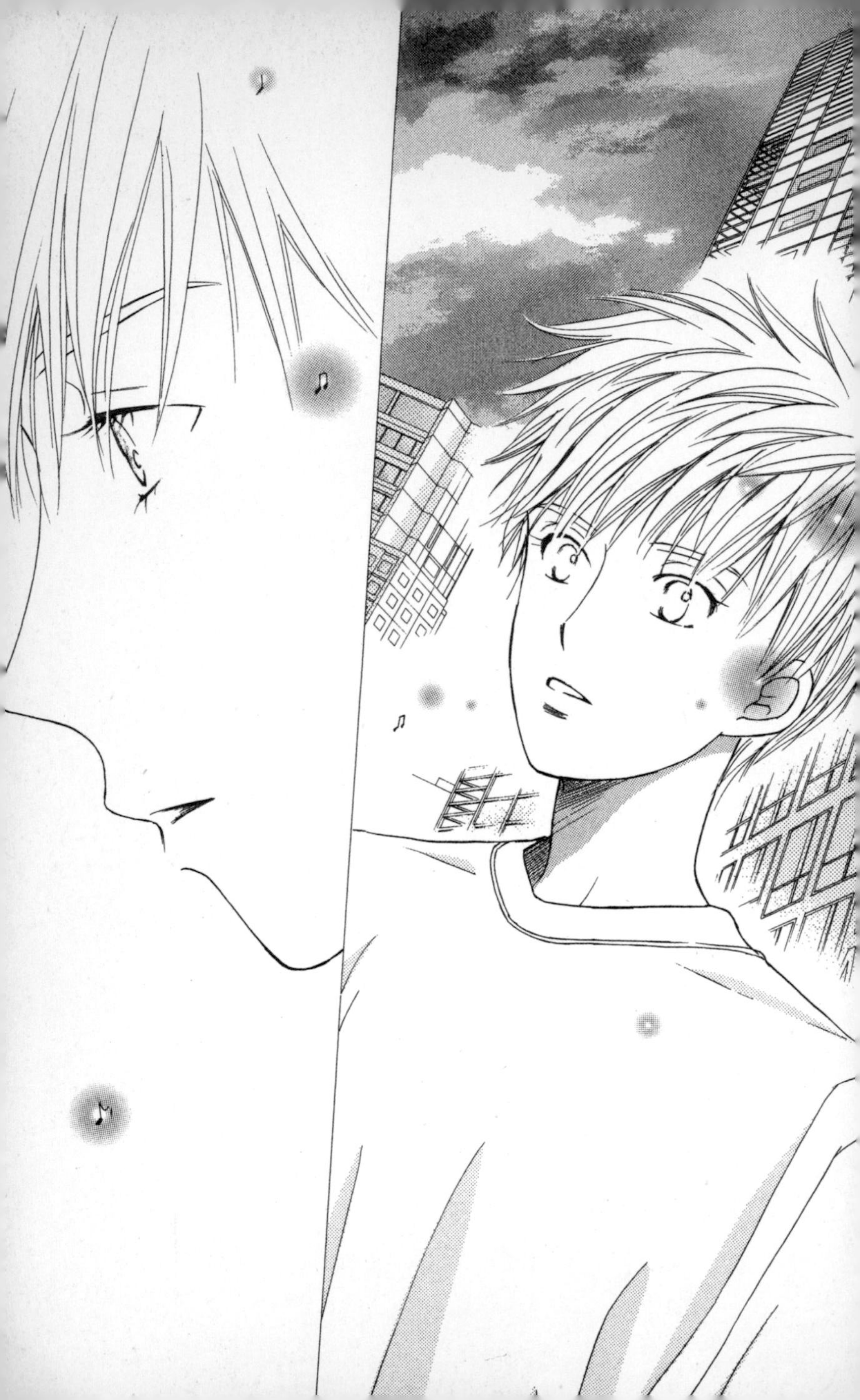

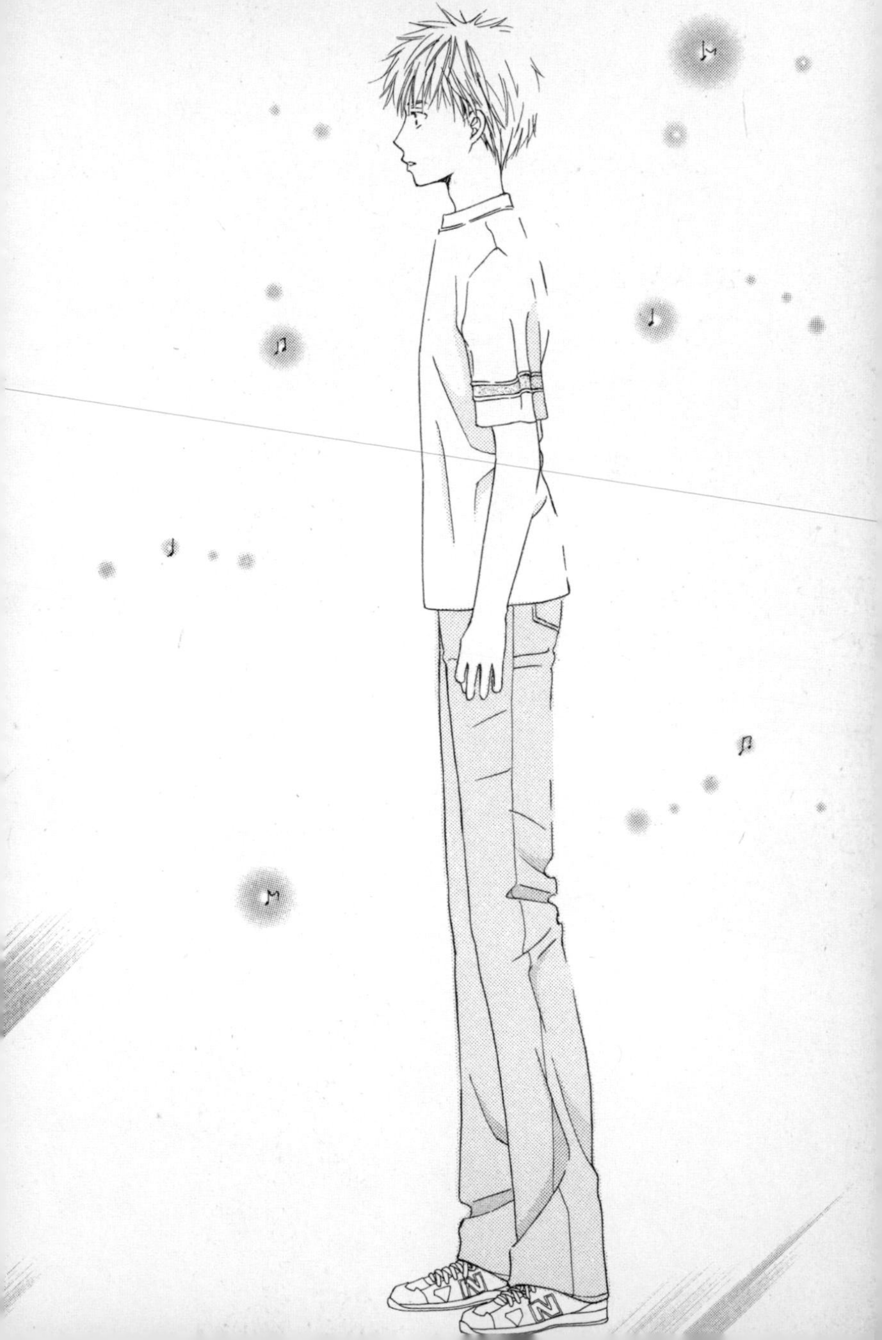

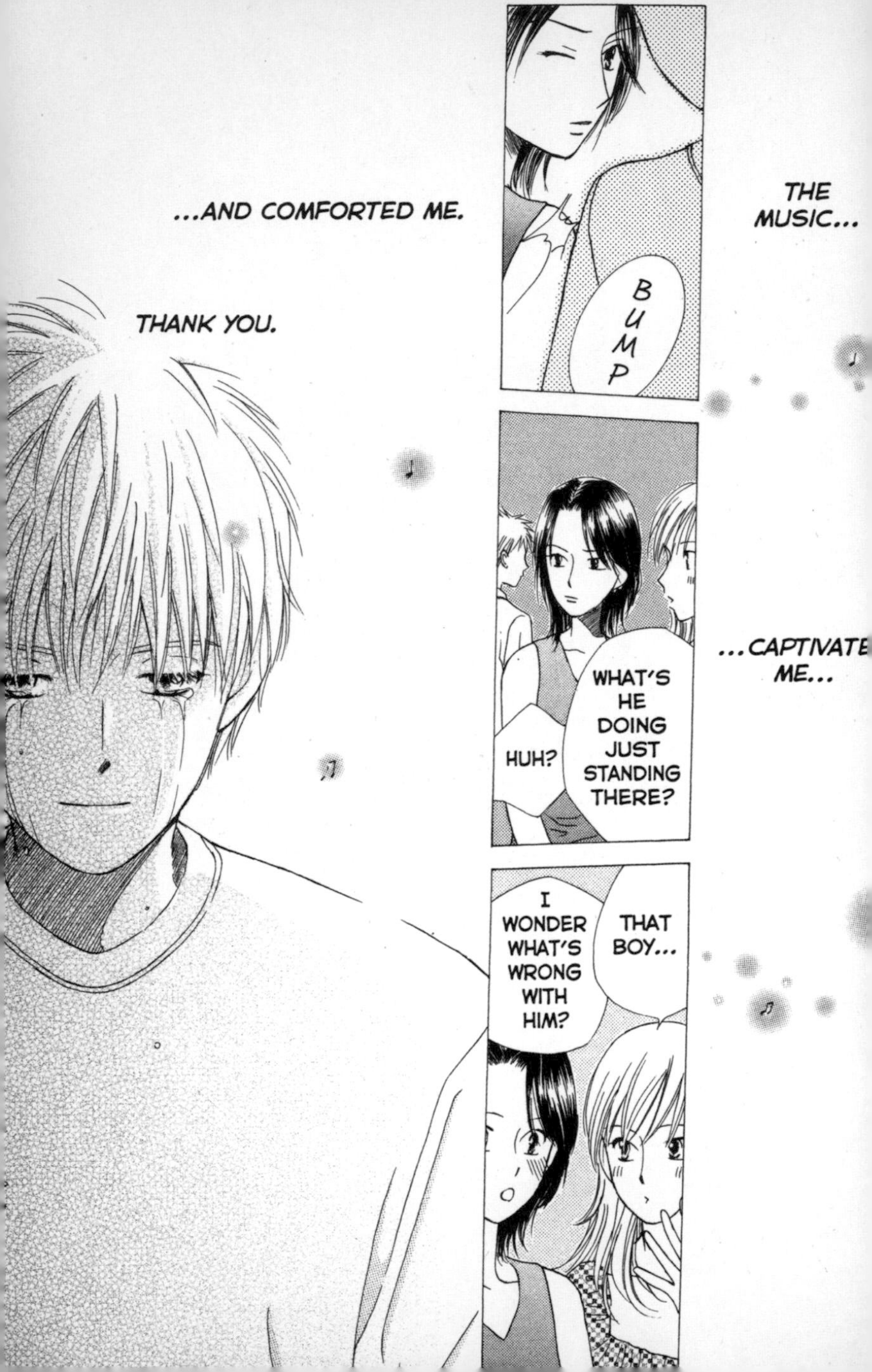
THE MUSIC...
BUMP
...CAPTIVATE ME...
WHAT'S HE DOING JUST STANDING THERE?
HUH?
THAT BOY...
I WONDER WHAT'S WRONG WITH HIM?
...AND COMFORTED ME.
THANK YOU.

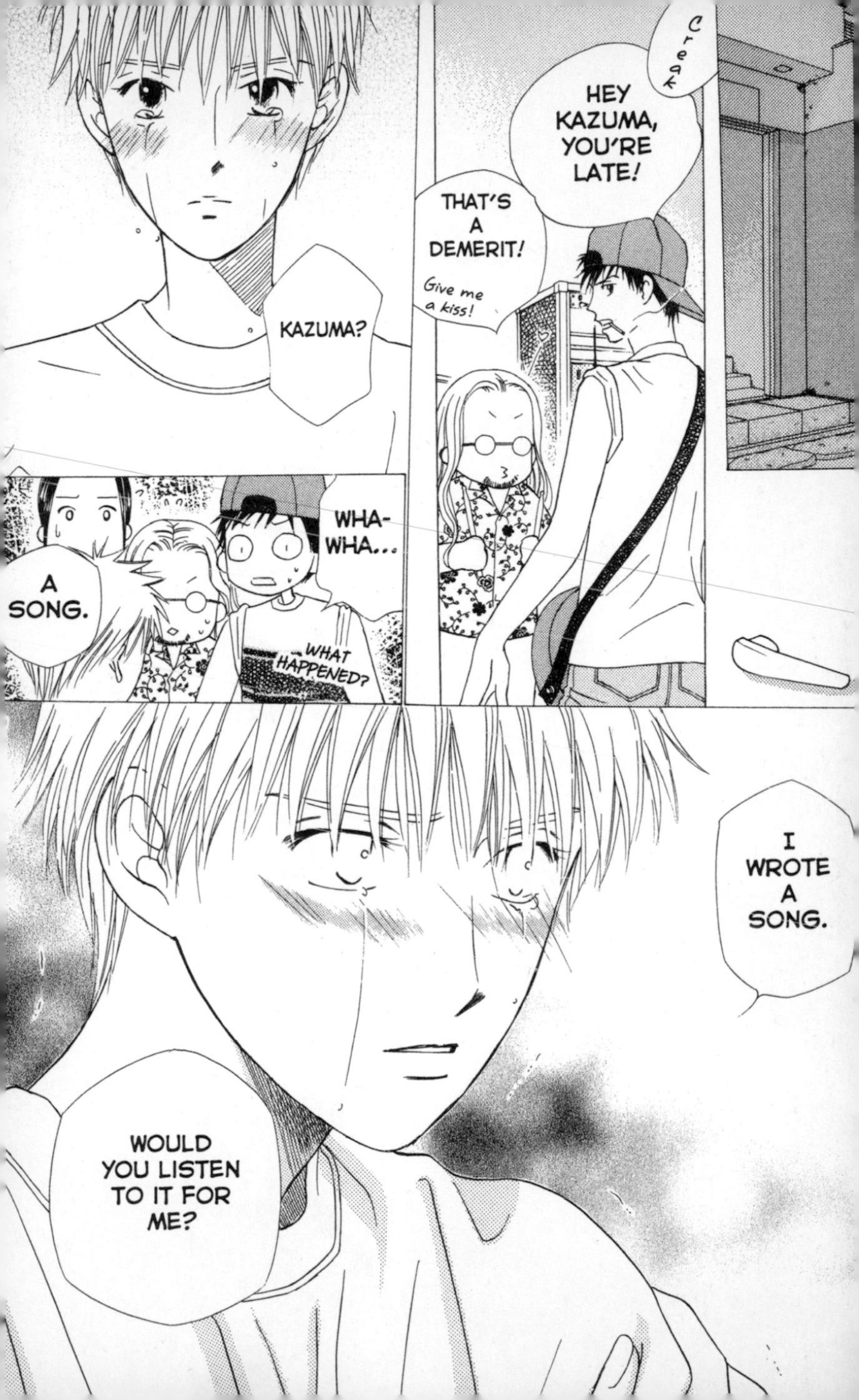
Creak
HEY KAZUMA, YOU'RE LATE!
THAT'S A DEMERIT!
Give me a kiss!
KAZUMA?
WHA-WHA...
WHAT HAPPENED?
A SONG.
I WROTE A SONG.
WOULD YOU LISTEN TO IT FOR ME?

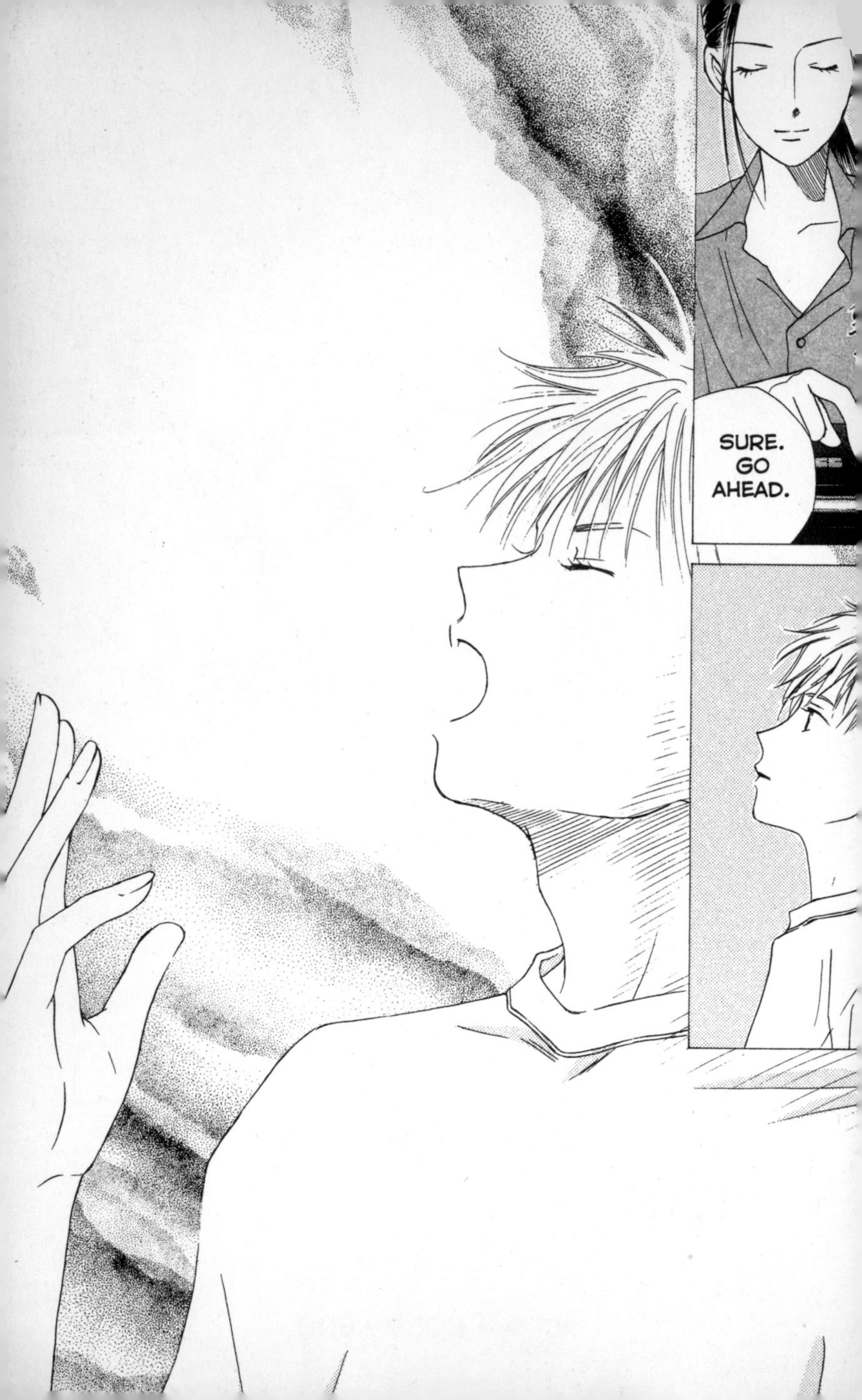
SURE. GO AHEAD.

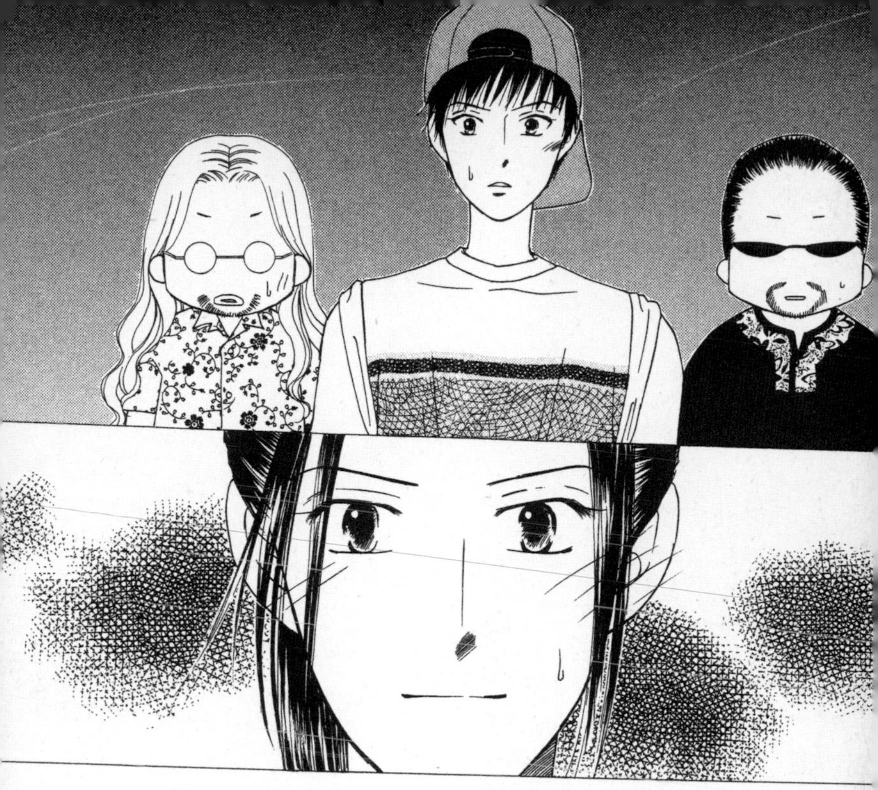

ON THAT DAY,
MY LIFE REALLY
BEGAN.

ACT 54 ★ BORN / END

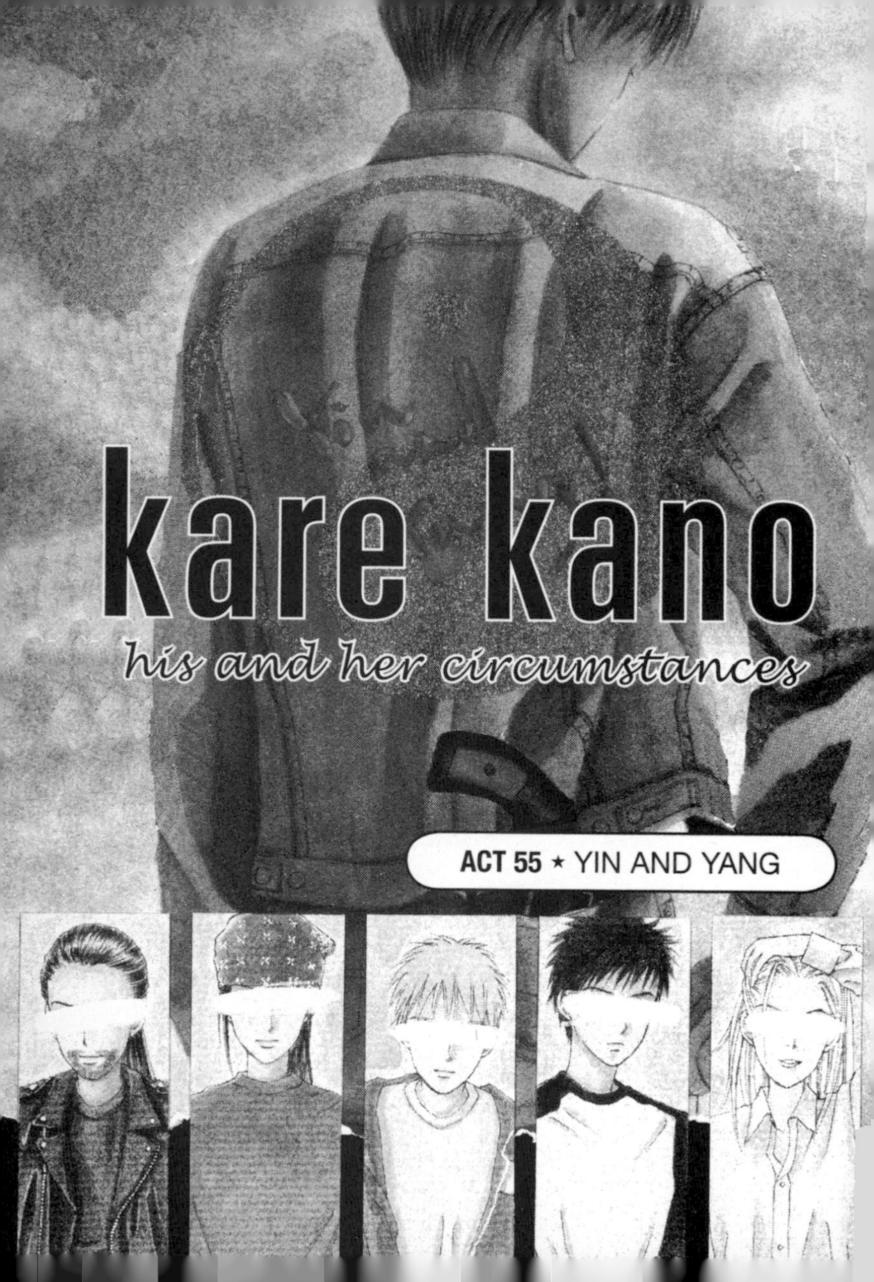
kare kano
his and her circumstances
ACT 55 ★ YIN AND YANG

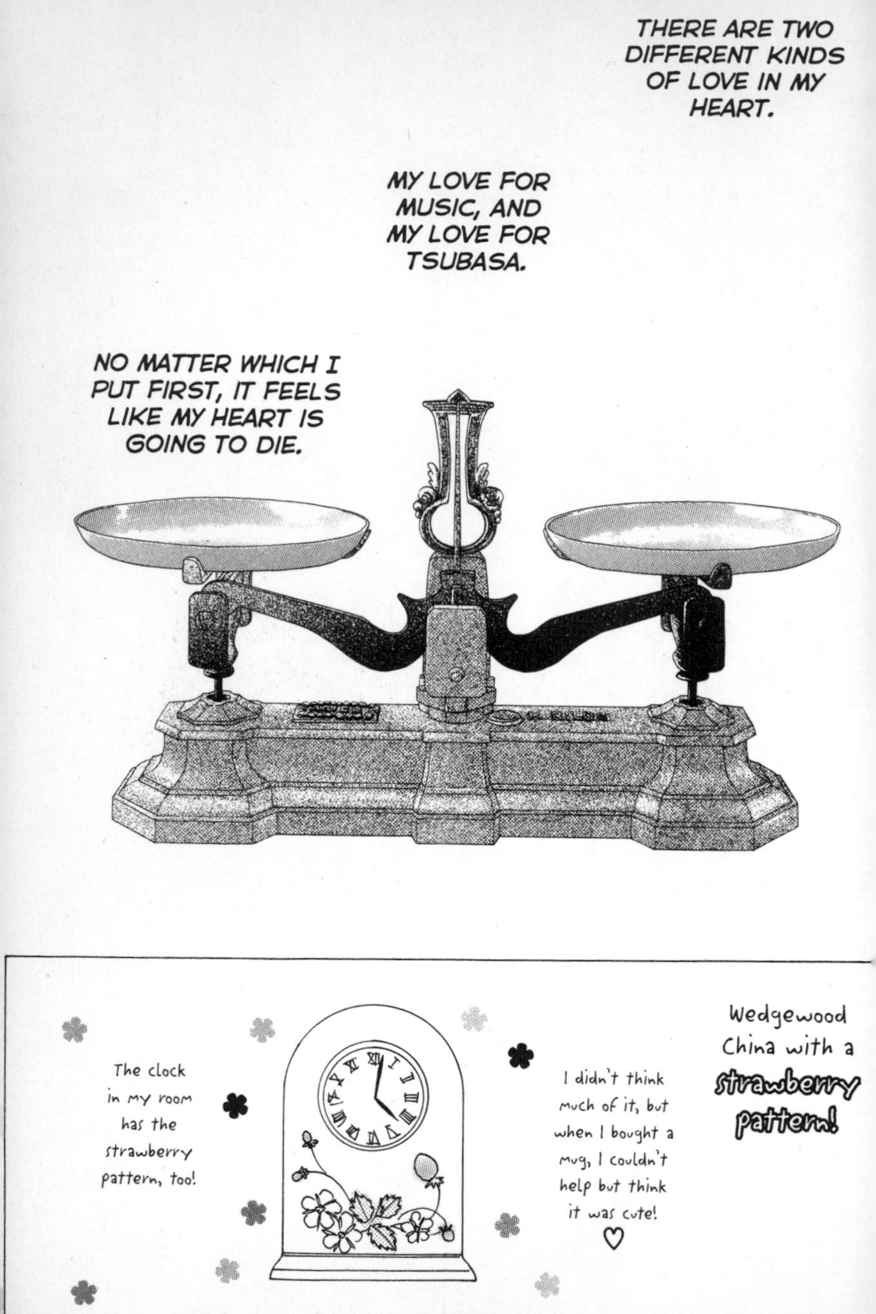
THERE ARE TWO DIFFERENT KINDS OF LOVE IN MY HEART.
MY LOVE FOR MUSIC, AND MY LOVE FOR TSUBASA.
NO MATTER WHICH I PUT FIRST, IT FEELS LIKE MY HEART IS GOING TO DIE.
Wedgewood China with a strawberry pattern!
I didn't think much of it, but when I bought a mug, I couldn't help but think it was cute! ♡
The clock in my room has the strawberry pattern, too!

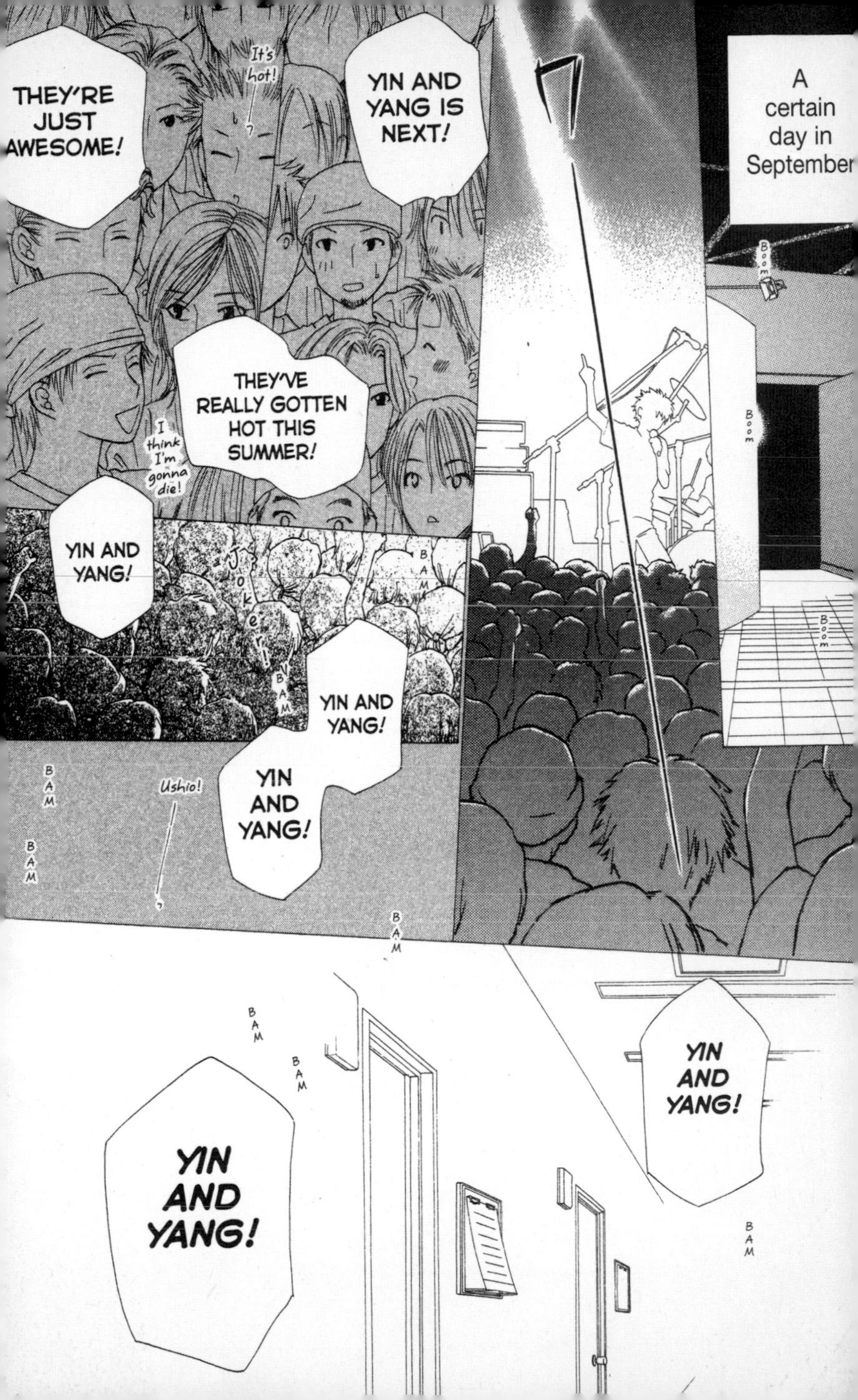
A certain day in September
Boom
Boom
Boom
YIN AND YANG IS NEXT!
It's hot!
THEY'RE JUST AWESOME!
THEY'VE REALLY GOTTEN HOT THIS SUMMER!
I think I'm gonna die!
YIN AND YANG!
BAM
Joker!
BAM
BAM
YIN AND YANG!
YIN AND YANG!
Ushio!
BAM
BAM
BAM
YIN AND YANG!
BAM
BAM
BAM
YIN AND YANG!

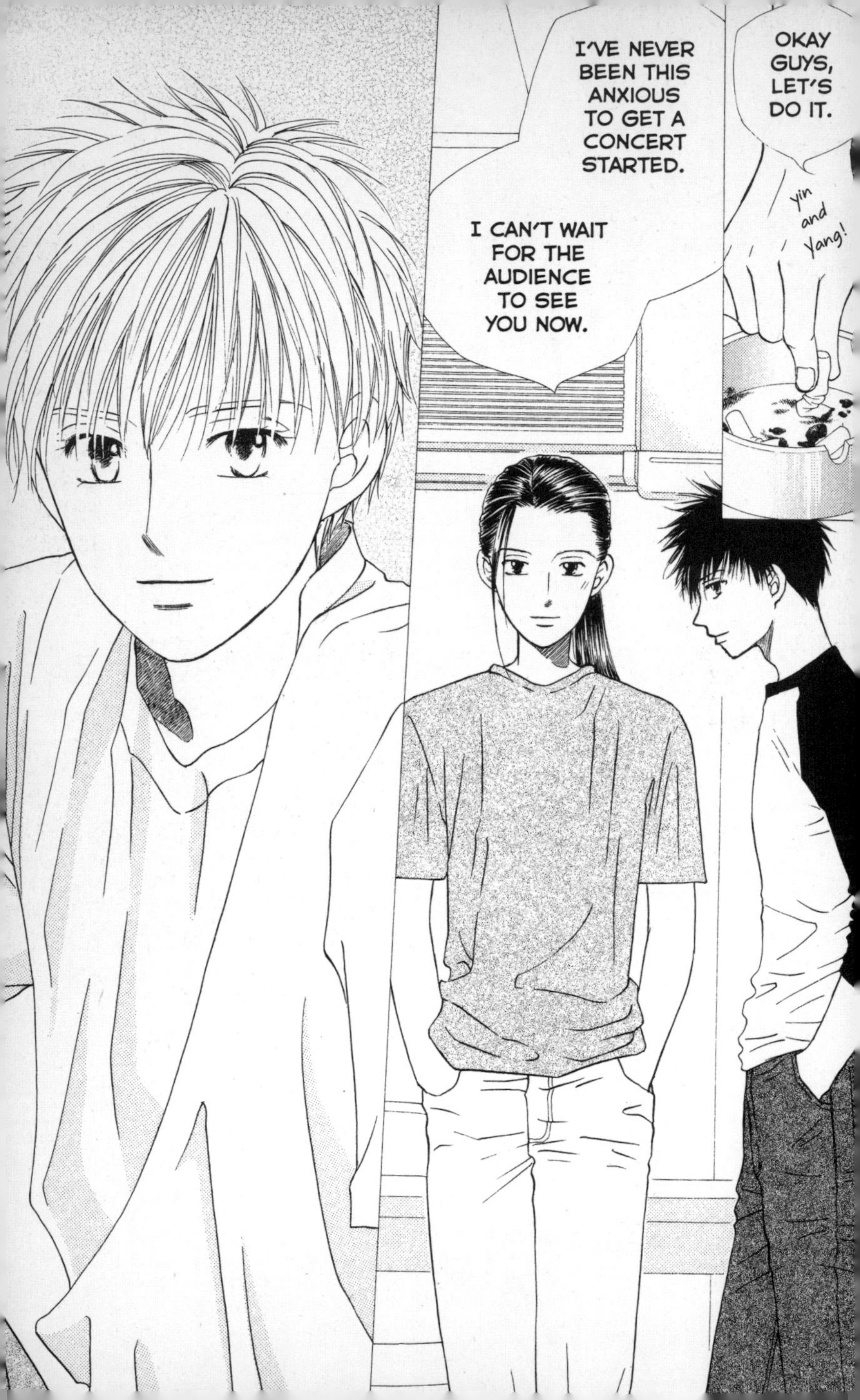
OKAY GUYS, LET'S DO IT.
yin and Yang!
I'VE NEVER BEEN THIS ANXIOUS TO GET A CONCERT STARTED.
I CAN'T WAIT FOR THE AUDIENCE TO SEE YOU NOW.

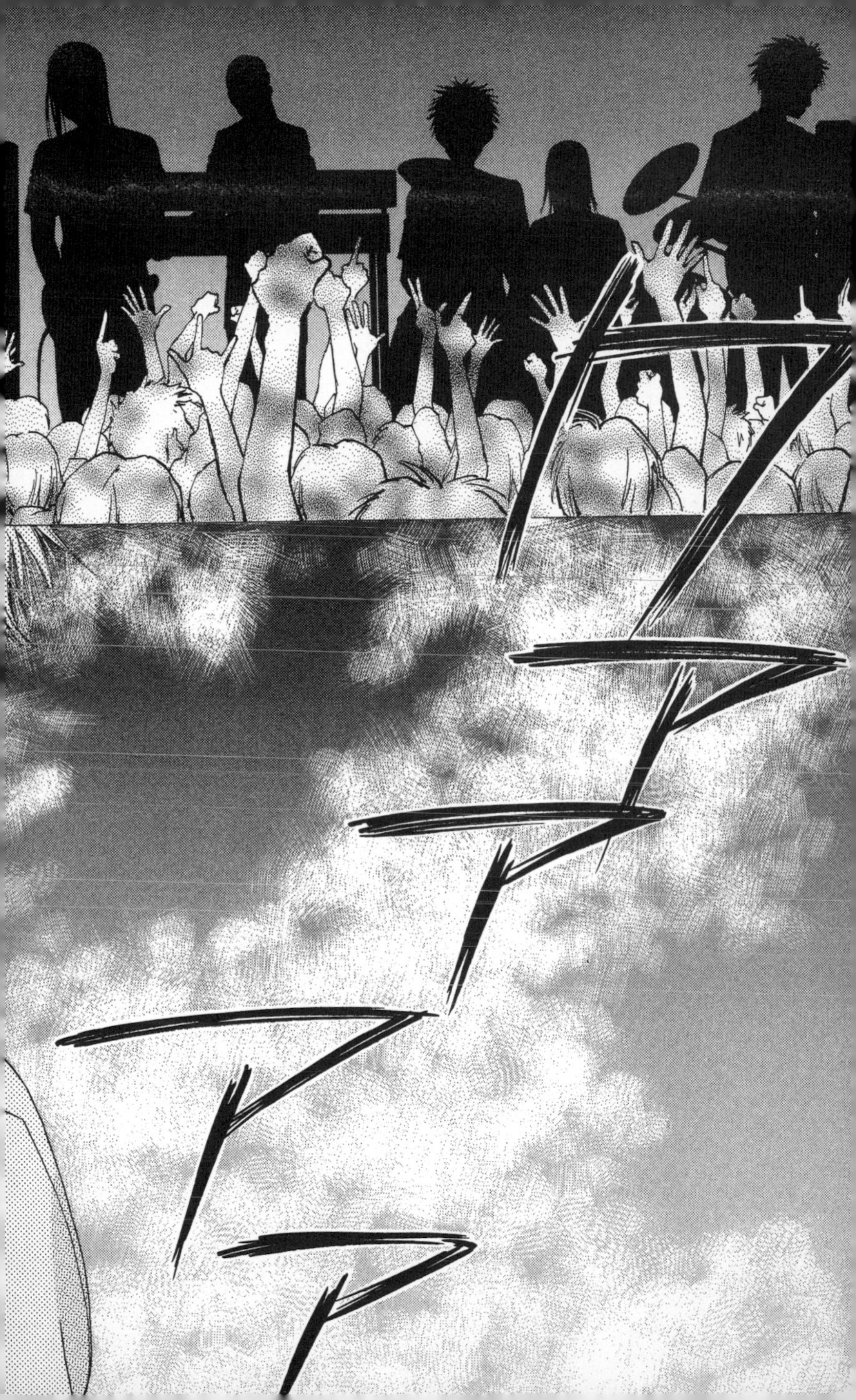
ワアアアア

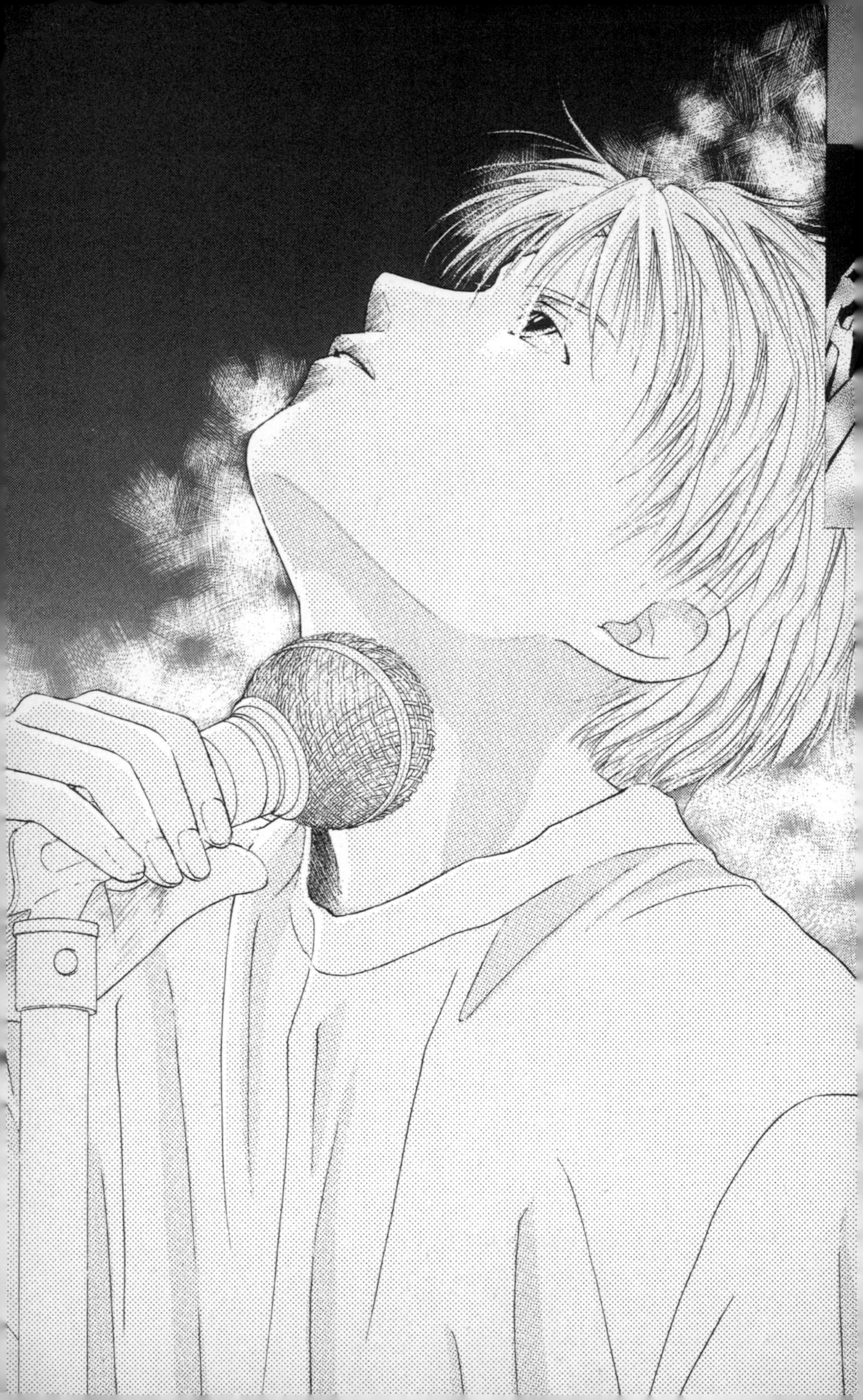

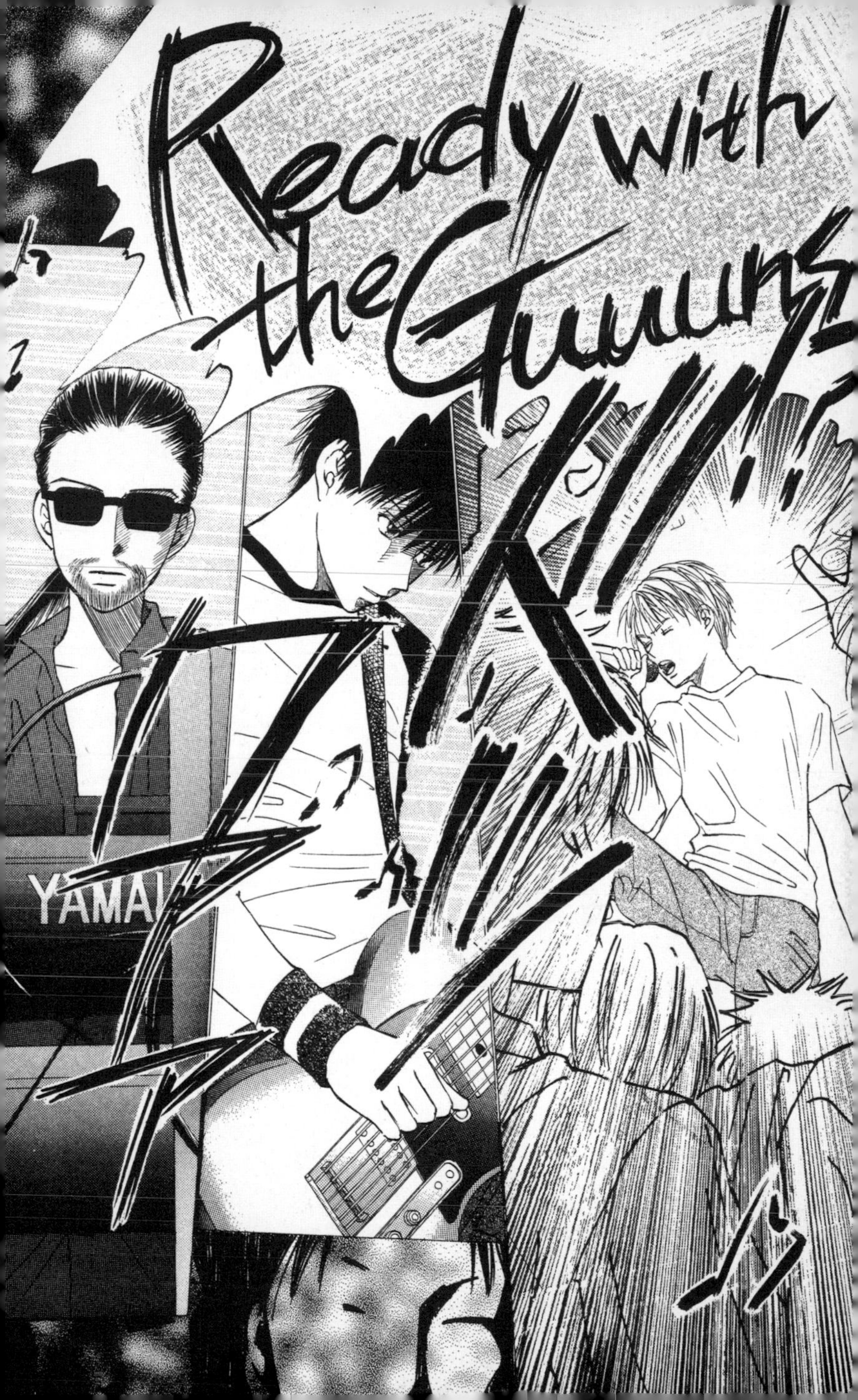
Ready with the Guuuuns
YAMA

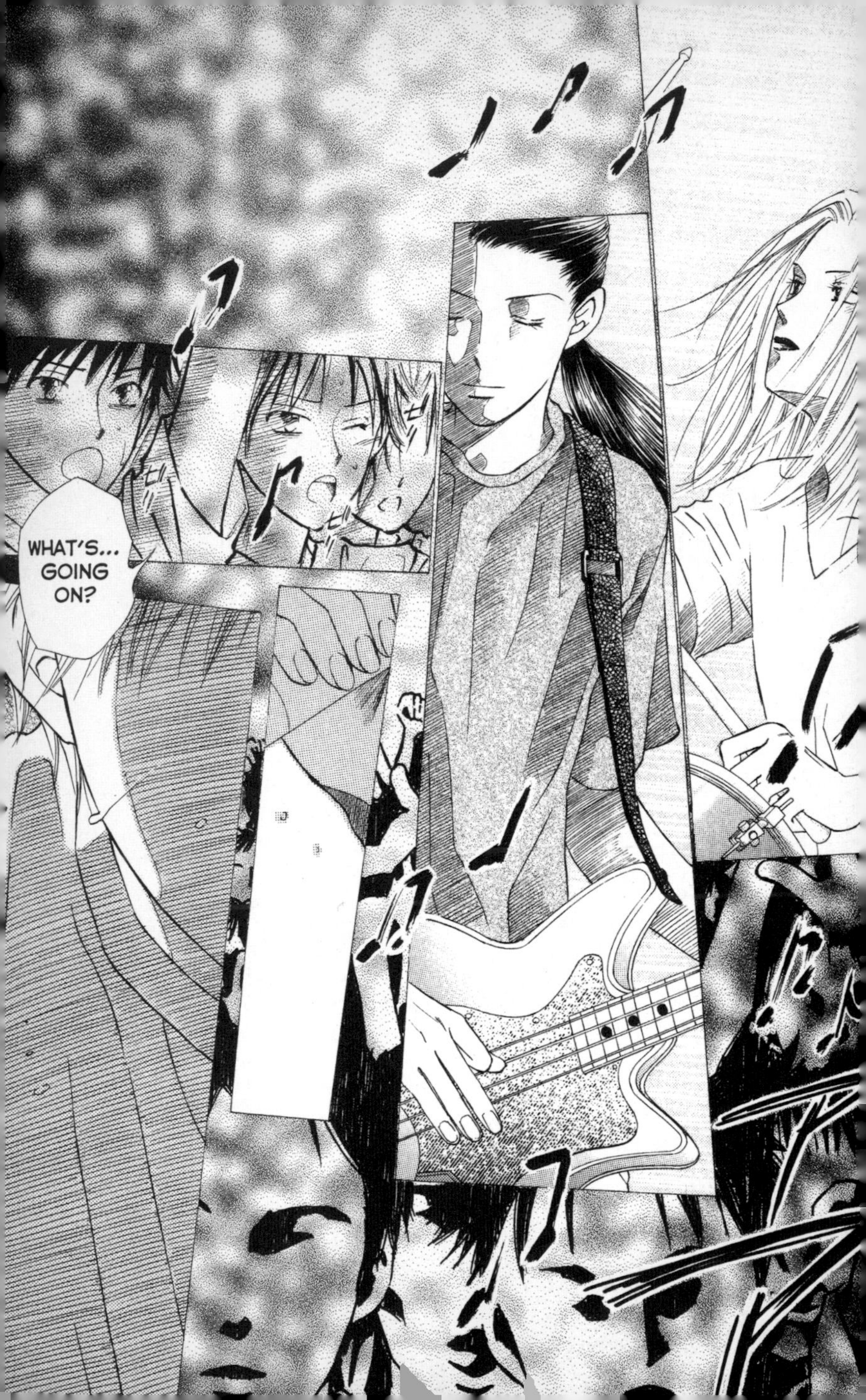
WHAT'S... GOING ON?

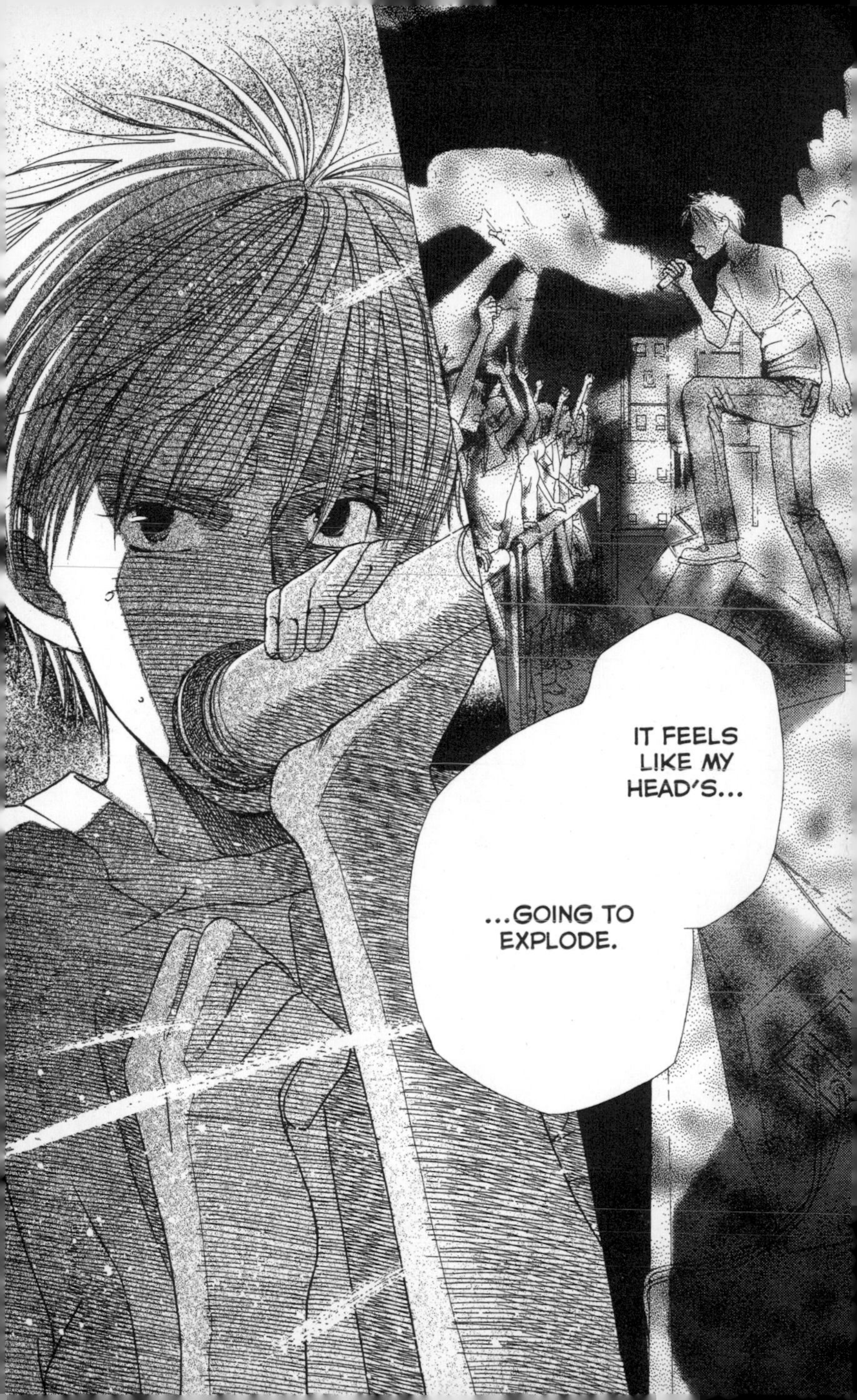
IT FEELS LIKE MY HEAD'S...
...GOING TO EXPLODE.

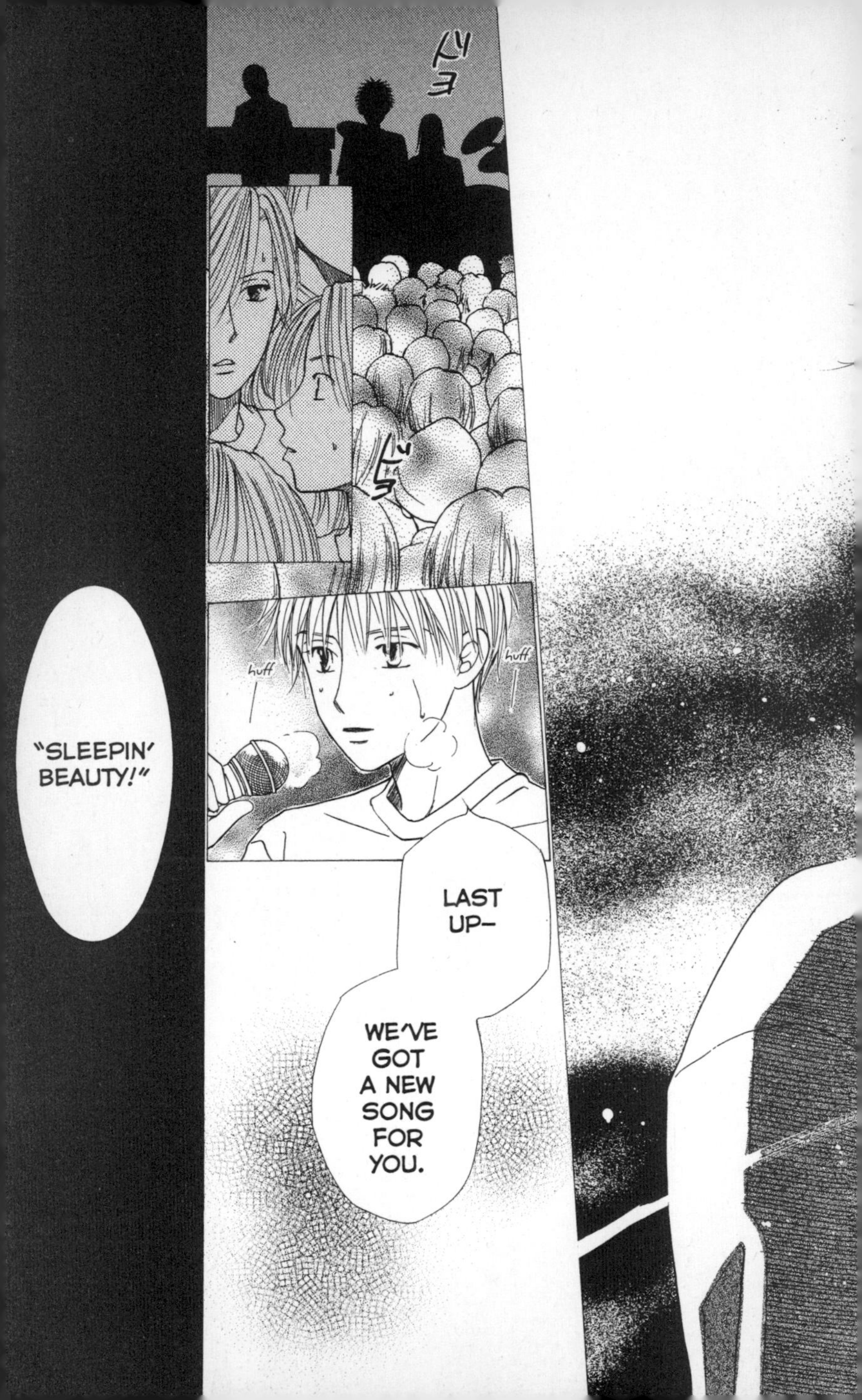
huff
huff
LAST UP–
WE'VE GOT A NEW SONG FOR YOU.
"SLEEPIN' BEAUTY!"

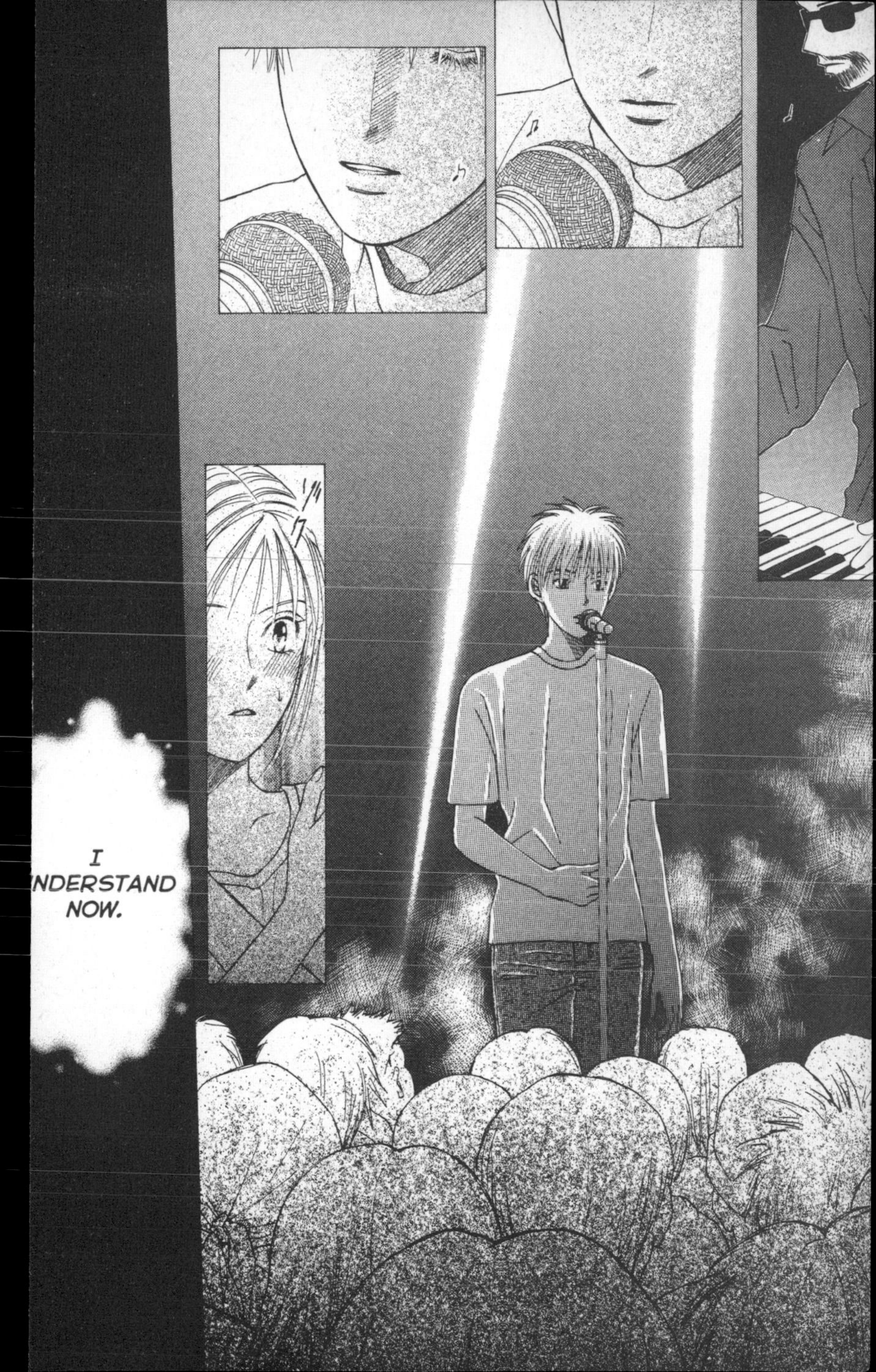
I UNDERSTAND NOW.

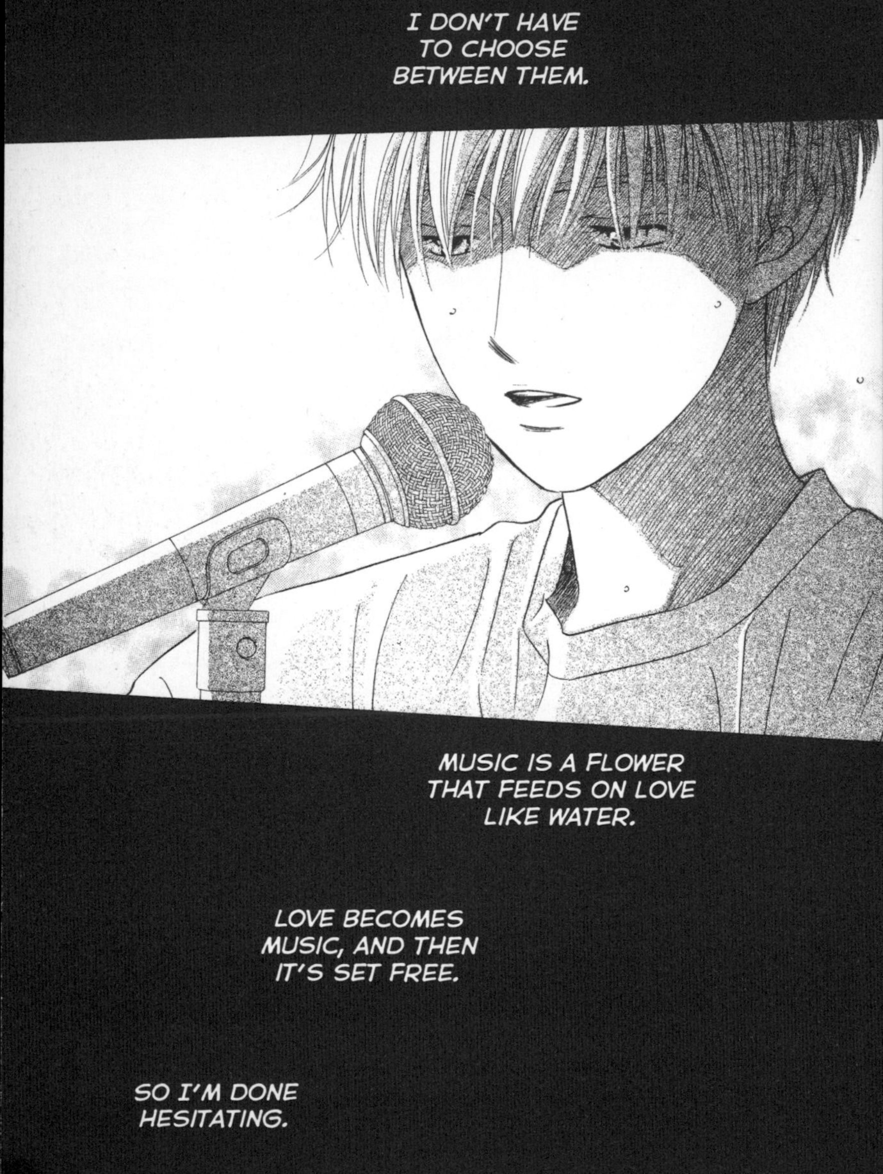
I DON'T HAVE TO CHOOSE BETWEEN THEM.
MUSIC IS A FLOWER THAT FEEDS ON LOVE LIKE WATER.
LOVE BECOMES MUSIC, AND THEN IT'S SET FREE.
SO I'M DONE HESITATING.

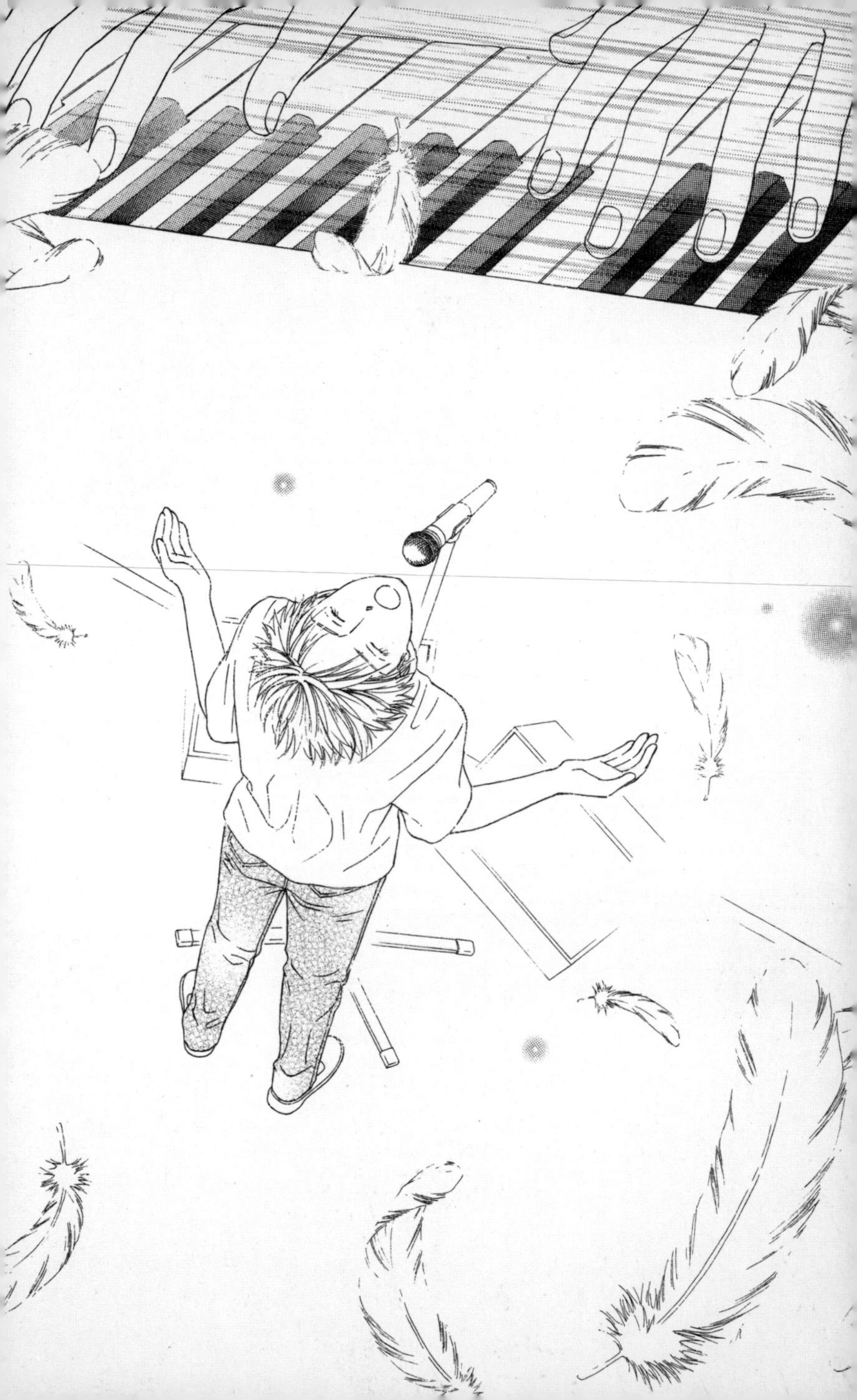

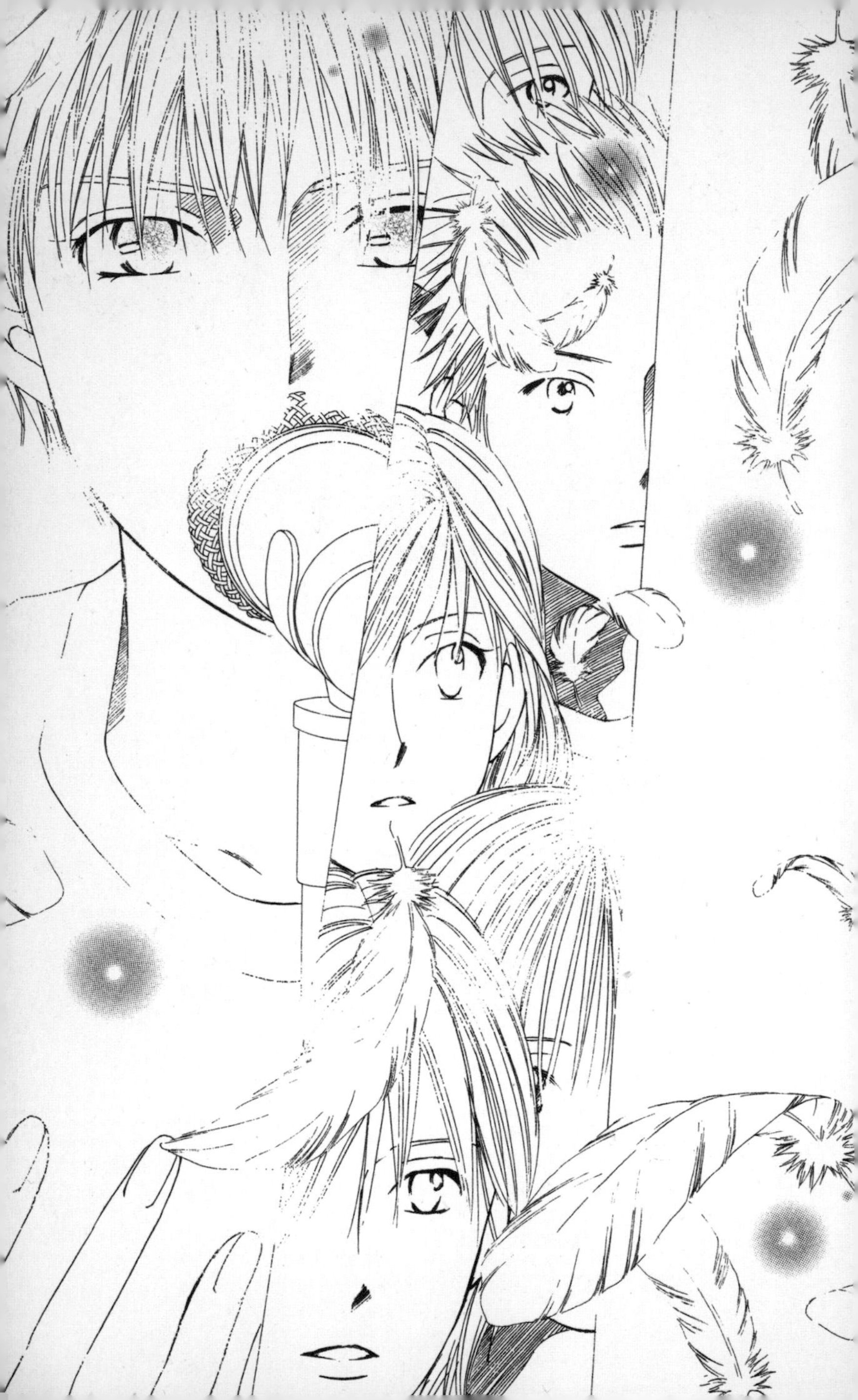

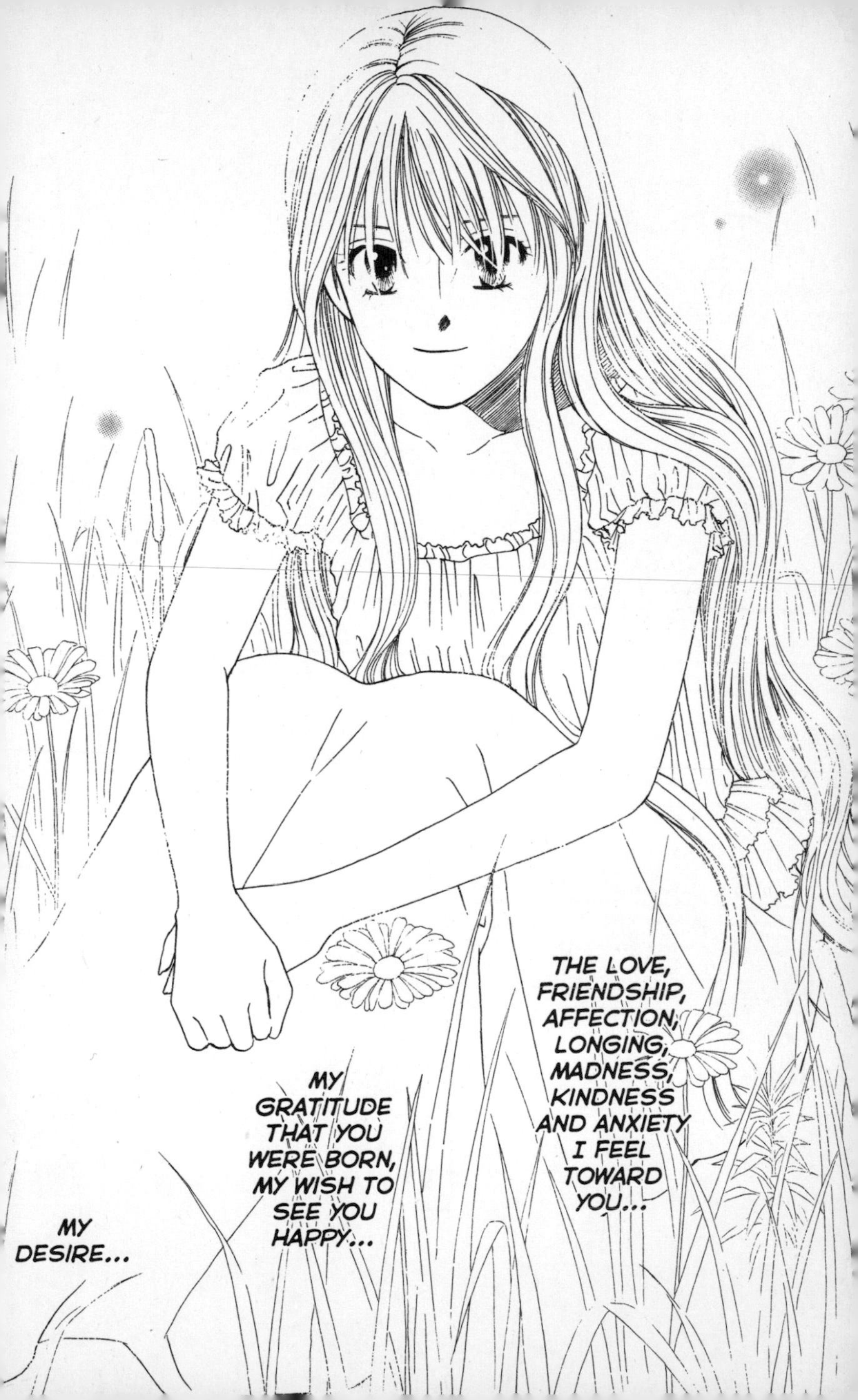
THE LOVE, FRIENDSHIP, AFFECTION, LONGING, MADNESS, KINDNESS AND ANXIETY I FEEL TOWARD YOU...
MY GRATITUDE THAT YOU WERE BORN, MY WISH TO SEE YOU HAPPY...
MY DESIRE...

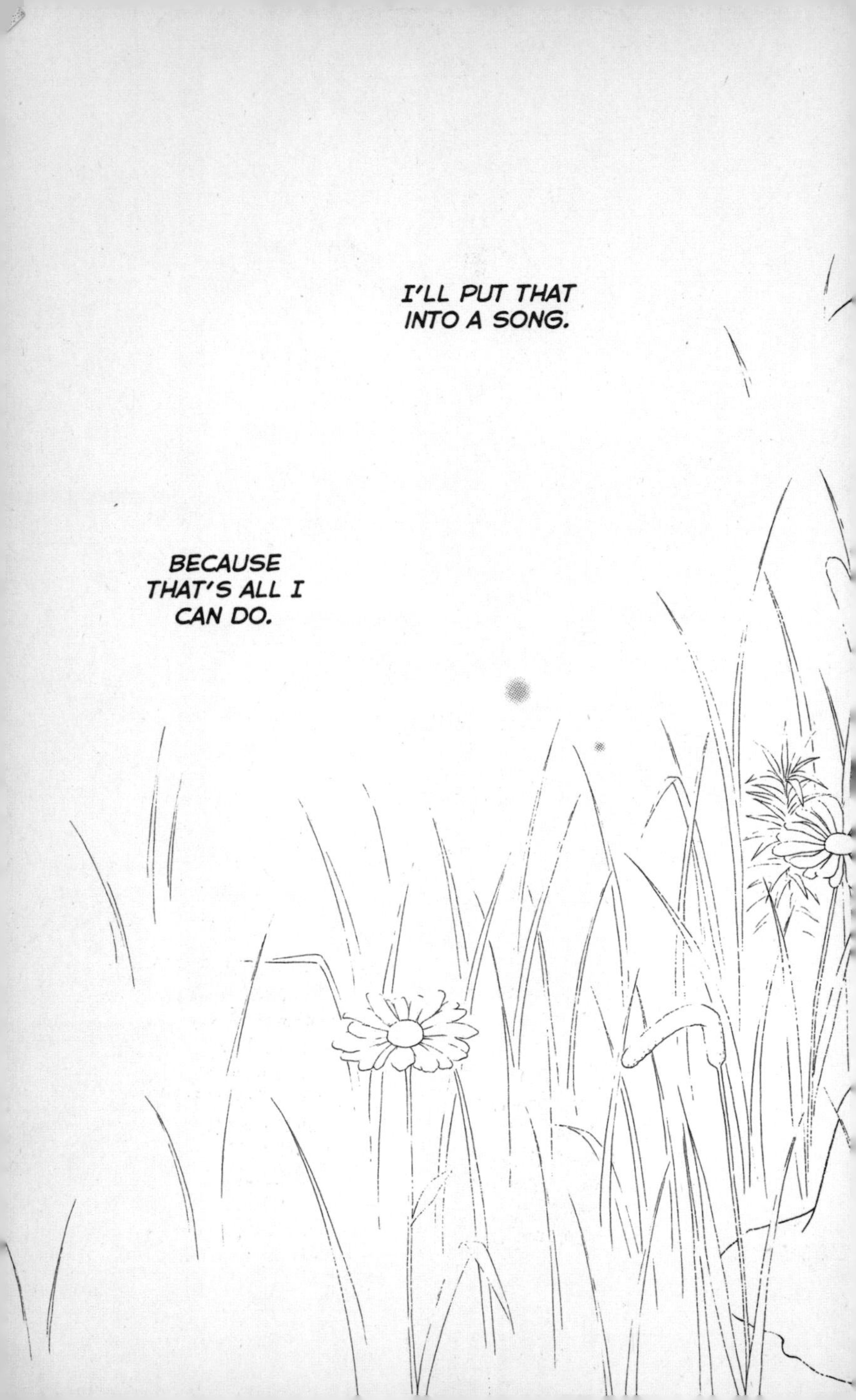
I'LL PUT THAT INTO A SONG.
BECAUSE THAT'S ALL I CAN DO.

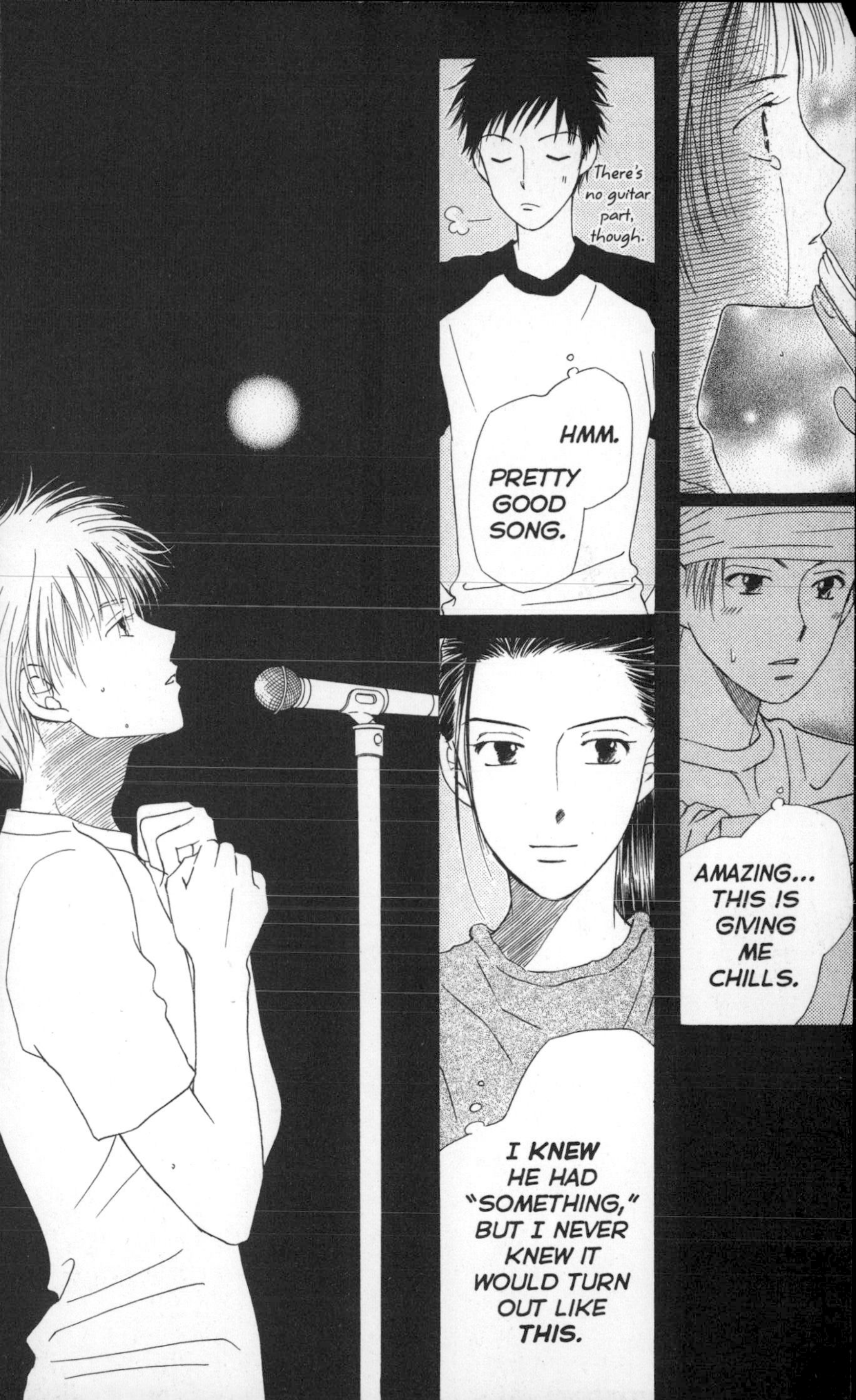
There's no guitar part, though.
HMM.
PRETTY GOOD SONG.
AMAZING... THIS IS GIVING ME CHILLS.
I KNEW HE HAD "SOMETHING," BUT I NEVER KNEW IT WOULD TURN OUT LIKE THIS.

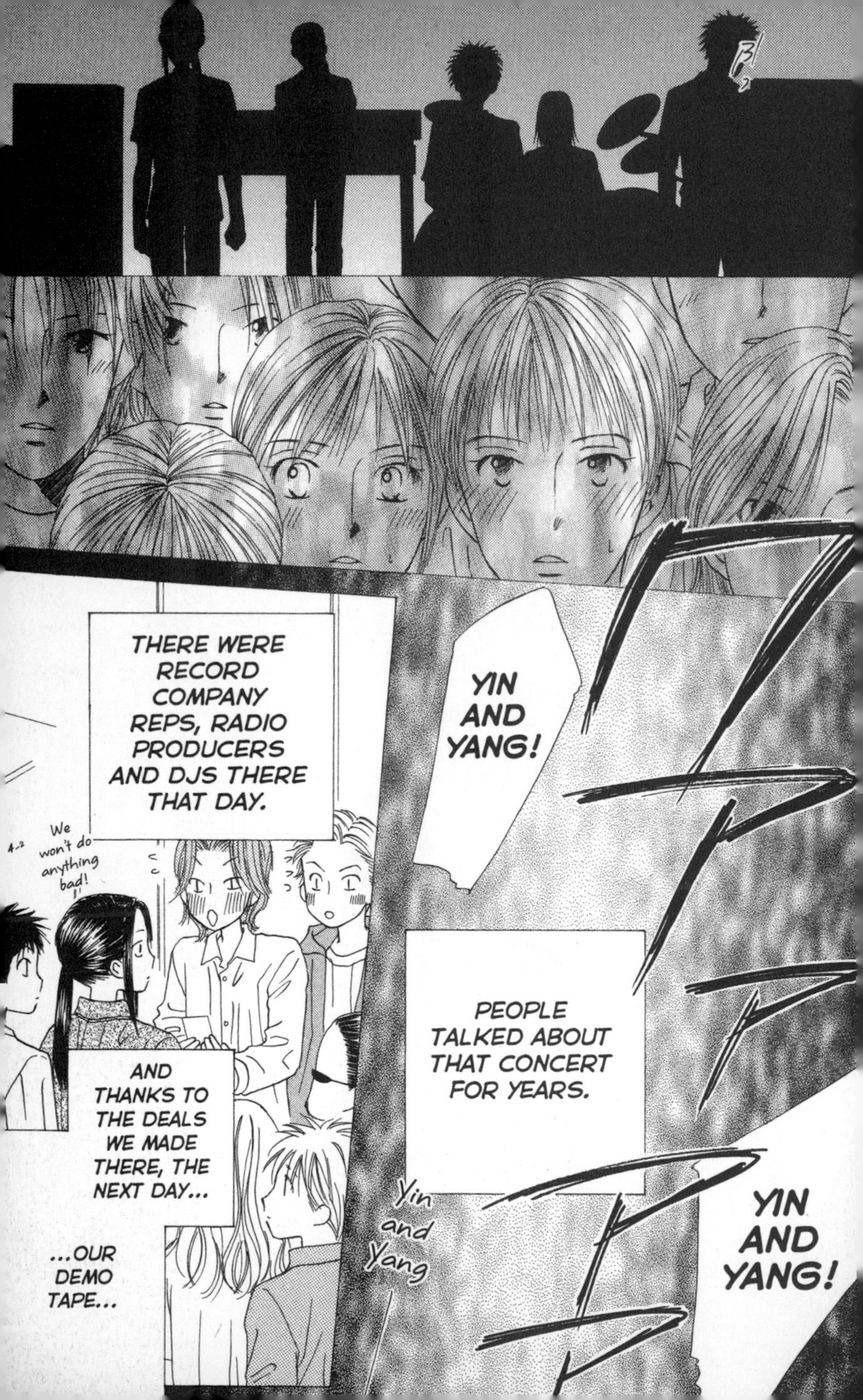
YIN AND YANG!
PEOPLE TALKED ABOUT THAT CONCERT FOR YEARS.
YIN AND YANG!
Yin and Yang
THERE WERE RECORD COMPANY REPS, RADIO PRODUCERS AND DJS THERE THAT DAY.
We won't do anything bad!
AND THANKS TO THE DEALS WE MADE THERE, THE NEXT DAY...
...OUR DEMO TAPE...

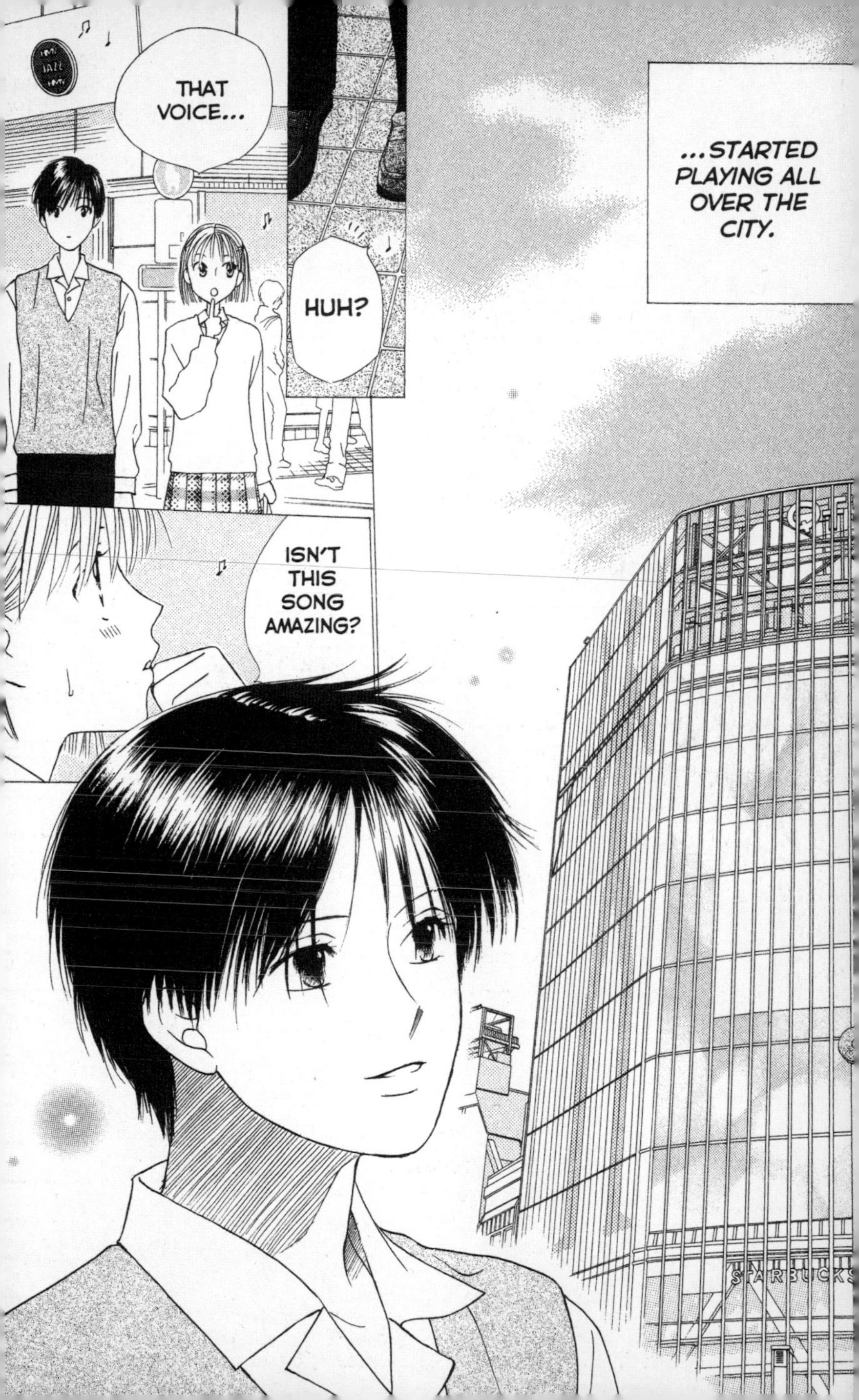
...STARTED PLAYING ALL OVER THE CITY.
HUH?
THAT VOICE...
ISN'T THIS SONG AMAZING?

2

I read Kare Kano for the first time.

I never read my own manga before, because I see nothing but the bad points and I hate it. And I wrote the first volume six years ago, too...

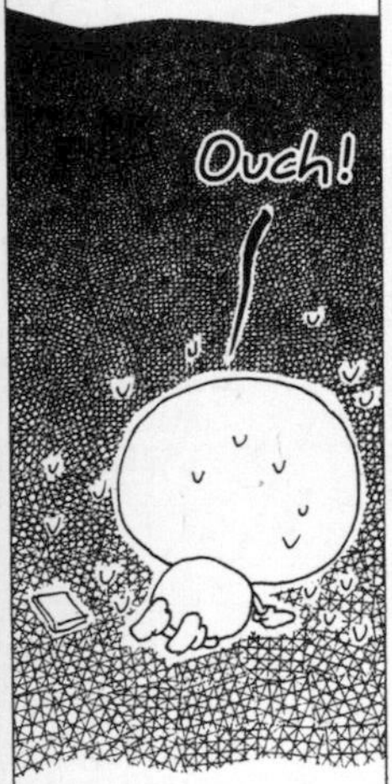
Ouch!

And to think there are some people who love the feeling the manga had in the very beginning. I'm so embarrassed.

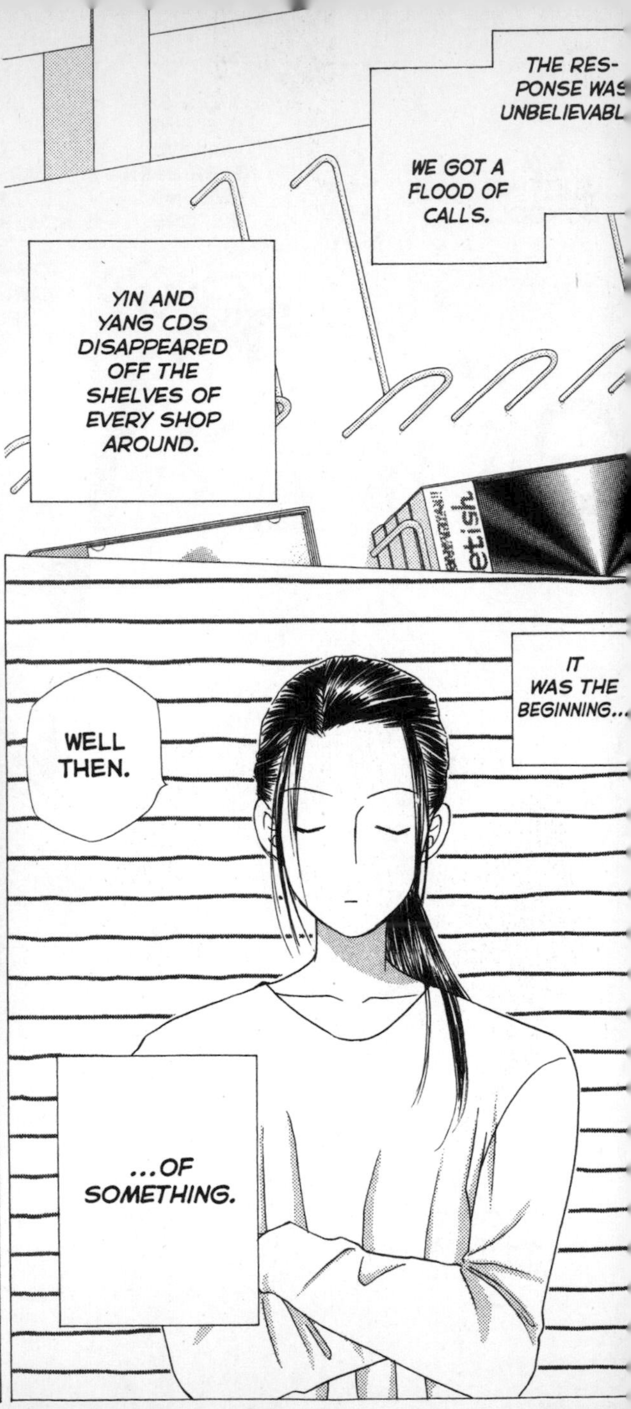
THE RES-PONSE WAS UNBELIEVABL
WE GOT A FLOOD OF CALLS.
YIN AND YANG CDS DISAPPEARED OFF THE SHELVES OF EVERY SHOP AROUND.
IT WAS THE BEGINNING...
WELL THEN.
...OF SOMETHING.

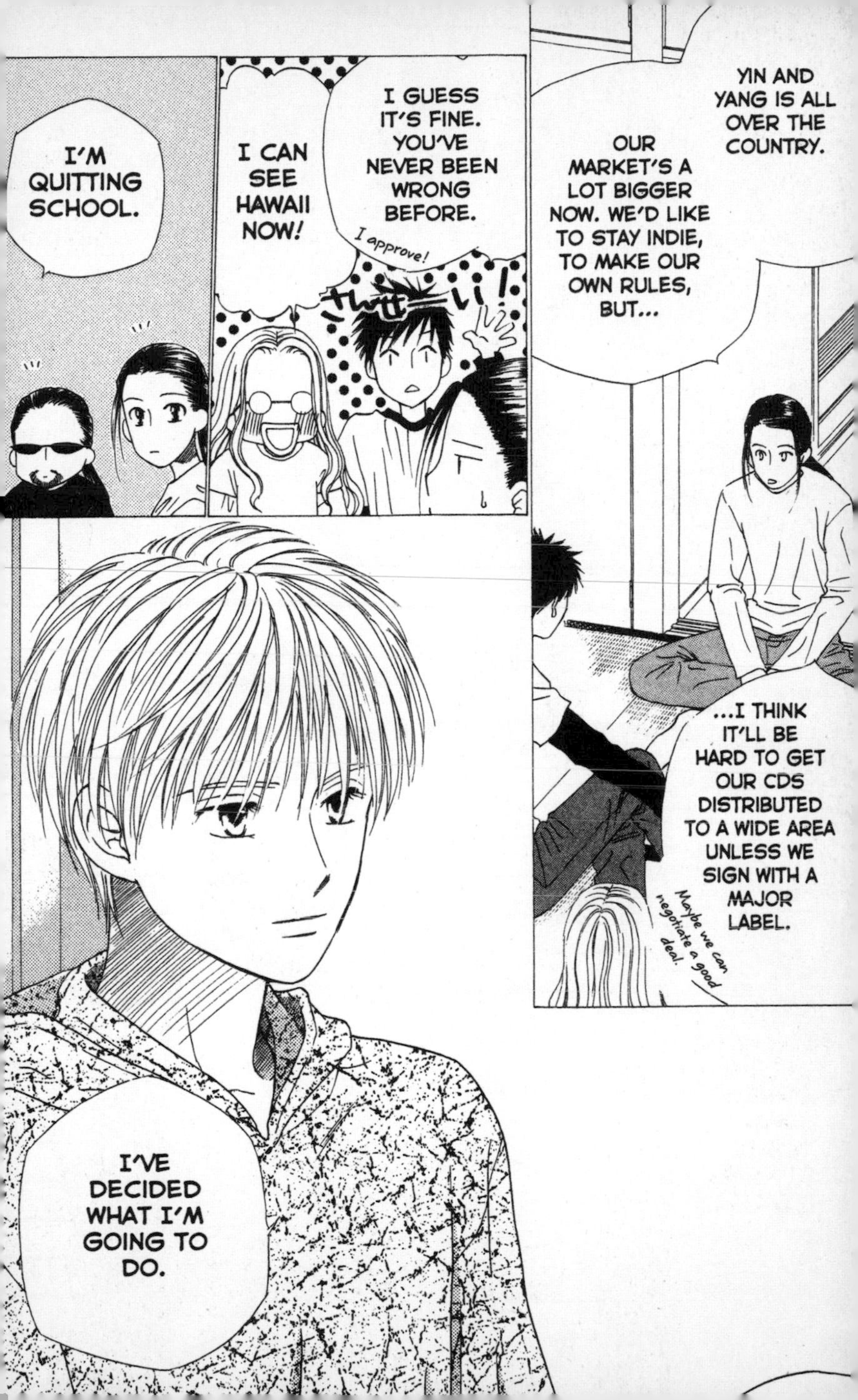
YIN AND YANG IS ALL OVER THE COUNTRY.
OUR MARKET'S A LOT BIGGER NOW. WE'D LIKE TO STAY INDIE, TO MAKE OUR OWN RULES, BUT...
...I THINK IT'LL BE HARD TO GET OUR CDS DISTRIBUTED TO A WIDE AREA UNLESS WE SIGN WITH A MAJOR LABEL.
Maybe we can negotiate a good deal.
I GUESS IT'S FINE. YOU'VE NEVER BEEN WRONG BEFORE.
I approve!
I CAN SEE HAWAII NOW!
I'M QUITTING SCHOOL.
I'VE DECIDED WHAT I'M GOING TO DO.

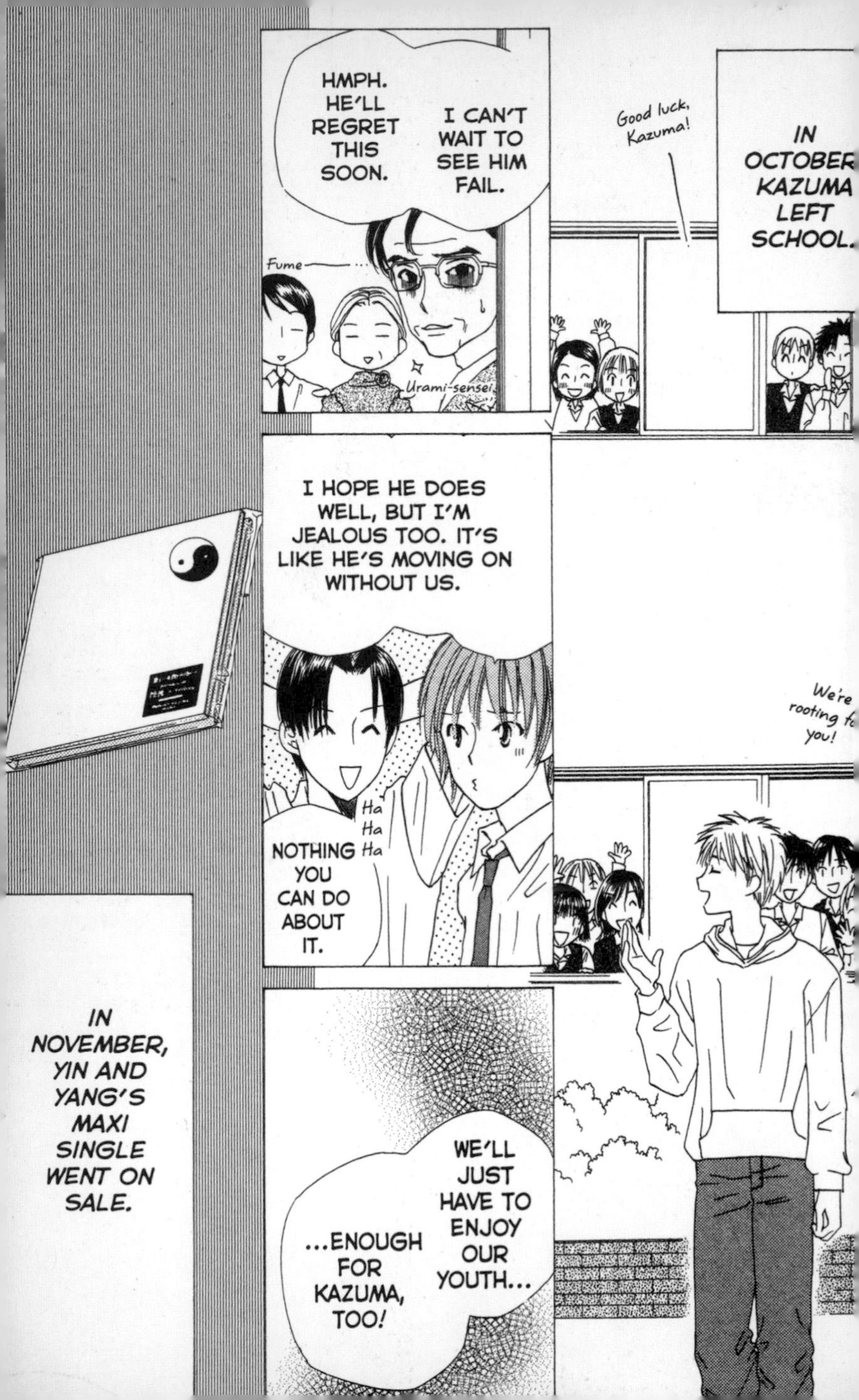
IN OCTOBER KAZUMA LEFT SCHOOL.
Good luck, Kazuma!
HMPH. HE'LL REGRET THIS SOON.
I CAN'T WAIT TO SEE HIM FAIL.
Fume......
Urami-sensei
We're rooting fo you!
I HOPE HE DOES WELL, BUT I'M JEALOUS TOO. IT'S LIKE HE'S MOVING ON WITHOUT US.
Ha Ha Ha
NOTHING YOU CAN DO ABOUT IT.
WE'LL JUST HAVE TO ENJOY OUR YOUTH...
...ENOUGH FOR KAZUMA, TOO!
IN NOVEMBER, YIN AND YANG'S MAXI SINGLE WENT ON SALE.

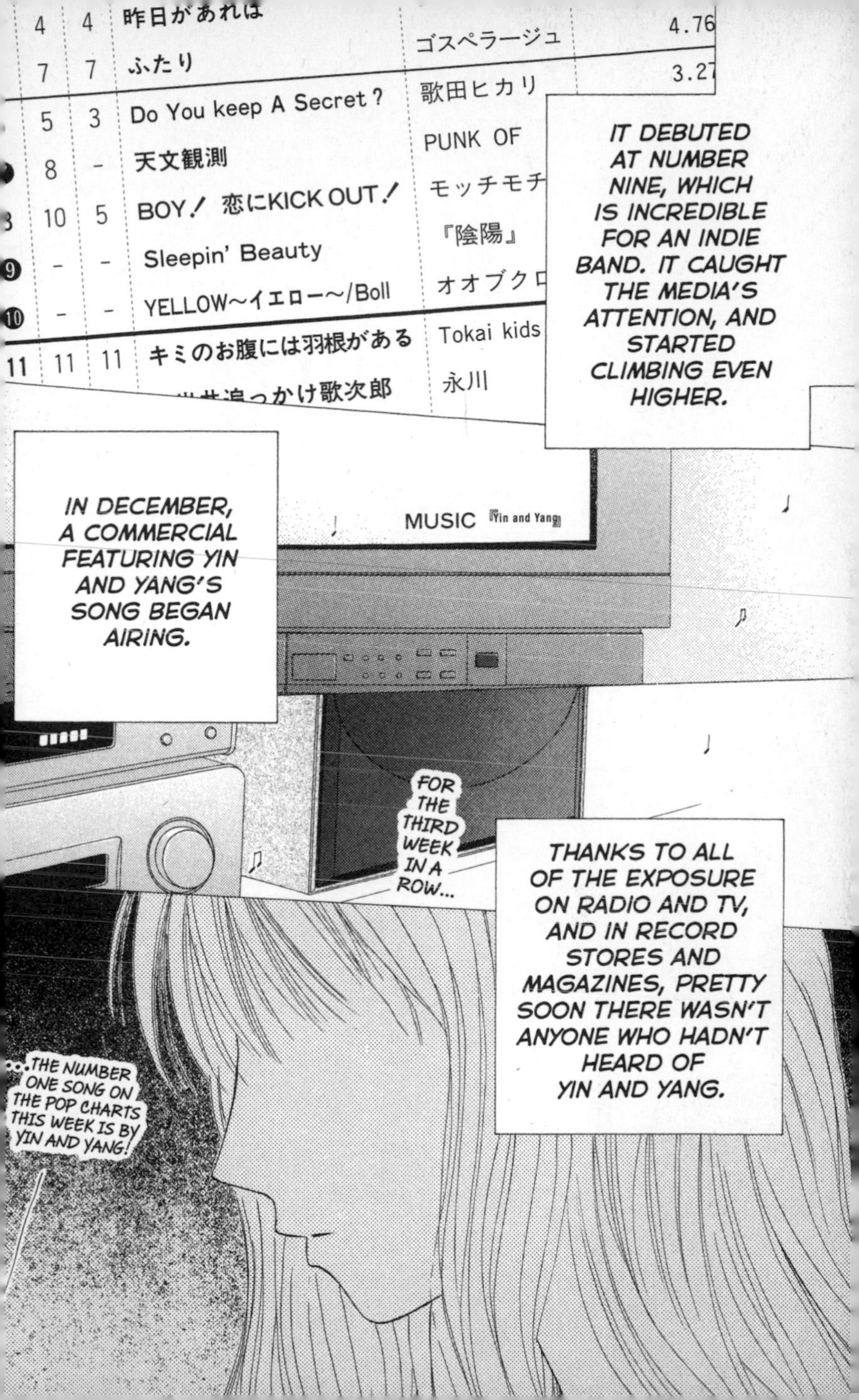
4 4 昨日があれは ゴスペラージュ 4.76
7 7 ふたり 3.27
5 3 Do You keep A Secret? 歌田ヒカリ
8 - 天文観測 PUNK OF
10 5 BOY! 恋にKICK OUT! モッチモチ
- - Sleepin' Beauty 『陰陽』
- - YELLOW〜イエロー〜/Boll オオブクロ
11 11 11 キミのお腹には羽根がある Tokai kids
永川
IT DEBUTED AT NUMBER NINE, WHICH IS INCREDIBLE FOR AN INDIE BAND. IT CAUGHT THE MEDIA'S ATTENTION, AND STARTED CLIMBING EVEN HIGHER.
IN DECEMBER, A COMMERCIAL FEATURING YIN AND YANG'S SONG BEGAN AIRING.
MUSIC 『Yin and Yang』
THANKS TO ALL OF THE EXPOSURE ON RADIO AND TV, AND IN RECORD STORES AND MAGAZINES, PRETTY SOON THERE WASN'T ANYONE WHO HADN'T HEARD OF YIN AND YANG.
FOR THE THIRD WEEK IN A ROW...
...THE NUMBER ONE SONG ON THE POP CHARTS THIS WEEK IS BY YIN AND YANG!

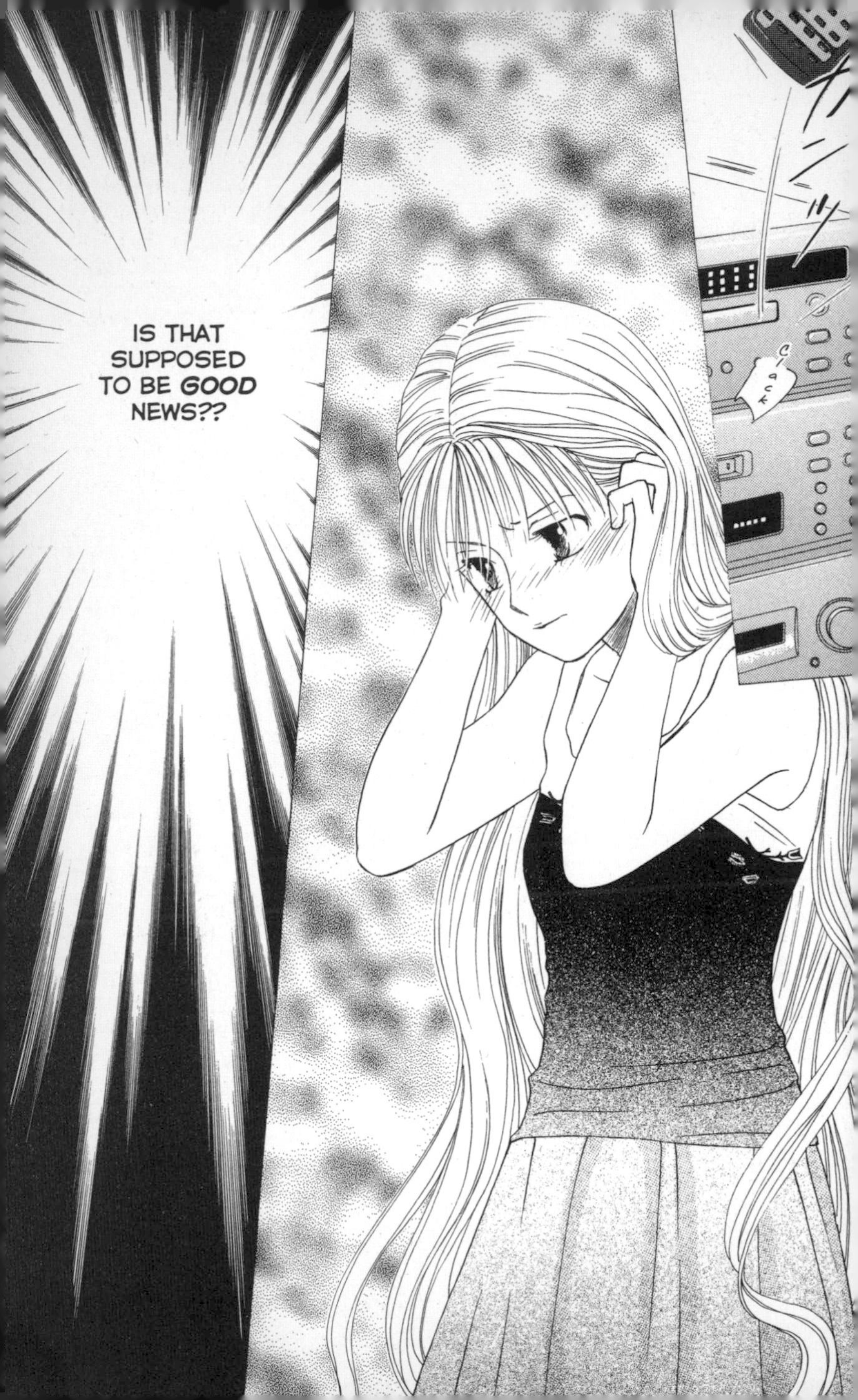
clack
IS THAT SUPPOSED TO BE GOOD NEWS??

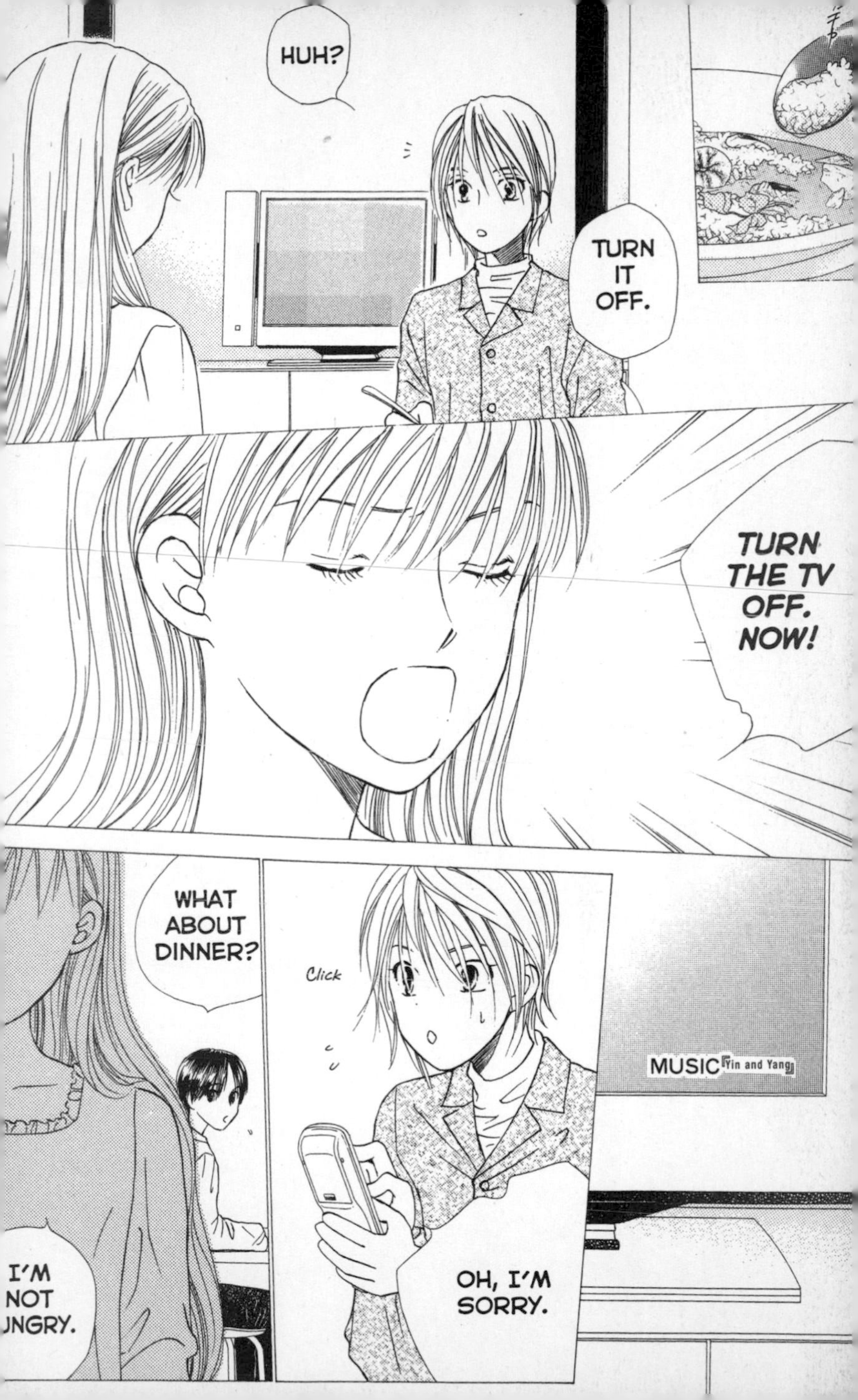
TURN IT OFF.
HUH?
TURN THE TV OFF. NOW!
MUSIC『Yin and Yang』
Click
OH, I'M SORRY.
WHAT ABOUT DINNER?
I'M NOT
NGRY.

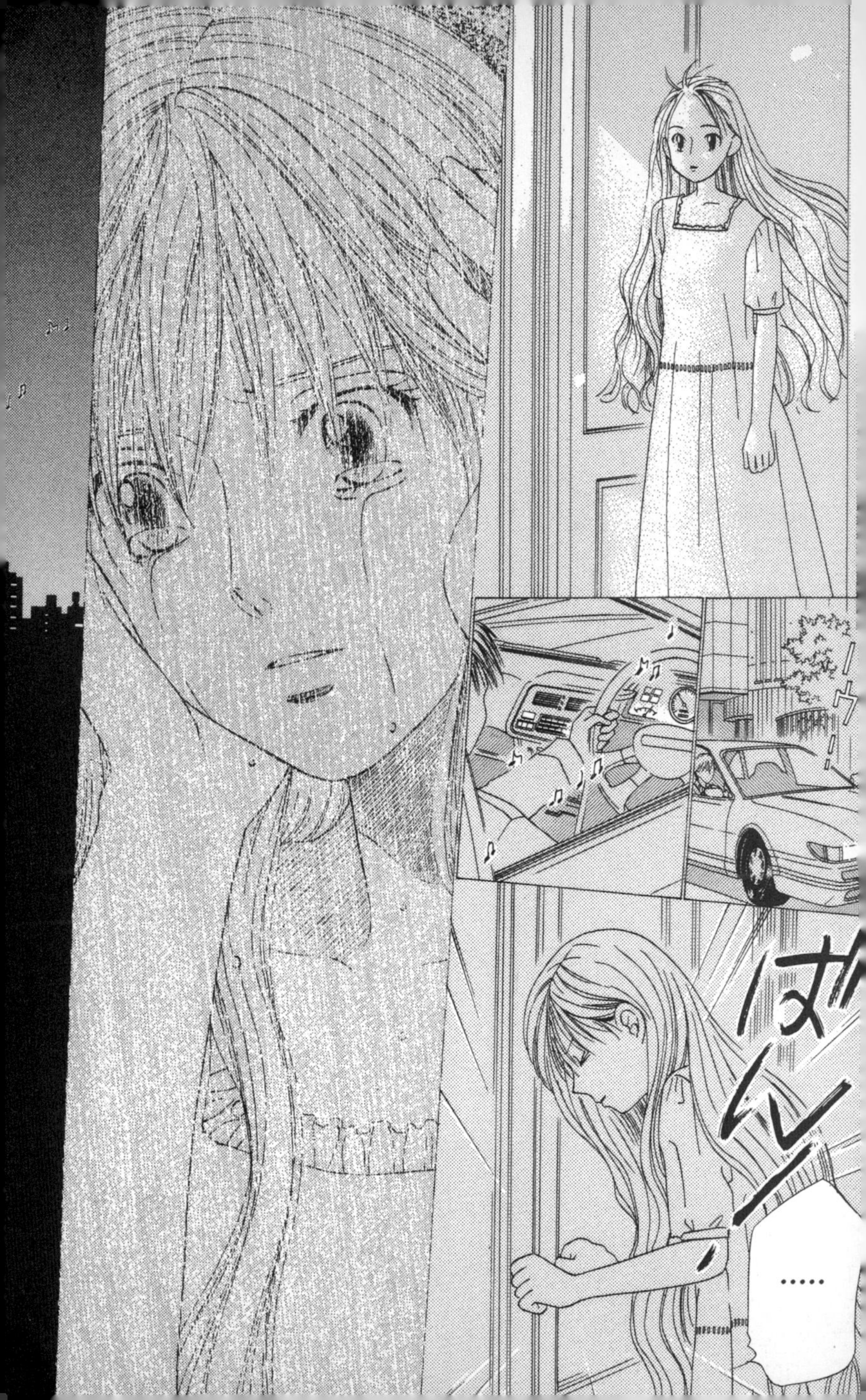
ばん
……

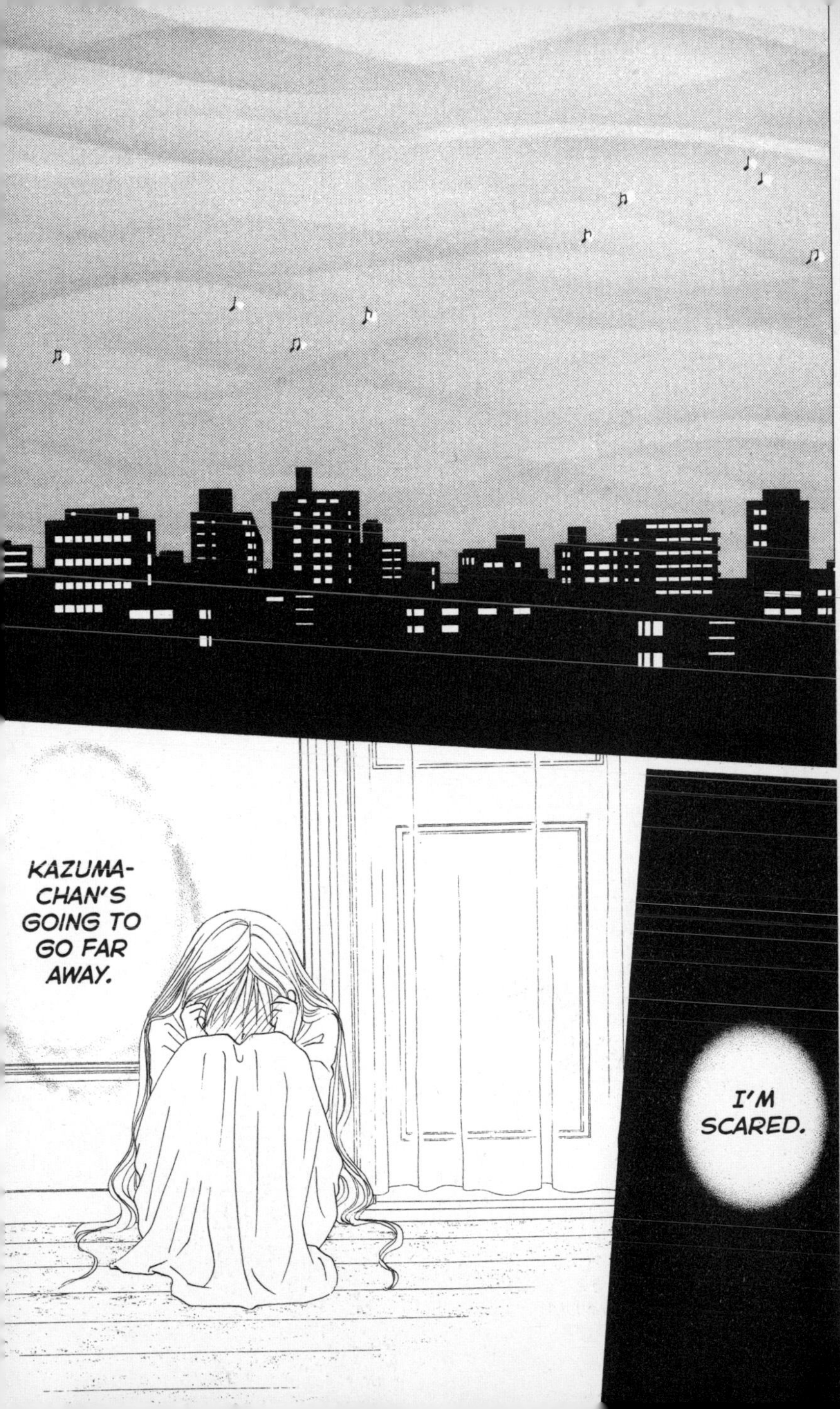
KAZUMA-CHAN'S GOING TO GO FAR AWAY.
I'M SCARED.

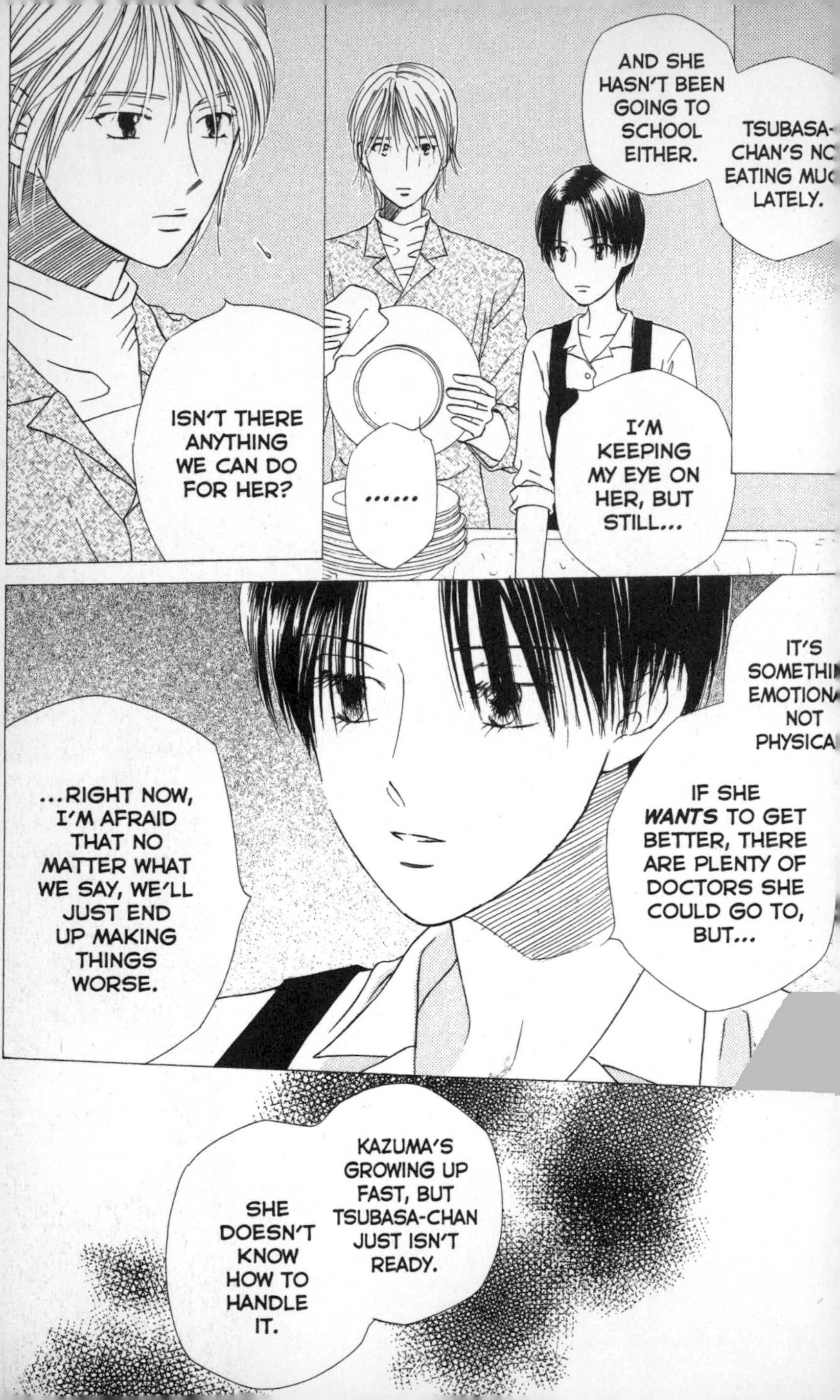
TSUBASA-CHAN'S NO EATING MUC LATELY.
AND SHE HASN'T BEEN GOING TO SCHOOL EITHER.
I'M KEEPING MY EYE ON HER, BUT STILL...
......
ISN'T THERE ANYTHING WE CAN DO FOR HER?
IT'S SOMETHI EMOTIONA NOT PHYSICA
IF SHE *WANTS* TO GET BETTER, THERE ARE PLENTY OF DOCTORS SHE COULD GO TO, BUT...
...RIGHT NOW, I'M AFRAID THAT NO MATTER WHAT WE SAY, WE'LL JUST END UP MAKING THINGS WORSE.
KAZUMA'S GROWING UP FAST, BUT TSUBASA-CHAN JUST ISN'T READY.
SHE DOESN'T KNOW HOW TO HANDLE IT.

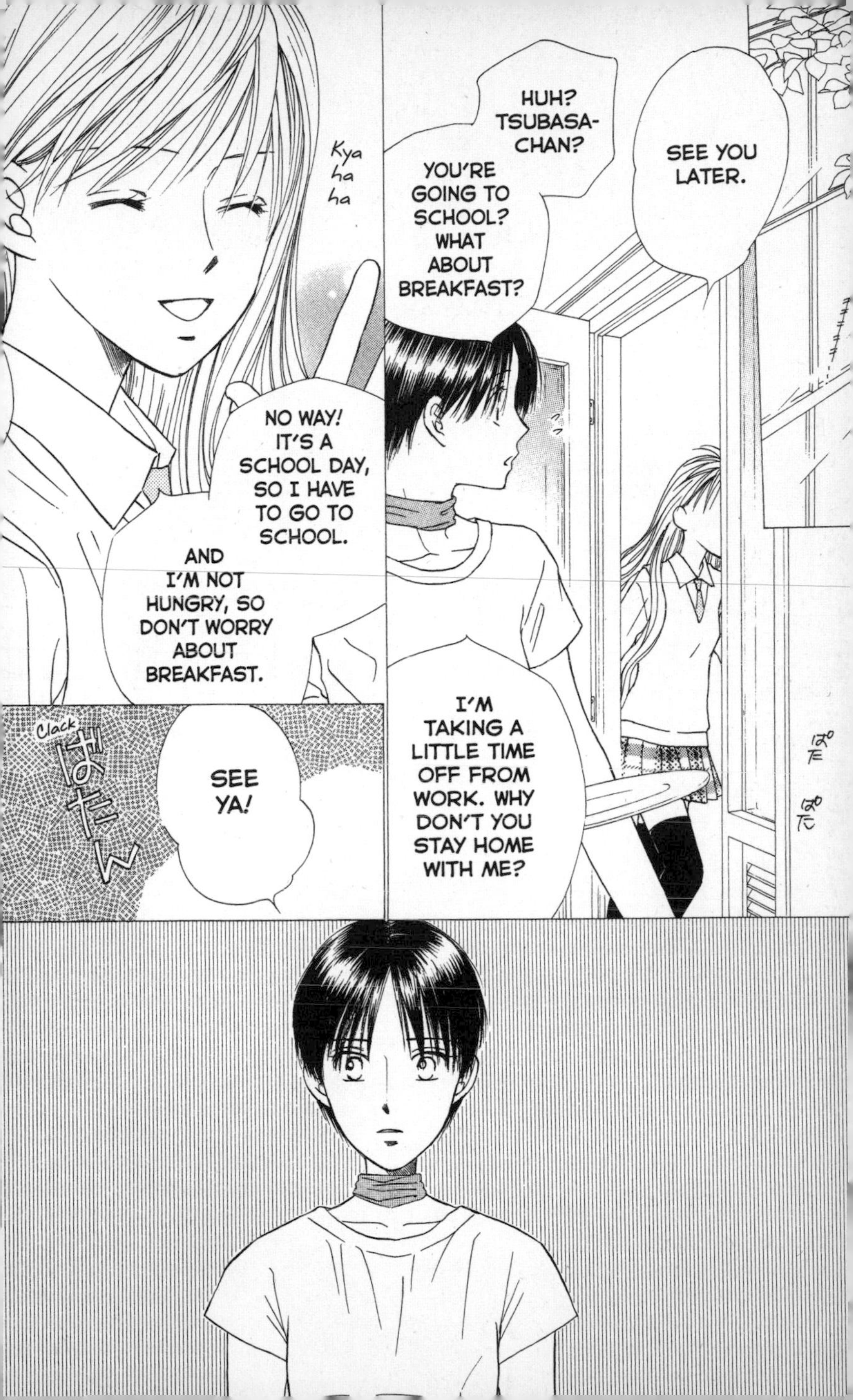
SEE YOU LATER.
HUH? TSUBASA-CHAN?
YOU'RE GOING TO SCHOOL? WHAT ABOUT BREAKFAST?
Kya ha ha
NO WAY! IT'S A SCHOOL DAY, SO I HAVE TO GO TO SCHOOL.
AND I'M NOT HUNGRY, SO DON'T WORRY ABOUT BREAKFAST.
ぱた ぱた
I'M TAKING A LITTLE TIME OFF FROM WORK. WHY DON'T YOU STAY HOME WITH ME?
Clack
ばたん
SEE YA!

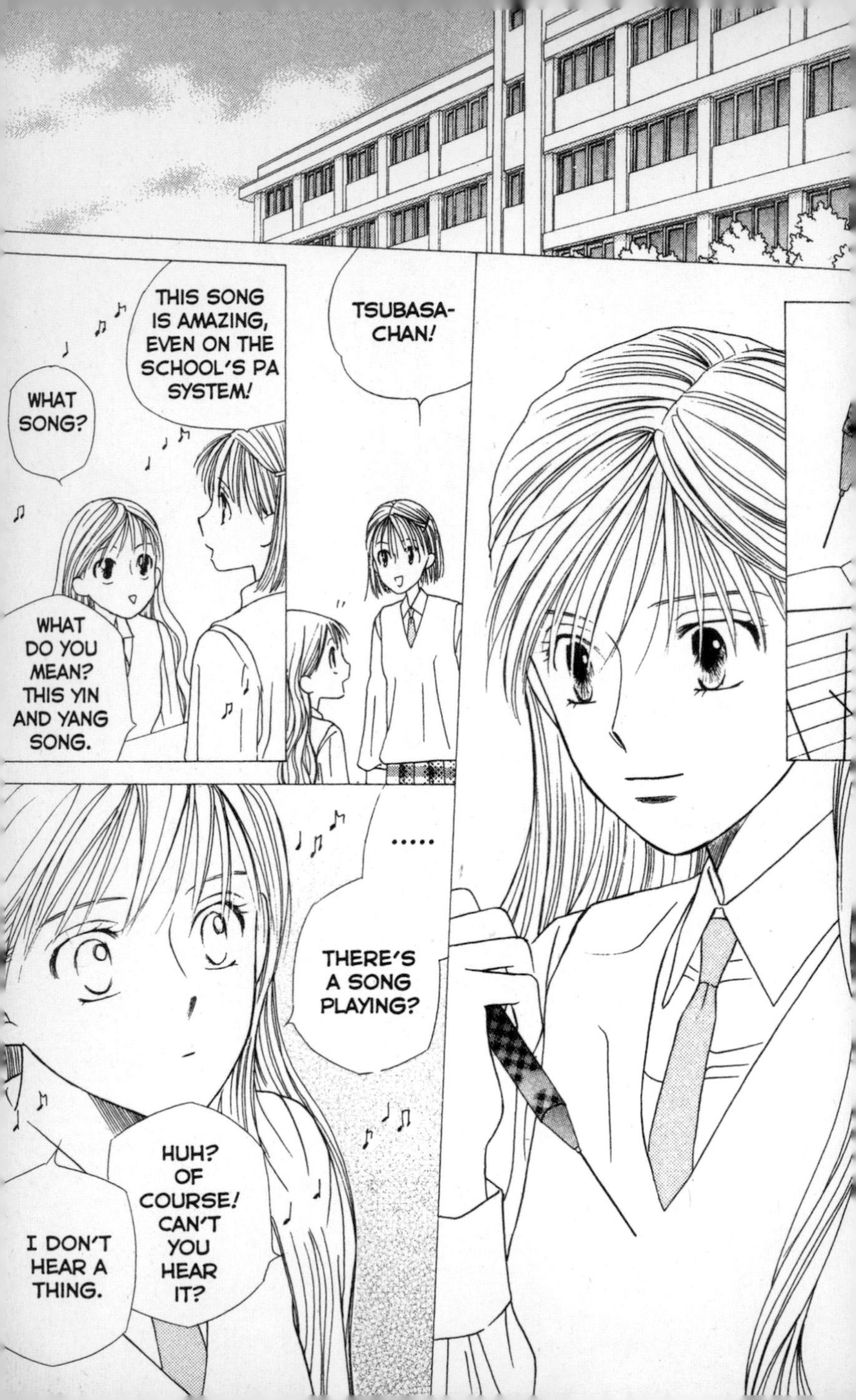
TSUBASA-CHAN!
THIS SONG IS AMAZING, EVEN ON THE SCHOOL'S PA SYSTEM!
WHAT SONG?
WHAT DO YOU MEAN? THIS YIN AND YANG SONG.
.....
THERE'S A SONG PLAYING?
HUH? OF COURSE! CAN'T YOU HEAR IT?
I DON'T HEAR A THING.

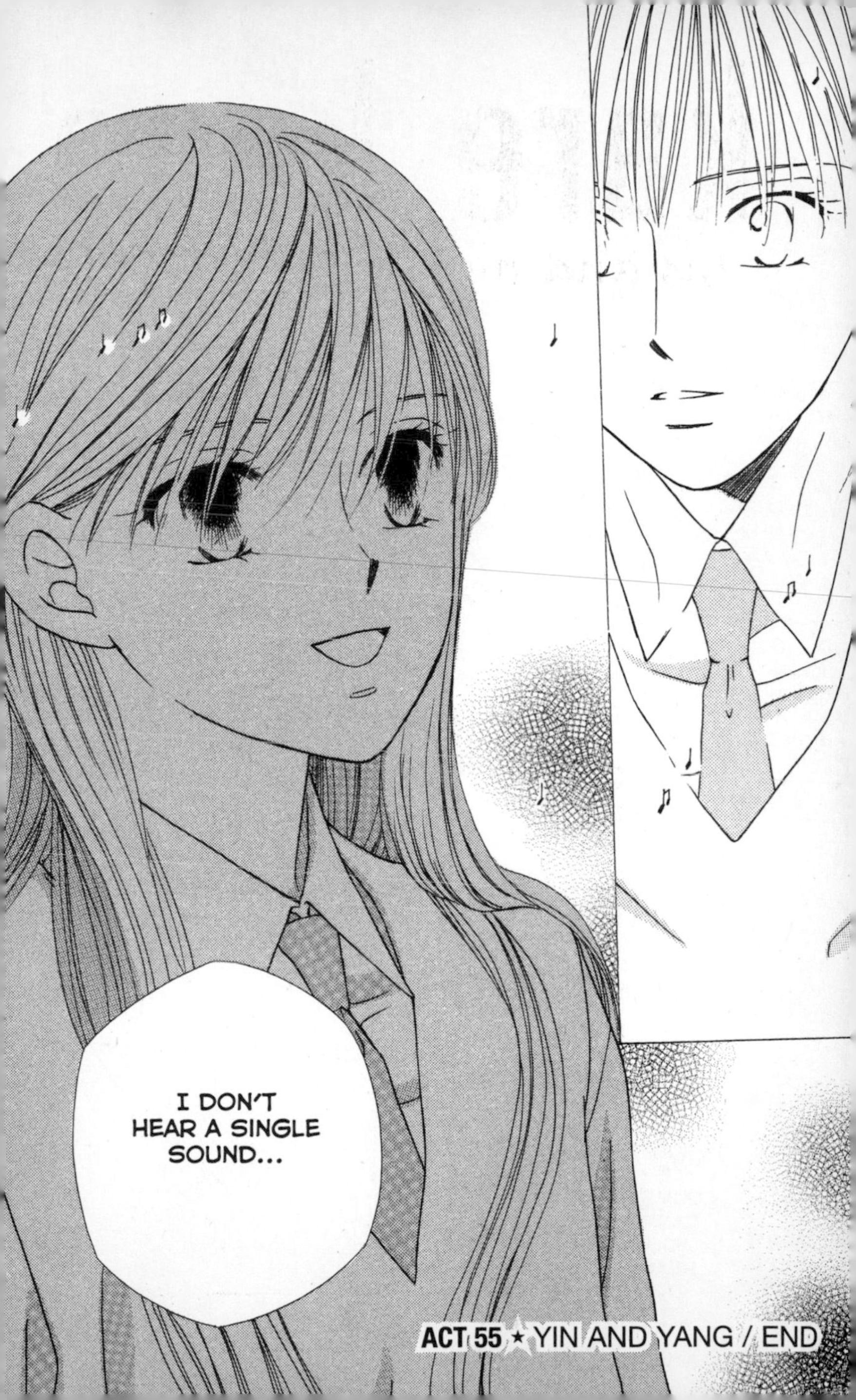
I DON'T HEAR A SINGLE SOUND...
ACT 55 ★ YIN AND YANG / END

kare kano

his and her circumstances

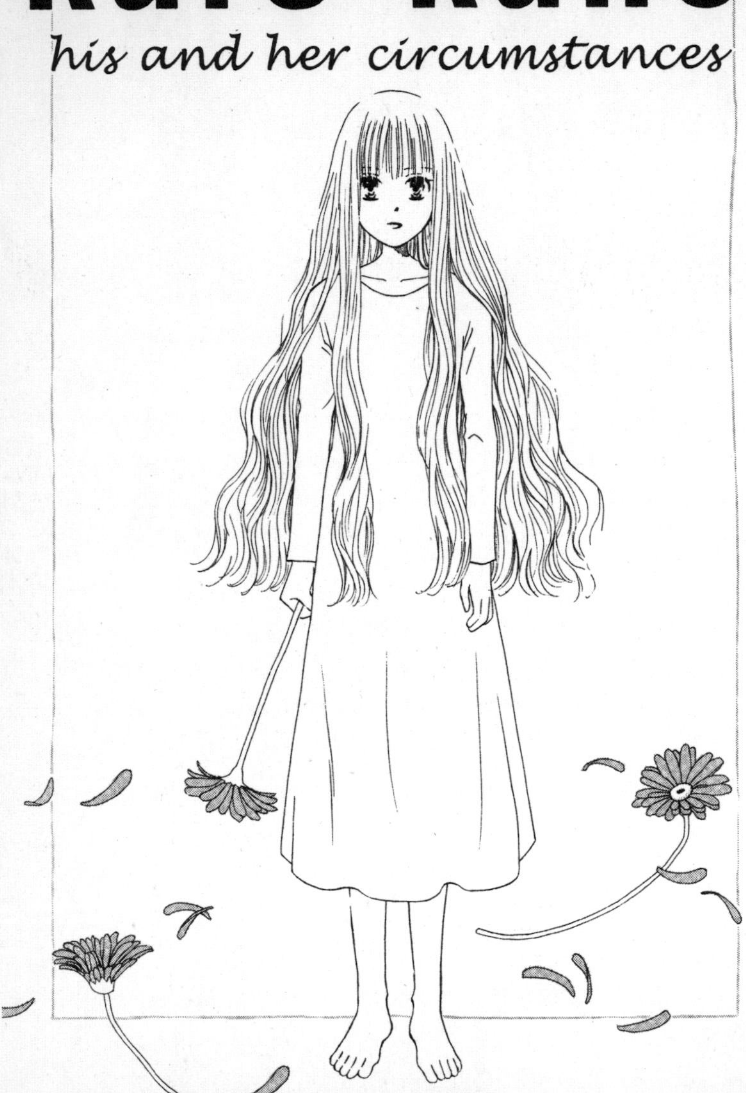

ACT 56 ★ TSUBASA

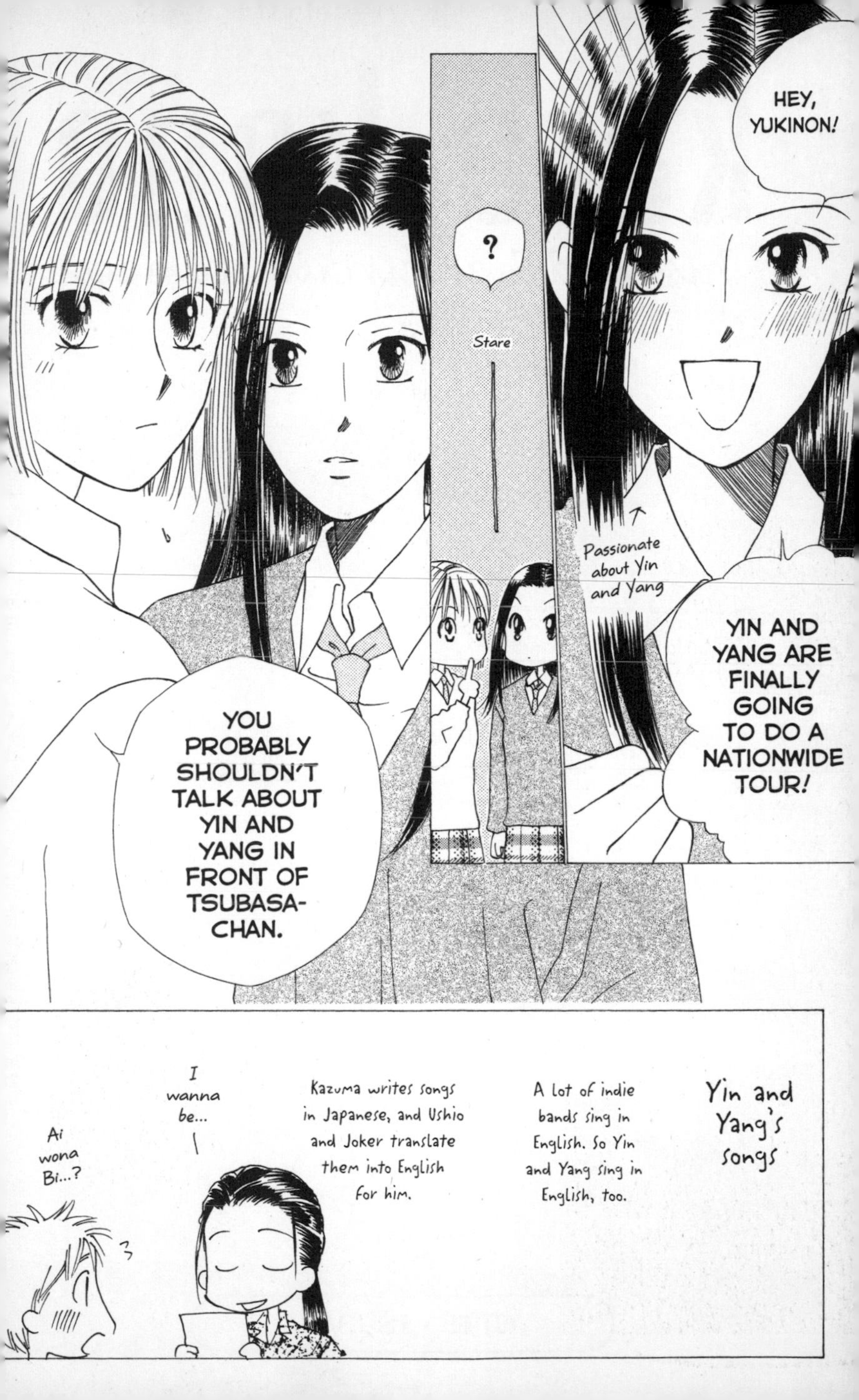
HEY, YUKINON!
YIN AND YANG ARE FINALLY GOING TO DO A NATIONWIDE TOUR!
Passionate about Yin and Yang
?
Stare
YOU PROBABLY SHOULDN'T TALK ABOUT YIN AND YANG IN FRONT OF TSUBASA-CHAN.
Yin and Yang's songs
A lot of indie bands sing in English. So Yin and Yang sing in English, too.
Kazuma writes songs in Japanese, and Ushio and Joker translate them into English for him.
I wanna be...
Ai wona Bi...?

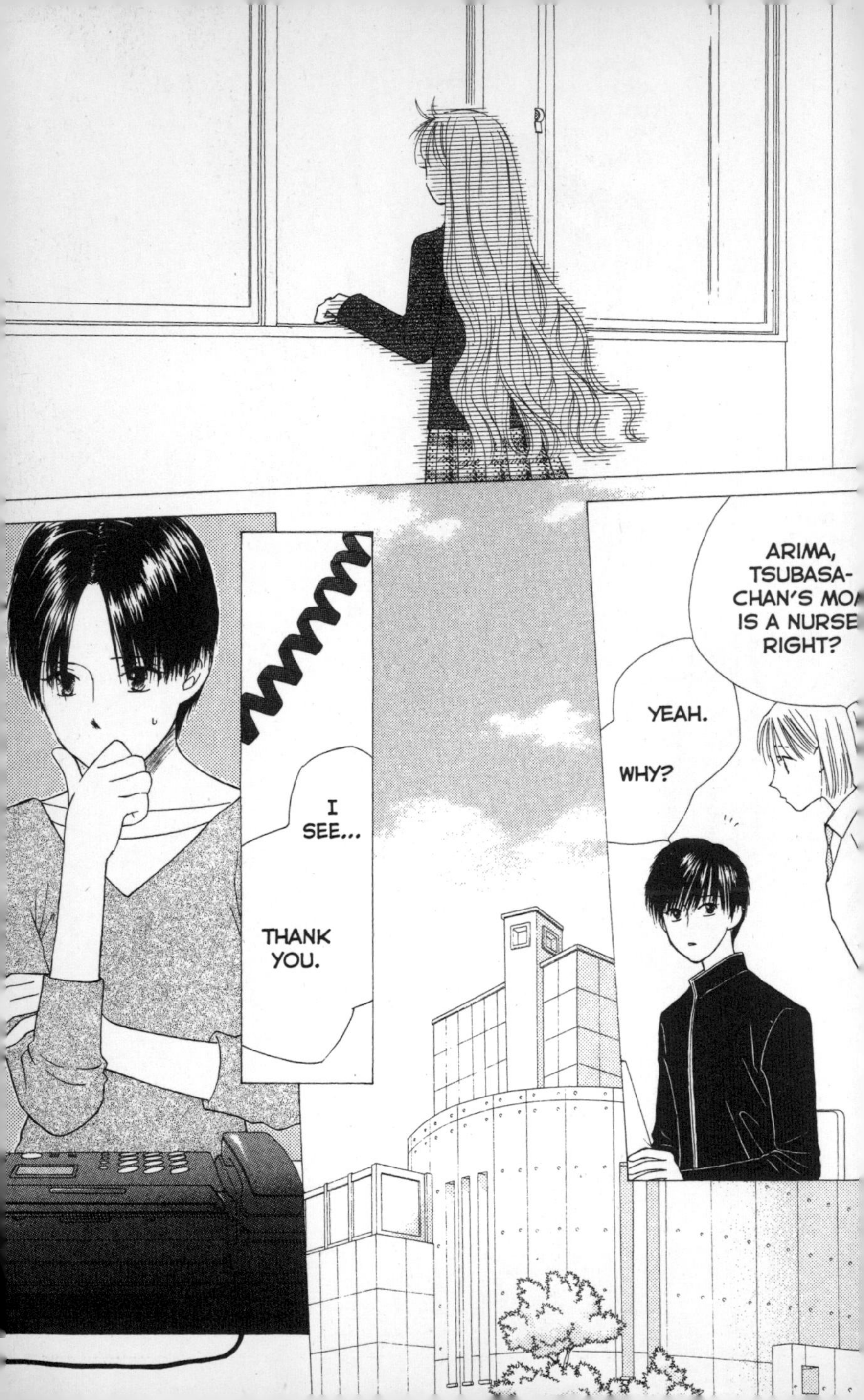
ARIMA, TSUBASA-CHAN'S MOA
IS A NURSE
RIGHT?
YEAH.
WHY?
I SEE...
THANK YOU.

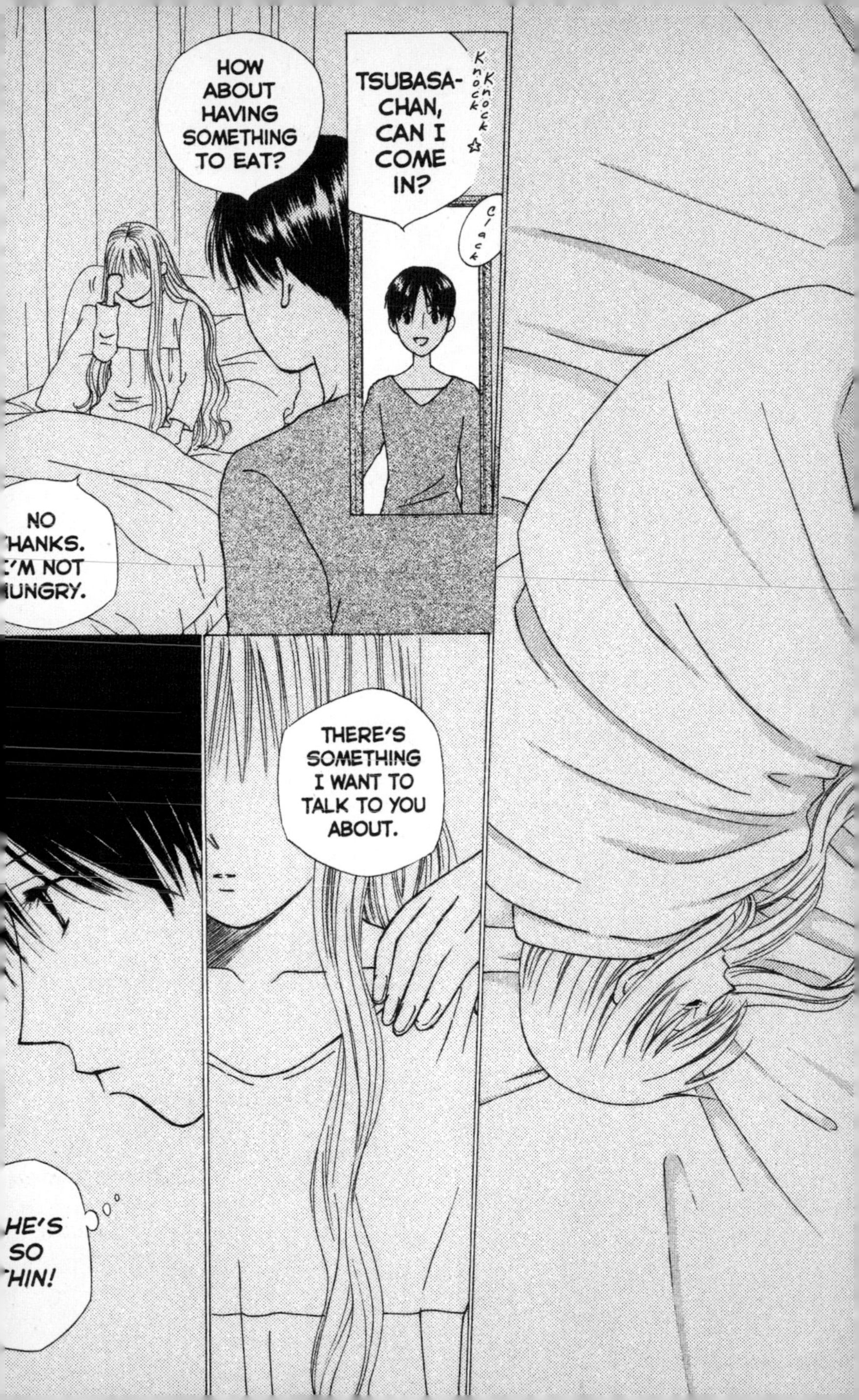
Knock Knock ☆
TSUBASA-CHAN, CAN I COME IN?
Clack
HOW ABOUT HAVING SOMETHING TO EAT?
NO HANKS. 'M NOT UNGRY.
THERE'S SOMETHING I WANT TO TALK TO YOU ABOUT.
HE'S SO HIN!

3

I've been hooked on tofu lately.

Zarudofu

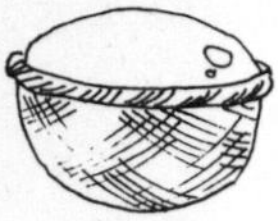

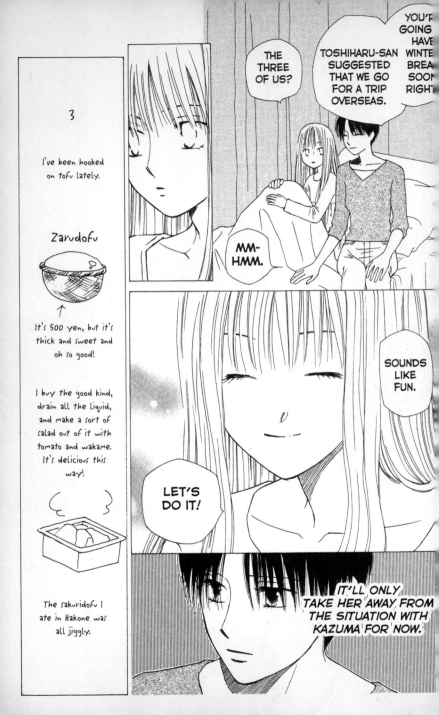

It's 500 yen, but it's thick and sweet and oh so good!

I buy the good kind, drain all the liquid, and make a sort of salad out of it with tomato and wakame. It's delicious this way!

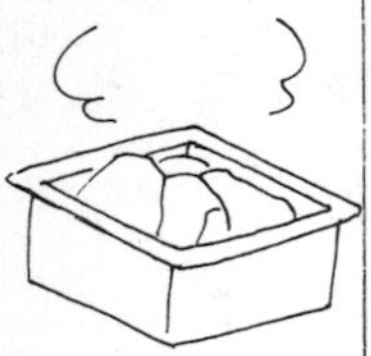

The sakuridofu I ate in Hakone was all jiggly.

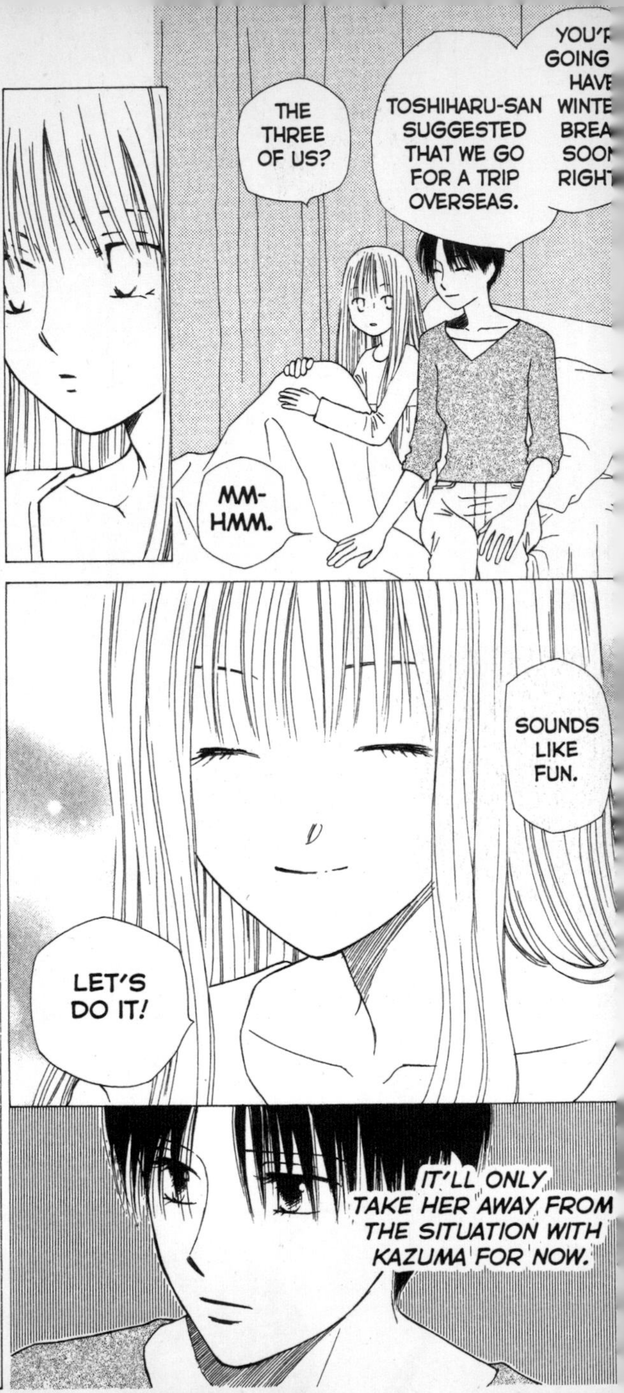
YOU'R GOING HAVE WINTE BREA SOON RIGHT
TOSHIHARU-SAN SUGGESTED THAT WE GO FOR A TRIP OVERSEAS.
THE THREE OF US?
MM-HMM.
SOUNDS LIKE FUN.
LET'S DO IT!
IT'LL ONLY TAKE HER AWAY FROM THE SITUATION WITH KAZUMA FOR NOW.

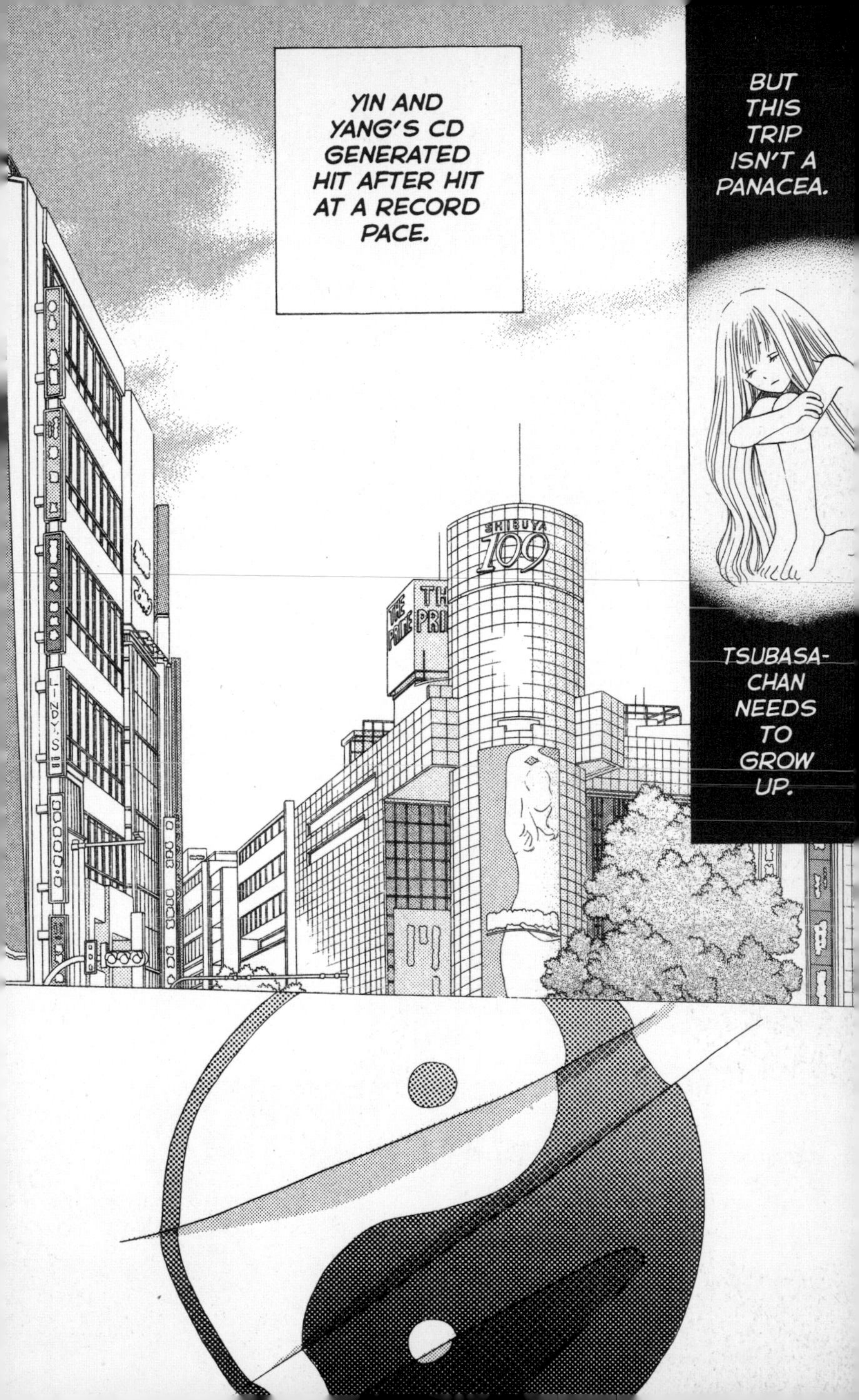
BUT THIS TRIP ISN'T A PANACEA.
YIN AND YANG'S CD GENERATED HIT AFTER HIT AT A RECORD PACE.
TSUBASA-CHAN NEEDS TO GROW UP.
SHIBUYA 109
THE PRIME

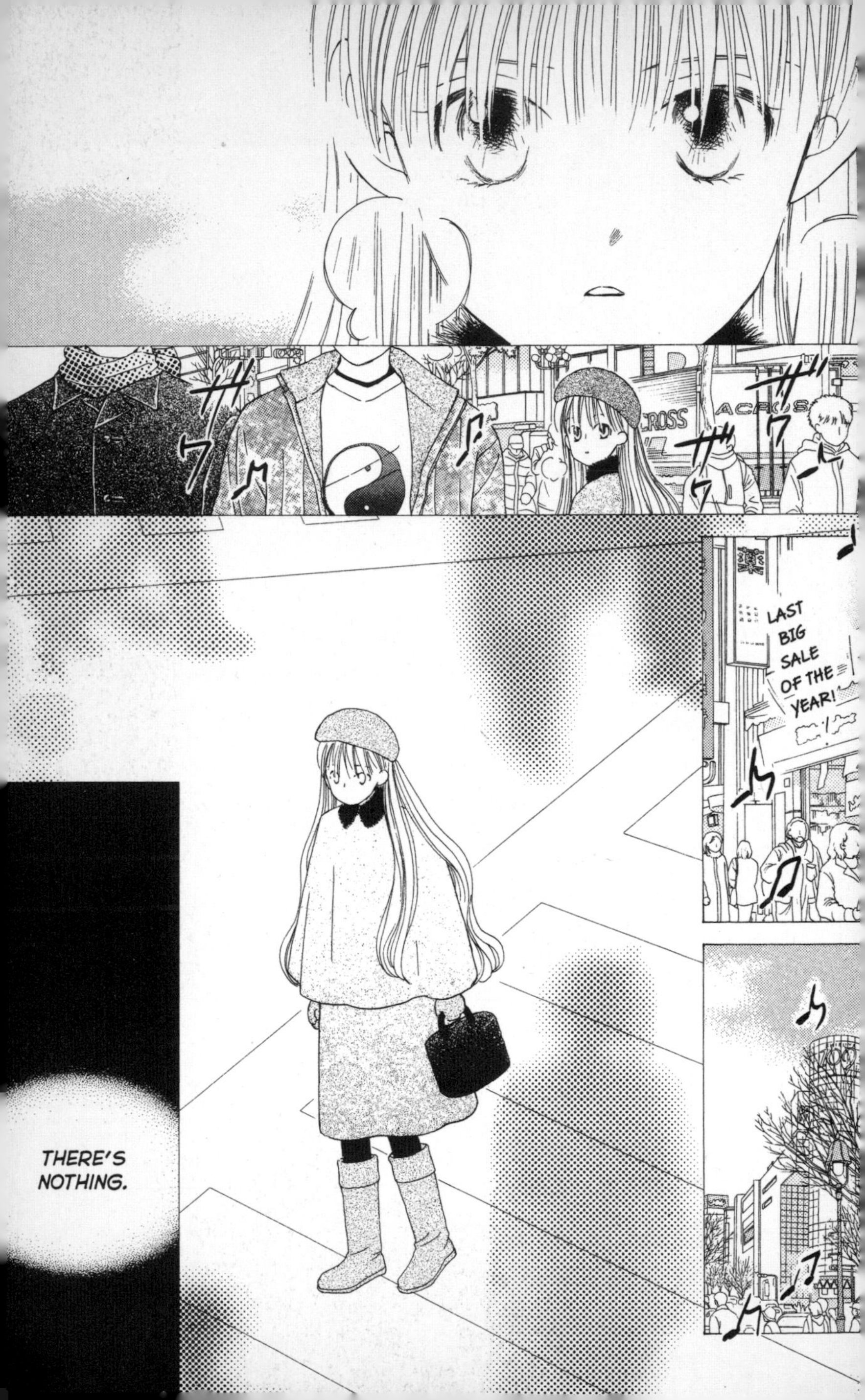
ザワ
ザワ
CROSS
ザワ
LAST BIG SALE OF THE YEAR!
THERE'S NOTHING.

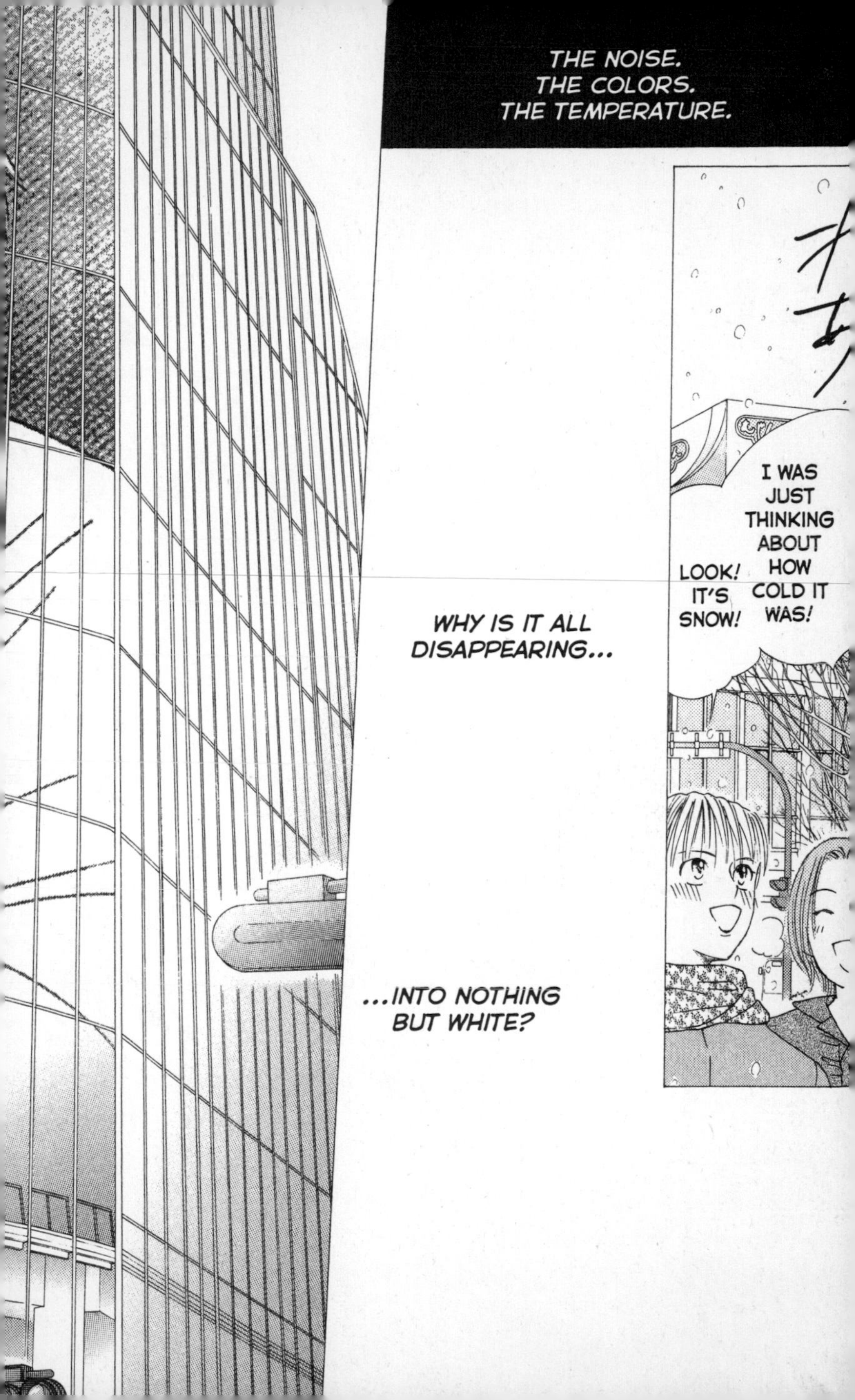
THE NOISE.
THE COLORS.
THE TEMPERATURE.
I WAS JUST THINKING ABOUT HOW COLD IT WAS!
LOOK! IT'S SNOW!
WHY IS IT ALL DISAPPEARING...
...INTO NOTHING BUT WHITE?

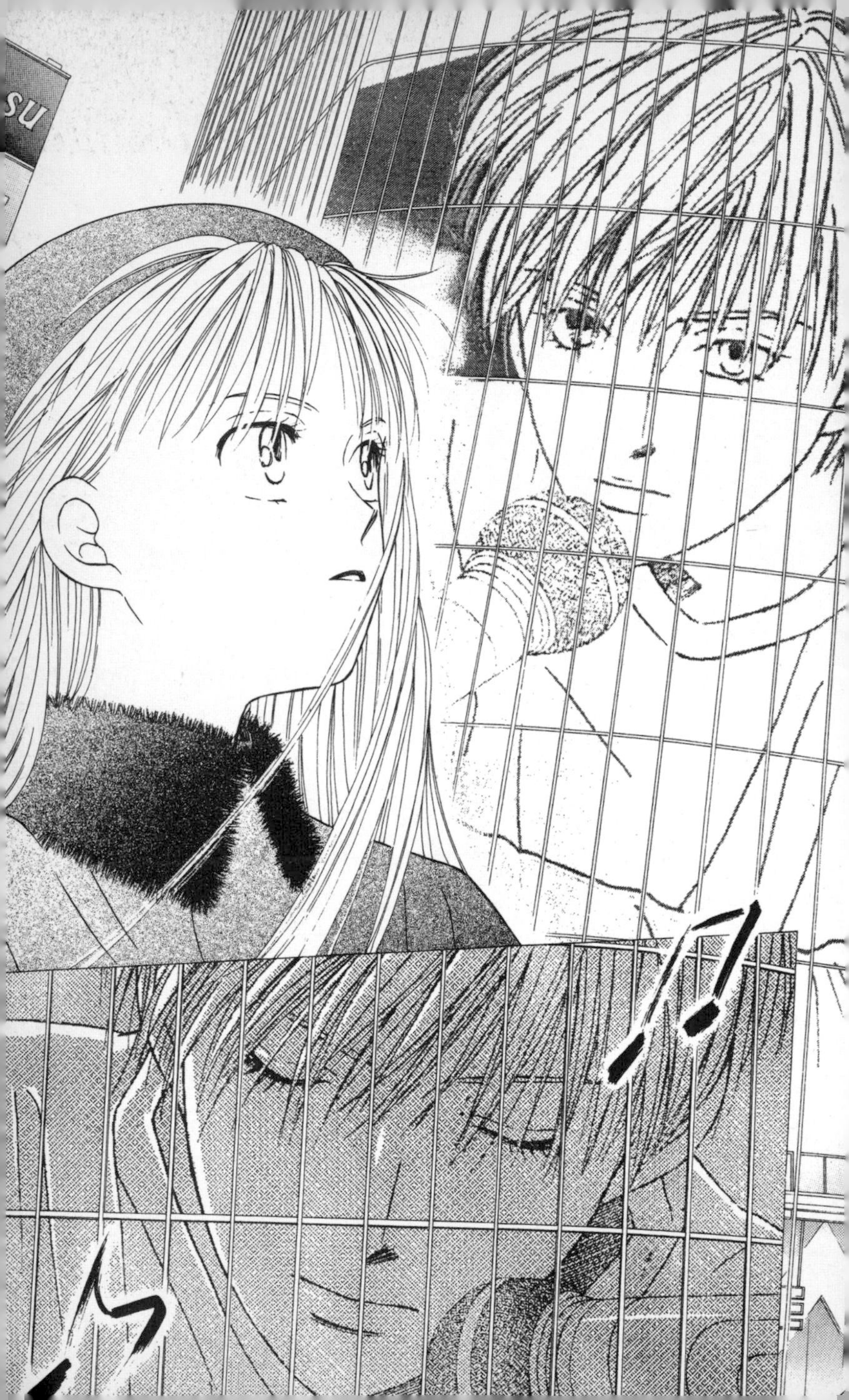

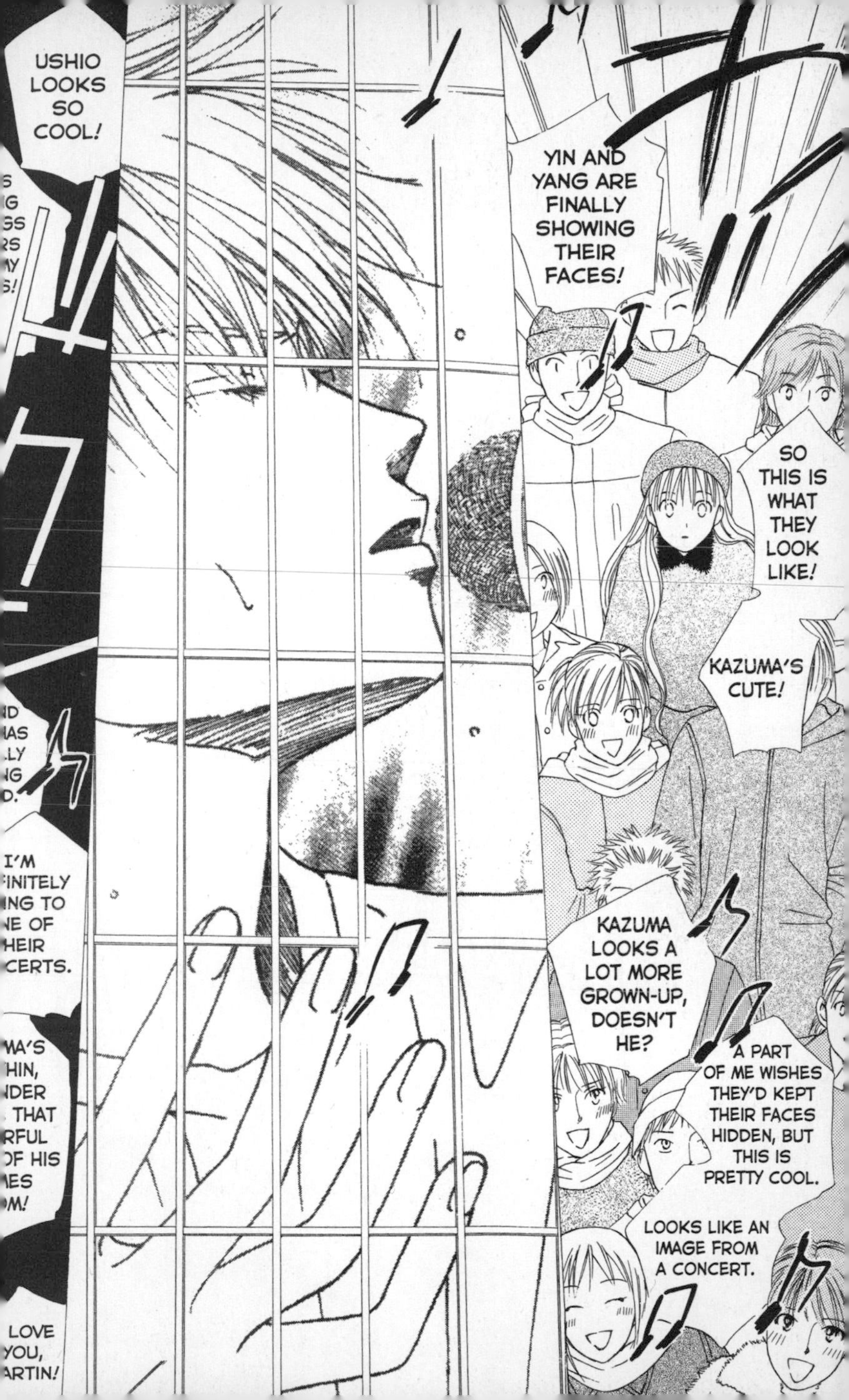
YIN AND YANG ARE FINALLY SHOWING THEIR FACES!
SO THIS IS WHAT THEY LOOK LIKE!
KAZUMA'S CUTE!
KAZUMA LOOKS A LOT MORE GROWN-UP, DOESN'T HE?
A PART OF ME WISHES THEY'D KEPT THEIR FACES HIDDEN, BUT THIS IS PRETTY COOL.
LOOKS LIKE AN IMAGE FROM A CONCERT.
USHIO LOOKS SO COOL!

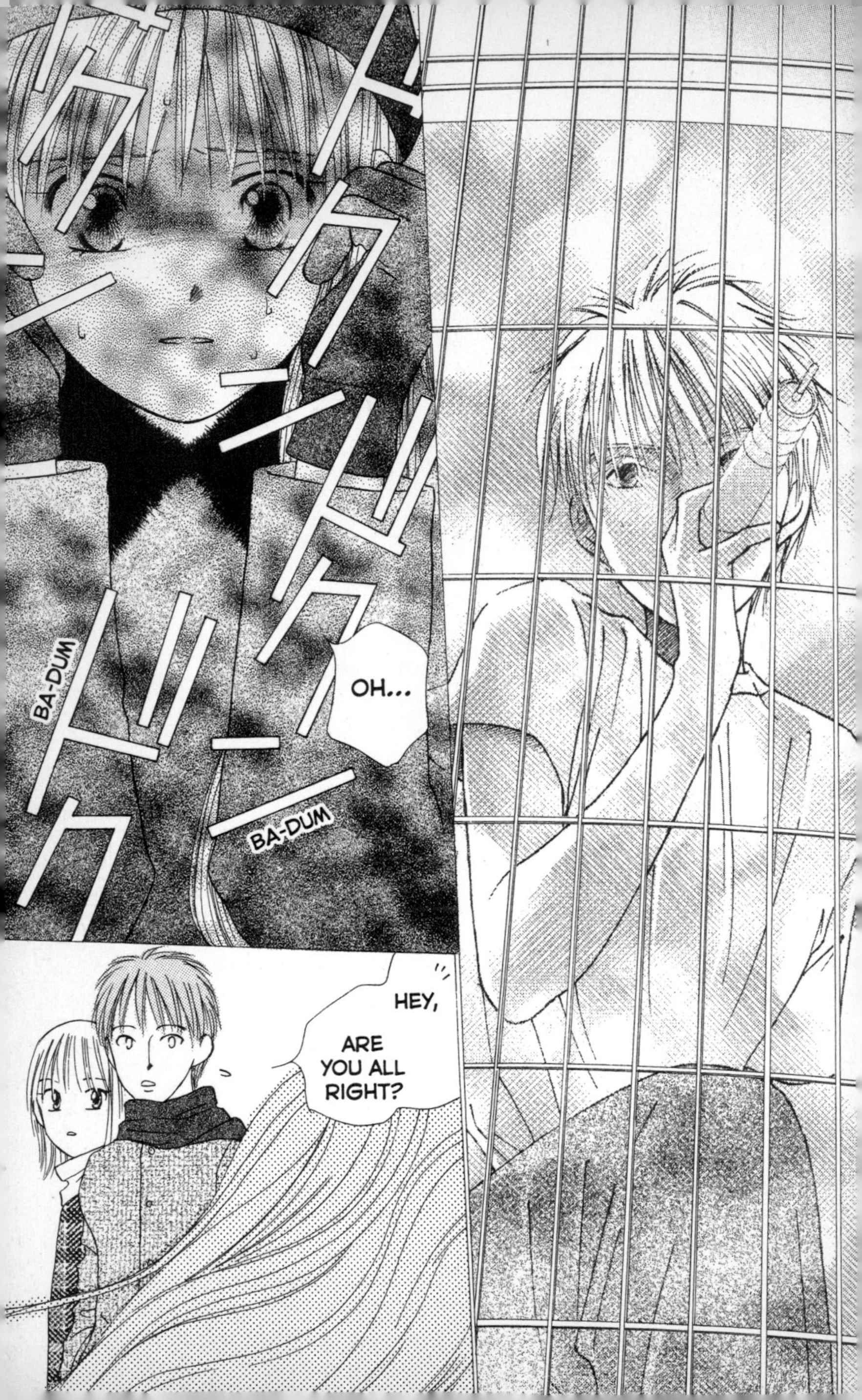
OH...
BA-DUM
BA-DUM
HEY,
ARE YOU ALL RIGHT?

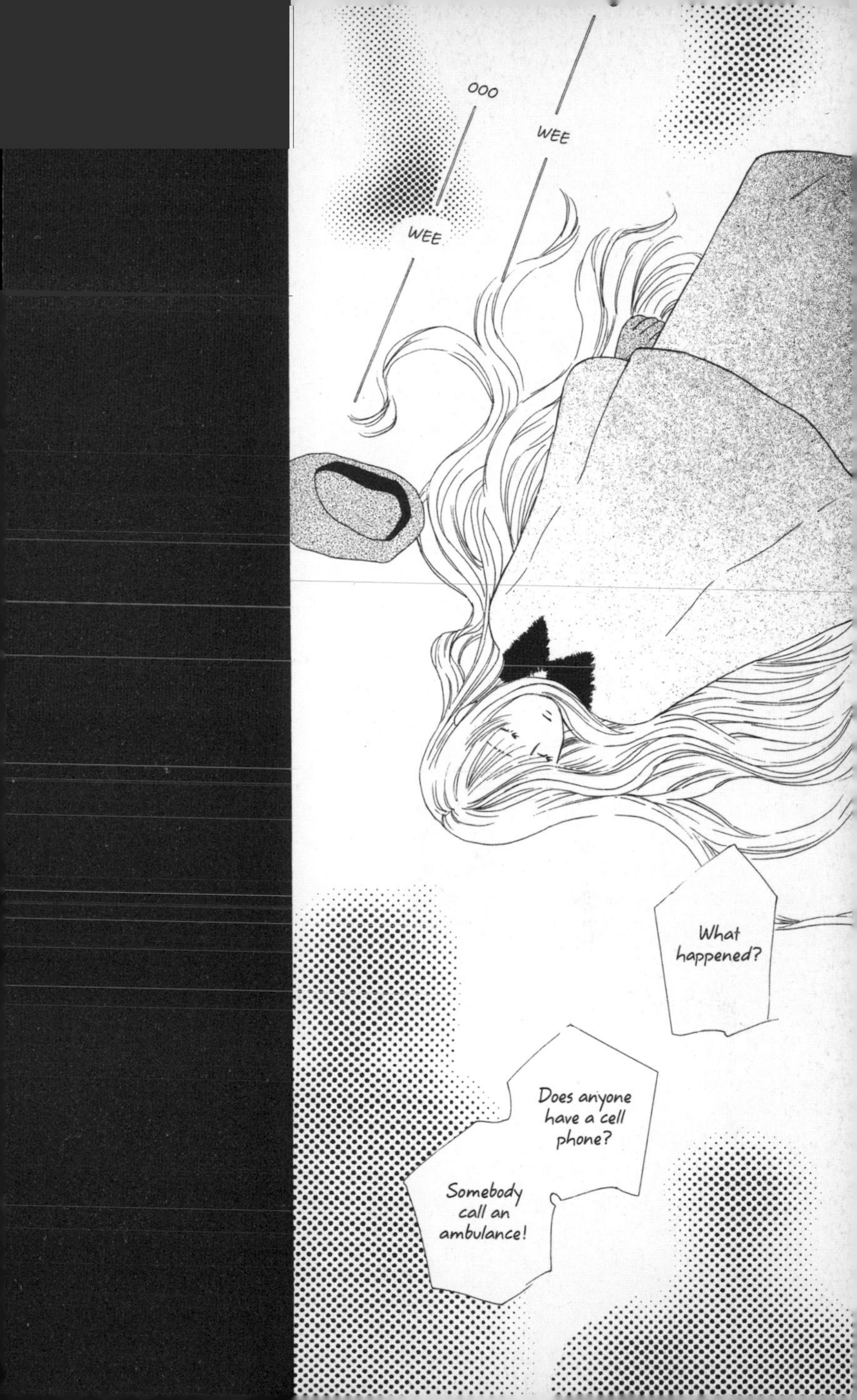
WEE
OOO
WEE
What happened?
Does anyone have a cell phone?
Somebody call an ambulance!

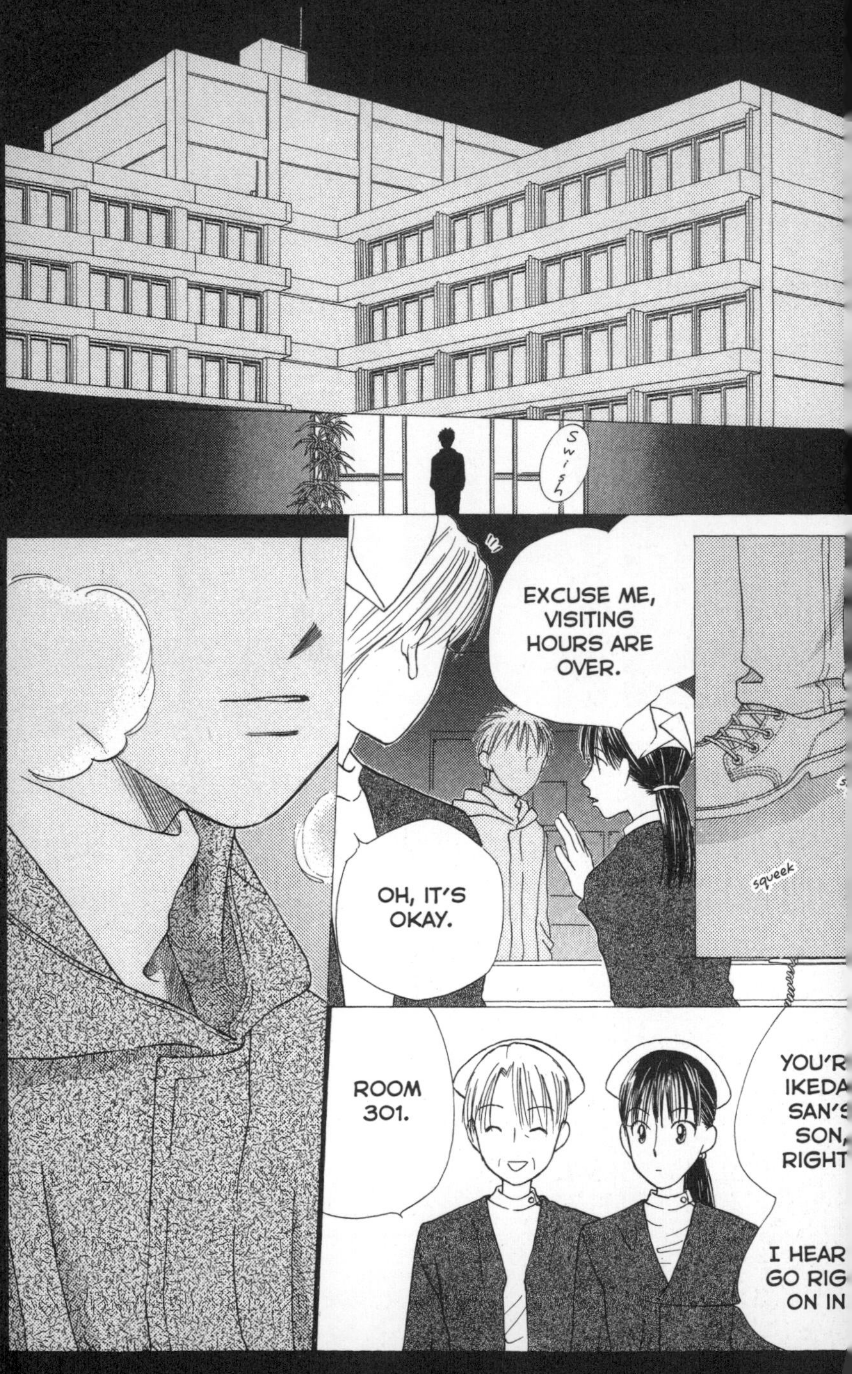
Swish
squeek
EXCUSE ME, VISITING HOURS ARE OVER.
OH, IT'S OKAY.
YOU'R IKEDA SAN'S SON, RIGHT
I HEAR GO RIG ON IN
ROOM 301.

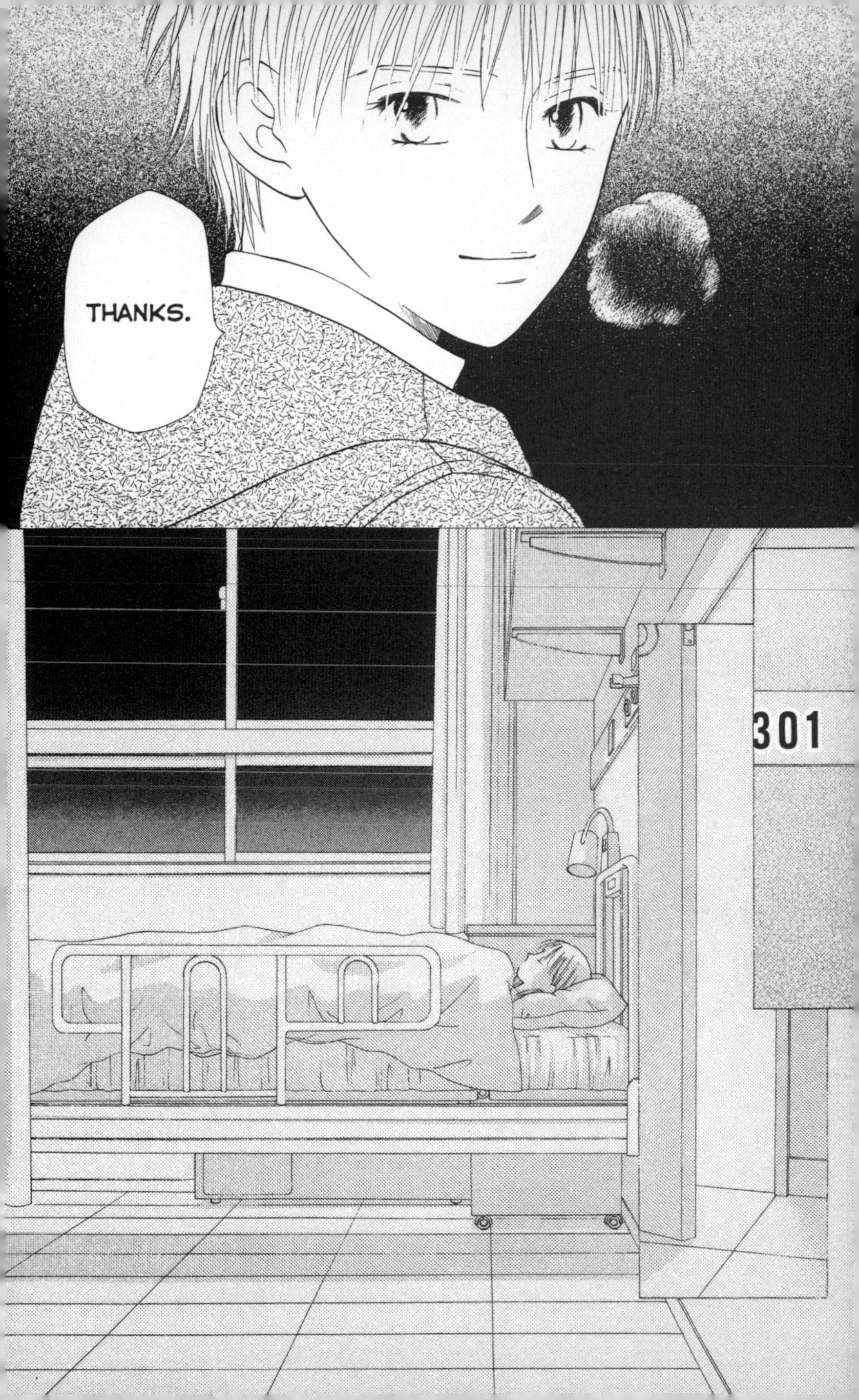
THANKS.
301

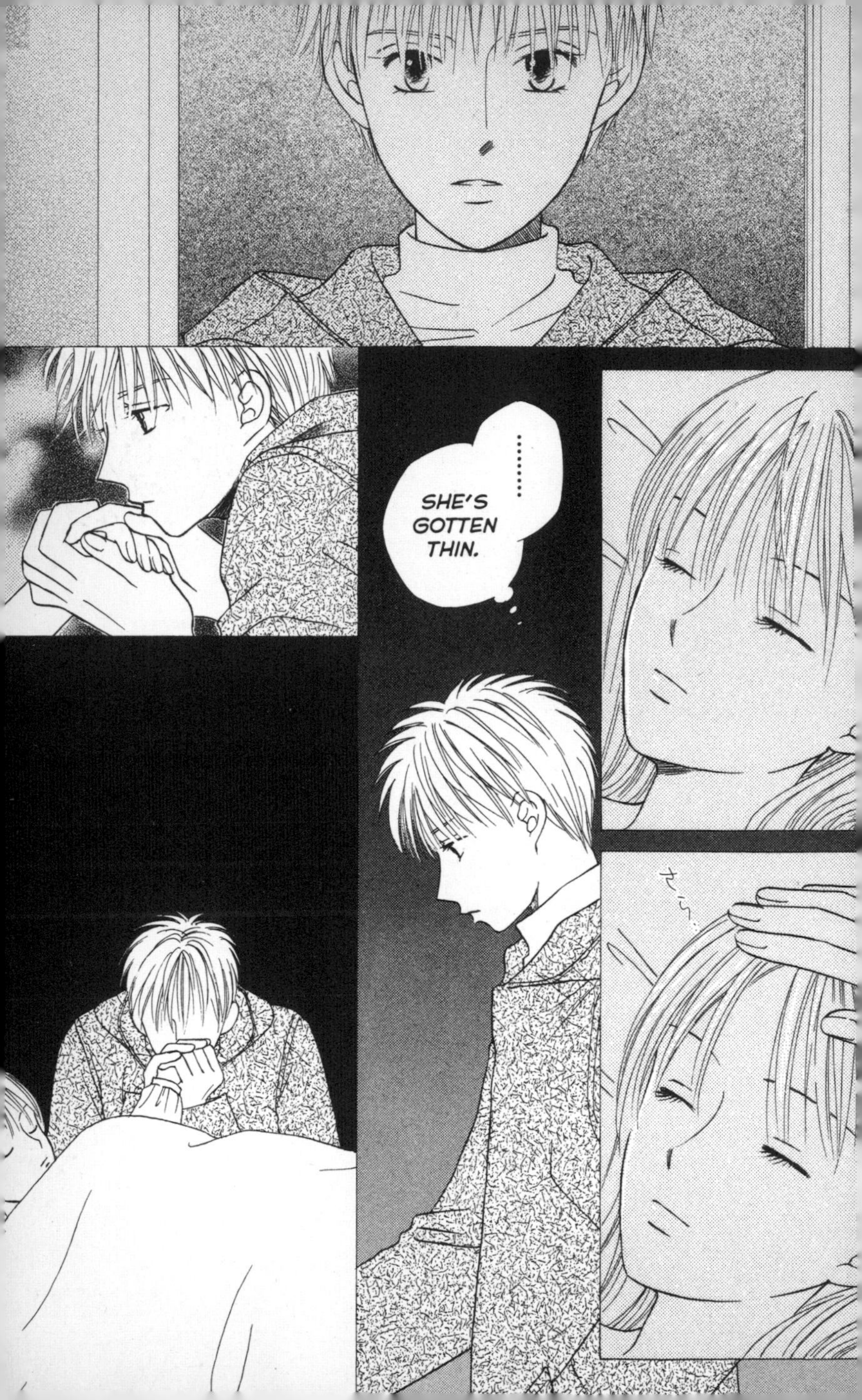
......
SHE'S GOTTEN THIN.

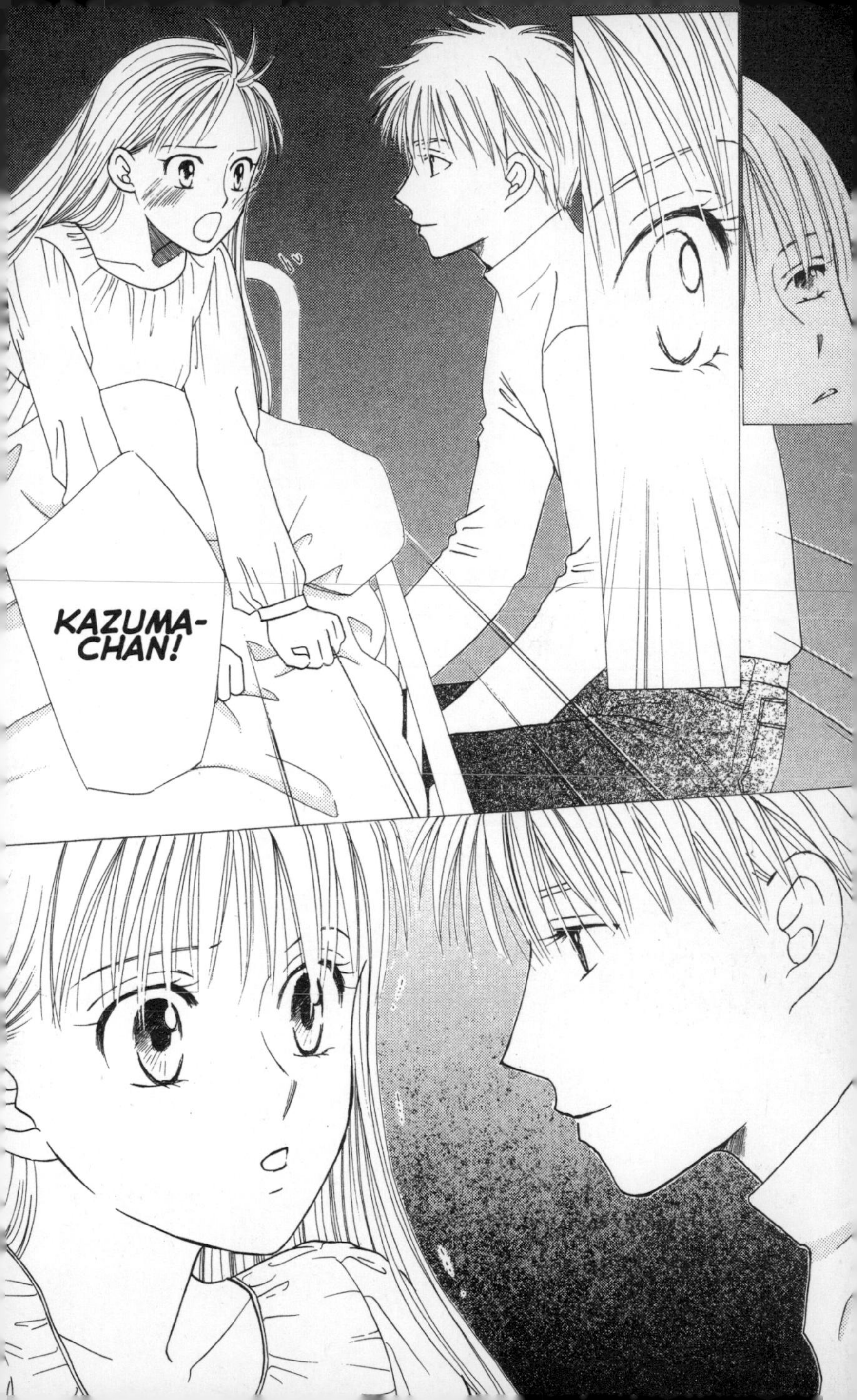
KAZUMA-CHAN!

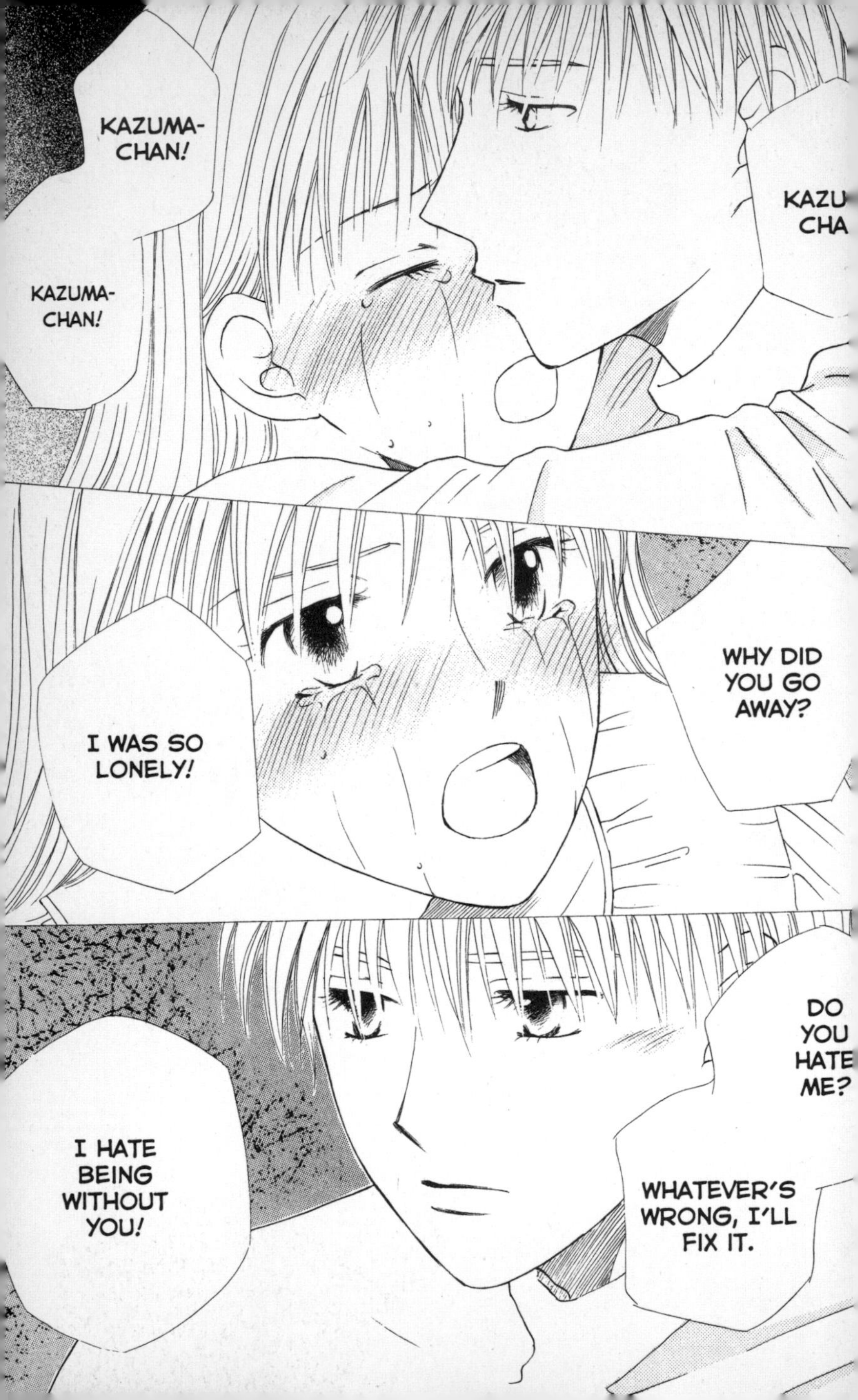
KAZU CHA
KAZUMA-CHAN!
KAZUMA-CHAN!
WHY DID YOU GO AWAY?
I WAS SO LONELY!
DO YOU HATE ME?
WHATEVER'S WRONG, I'LL FIX IT.
I HATE BEING WITHOUT YOU!

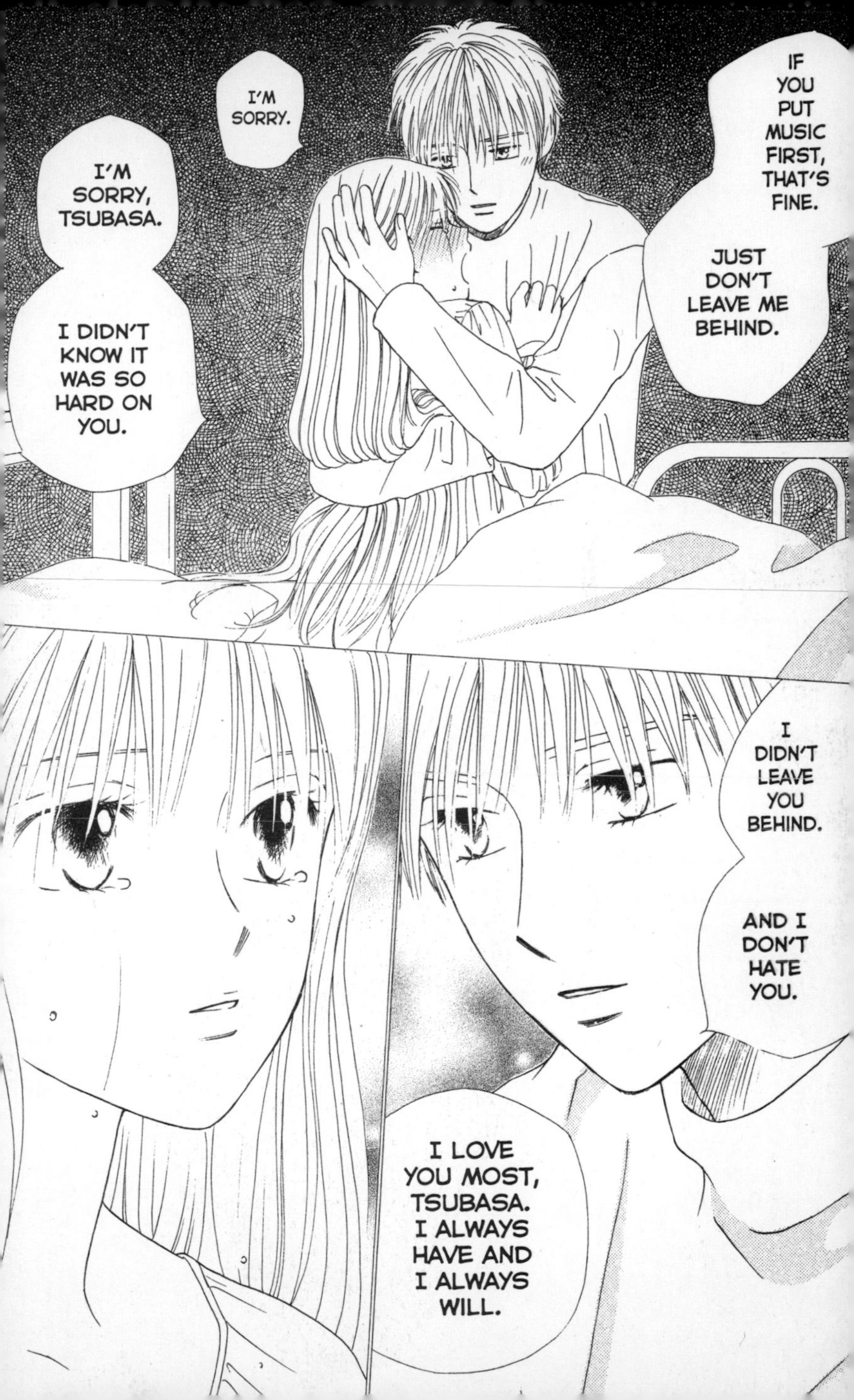
IF YOU PUT MUSIC FIRST, THAT'S FINE.
JUST DON'T LEAVE ME BEHIND.
I'M SORRY.
I'M SORRY, TSUBASA.
I DIDN'T KNOW IT WAS SO HARD ON YOU.
I DIDN'T LEAVE YOU BEHIND.
AND I DON'T HATE YOU.
I LOVE YOU MOST, TSUBASA. I ALWAYS HAVE AND I ALWAYS WILL.

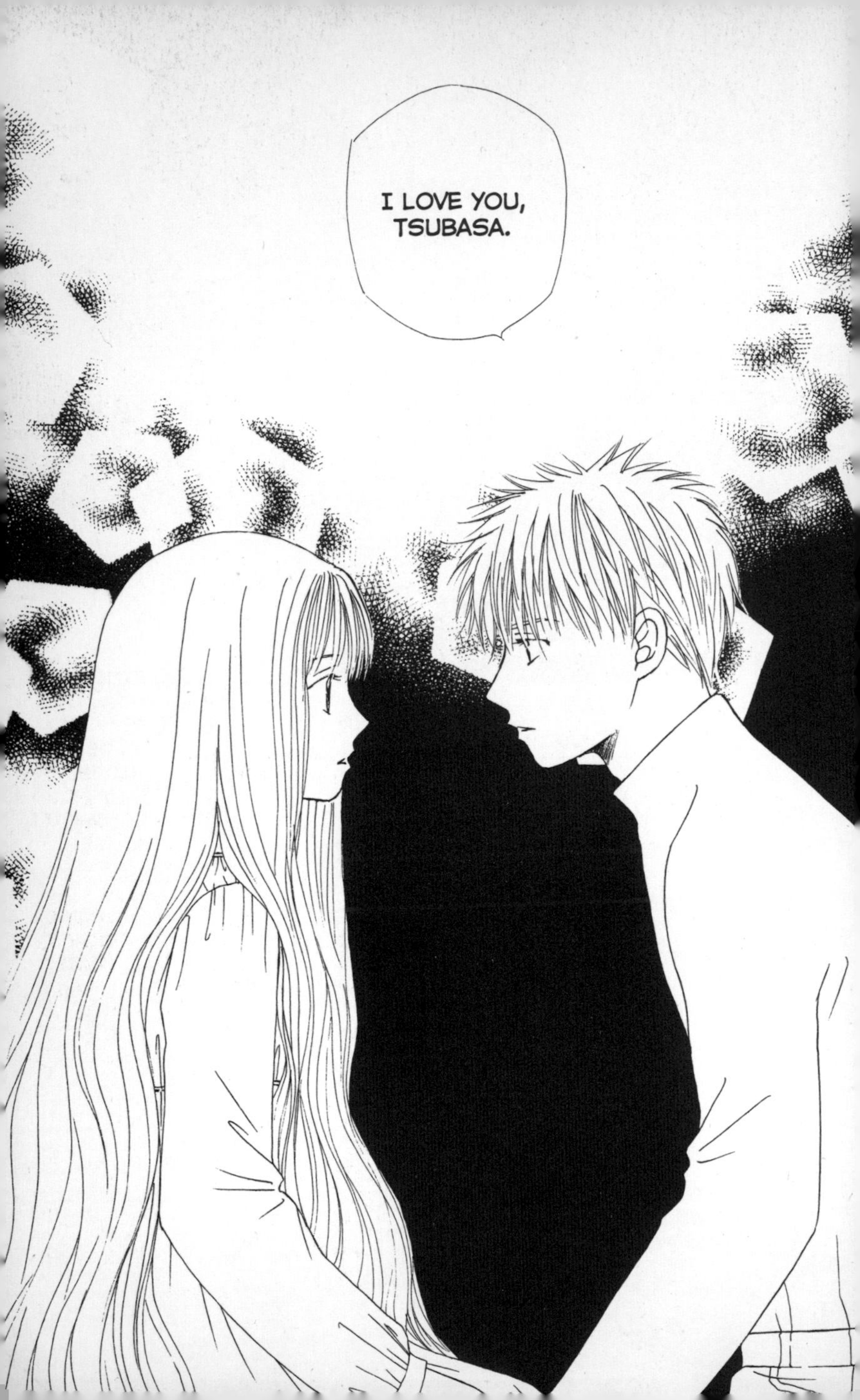
I LOVE YOU, TSUBASA.

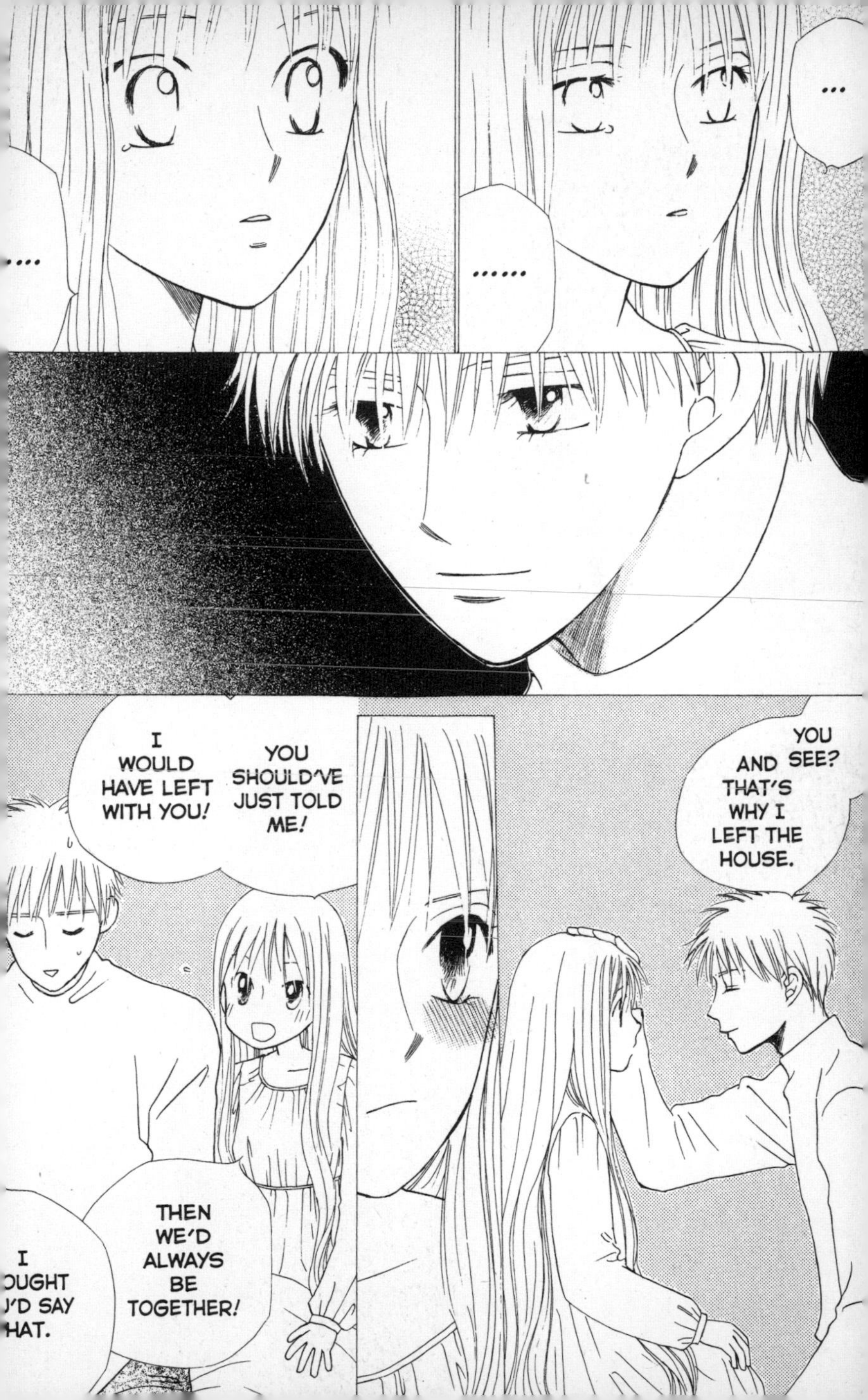
...
......
....
YOU SEE?
AND THAT'S WHY I LEFT THE HOUSE.
YOU SHOULD'VE JUST TOLD ME!
I WOULD HAVE LEFT WITH YOU!
THEN WE'D ALWAYS BE TOGETHER!
I OUGHT 'D SAY HAT.

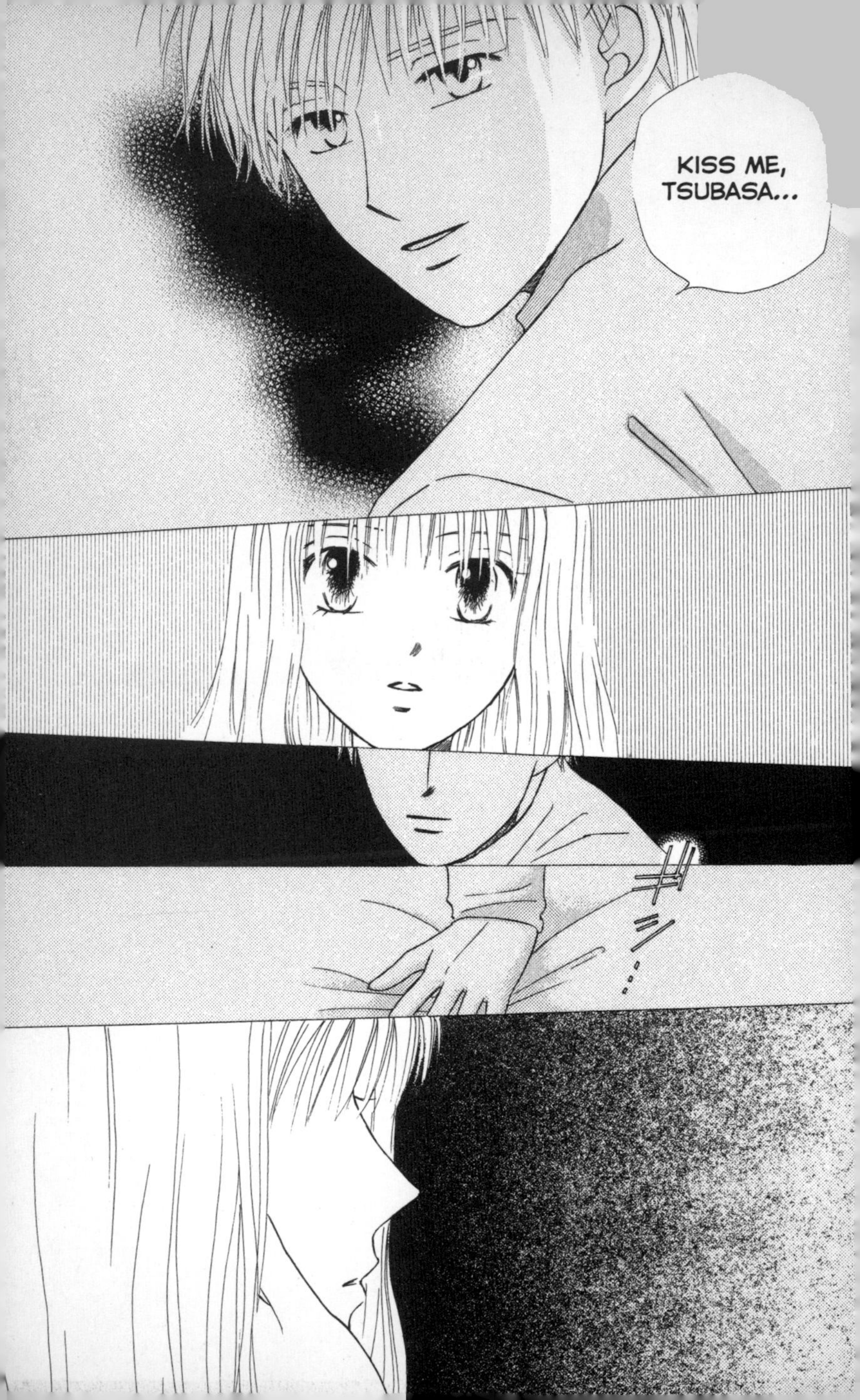
KISS ME, TSUBASA...

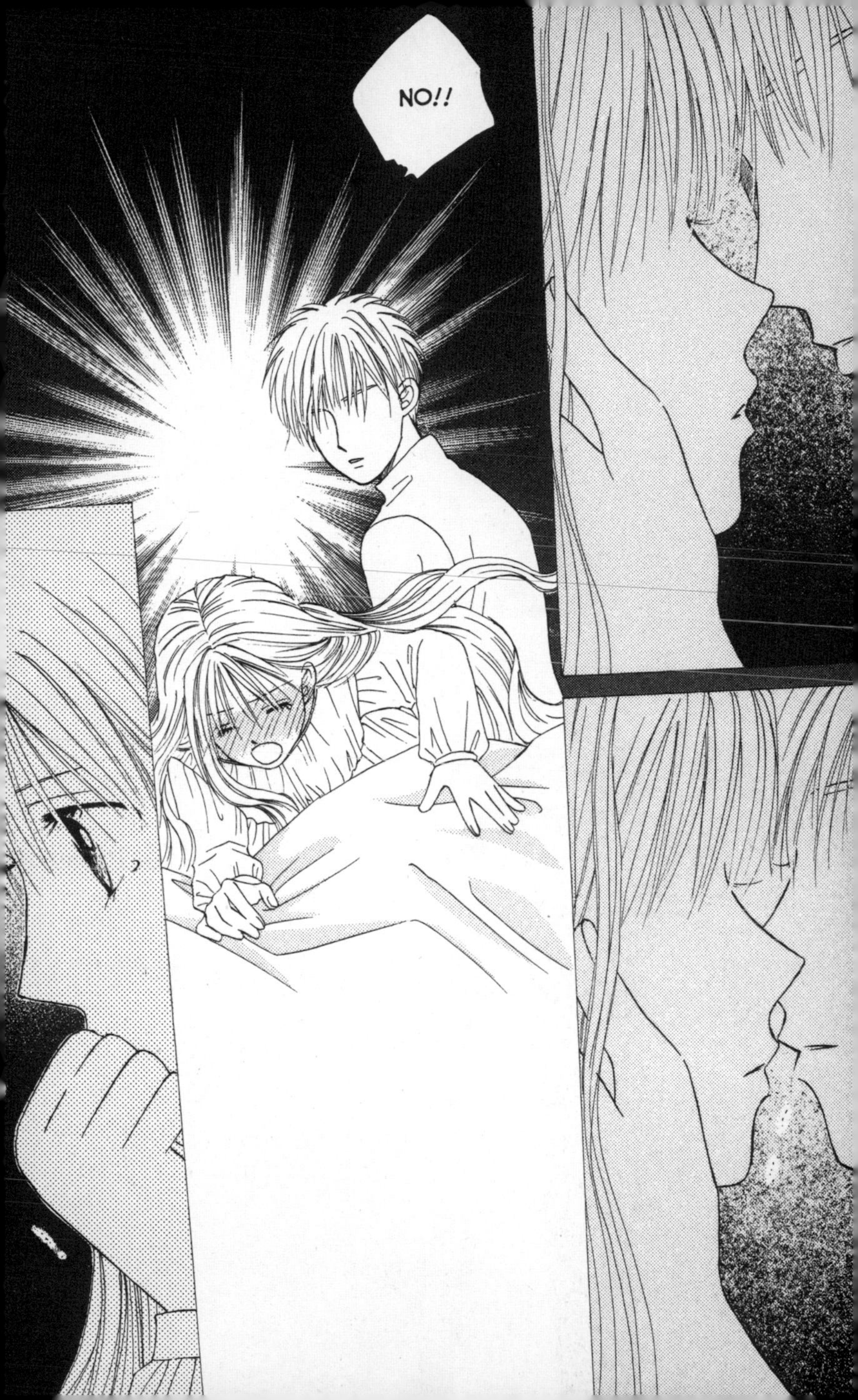
NO!!

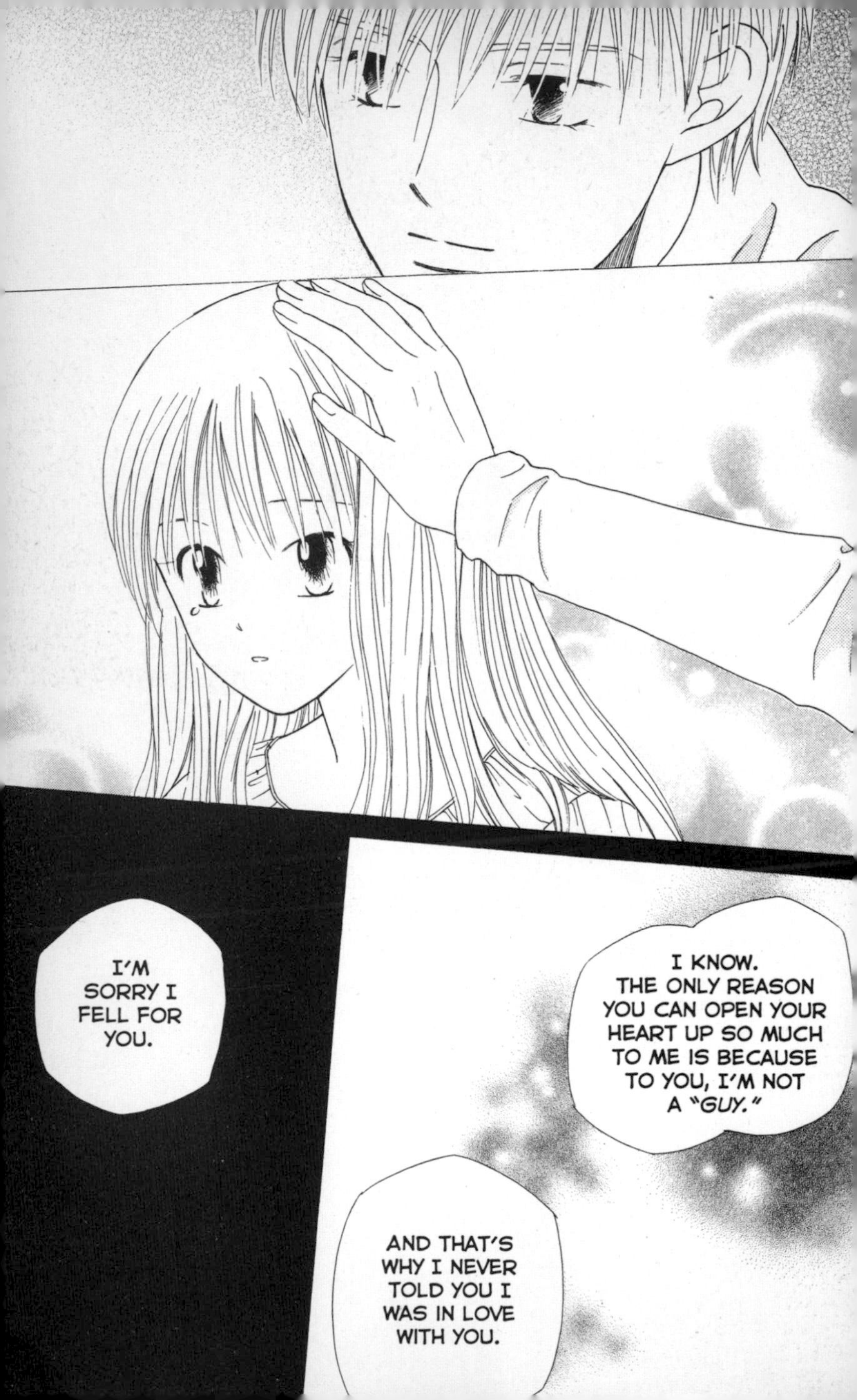
I KNOW. THE ONLY REASON YOU CAN OPEN YOUR HEART UP SO MUCH TO ME IS BECAUSE TO YOU, I'M NOT A "GUY."
AND THAT'S WHY I NEVER TOLD YOU I WAS IN LOVE WITH YOU.
I'M SORRY I FELL FOR YOU.

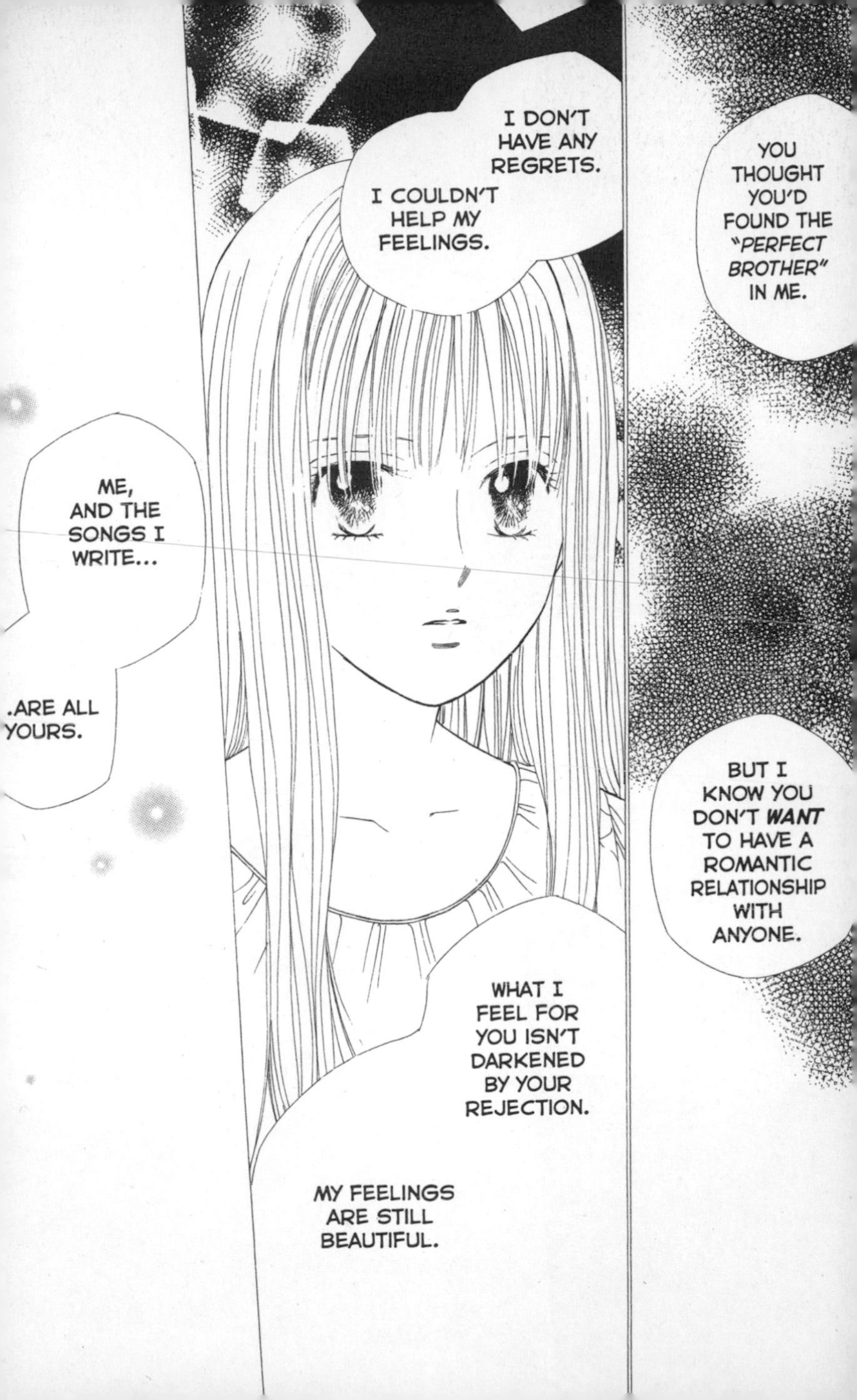
YOU THOUGHT YOU'D FOUND THE "PERFECT BROTHER" IN ME.
BUT I KNOW YOU DON'T *WANT* TO HAVE A ROMANTIC RELATIONSHIP WITH ANYONE.
I DON'T HAVE ANY REGRETS.
I COULDN'T HELP MY FEELINGS.
WHAT I FEEL FOR YOU ISN'T DARKENED BY YOUR REJECTION.
MY FEELINGS ARE STILL BEAUTIFUL.
ME, AND THE SONGS I WRITE...
.ARE ALL YOURS.

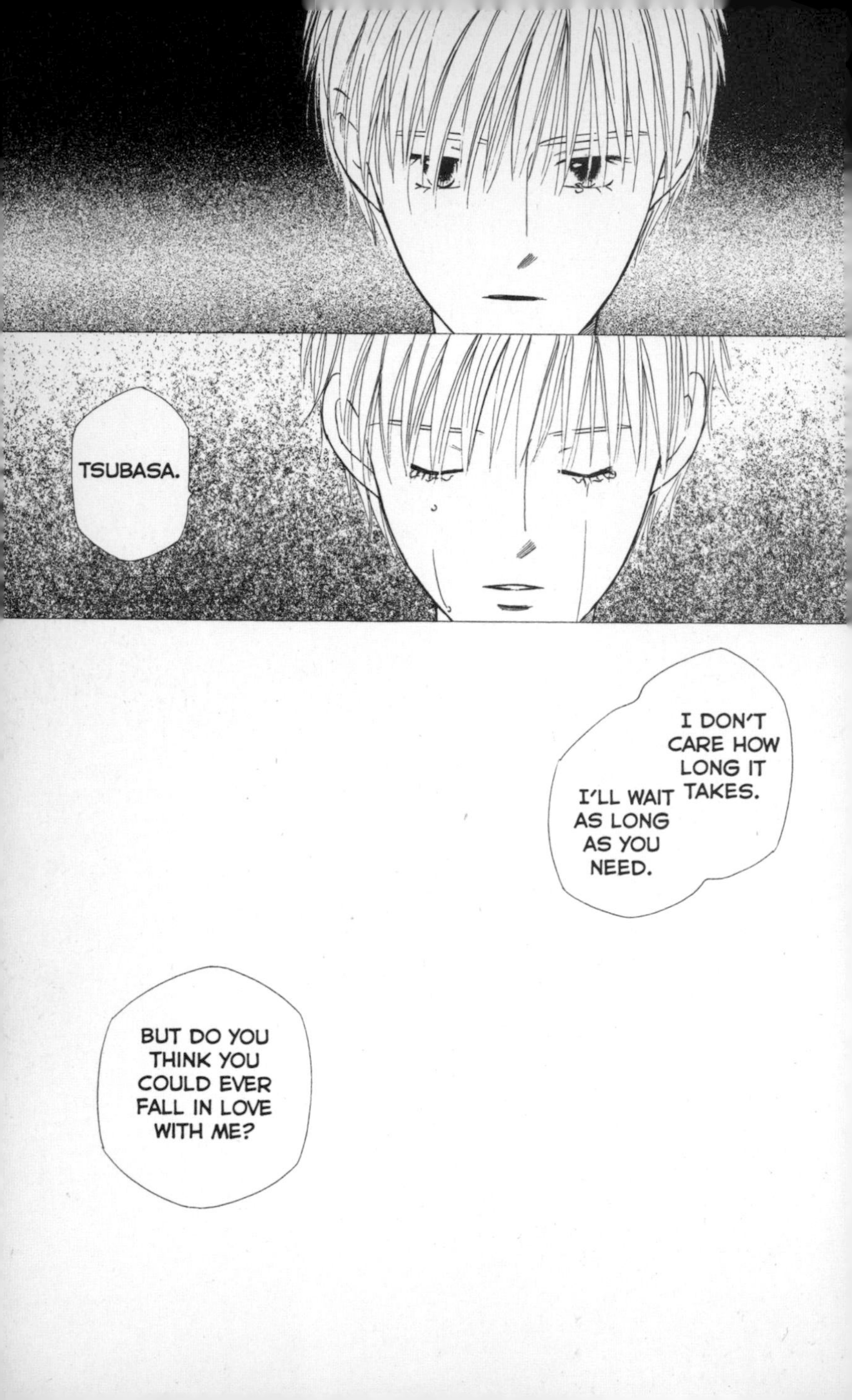
TSUBASA.
I DON'T CARE HOW LONG IT TAKES.
I'LL WAIT AS LONG AS YOU NEED.
BUT DO YOU THINK YOU COULD EVER FALL IN LOVE WITH ME?

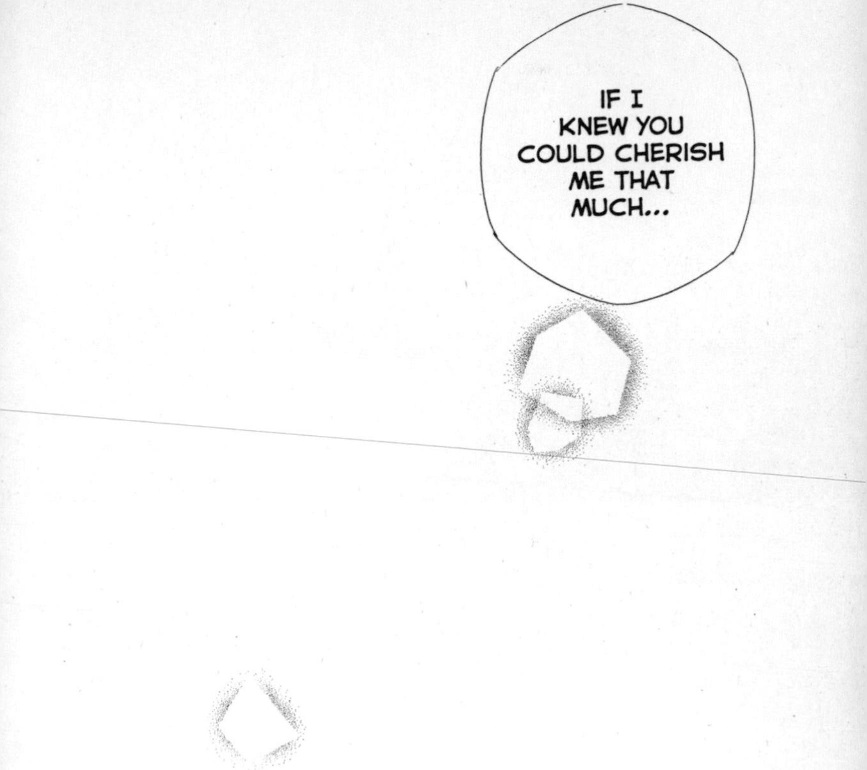
IF I KNEW YOU COULD CHERISH ME THAT MUCH...

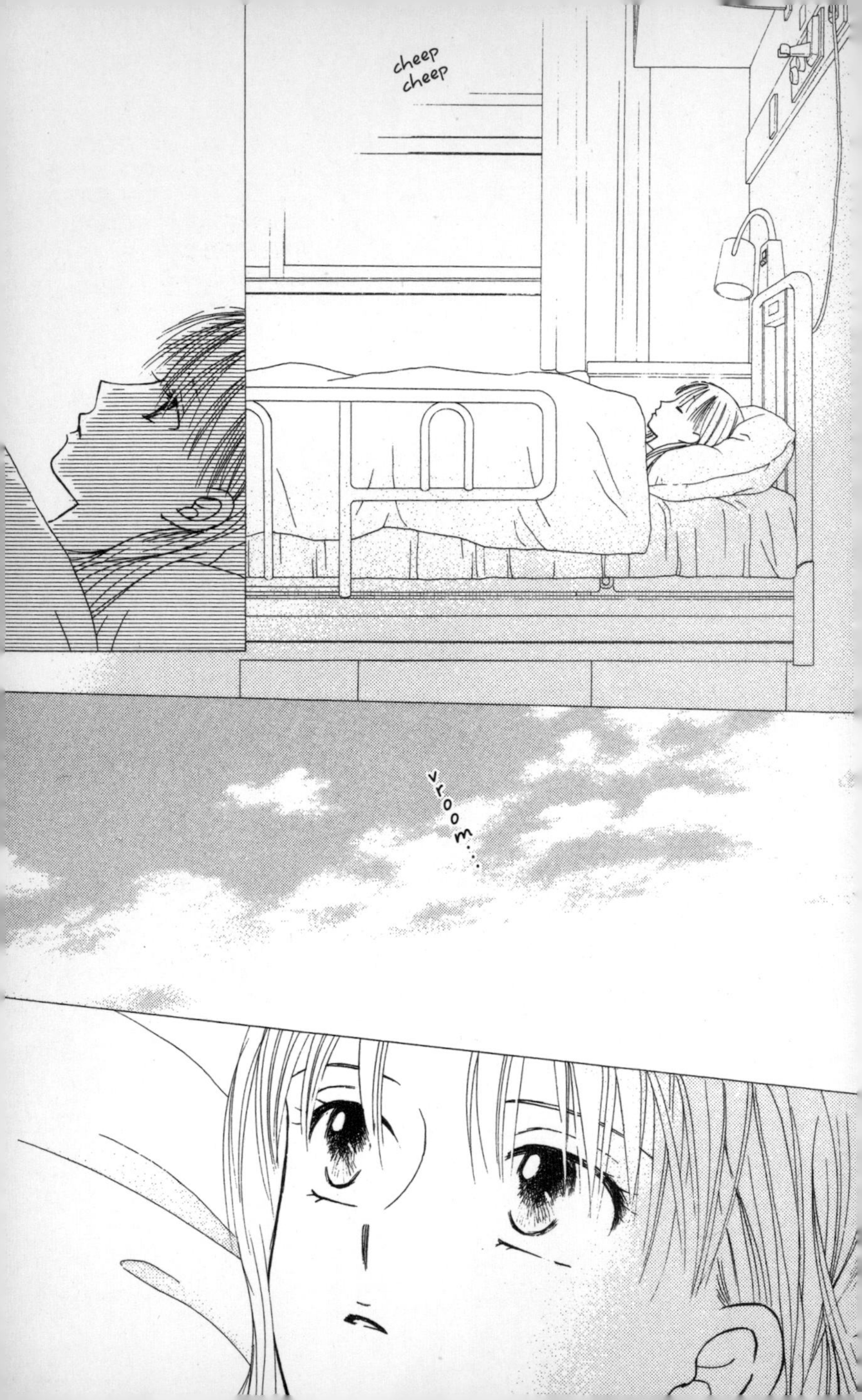
cheep
cheep
vroom...

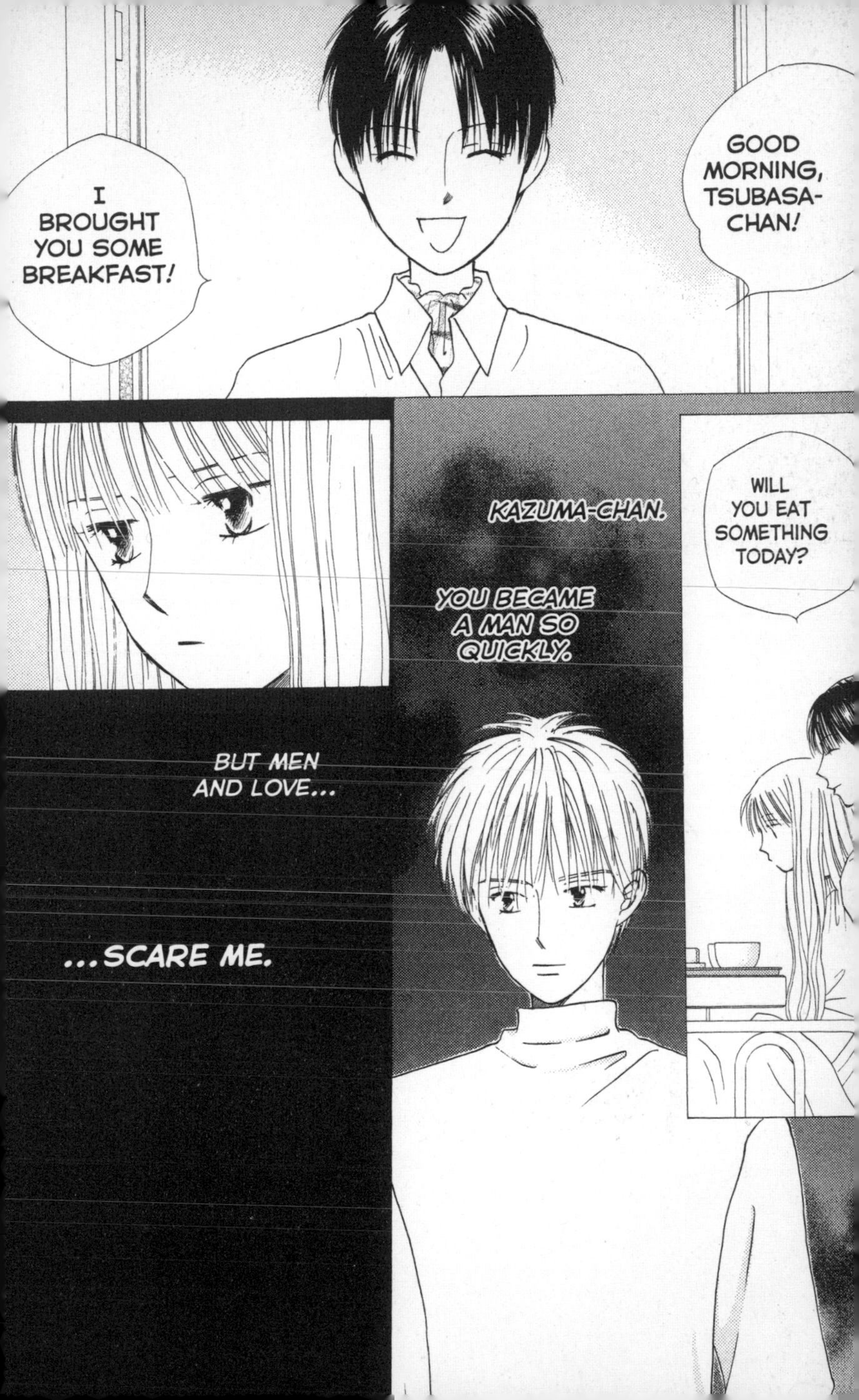
GOOD MORNING, TSUBASA-CHAN!
I BROUGHT YOU SOME BREAKFAST!
WILL YOU EAT SOMETHING TODAY?
KAZUMA-CHAN.
YOU BECAME A MAN SO QUICKLY.
BUT MEN AND LOVE...
...SCARE ME.

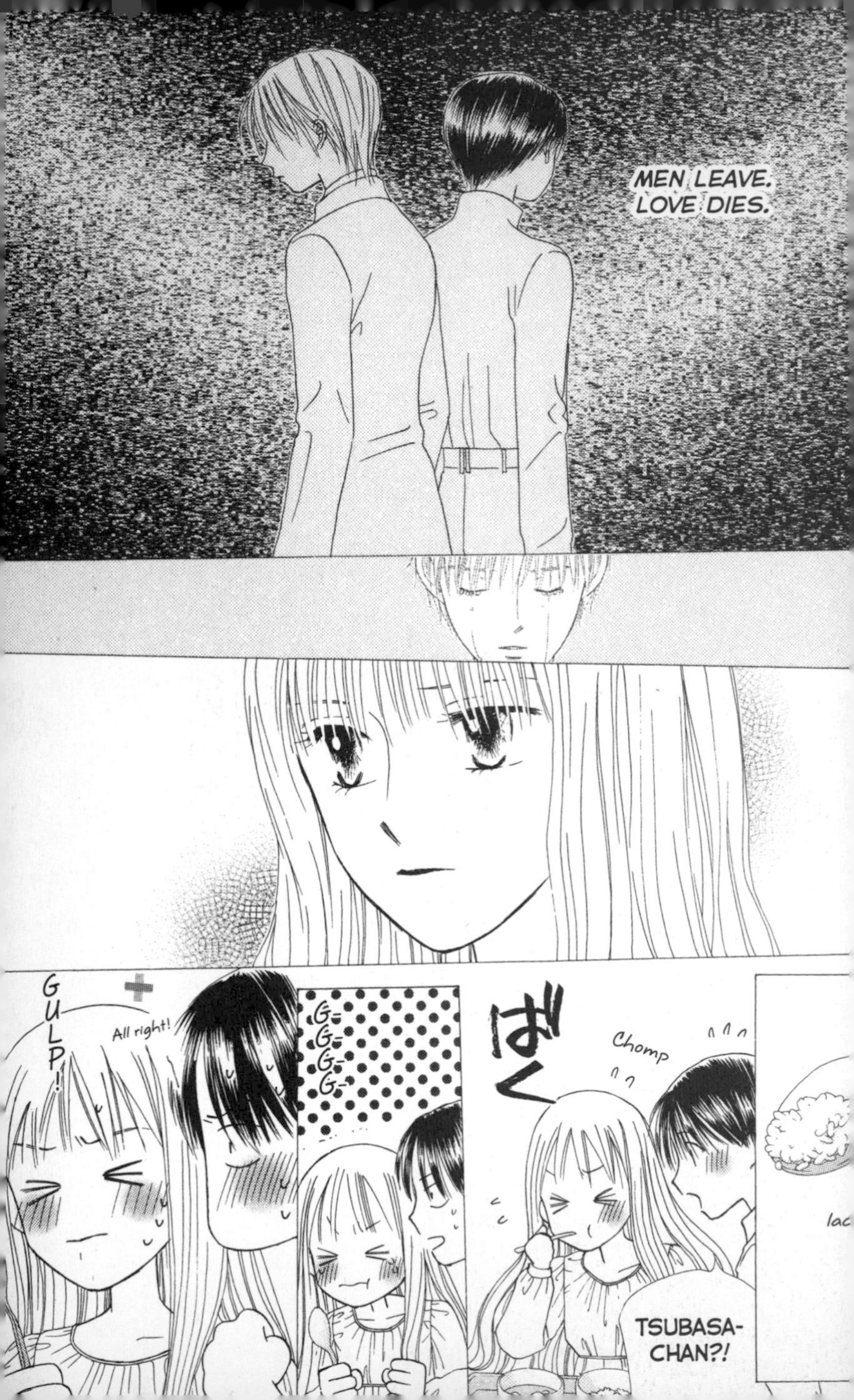
MEN LEAVE. LOVE DIES.
ぱく
Chomp
TSUBASA-CHAN?!
G-G-G-G-
All right!
GULP!

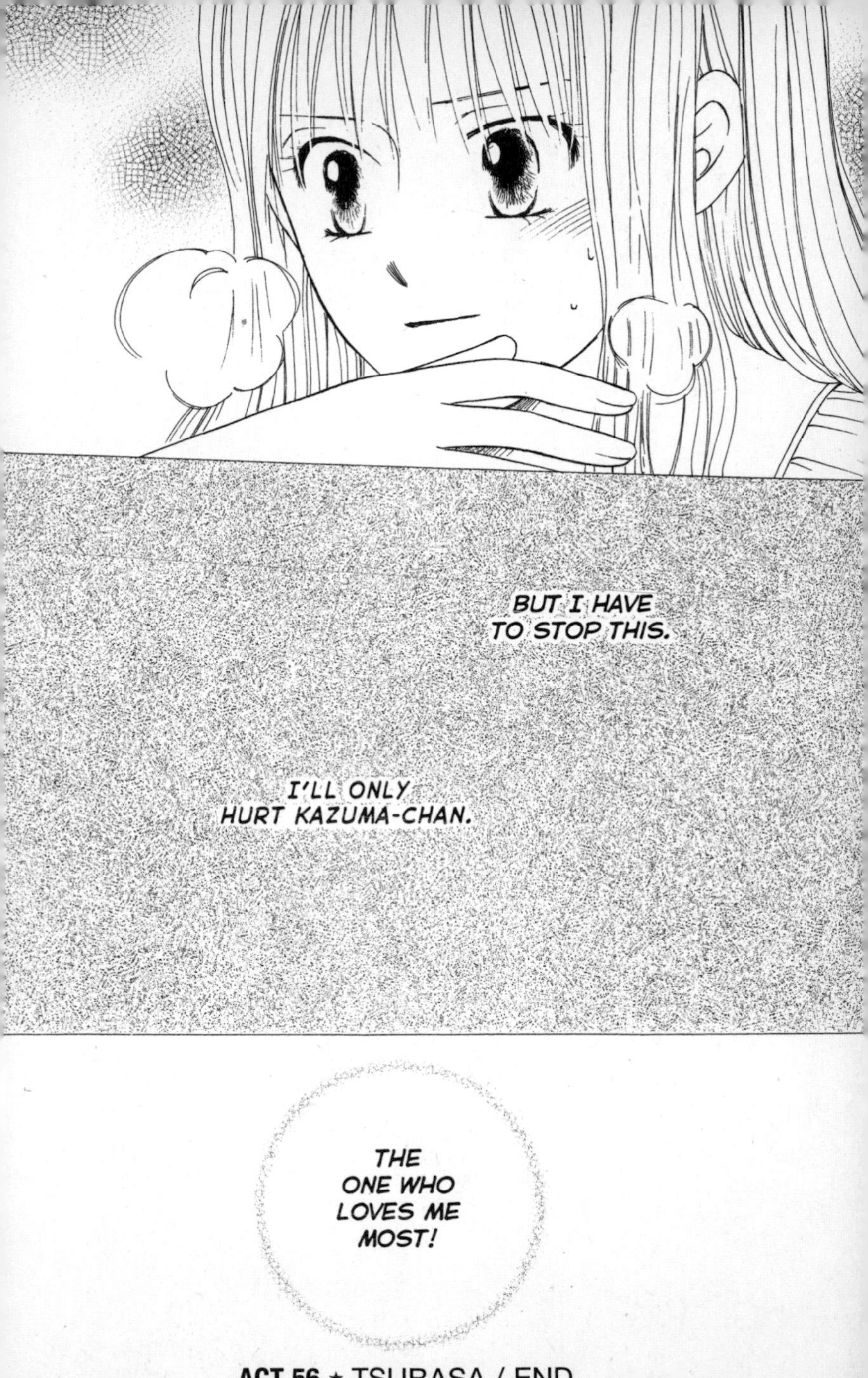
BUT I HAVE TO STOP THIS.
I'LL ONLY HURT KAZUMA-CHAN.
THE ONE WHO LOVES ME MOST!

ACT 56 ★ TSUBASA / END

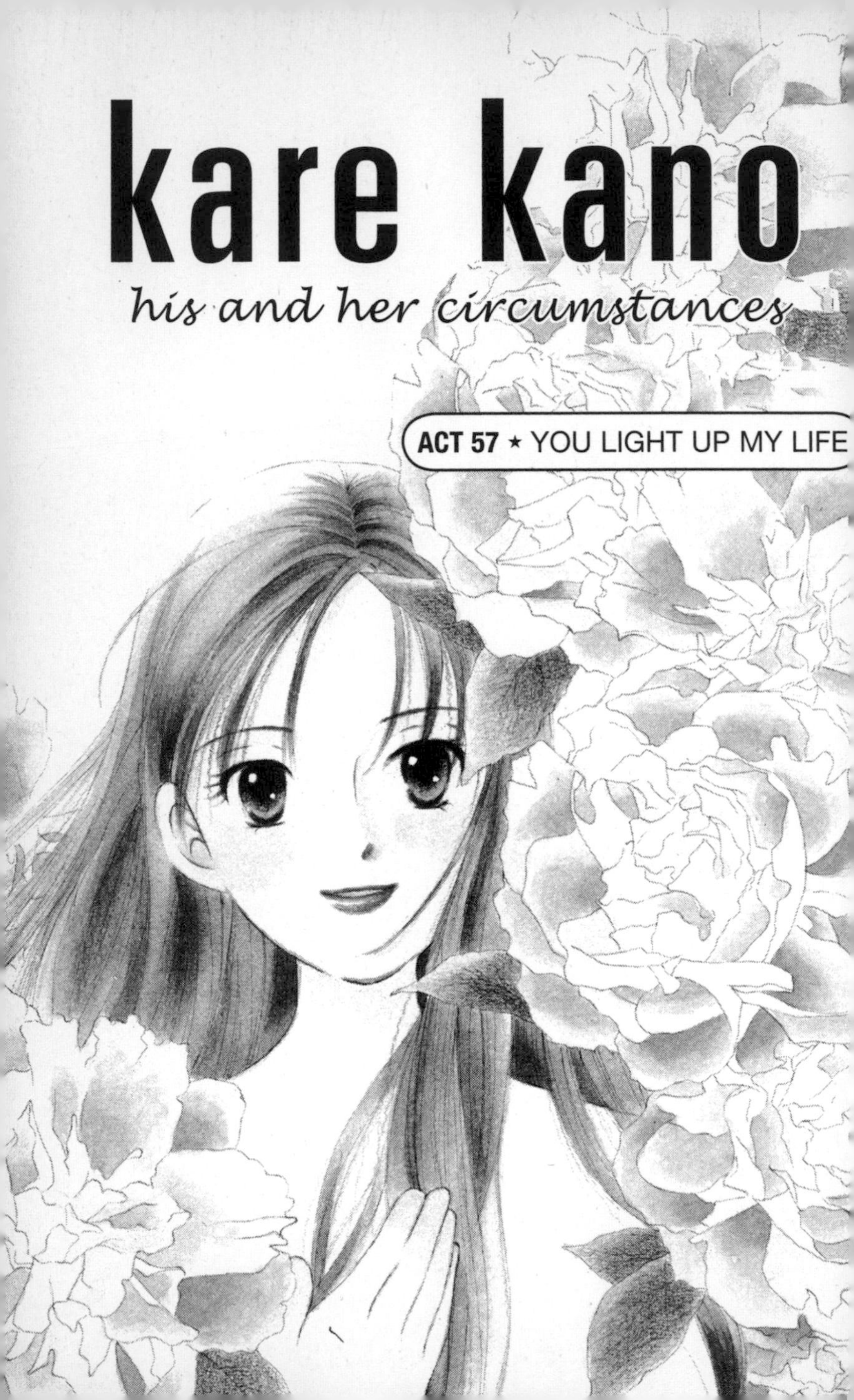
kare kano
his and her circumstances
ACT 57 ★ YOU LIGHT UP MY LIFE

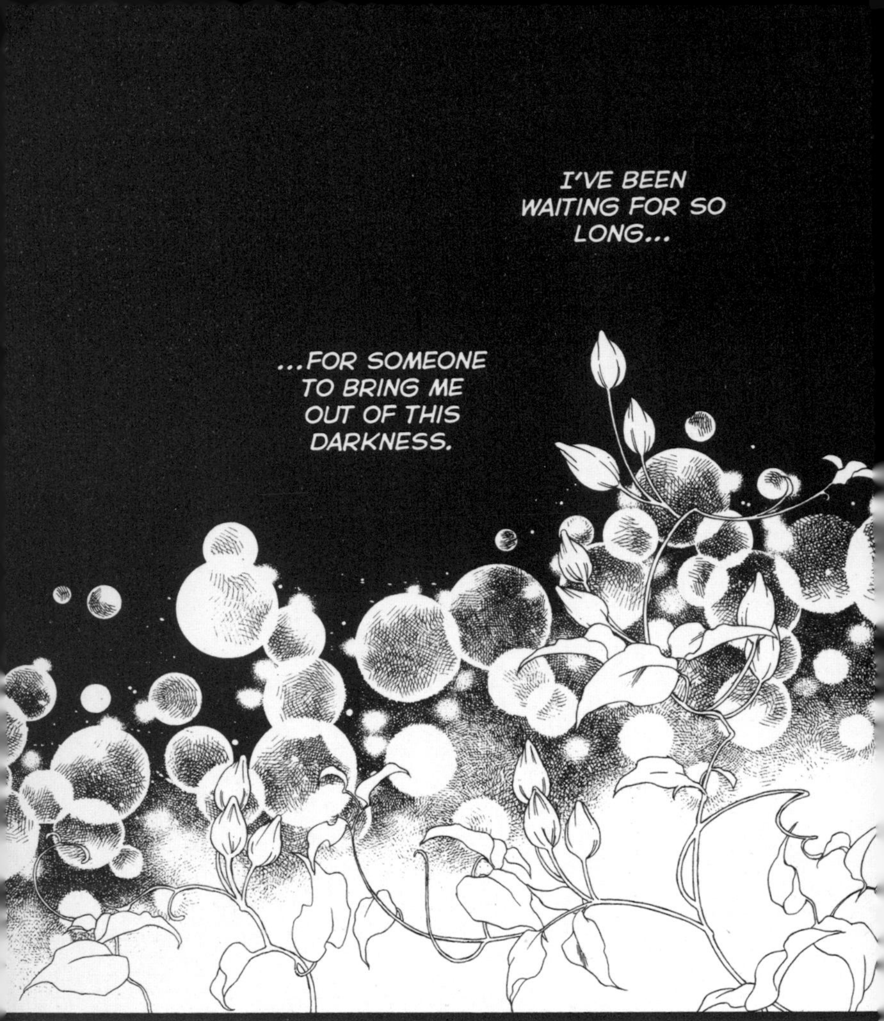
I'VE BEEN WAITING FOR SO LONG...
...FOR SOMEONE TO BRING ME OUT OF THIS DARKNESS.

About the songs I used in the story

"You Light Up My Life."
The version I have of this song is the one on the "Voices" album. Right in the middle of writing this story, I thought, "Wow, what a great song." And when I looked at the Japanese translation of the lyrics, I thought it would be PERFECT for the last part, so I got permission to use it (but only in Japan -Ed.) Since it's an actual song, if you happen to hear it sometime, then maybe the story can become more real for you. They probably have it at the CD shop, just for reference. "Chohatsu Mugendai" is the song Yin and Yang sang in Act 50. Come on everybody, let's listen to Shibugakitai!
I'm just bursting with excitement!

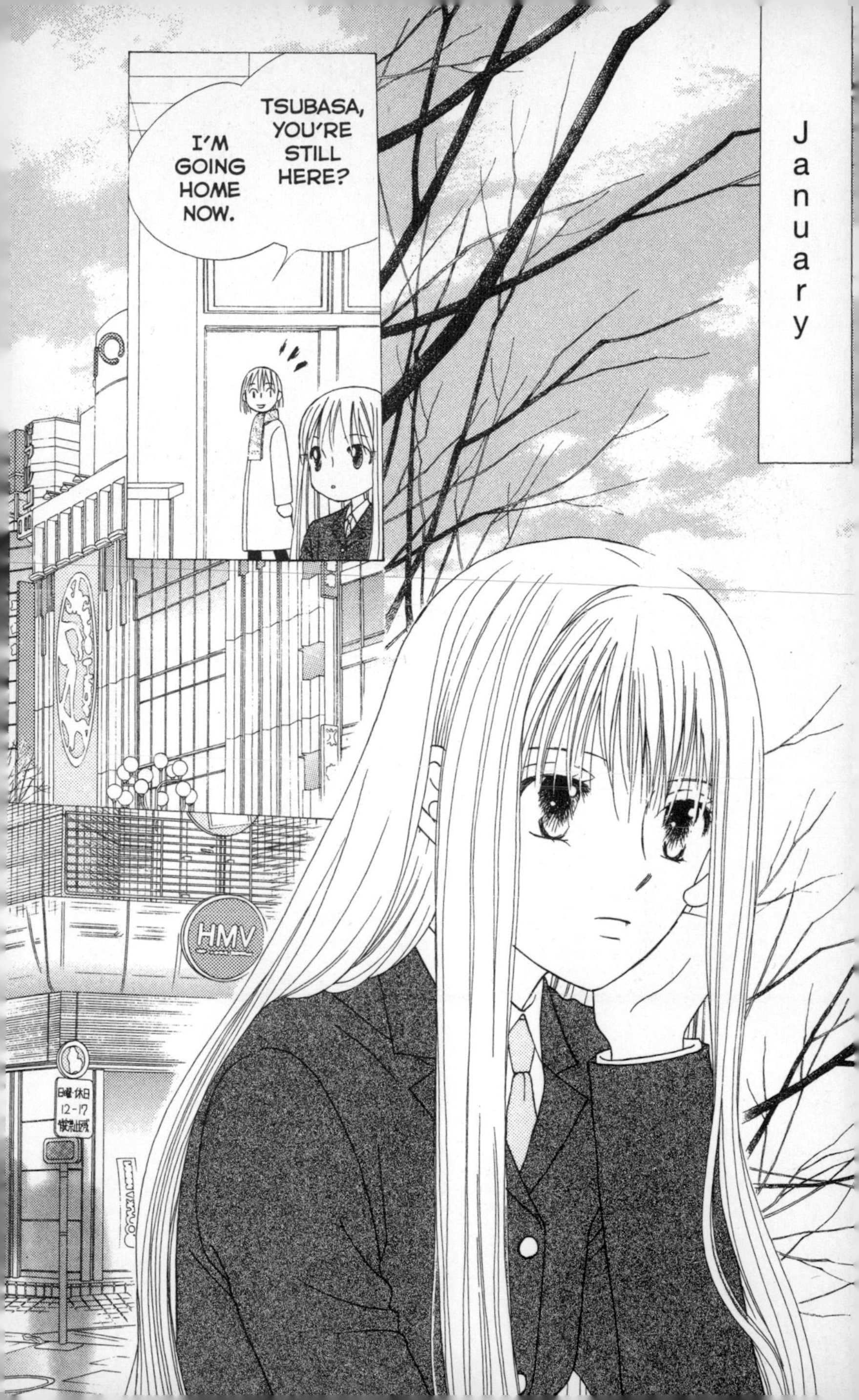
January
TSUBASA, YOU'RE STILL HERE?
I'M GOING HOME NOW.
HMV
日曜·休日
12-17

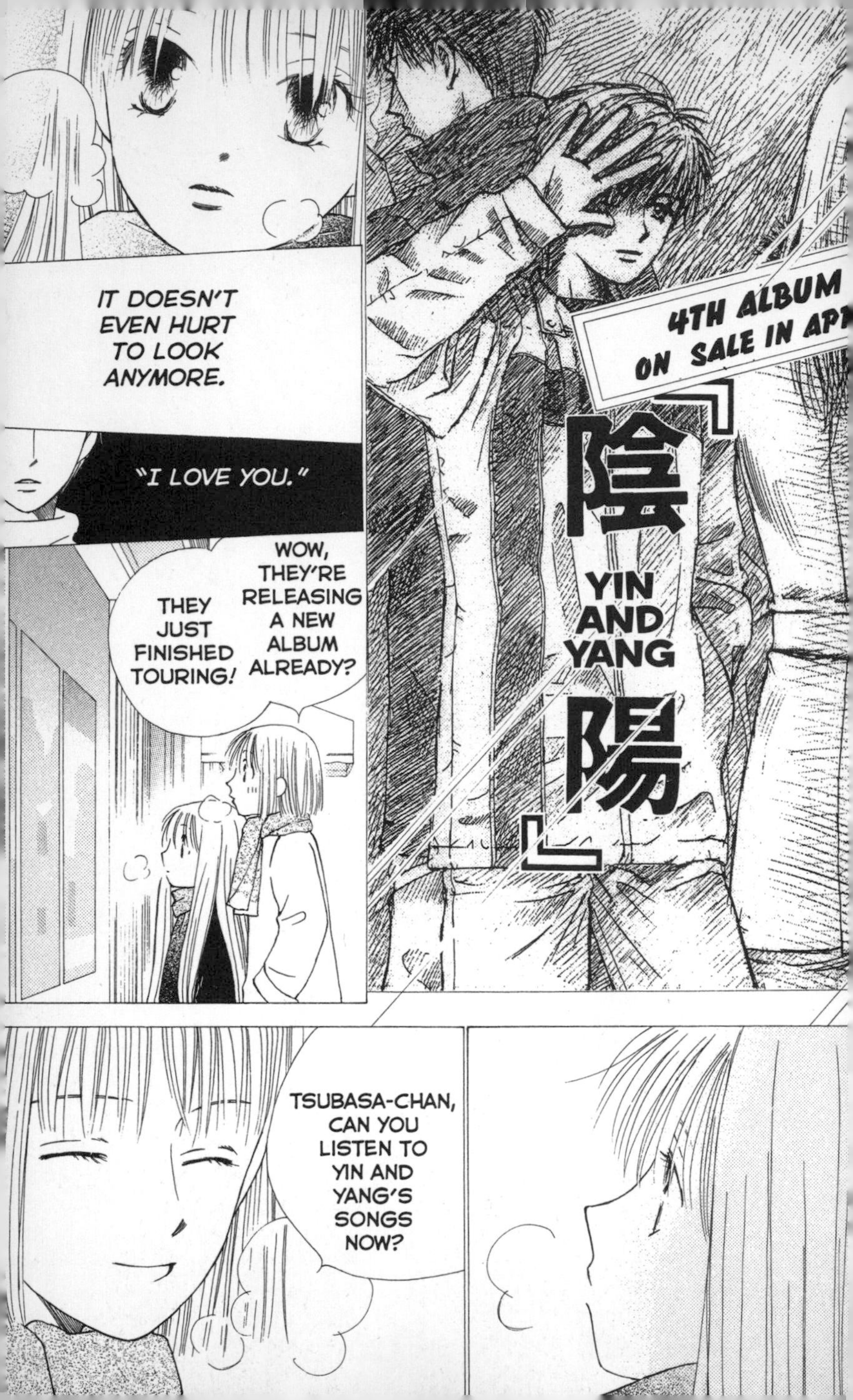
4TH ALBUM
ON SALE IN AP
『陰
YIN AND YANG
陽』
IT DOESN'T EVEN HURT TO LOOK ANYMORE.
"I LOVE YOU."
WOW, THEY'RE RELEASING A NEW ALBUM ALREADY?
THEY JUST FINISHED TOURING!
TSUBASA-CHAN, CAN YOU LISTEN TO YIN AND YANG'S SONGS NOW?

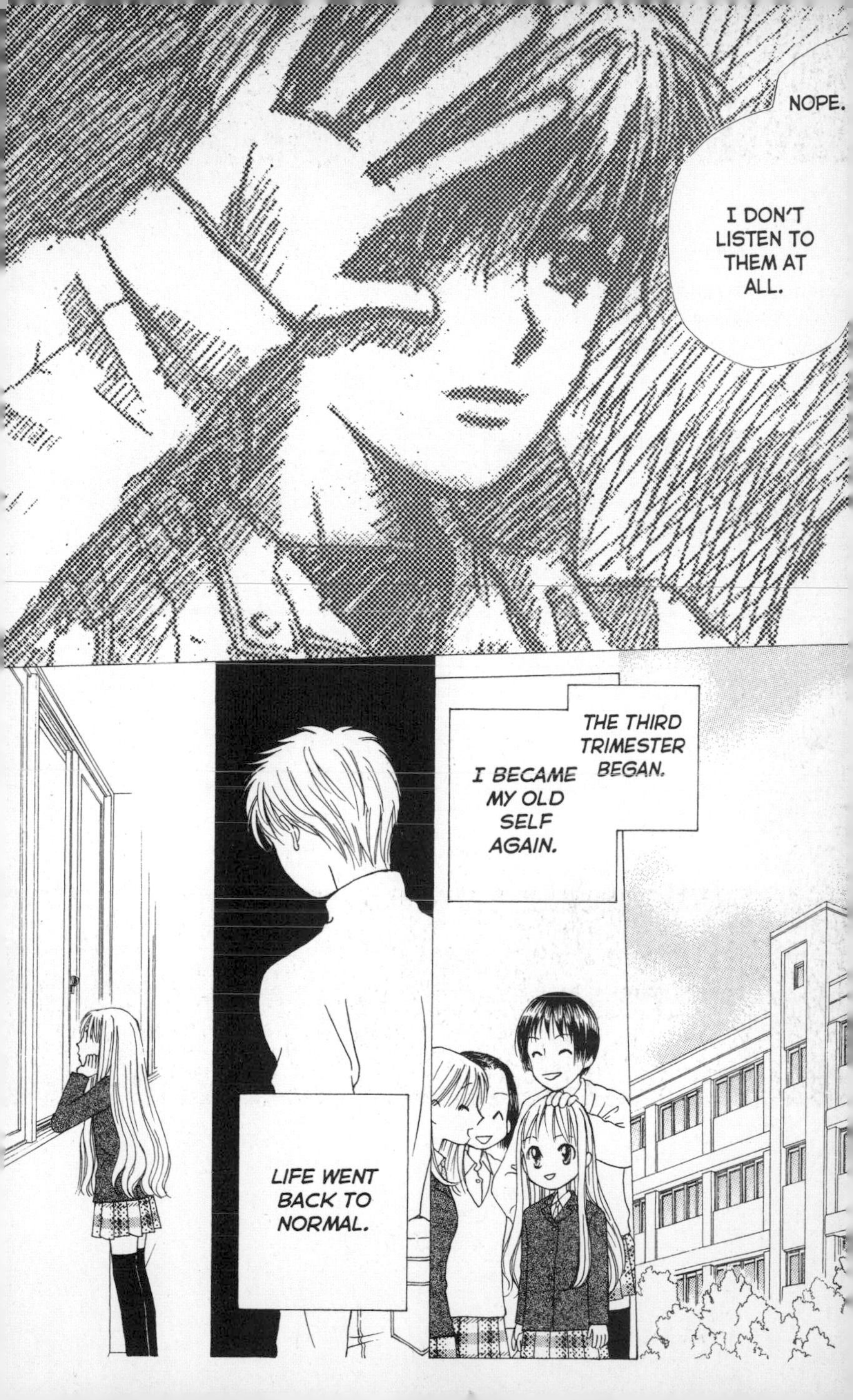
NOPE.
I DON'T LISTEN TO THEM AT ALL.
THE THIRD TRIMESTER BEGAN.
I BECAME MY OLD SELF AGAIN.
LIFE WENT BACK TO NORMAL.

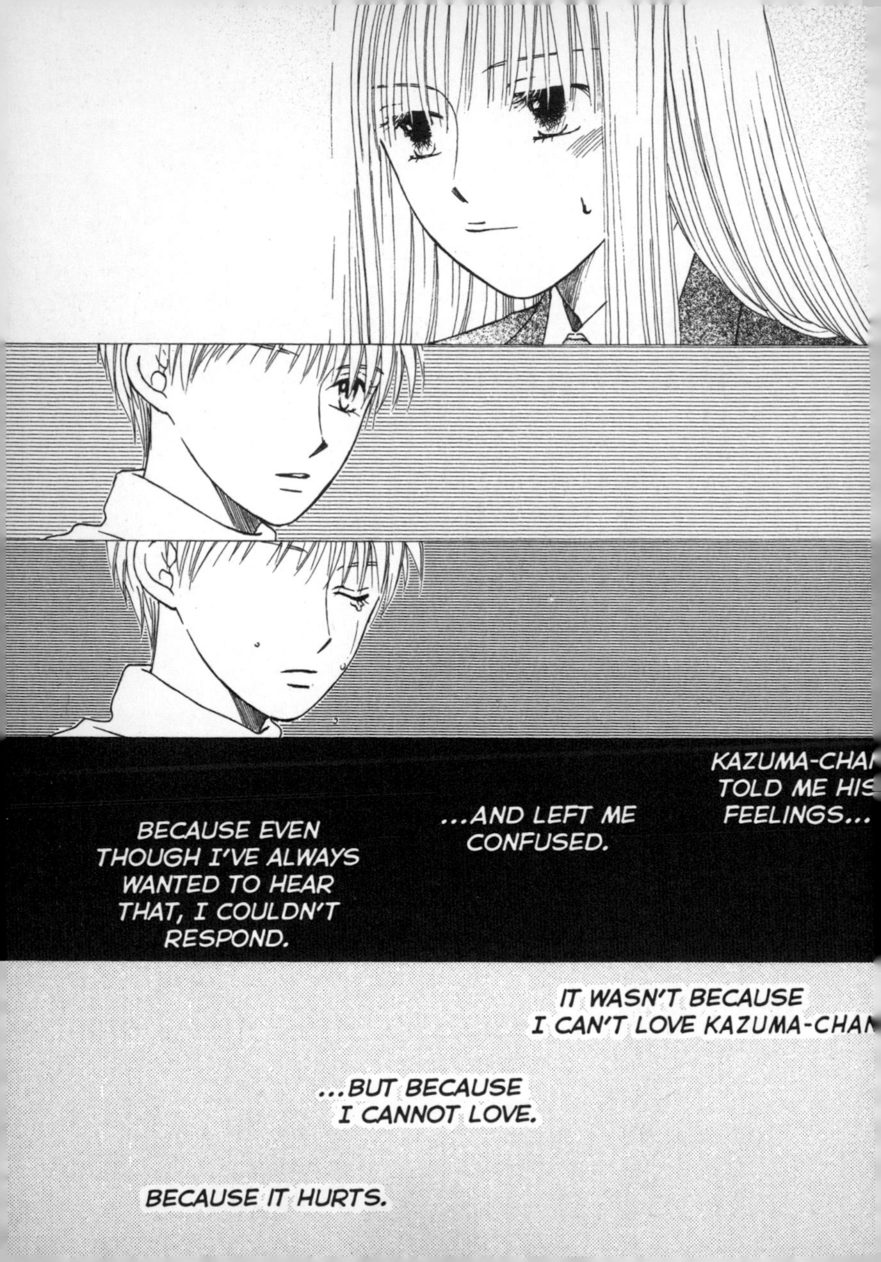
KAZUMA-CHAN TOLD ME HIS FEELINGS...
...AND LEFT ME CONFUSED.
BECAUSE EVEN THOUGH I'VE ALWAYS WANTED TO HEAR THAT, I COULDN'T RESPOND.
IT WASN'T BECAUSE I CAN'T LOVE KAZUMA-CHAN
...BUT BECAUSE I CANNOT LOVE.
BECAUSE IT HURTS.

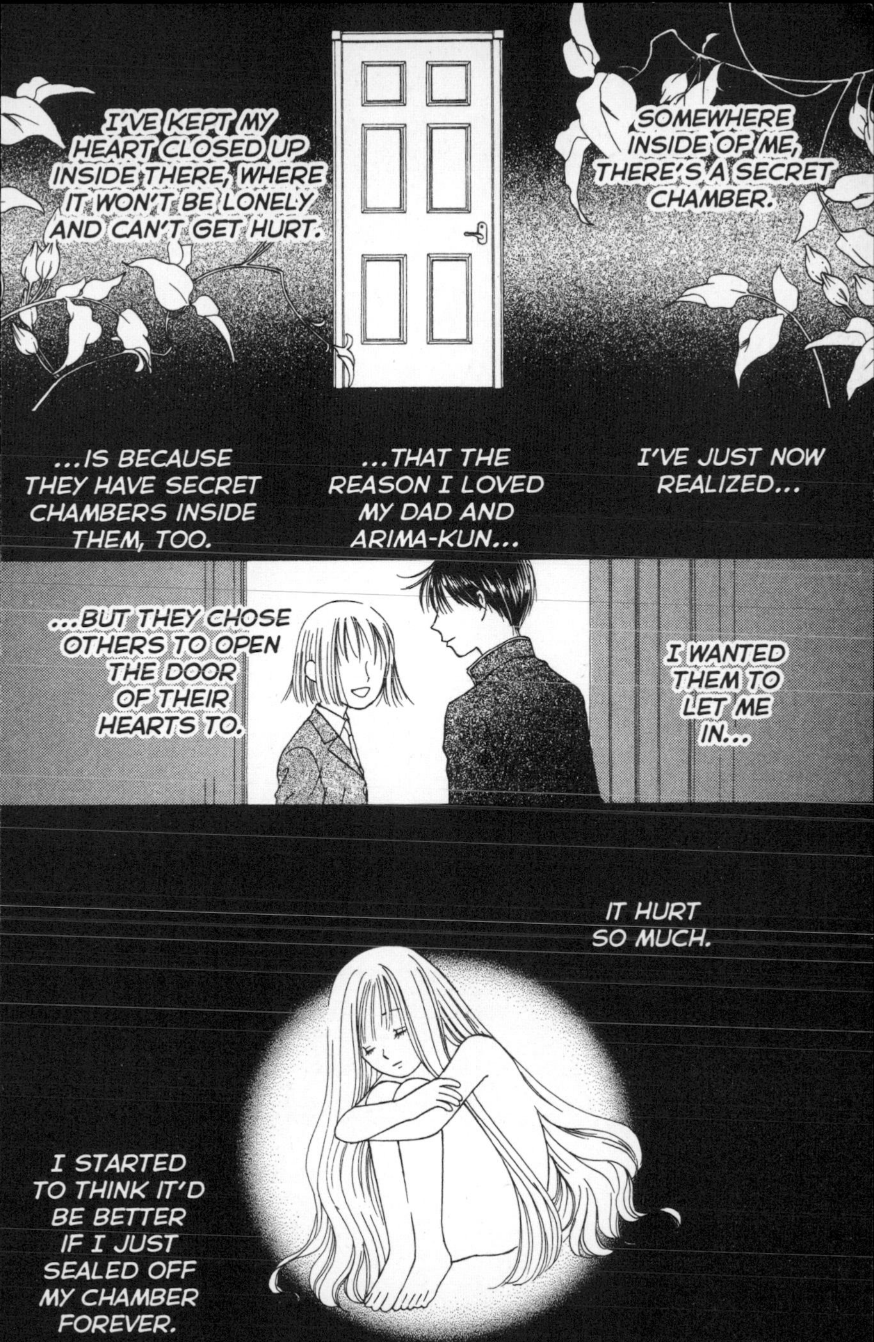
SOMEWHERE INSIDE OF ME, THERE'S A SECRET CHAMBER.
I'VE KEPT MY HEART CLOSED UP INSIDE THERE, WHERE IT WON'T BE LONELY AND CAN'T GET HURT.
I'VE JUST NOW REALIZED...
...THAT THE REASON I LOVED MY DAD AND ARIMA-KUN...
...IS BECAUSE THEY HAVE SECRET CHAMBERS INSIDE THEM, TOO.
I WANTED THEM TO LET ME IN...
...BUT THEY CHOSE OTHERS TO OPEN THE DOOR OF THEIR HEARTS TO.
IT HURT SO MUCH.
I STARTED TO THINK IT'D BE BETTER IF I JUST SEALED OFF MY CHAMBER FOREVER.

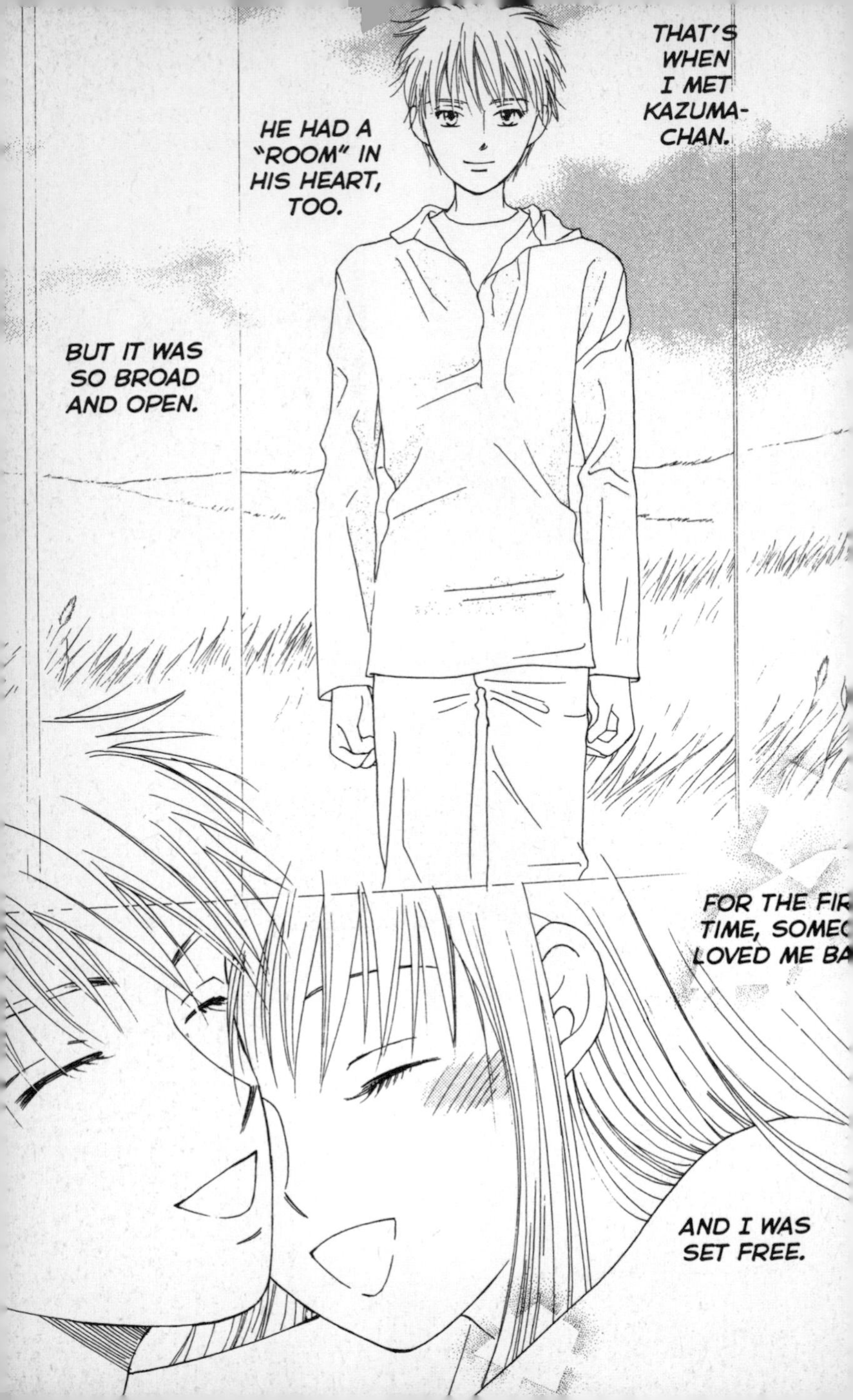
THAT'S WHEN I MET KAZUMA-CHAN.
HE HAD A "ROOM" IN HIS HEART, TOO.
BUT IT WAS SO BROAD AND OPEN.
FOR THE FIR TIME, SOME LOVED ME BA
AND I WAS SET FREE.

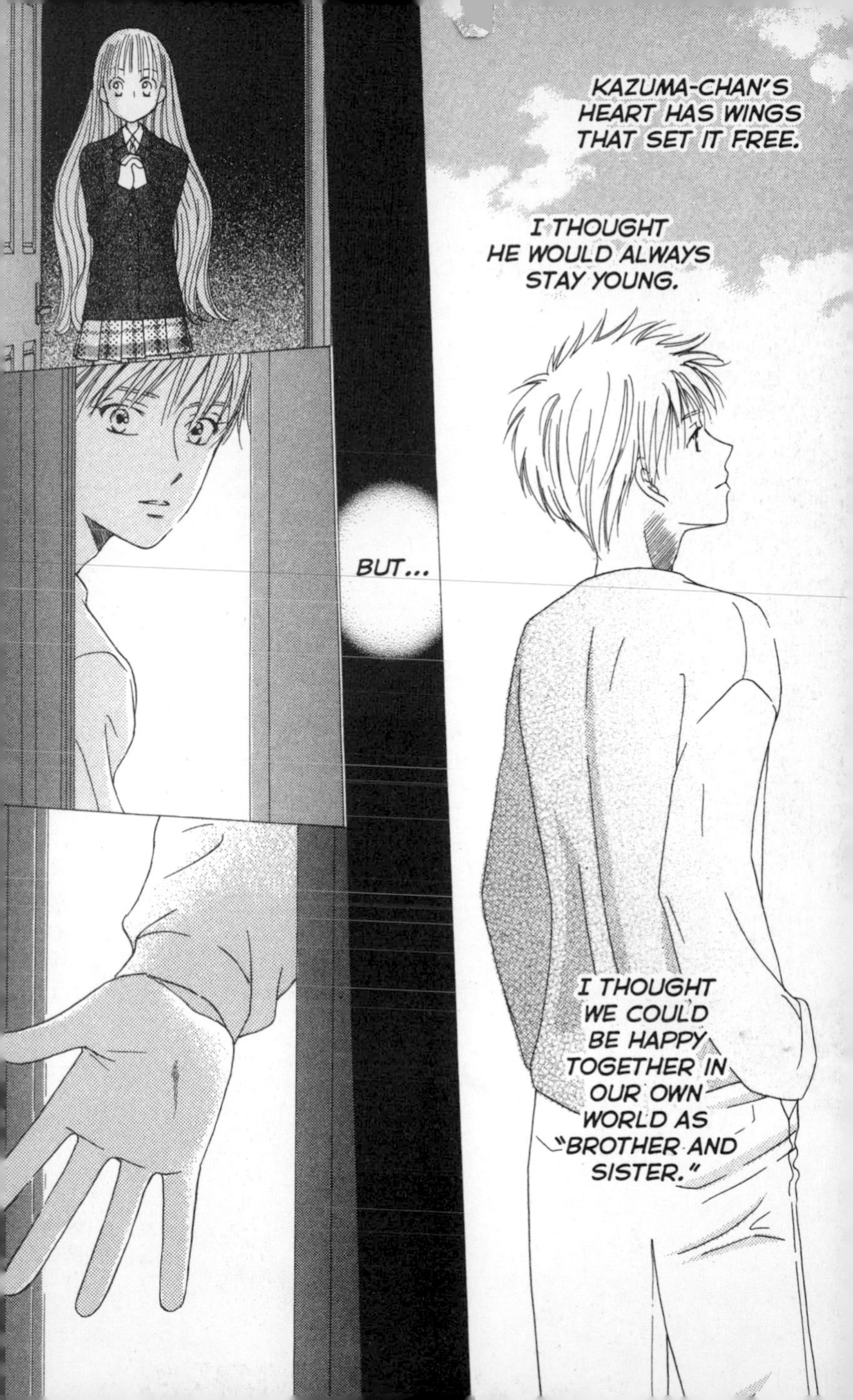
KAZUMA-CHAN'S HEART HAS WINGS THAT SET IT FREE.
I THOUGHT HE WOULD ALWAYS STAY YOUNG.
BUT...
I THOUGHT WE COULD BE HAPPY TOGETHER IN OUR OWN WORLD AS "BROTHER AND SISTER."

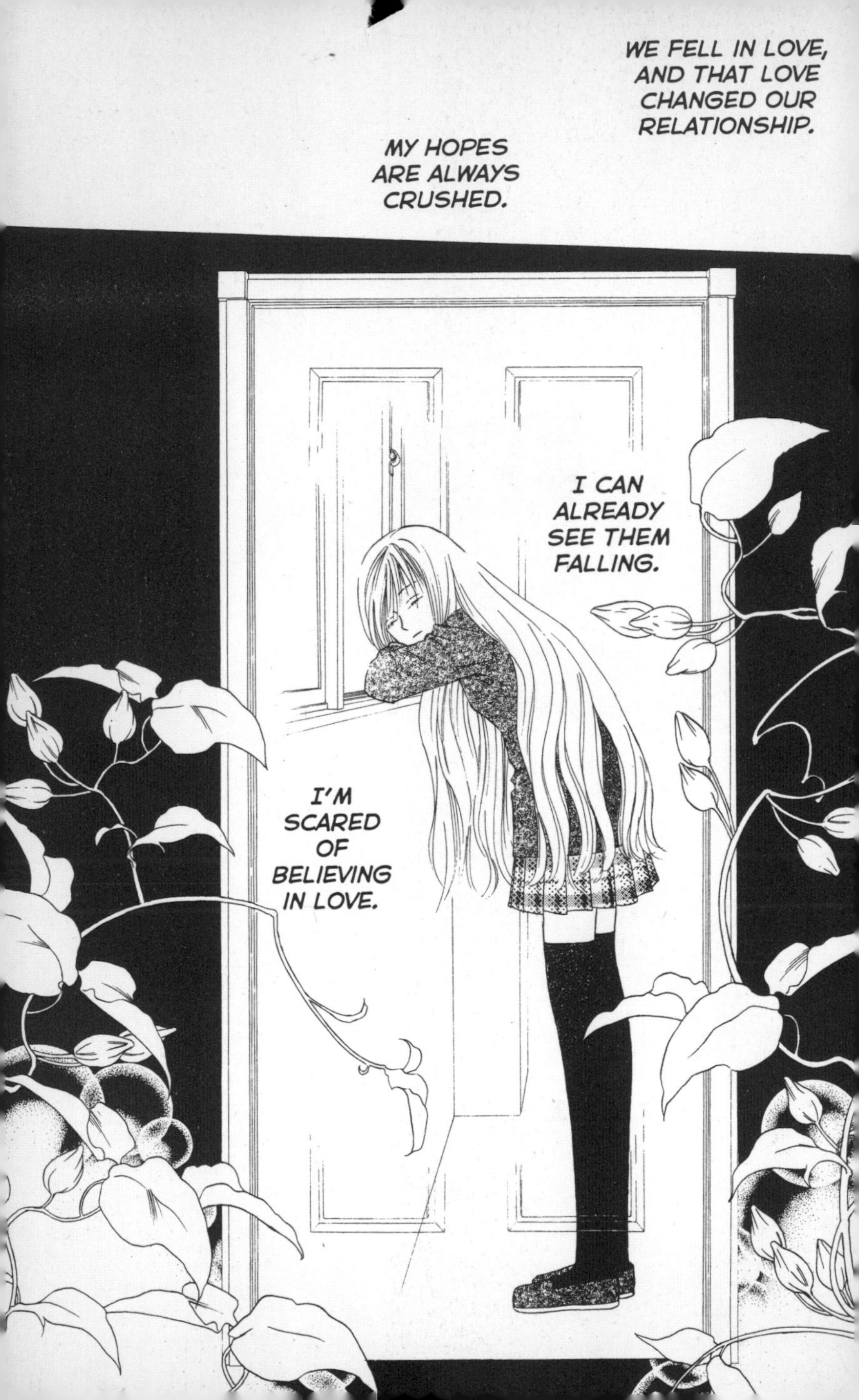
WE FELL IN LOVE, AND THAT LOVE CHANGED OUR RELATIONSHIP.
MY HOPES ARE ALWAYS CRUSHED.
I CAN ALREADY SEE THEM FALLING.
I'M SCARED OF BELIEVING IN LOVE.

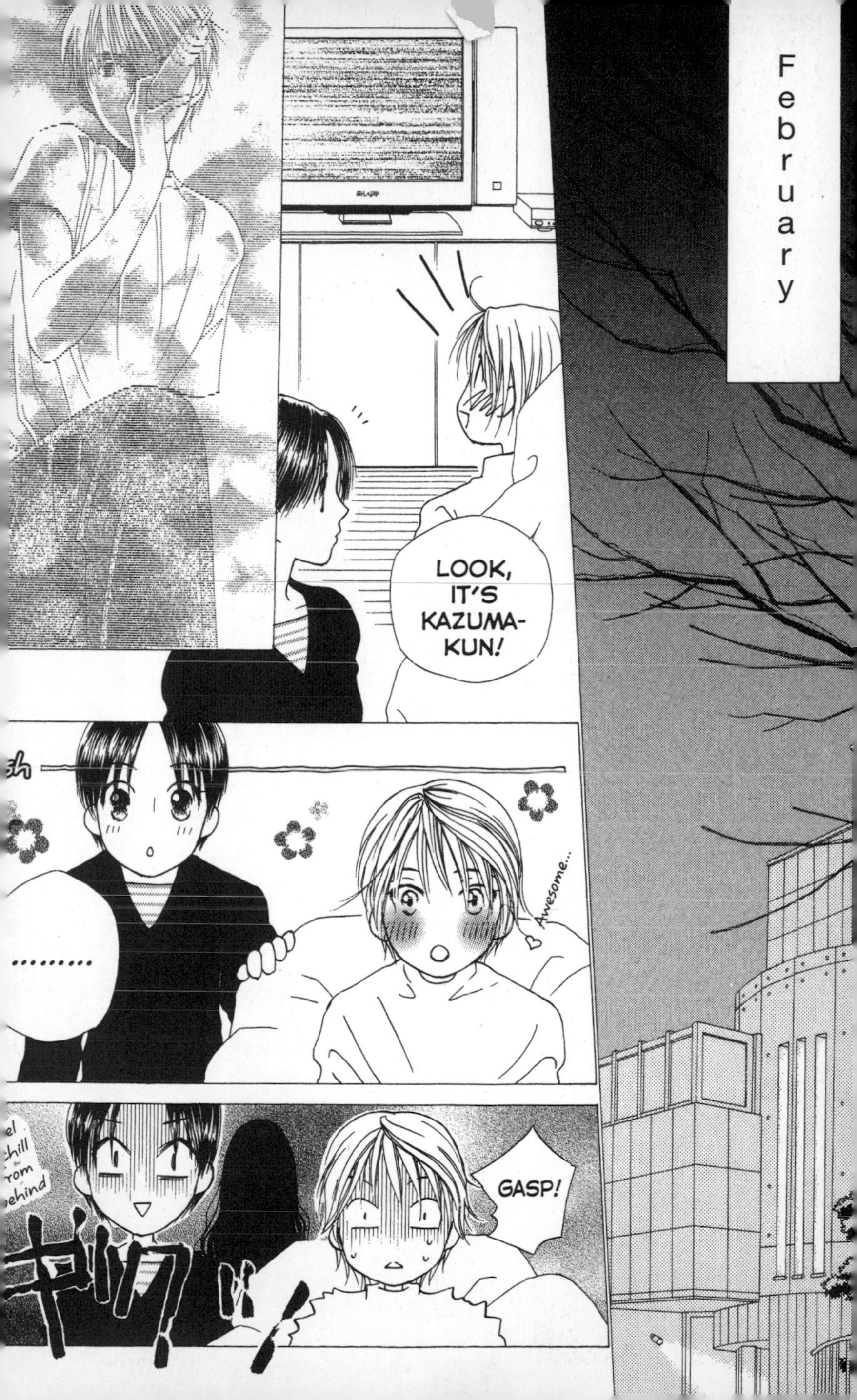
February
LOOK, IT'S KAZUMA-KUN!
Awesome...
....
GASP!

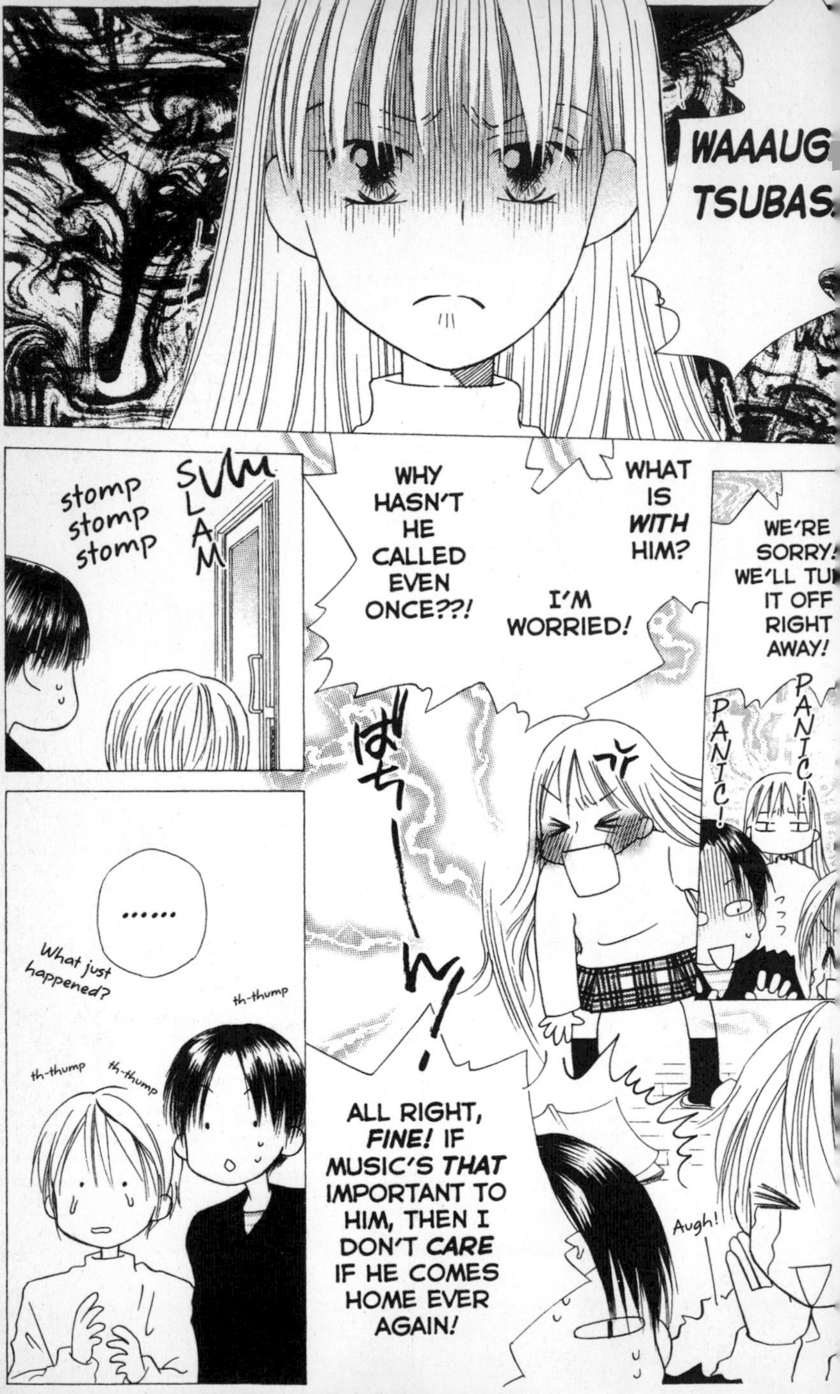
WAAAUG
TSUBAS
WE'RE SORRY! WE'LL TU
IT OFF RIGHT AWAY!
PANIC!
PANIC!
WHAT IS WITH HIM?
I'M WORRIED!
WHY HASN'T HE CALLED EVEN ONCE??!
ALL RIGHT, FINE! IF MUSIC'S THAT IMPORTANT TO HIM, THEN I DON'T CARE IF HE COMES HOME EVER AGAIN!
Augh!
stomp stomp stomp
SLAM
......
What just happened?
th-thump
th-thump
th-thump

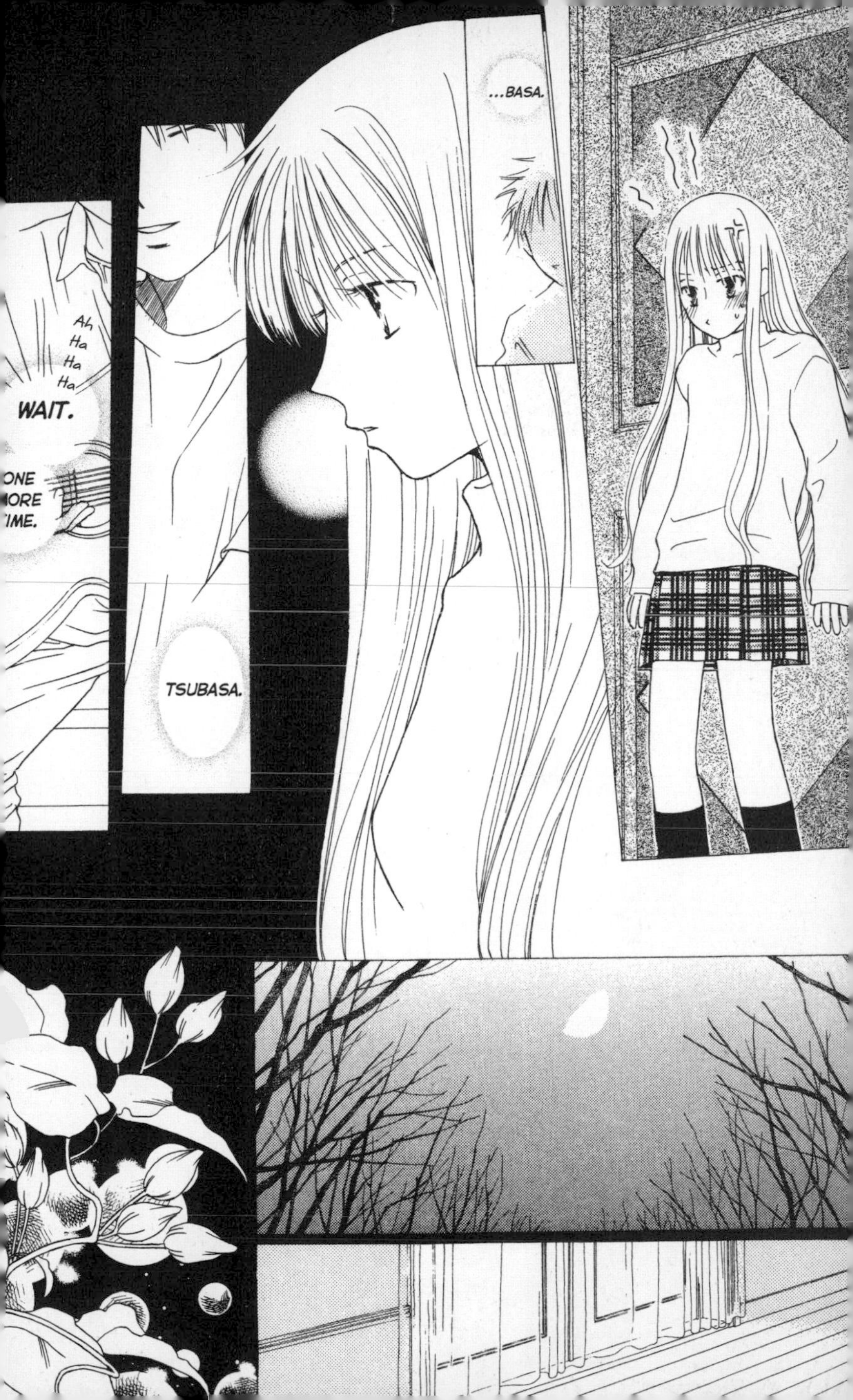
...BASA.
TSUBASA.
Ah Ha Ha Ha
WAIT.

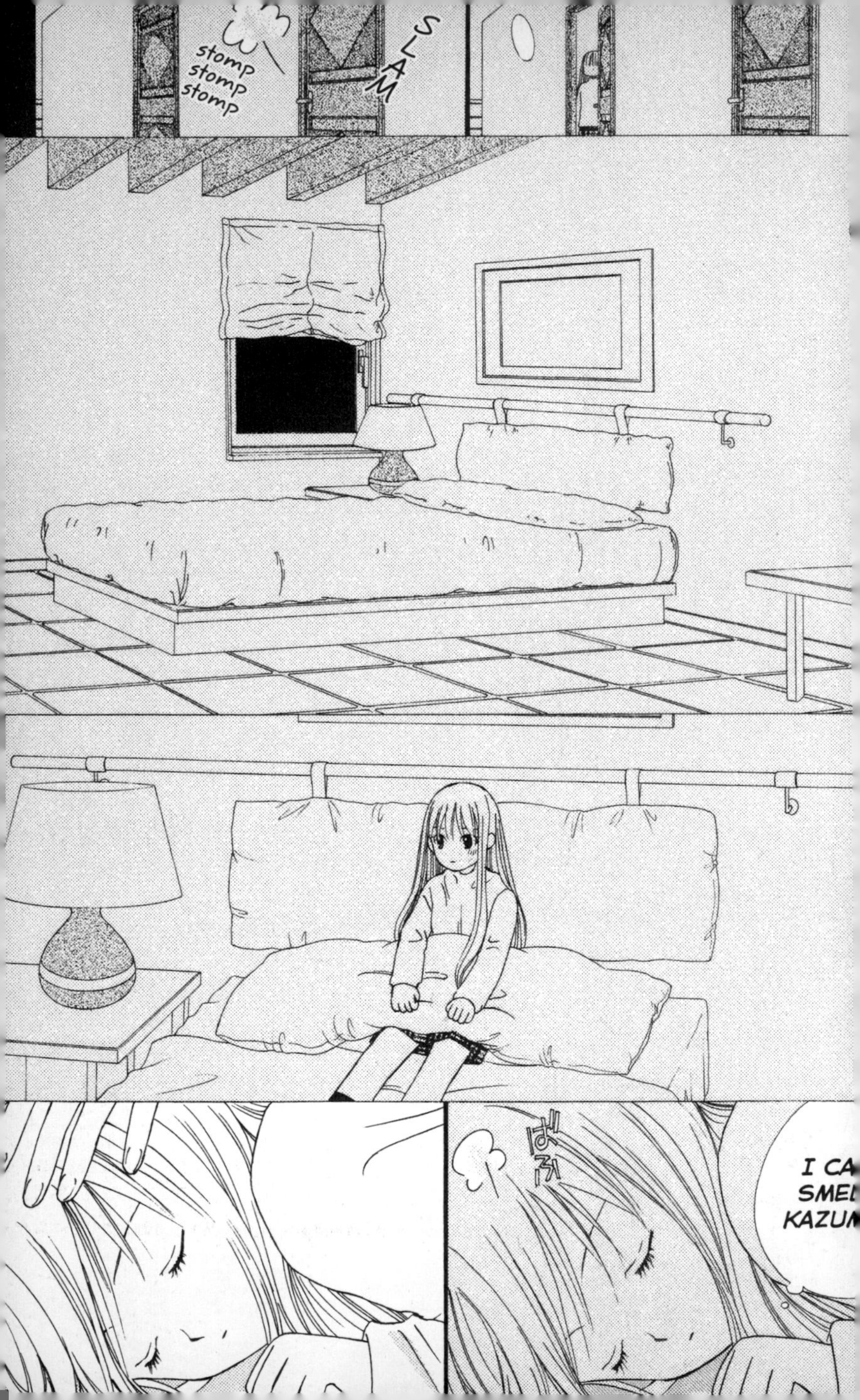
SLAM
stomp stomp stomp
I CA
SMEL
KAZUM

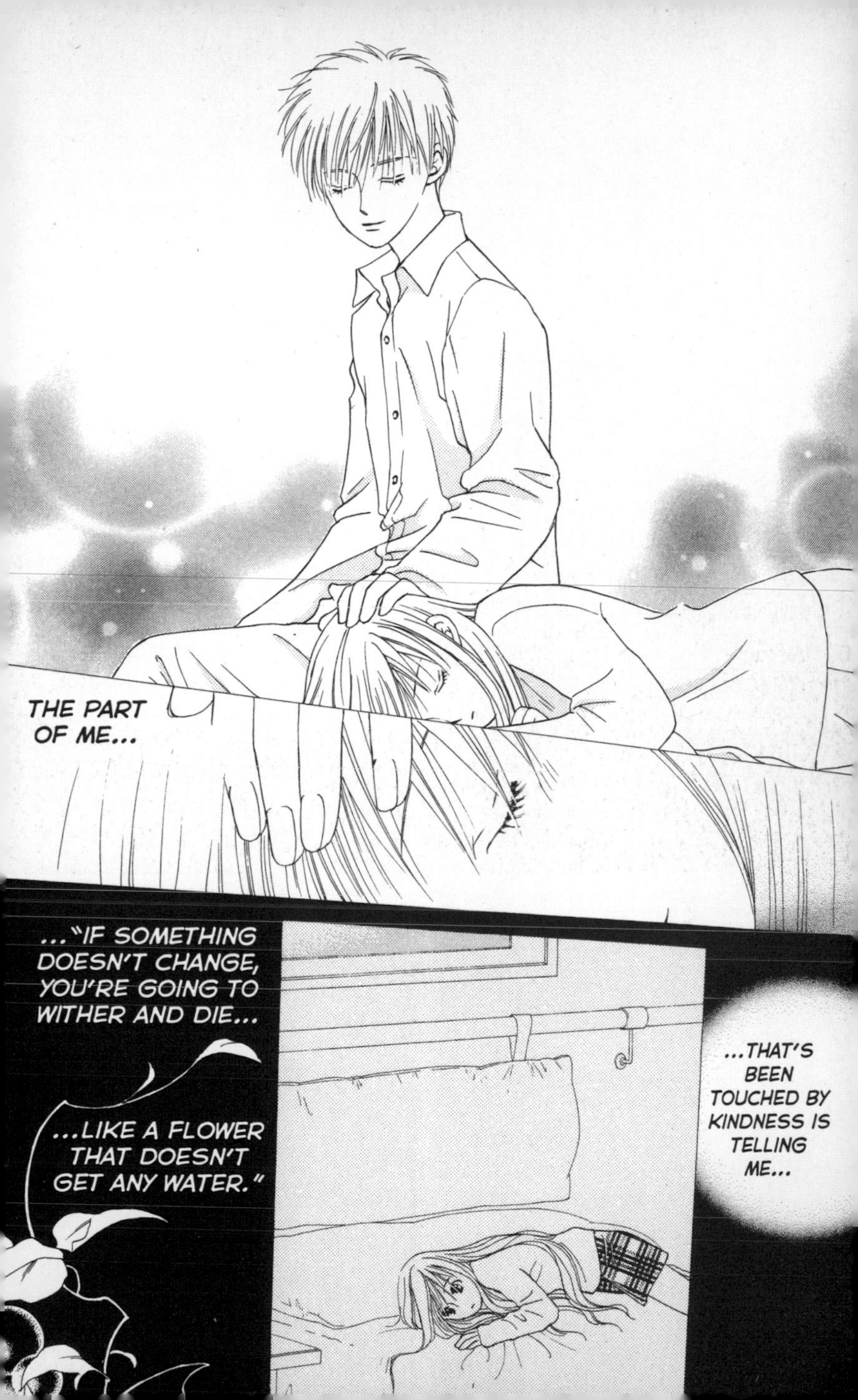
THE PART OF ME...
...THAT'S BEEN TOUCHED BY KINDNESS IS TELLING ME...
..."IF SOMETHING DOESN'T CHANGE, YOU'RE GOING TO WITHER AND DIE...
...LIKE A FLOWER THAT DOESN'T GET ANY WATER."

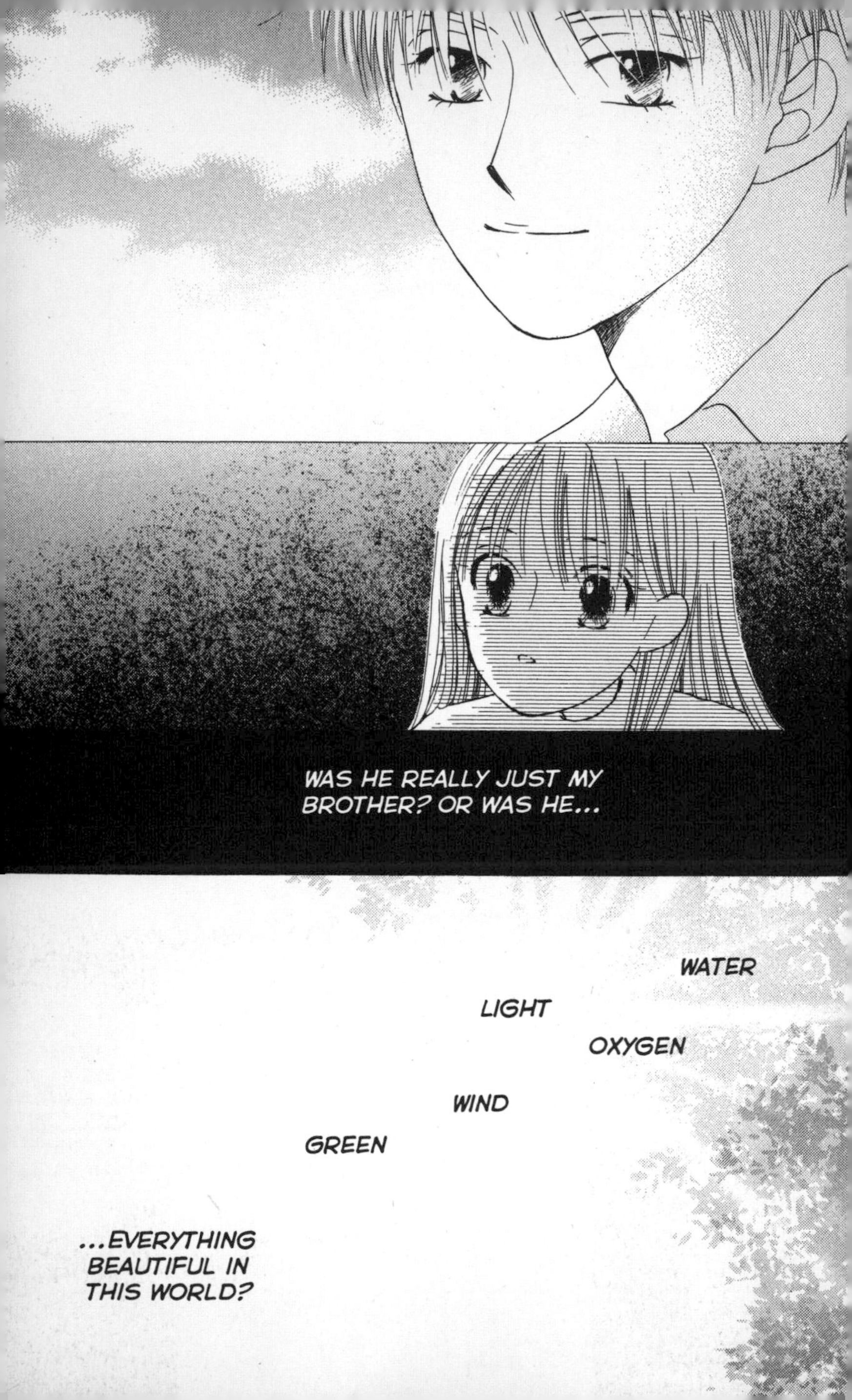
WAS HE REALLY JUST MY BROTHER? OR WAS HE...
WATER
LIGHT
OXYGEN
WIND
GREEN
...EVERYTHING BEAUTIFUL IN THIS WORLD?

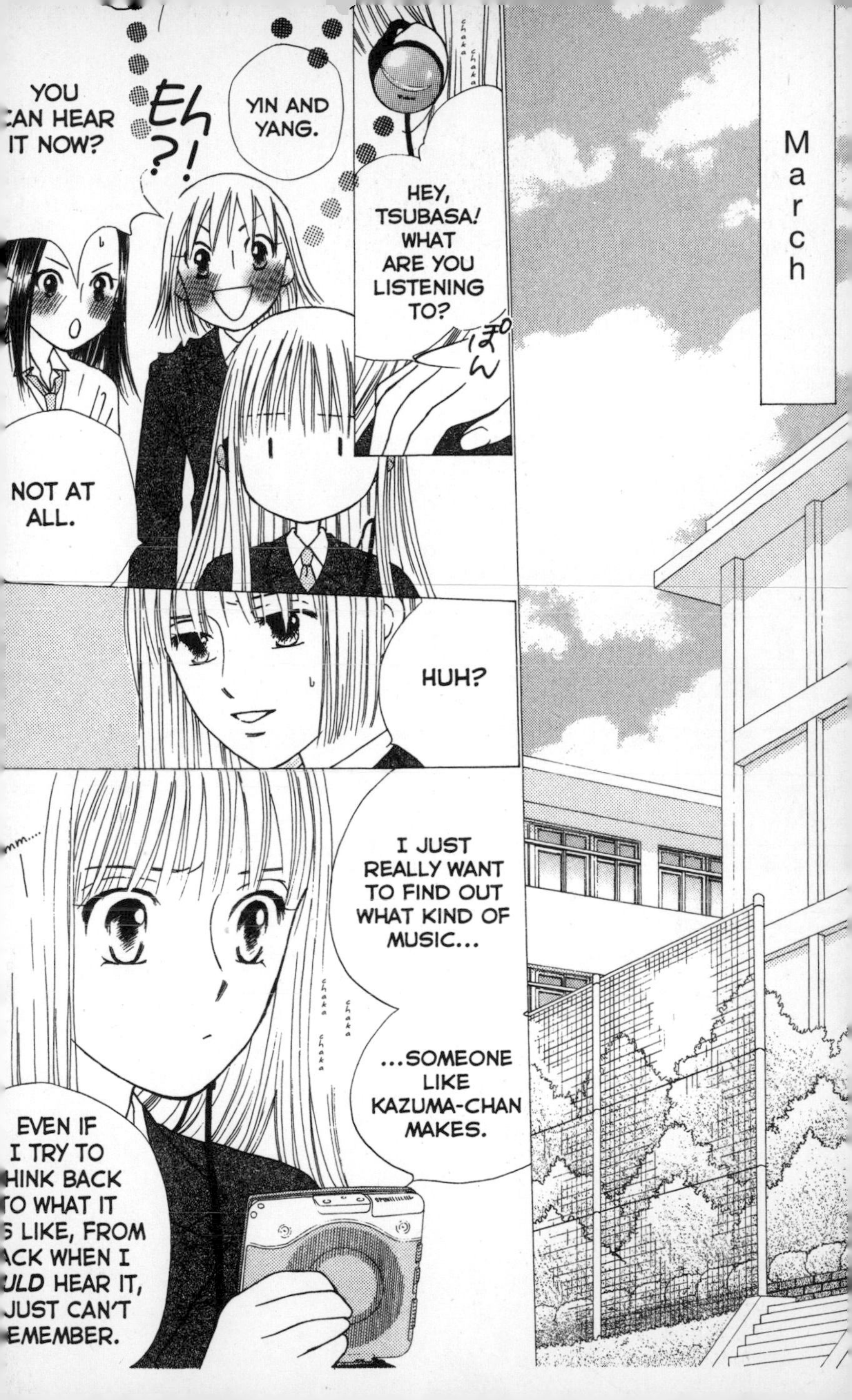
March
chaka chaka
HEY, TSUBASA! WHAT ARE YOU LISTENING TO?
ぽん
YIN AND YANG.
Eh?!
YOU CAN HEAR IT NOW?
NOT AT ALL.
HUH?
mm....
chaka chaka chaka
I JUST REALLY WANT TO FIND OUT WHAT KIND OF MUSIC...
...SOMEONE LIKE KAZUMA-CHAN MAKES.
EVEN IF I TRY TO HINK BACK TO WHAT IT S LIKE, FROM ACK WHEN I ULD HEAR IT, JUST CAN'T EMEMBER.

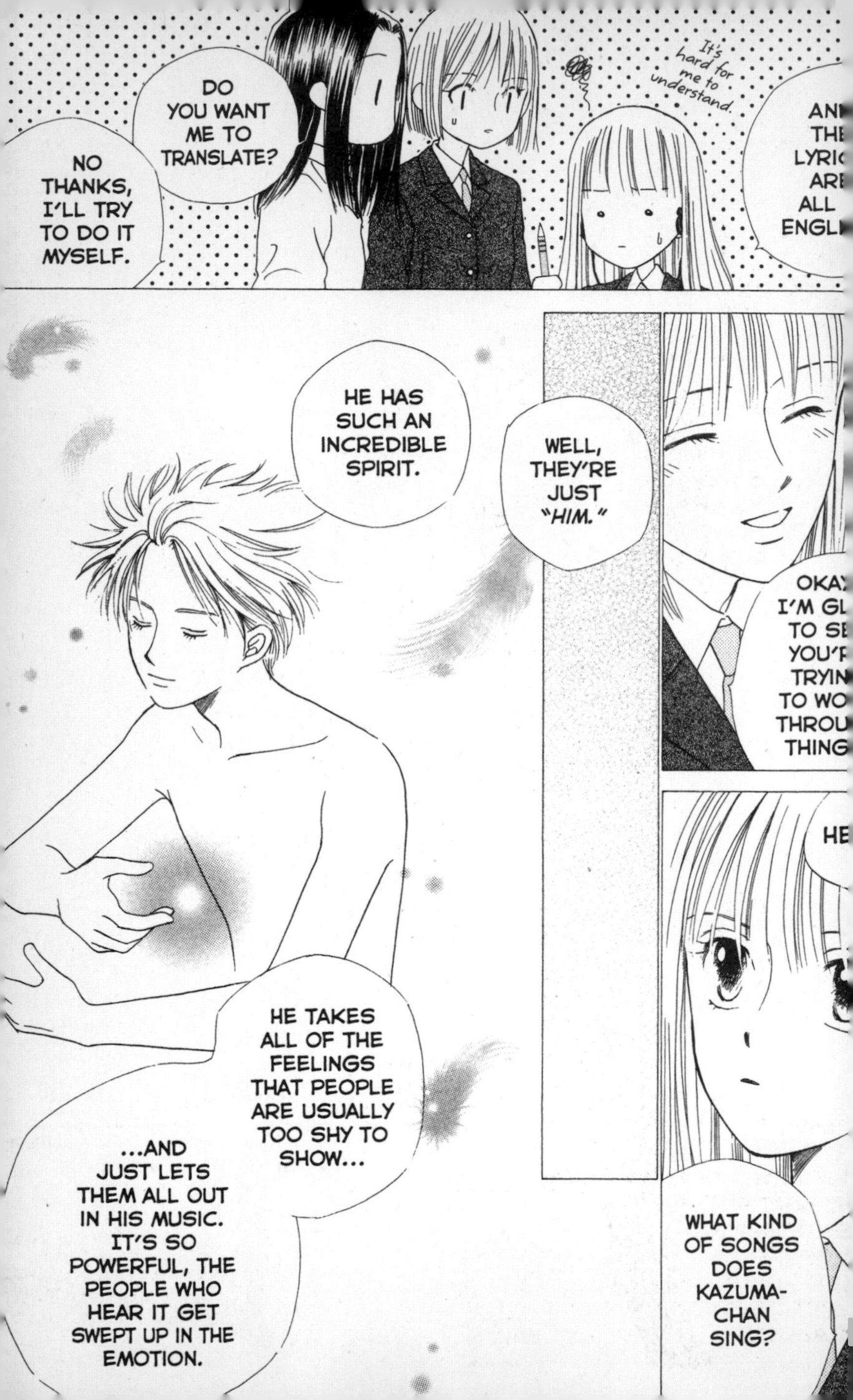
AN THE LYRIC ARE ALL ENGL
It's hard for me to understand.
DO YOU WANT ME TO TRANSLATE?
NO THANKS, I'LL TRY TO DO IT MYSELF.
OKAY I'M GL TO SE YOU'R TRYIN TO WO THROU THING
WELL, THEY'RE JUST "HIM."
HE
WHAT KIND OF SONGS DOES KAZUMA-CHAN SING?
HE HAS SUCH AN INCREDIBLE SPIRIT.
HE TAKES ALL OF THE FEELINGS THAT PEOPLE ARE USUALLY TOO SHY TO SHOW...
...AND JUST LETS THEM ALL OUT IN HIS MUSIC. IT'S SO POWERFUL, THE PEOPLE WHO HEAR IT GET SWEPT UP IN THE EMOTION.

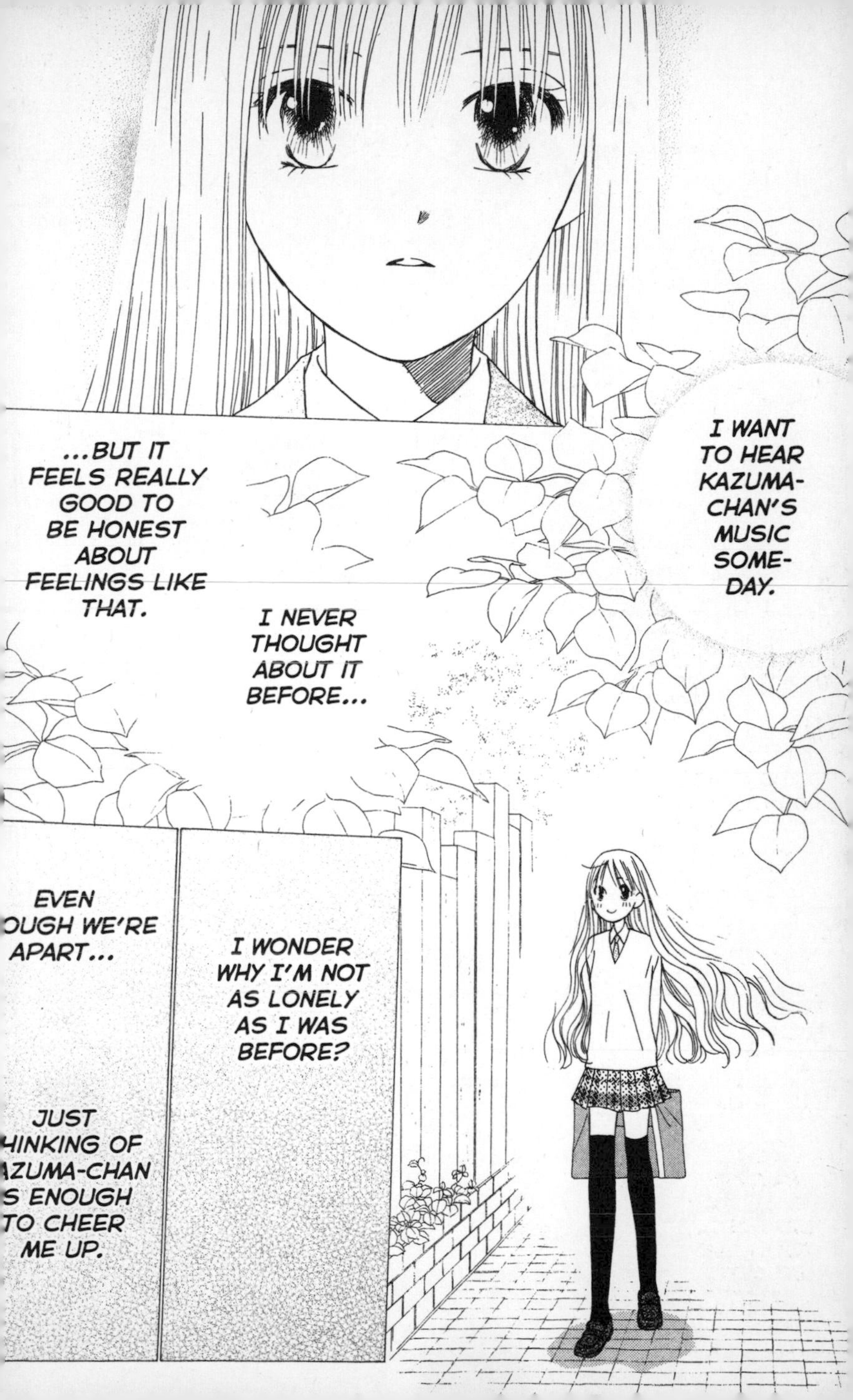
I WANT TO HEAR KAZUMA-CHAN'S MUSIC SOME-DAY.
I NEVER THOUGHT ABOUT IT BEFORE...
...BUT IT FEELS REALLY GOOD TO BE HONEST ABOUT FEELINGS LIKE THAT.
I WONDER WHY I'M NOT AS LONELY AS I WAS BEFORE?
EVEN OUGH WE'RE APART...
JUST HINKING OF AZUMA-CHAN S ENOUGH TO CHEER ME UP.

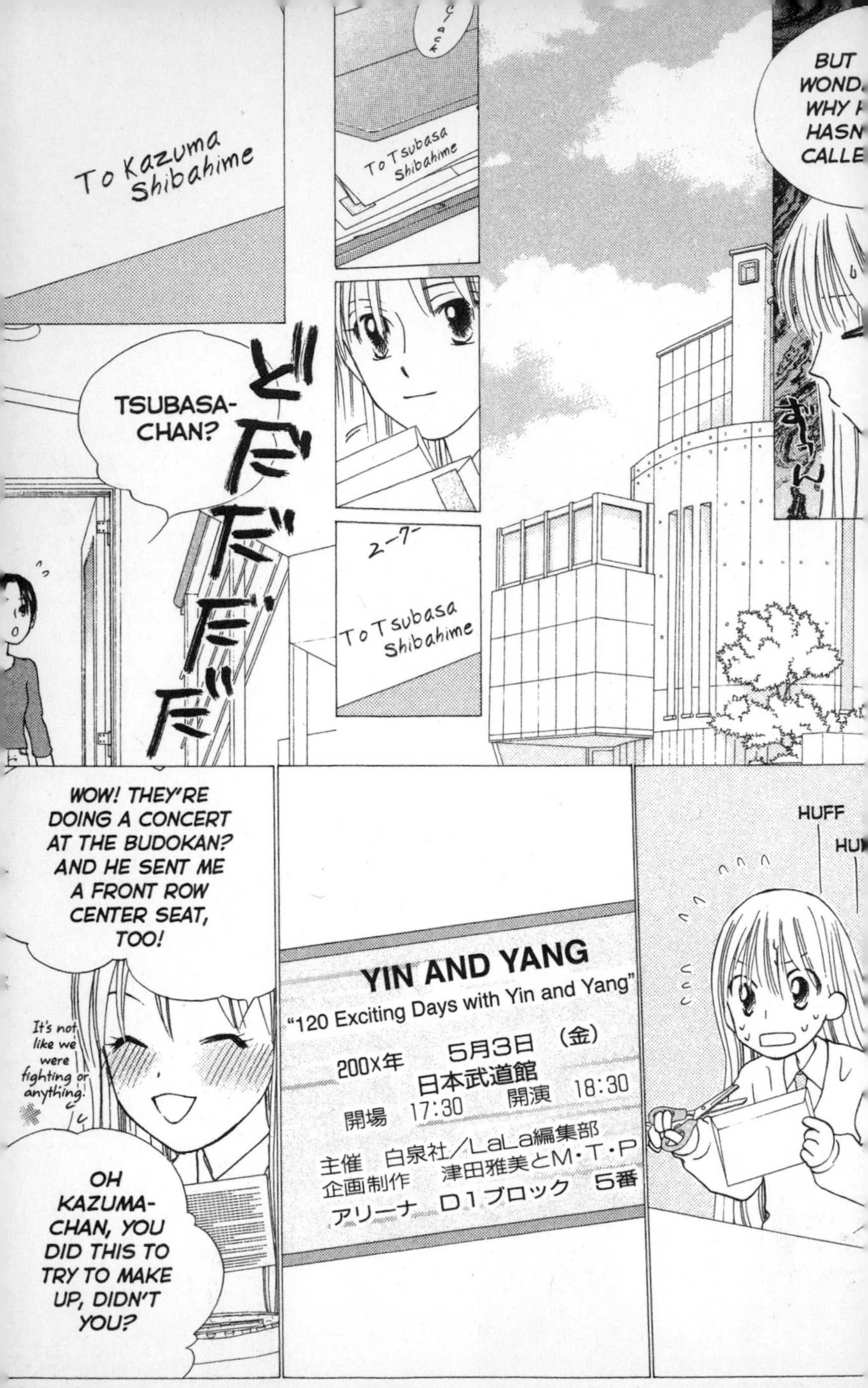
BUT
WOND
WHY H
HASN
CALLE
Crack
To Tsubasa Shibahime
To Kazuma Shibahime
To Tsubasa Shibahime
TSUBASA-CHAN?
どだだだだ
HUFF
HU
YIN AND YANG
"120 Exciting Days with Yin and Yang"
200X年 5月3日 (金)
日本武道館
開場 17:30 開演 18:30
主催 白泉社／LaLa編集部
企画制作 津田雅美とM・T・P
アリーナ D1ブロック 5番
WOW! THEY'RE DOING A CONCERT AT THE BUDOKAN? AND HE SENT ME A FRONT ROW CENTER SEAT, TOO!
It's not like we were fighting or anything.
OH KAZUMA-CHAN, YOU DID THIS TO TRY TO MAKE UP, DIDN'T YOU?

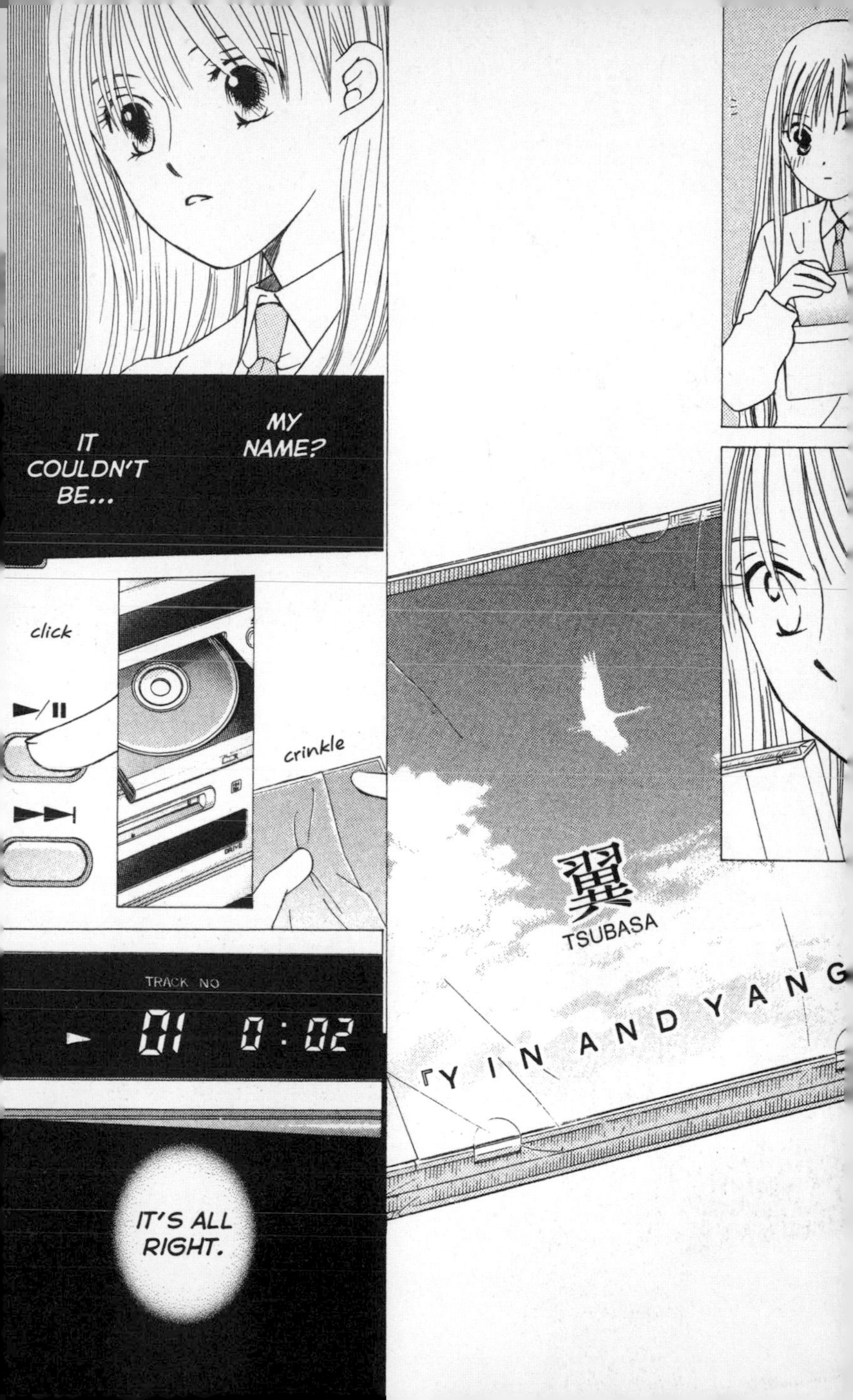
翼
TSUBASA
『Y IN AND YANG
MY NAME?
IT COULDN'T BE...
crinkle
click
►/II
►►I
TRACK NO
► 01 0:02
IT'S ALL RIGHT.

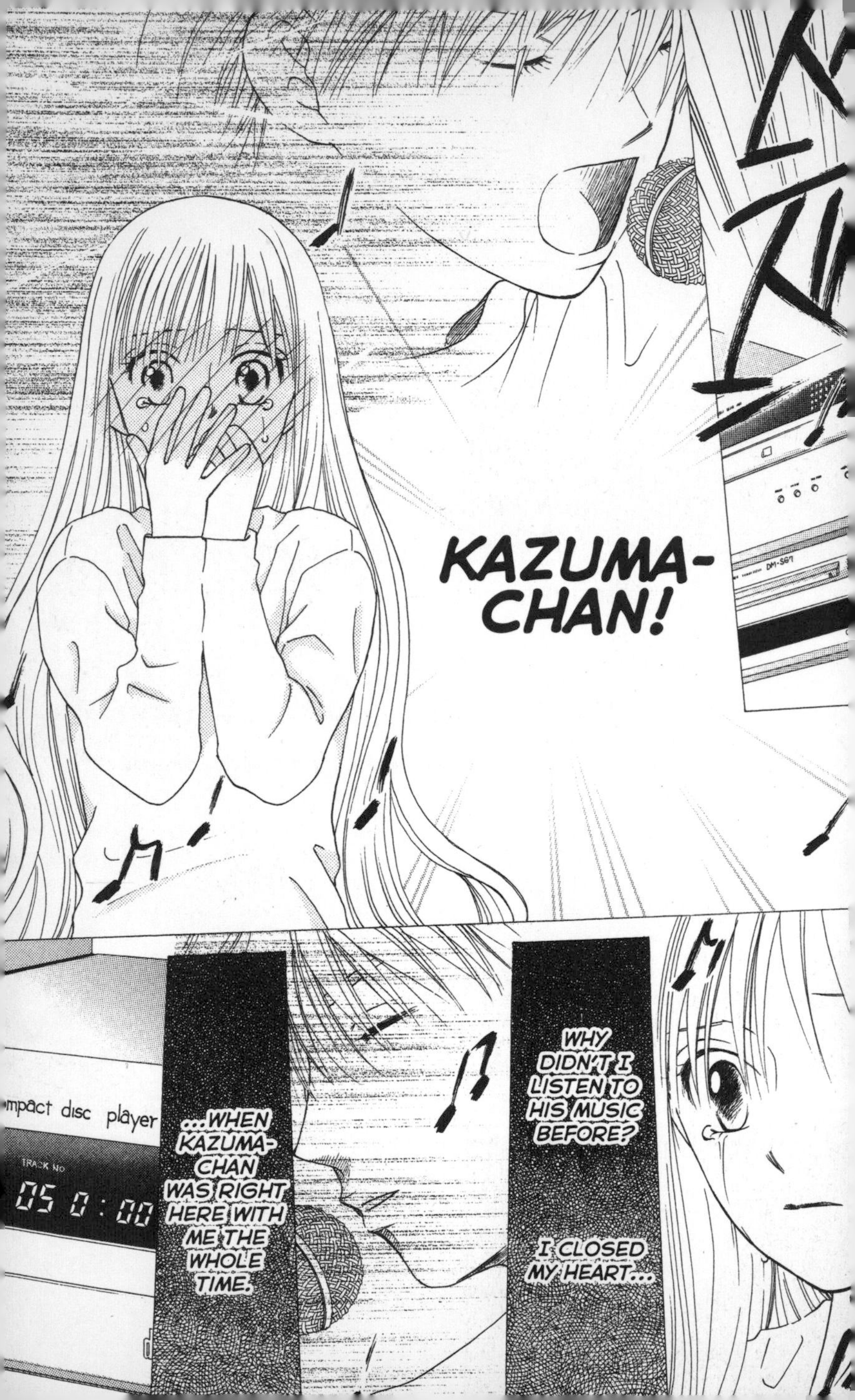
KAZUMA-CHAN!
WHY DIDN'T I LISTEN TO HIS MUSIC BEFORE?
I CLOSED MY HEART...
...WHEN KAZUMA-CHAN WAS RIGHT HERE WITH ME THE WHOLE TIME.
mpact disc player
TRACK NO
05 0:00
DM-S67

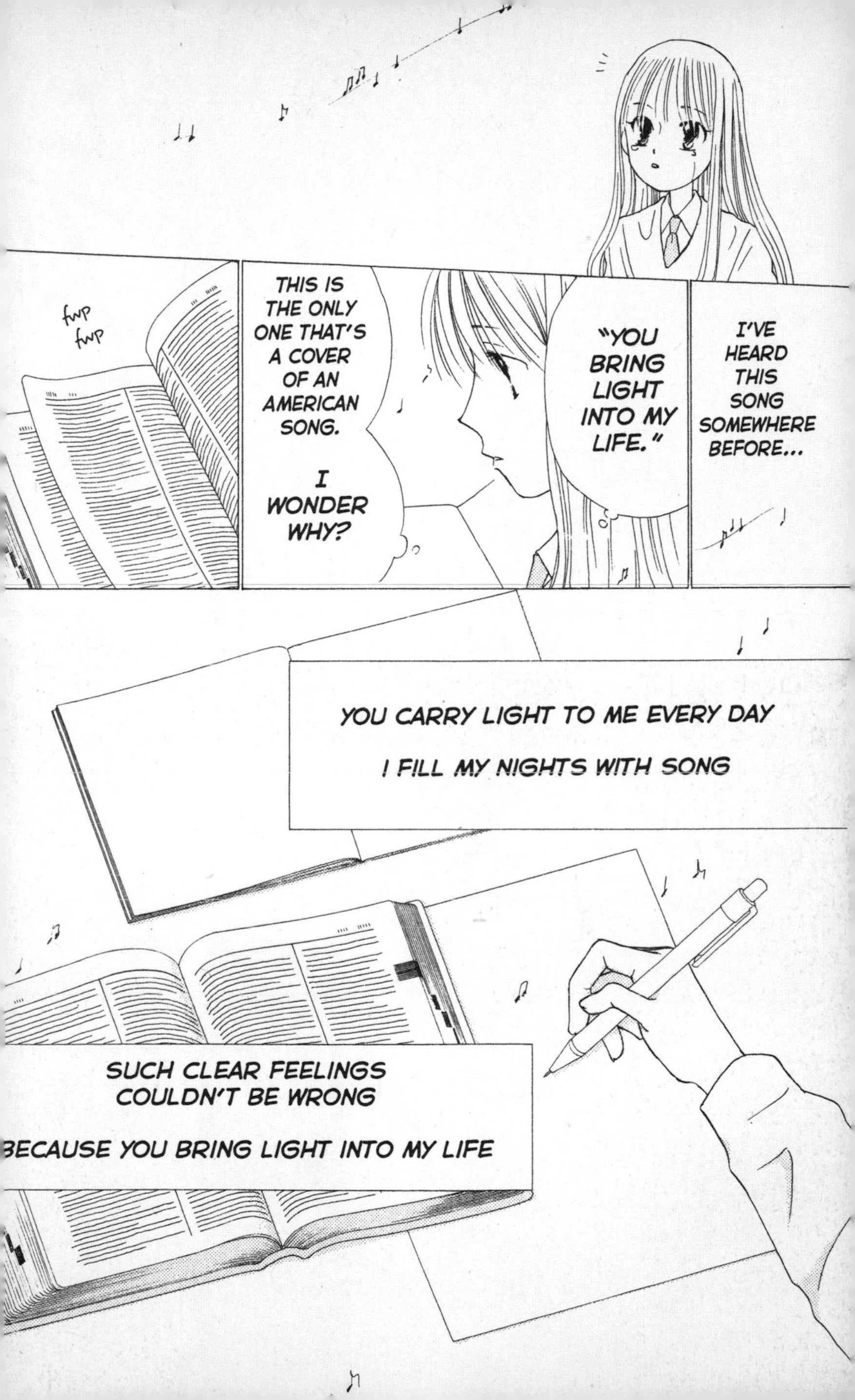
I'VE HEARD THIS SONG SOMEWHERE BEFORE...
"YOU BRING LIGHT INTO MY LIFE."
THIS IS THE ONLY ONE THAT'S A COVER OF AN AMERICAN SONG.
I WONDER WHY?
fwp fwp
YOU CARRY LIGHT TO ME EVERY DAY
I FILL MY NIGHTS WITH SONG
SUCH CLEAR FEELINGS COULDN'T BE WRONG
BECAUSE YOU BRING LIGHT INTO MY LIFE

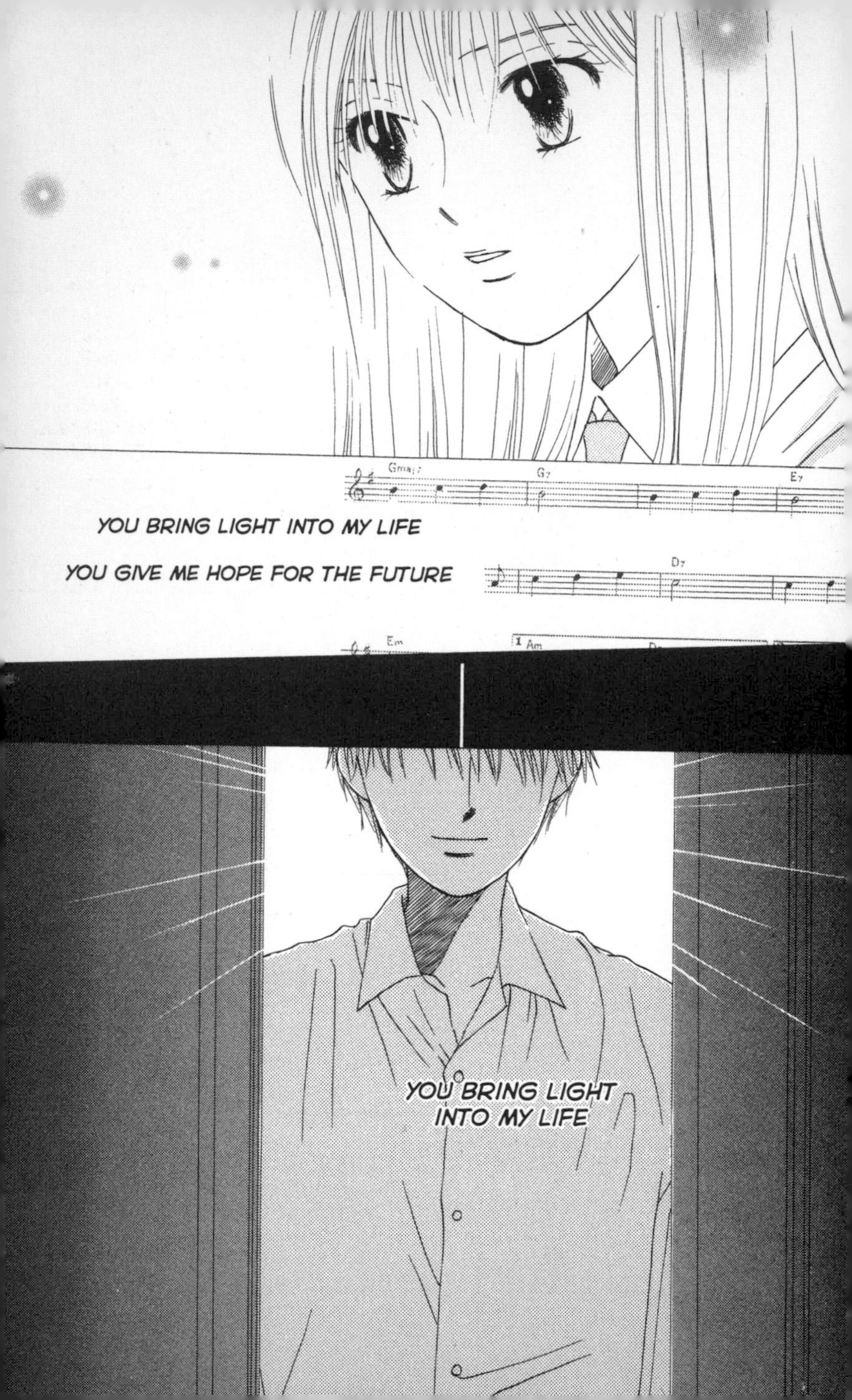
YOU BRING LIGHT INTO MY LIFE
YOU GIVE ME HOPE FOR THE FUTURE
YOU BRING LIGHT INTO MY LIFE

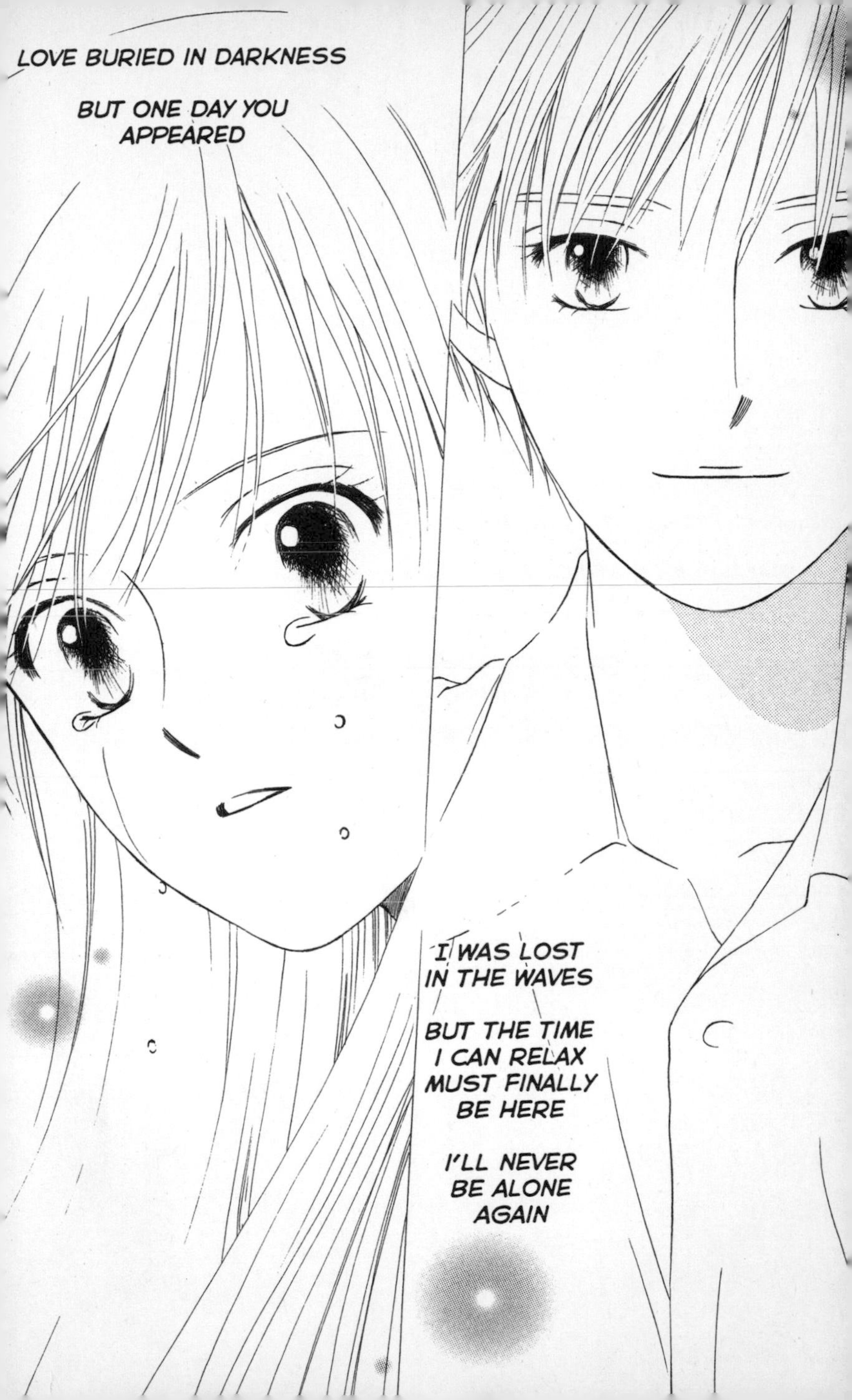
LOVE BURIED IN DARKNESS
BUT ONE DAY YOU APPEARED
I WAS LOST IN THE WAVES
BUT THE TIME I CAN RELAX MUST FINALLY BE HERE
I'LL NEVER BE ALONE AGAIN

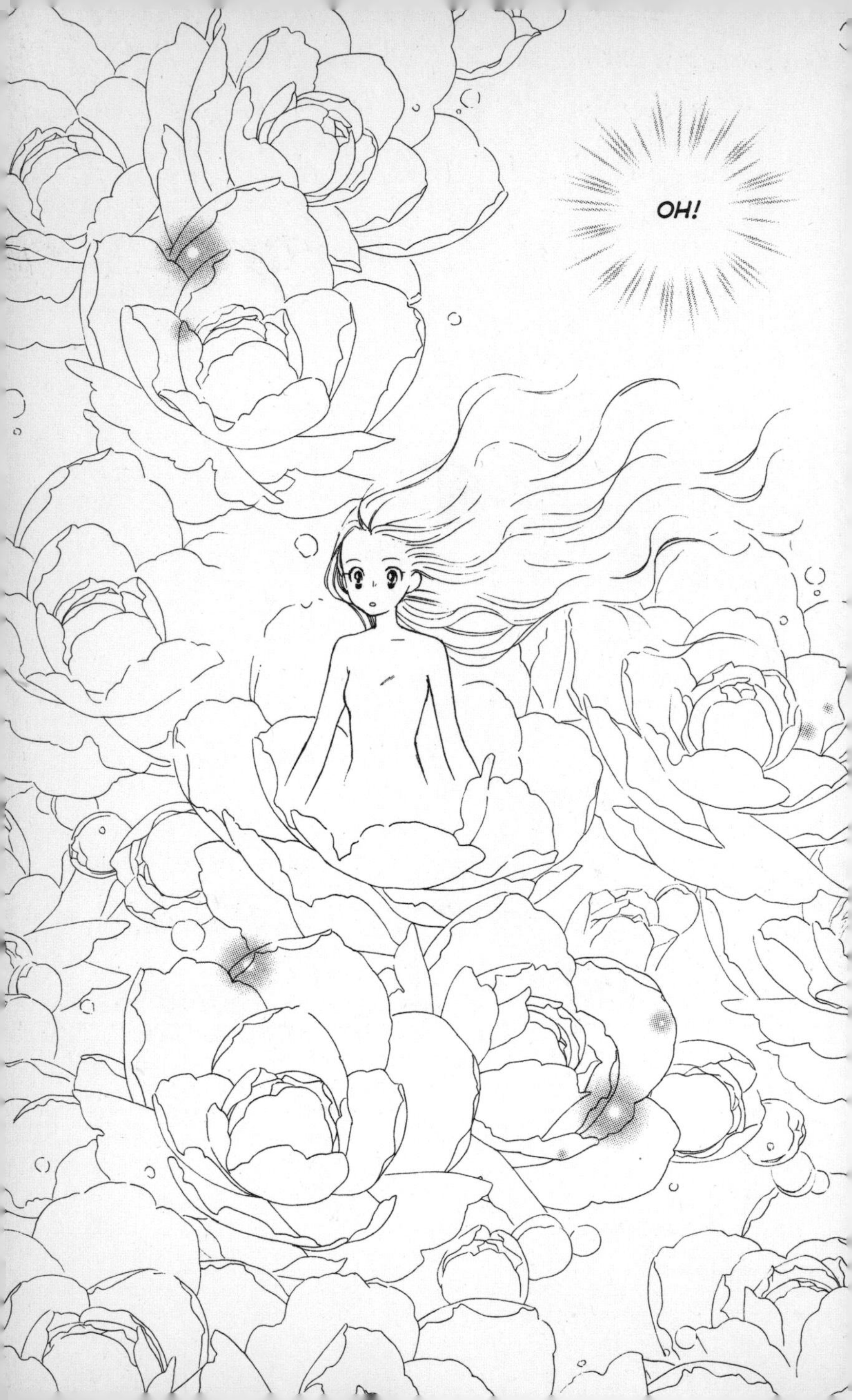
OH!

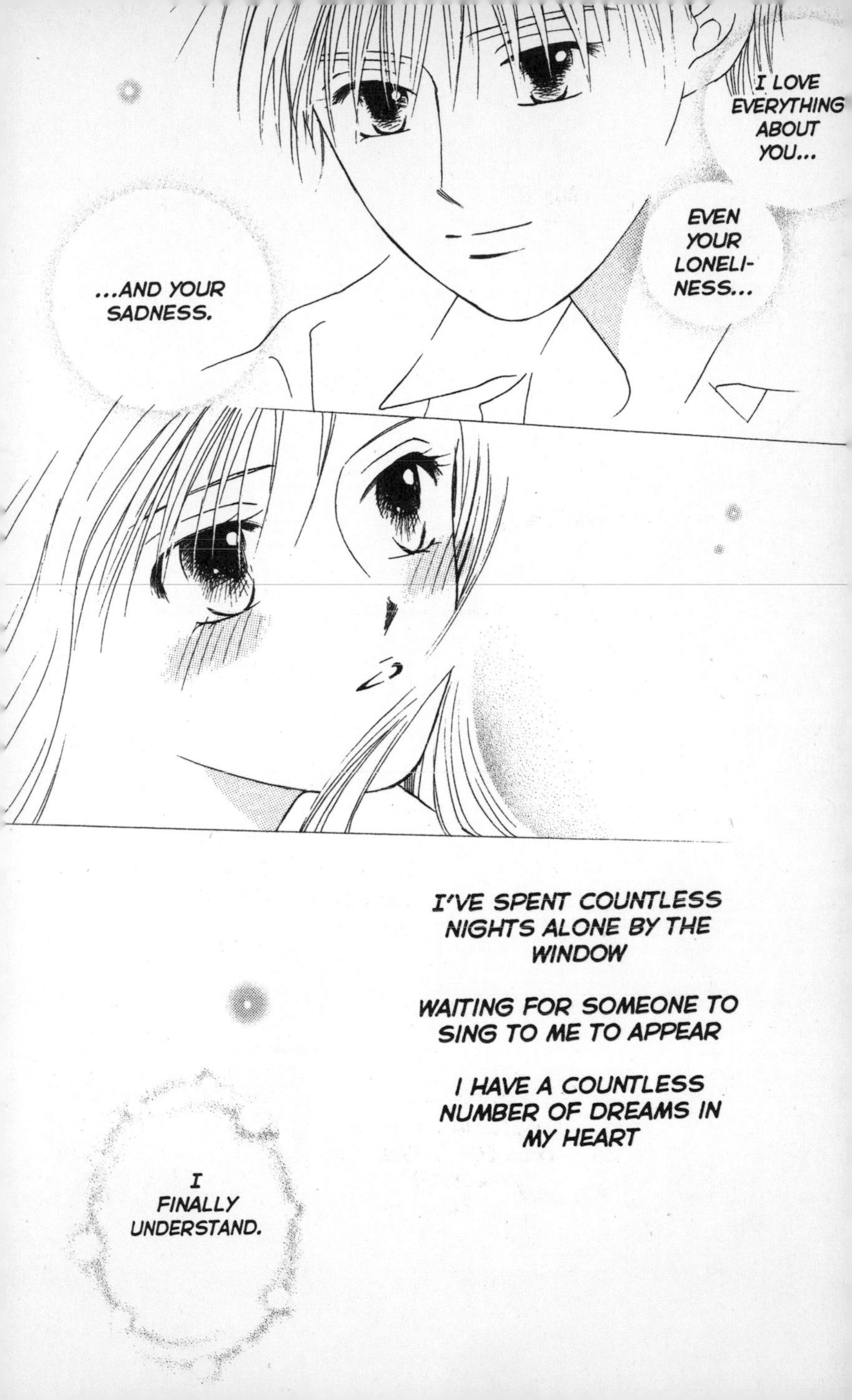
I LOVE EVERYTHING ABOUT YOU...
EVEN YOUR LONELI-NESS...
...AND YOUR SADNESS.
I'VE SPENT COUNTLESS NIGHTS ALONE BY THE WINDOW
WAITING FOR SOMEONE TO SING TO ME TO APPEAR
I HAVE A COUNTLESS NUMBER OF DREAMS IN MY HEART
I FINALLY UNDERSTAND.

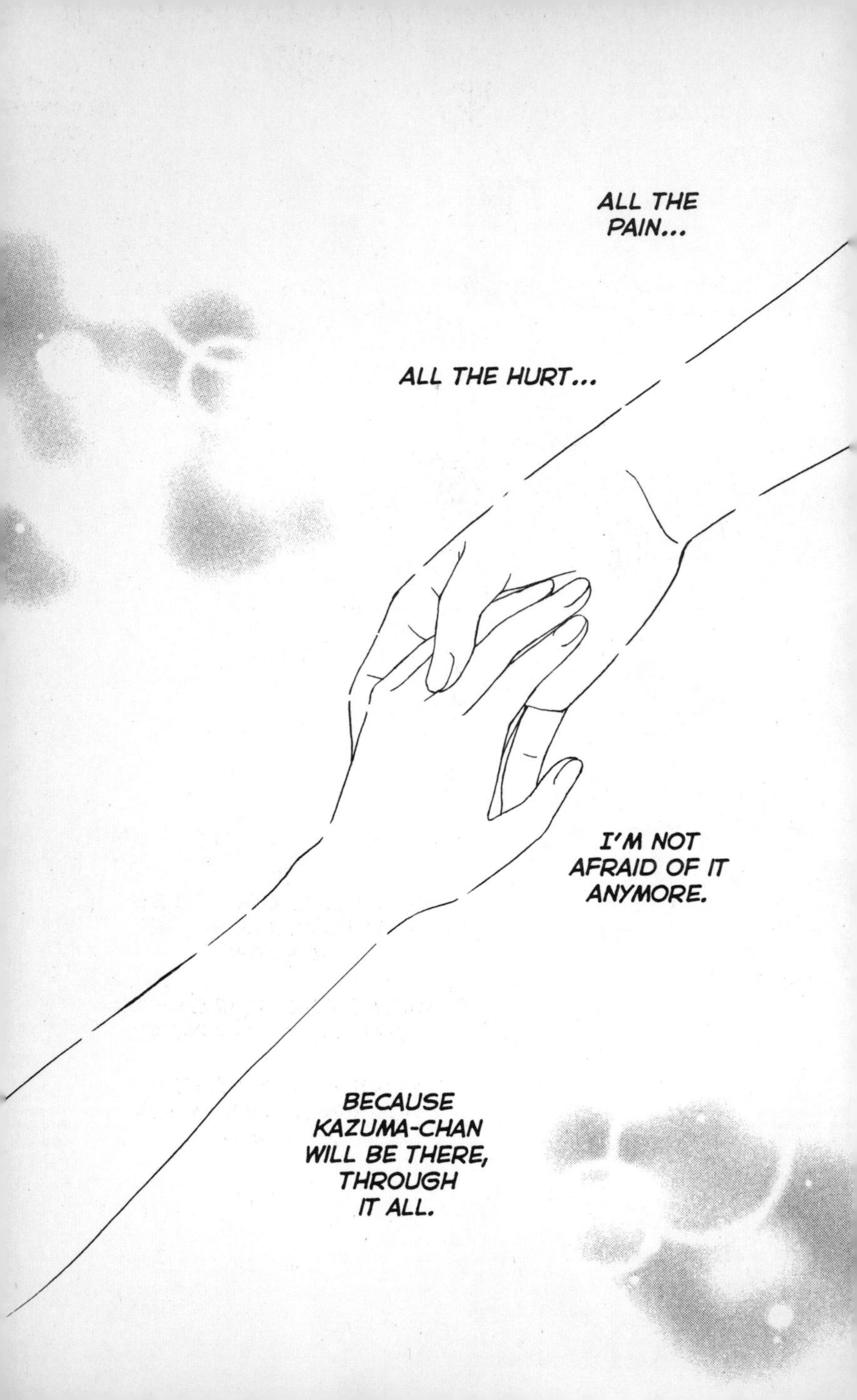

ALL THE PAIN...
ALL THE HURT...
I'M NOT AFRAID OF IT ANYMORE.
BECAUSE KAZUMA-CHAN WILL BE THERE, THROUGH IT ALL.

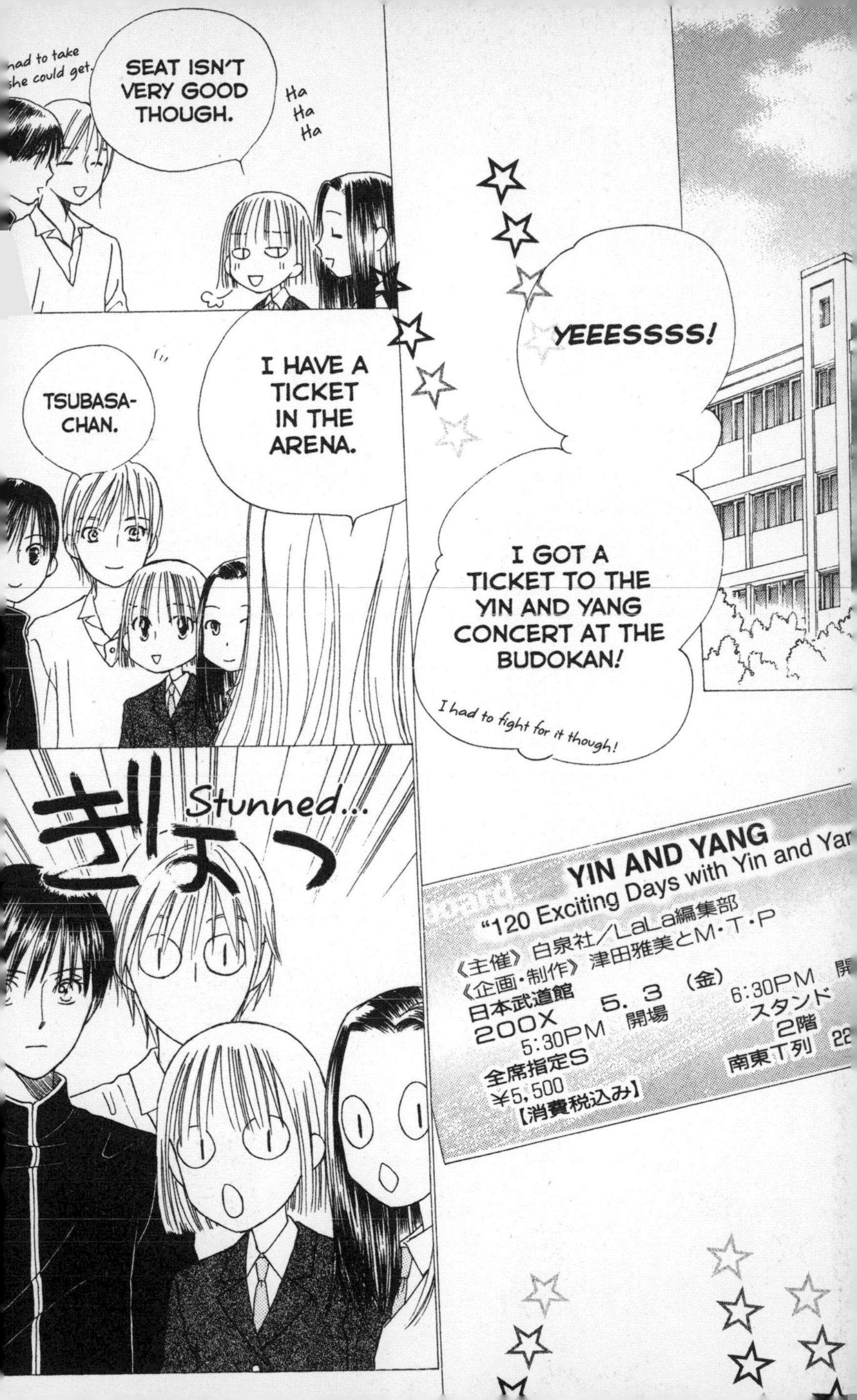

YEEESSSS!
I GOT A TICKET TO THE YIN AND YANG CONCERT AT THE BUDOKAN!
I had to fight for it though!
YIN AND YANG
"120 Exciting Days with Yin and
白泉社／LaLa編集部
《主催》
《企画・制作》 津田雅美とM・T・P
日本武道館
200X 5. 3 (金)
5:30PM 開場
6:30PM
スタンド
2階
南東T列
全席指定S
¥5,500
【消費税込み】
had to take
she could get.
SEAT ISN'T VERY GOOD THOUGH.
Ha Ha Ha
I HAVE A TICKET IN THE ARENA.
TSUBASA-CHAN.
Stunned...

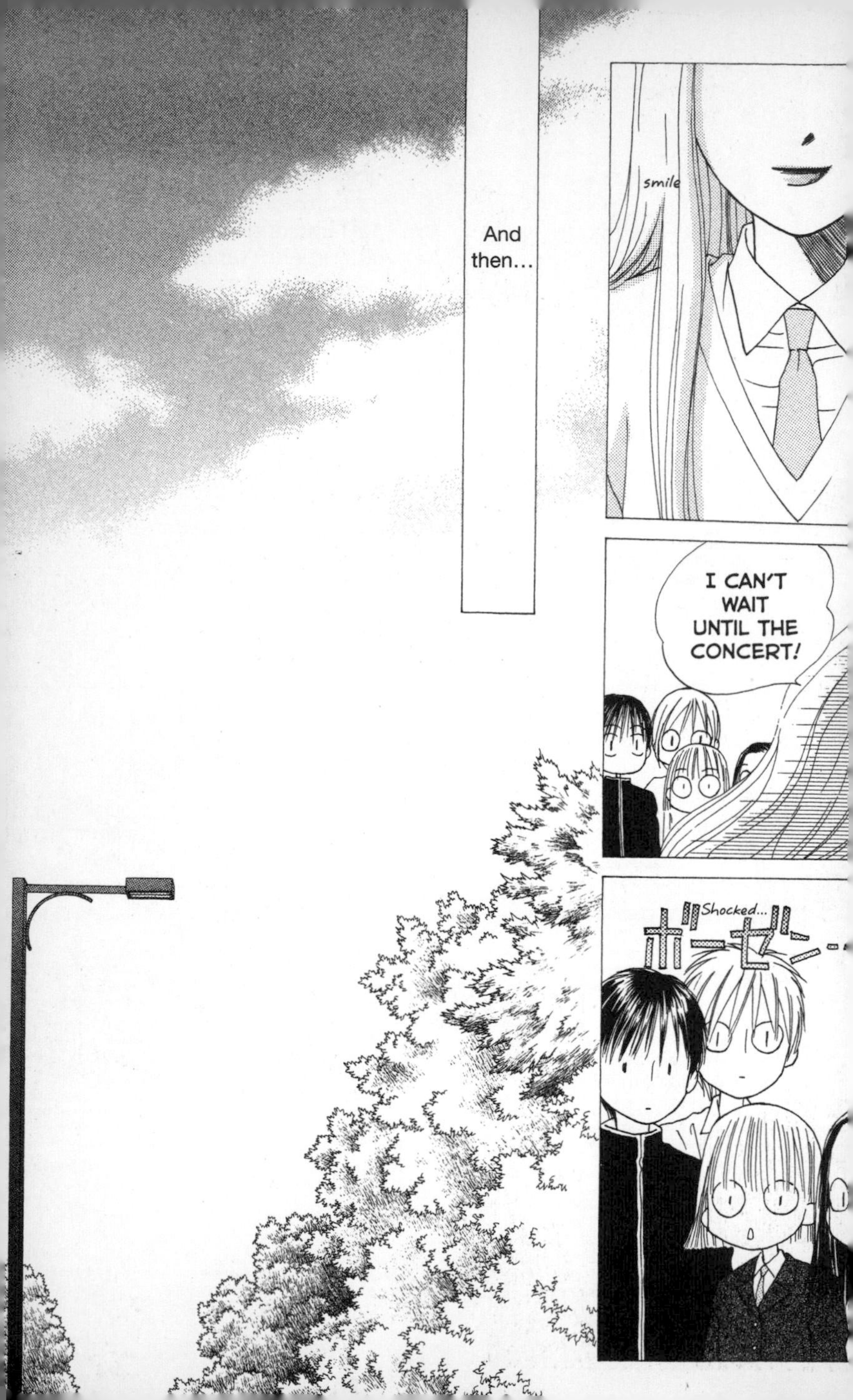
smile
I CAN'T WAIT UNTIL THE CONCERT!
Shocked...
And then...

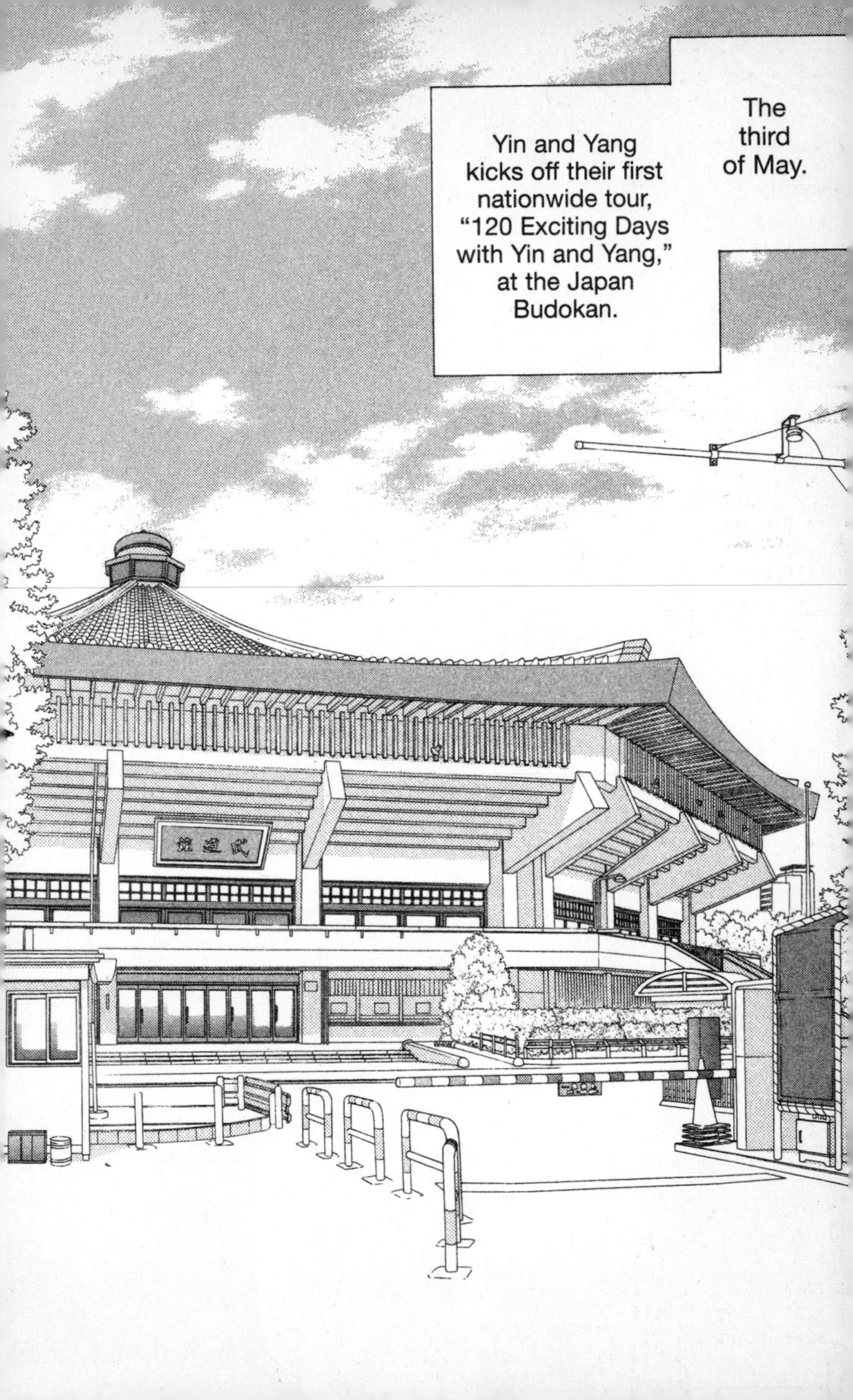
The third of May.
Yin and Yang kicks off their first nationwide tour, "120 Exciting Days with Yin and Yang," at the Japan Budokan.

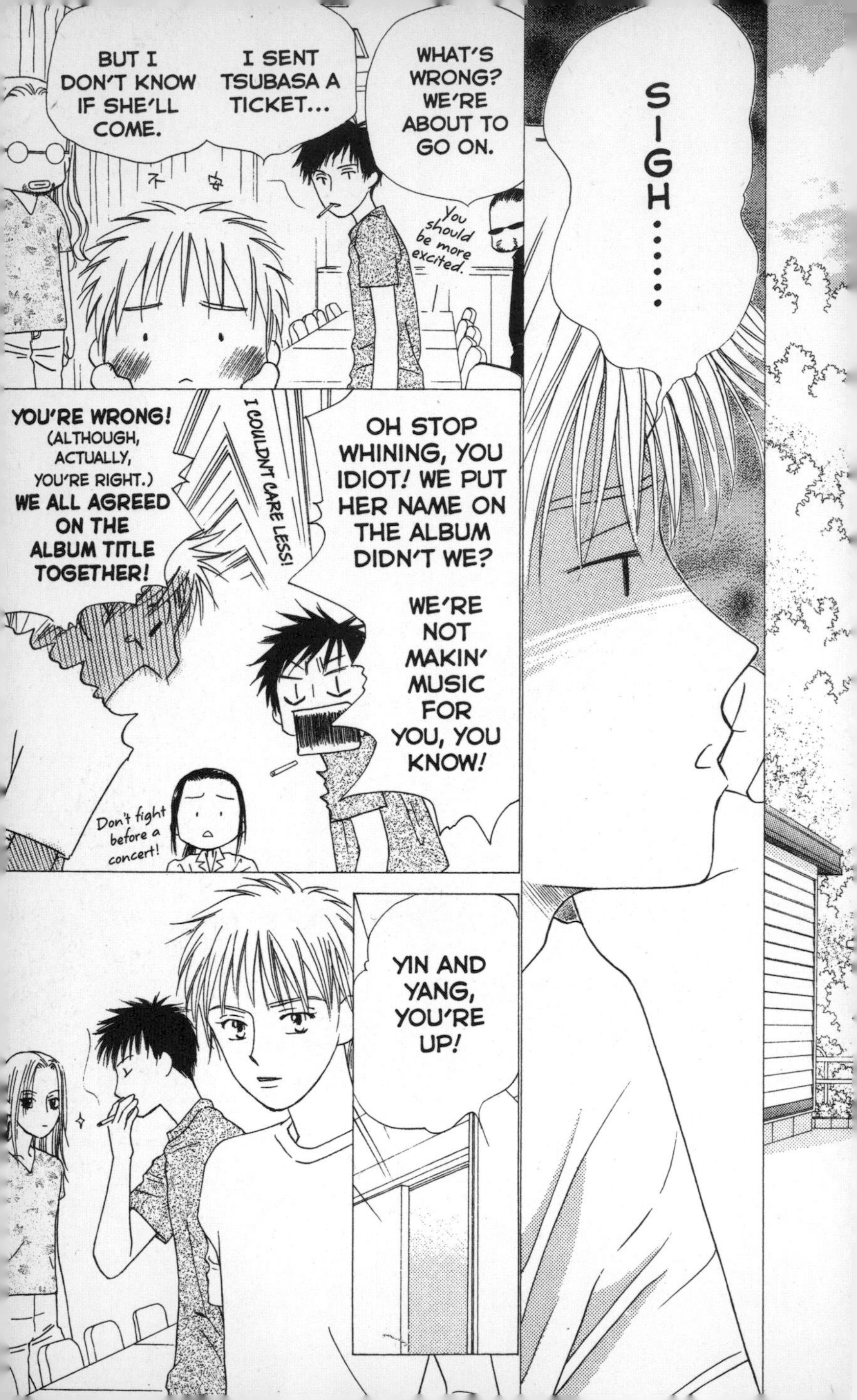
SIGH.....
WHAT'S WRONG? WE'RE ABOUT TO GO ON.
You should be more excited.
I SENT TSUBASA A TICKET...
BUT I DON'T KNOW IF SHE'LL COME.
OH STOP WHINING, YOU IDIOT! WE PUT HER NAME ON THE ALBUM DIDN'T WE?
WE'RE NOT MAKIN' MUSIC FOR YOU, YOU KNOW!
I COULDN'T CARE LESS!
YOU'RE WRONG! (ALTHOUGH, ACTUALLY, YOU'RE RIGHT.) WE ALL AGREED ON THE ALBUM TITLE TOGETHER!
Don't fight before a concert!
YIN AND YANG, YOU'RE UP!

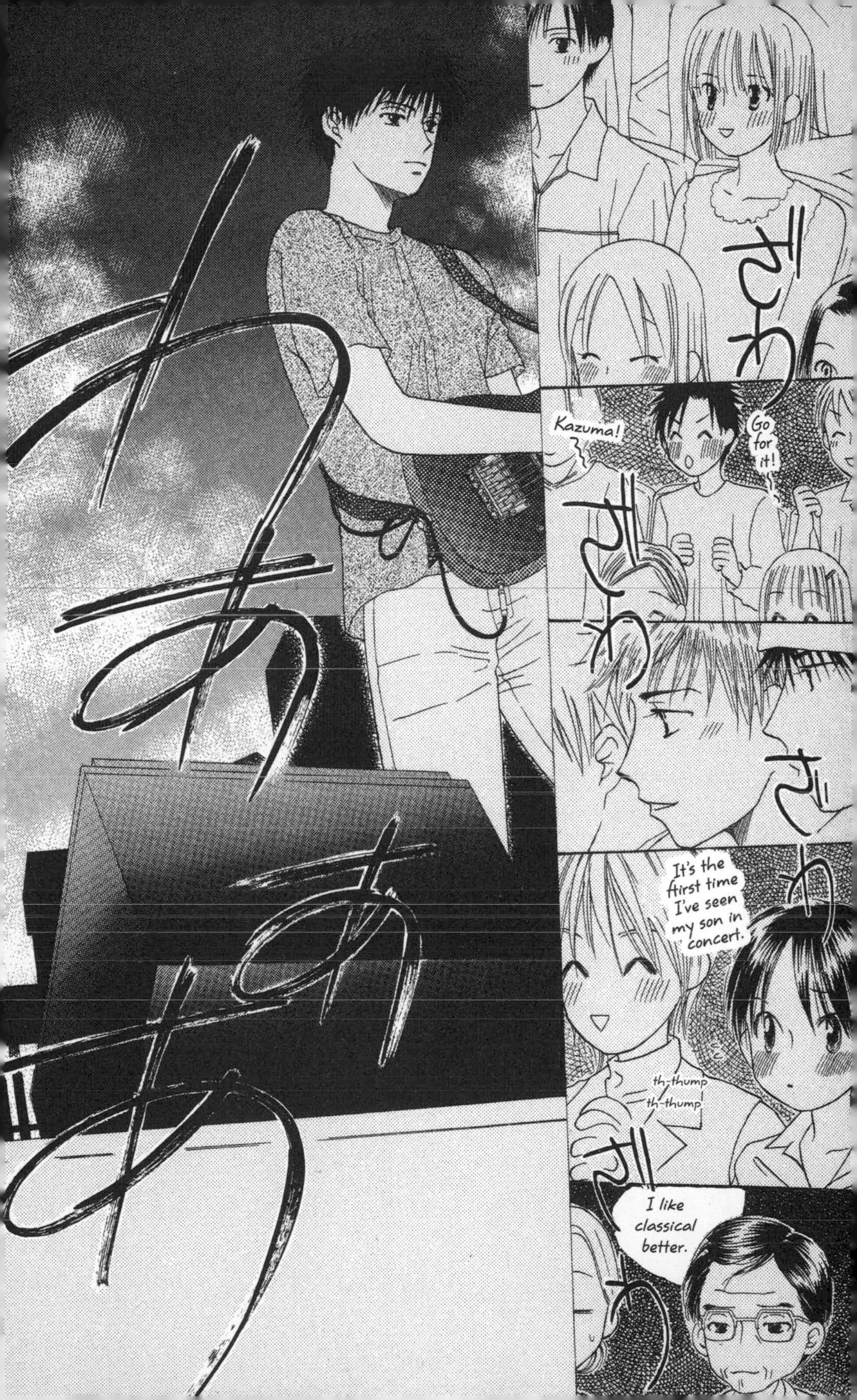
ざわ
Go for it!
Kazuma!
ざわ
ざわ
It's the first time I've seen my son in concert.
th-thump th-thump
ざわ
I like classical better.
わあああ

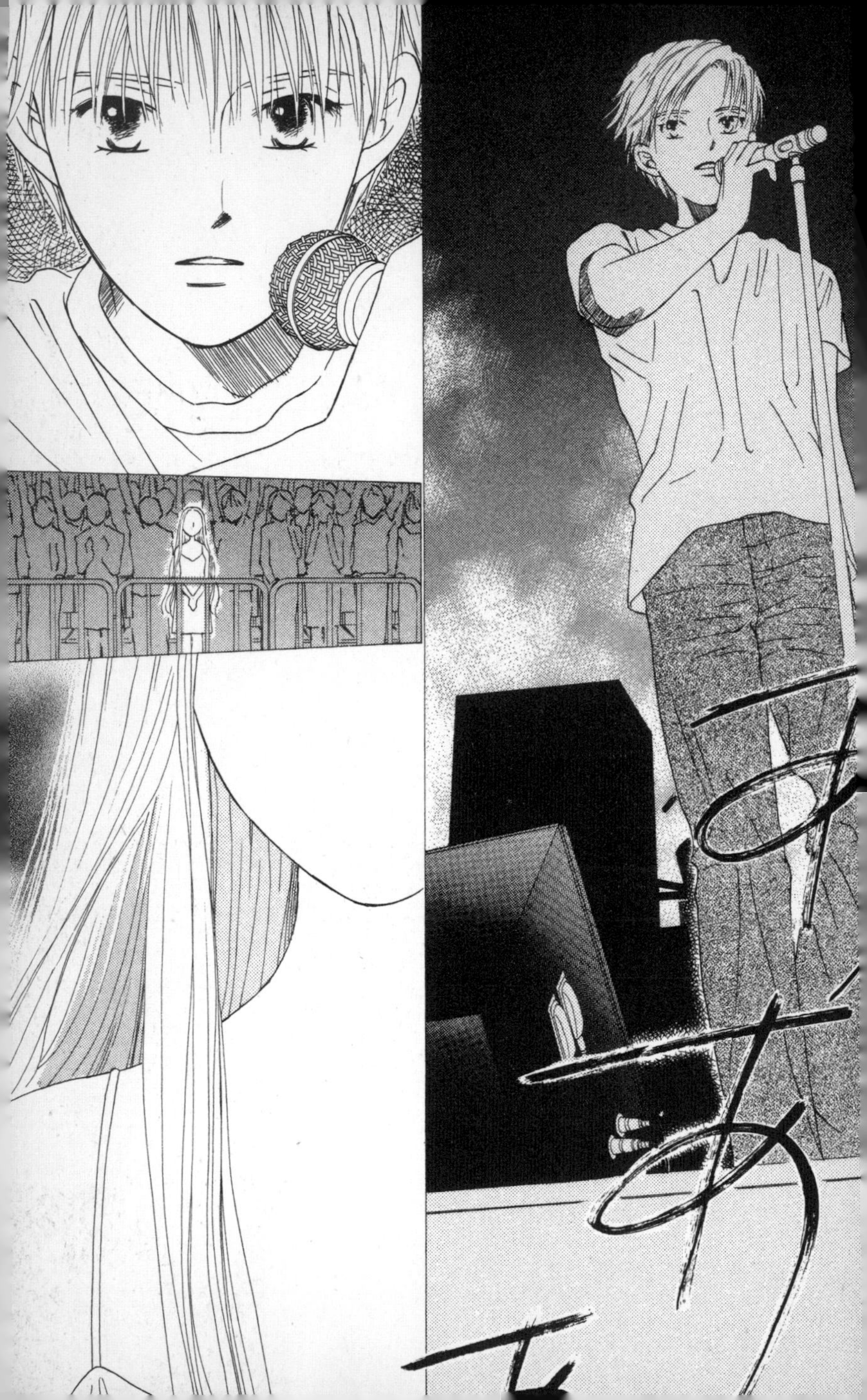

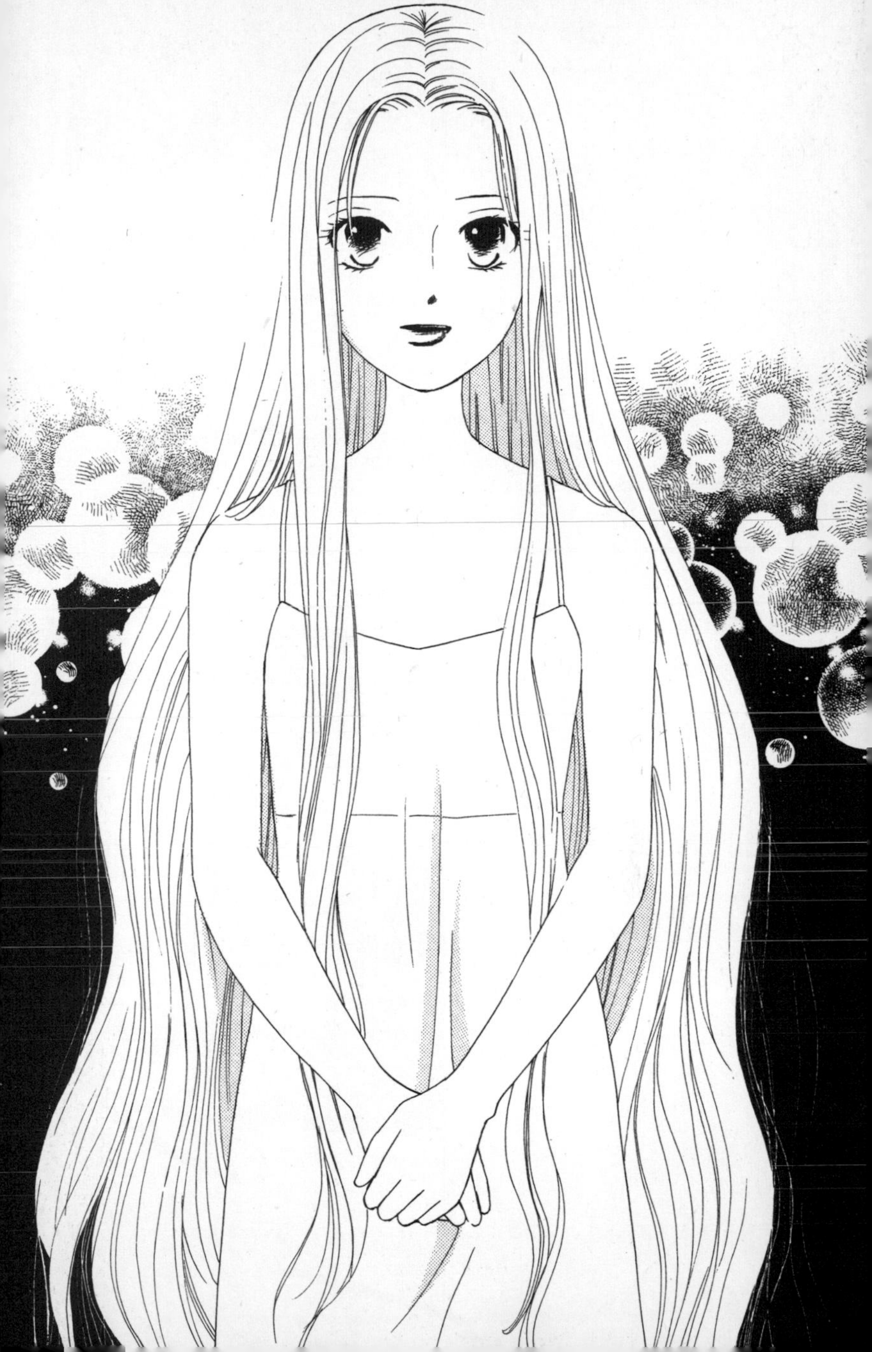

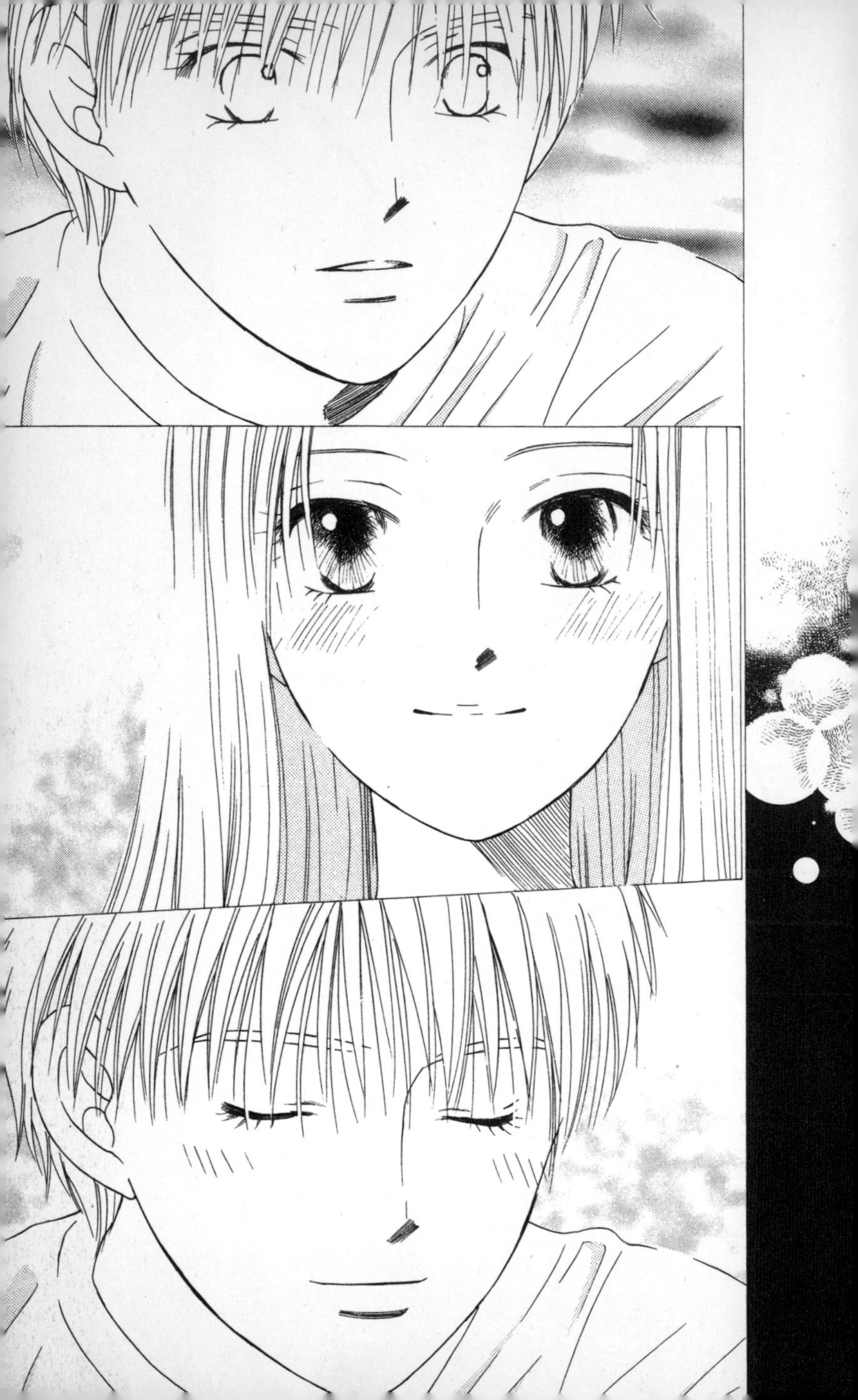

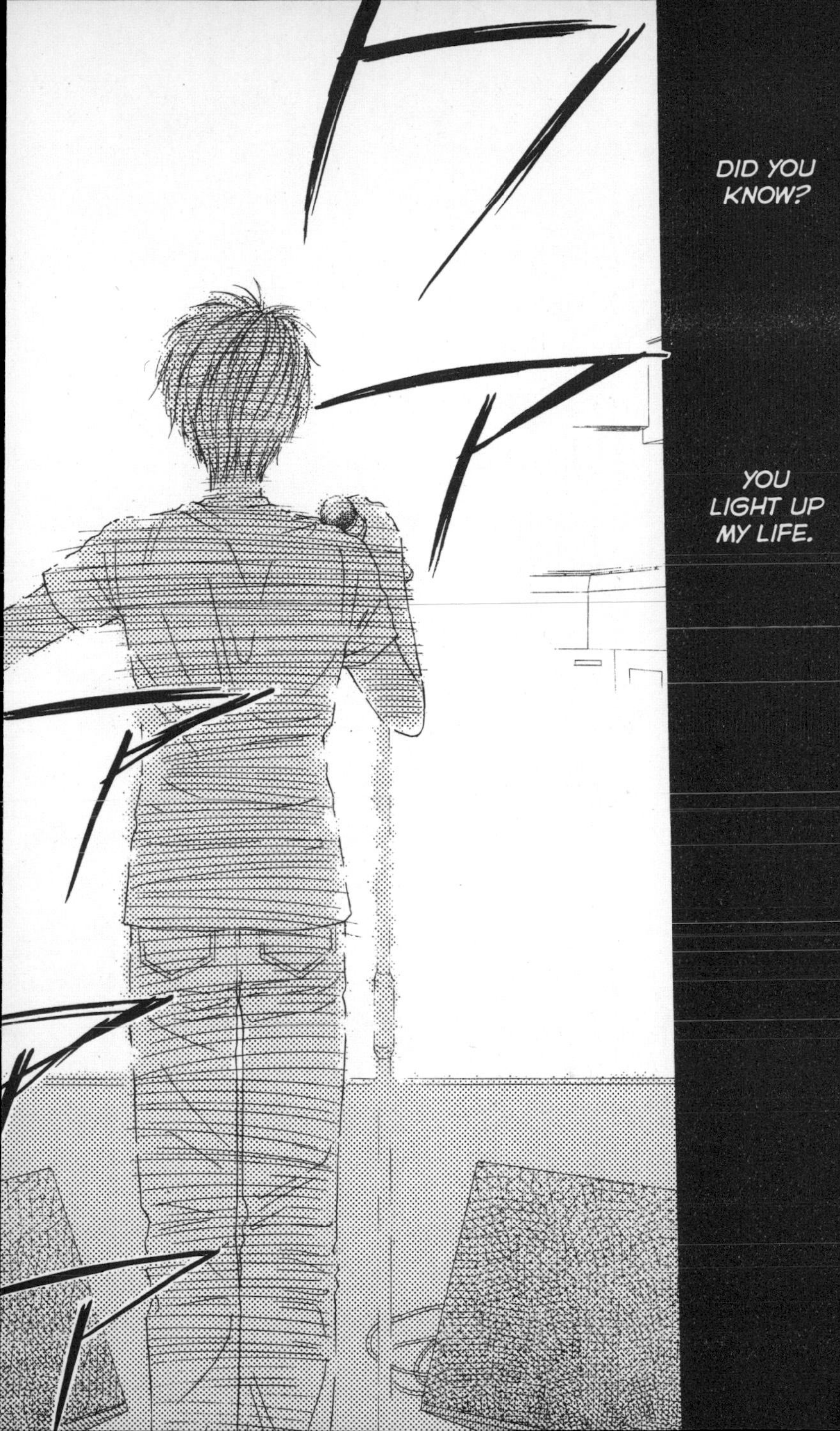
DID YOU KNOW?
YOU LIGHT UP MY LIFE.

4

Yours truly has mentioned how she loves Japanese hot springs, but all of a sudden I really want to go visit a foreign country. Since I want to visit a lot of different countries, I think I'm going to have to master English. So next year I'm going to start studying it a LOT.

Right now, the amount of English yours truly can speak is about on this level...

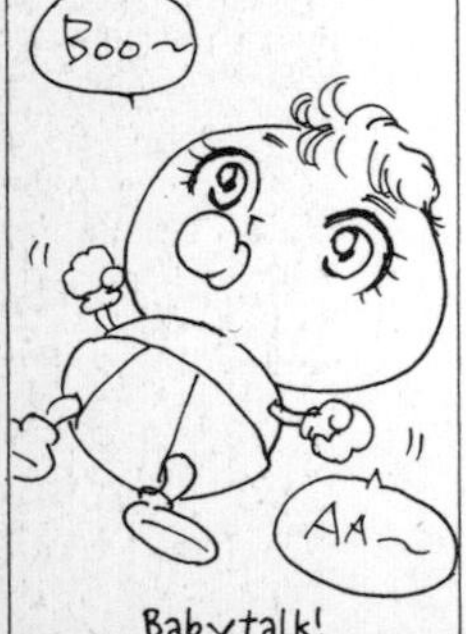
Boo~
AA~

Babytalk!

I studied English in middle and high school, but I've completely forgotten every word of it.

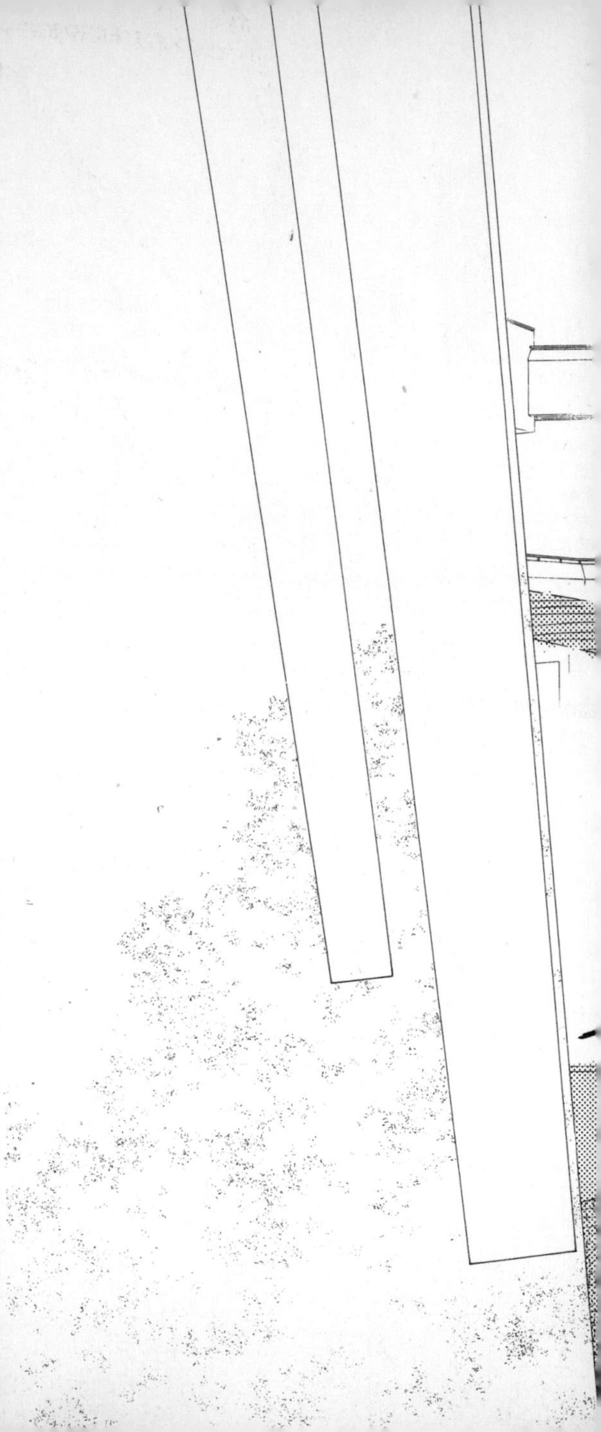

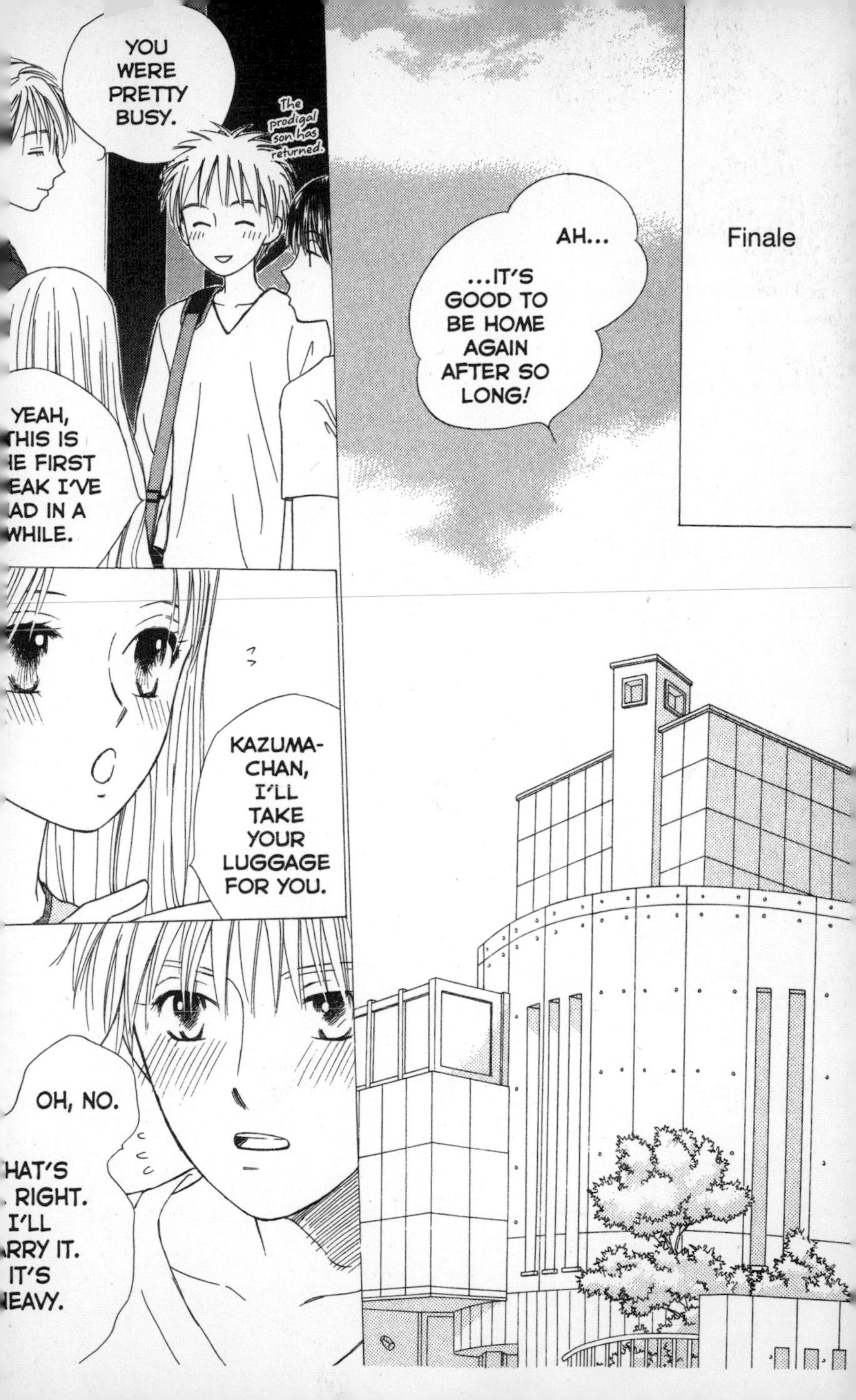
Finale
AH...
...IT'S GOOD TO BE HOME AGAIN AFTER SO LONG!
YOU WERE PRETTY BUSY.
The prodigal son has returned.
YEAH, THIS IS HE FIRST EAK I'VE AD IN A WHILE.
KAZUMA-CHAN, I'LL TAKE YOUR LUGGAGE FOR YOU.
OH, NO.
HAT'S RIGHT. I'LL RRY IT. IT'S EAVY.

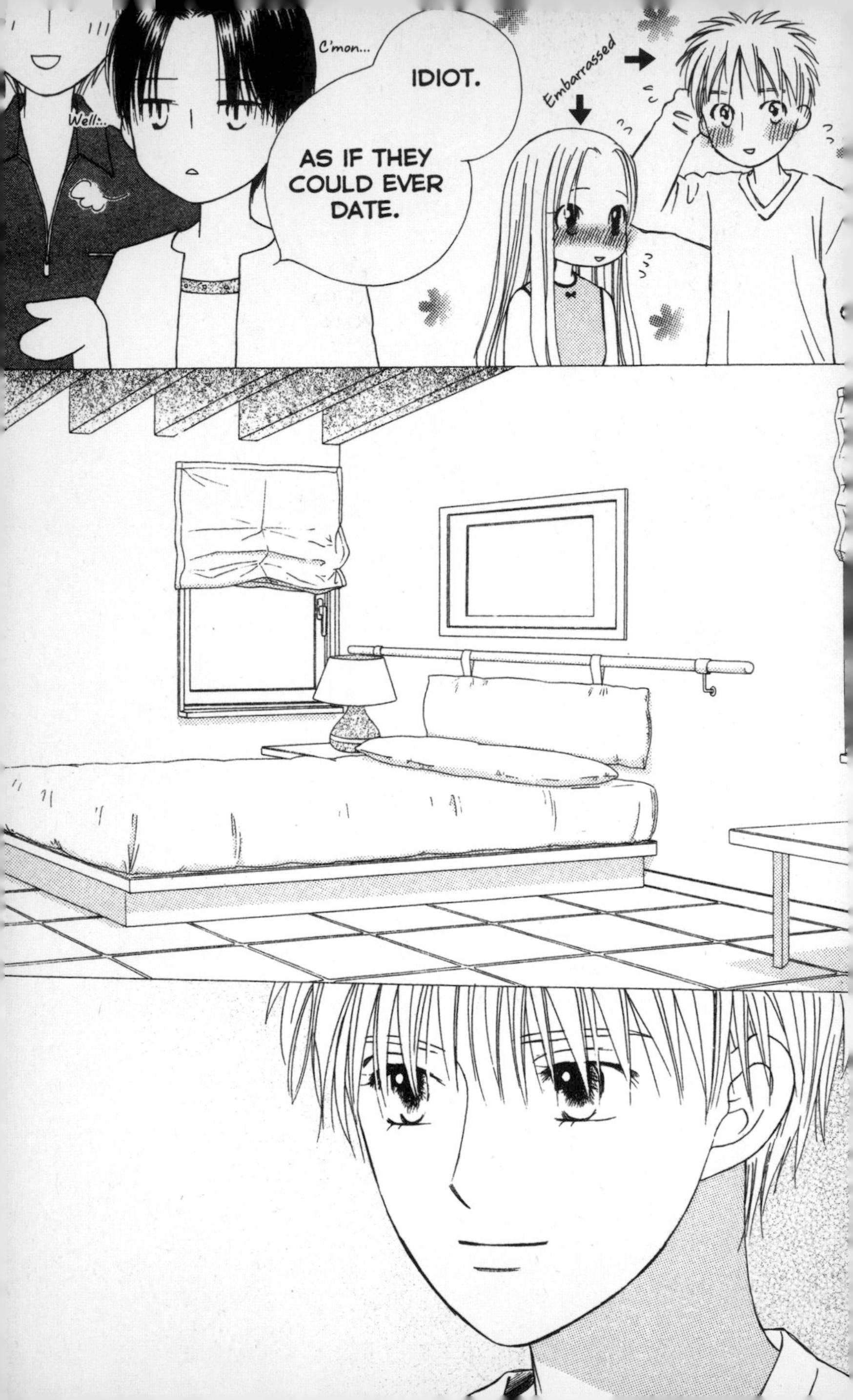

Embarrassed
IDIOT.
AS IF THEY COULD EVER DATE.
C'mon...
Well...

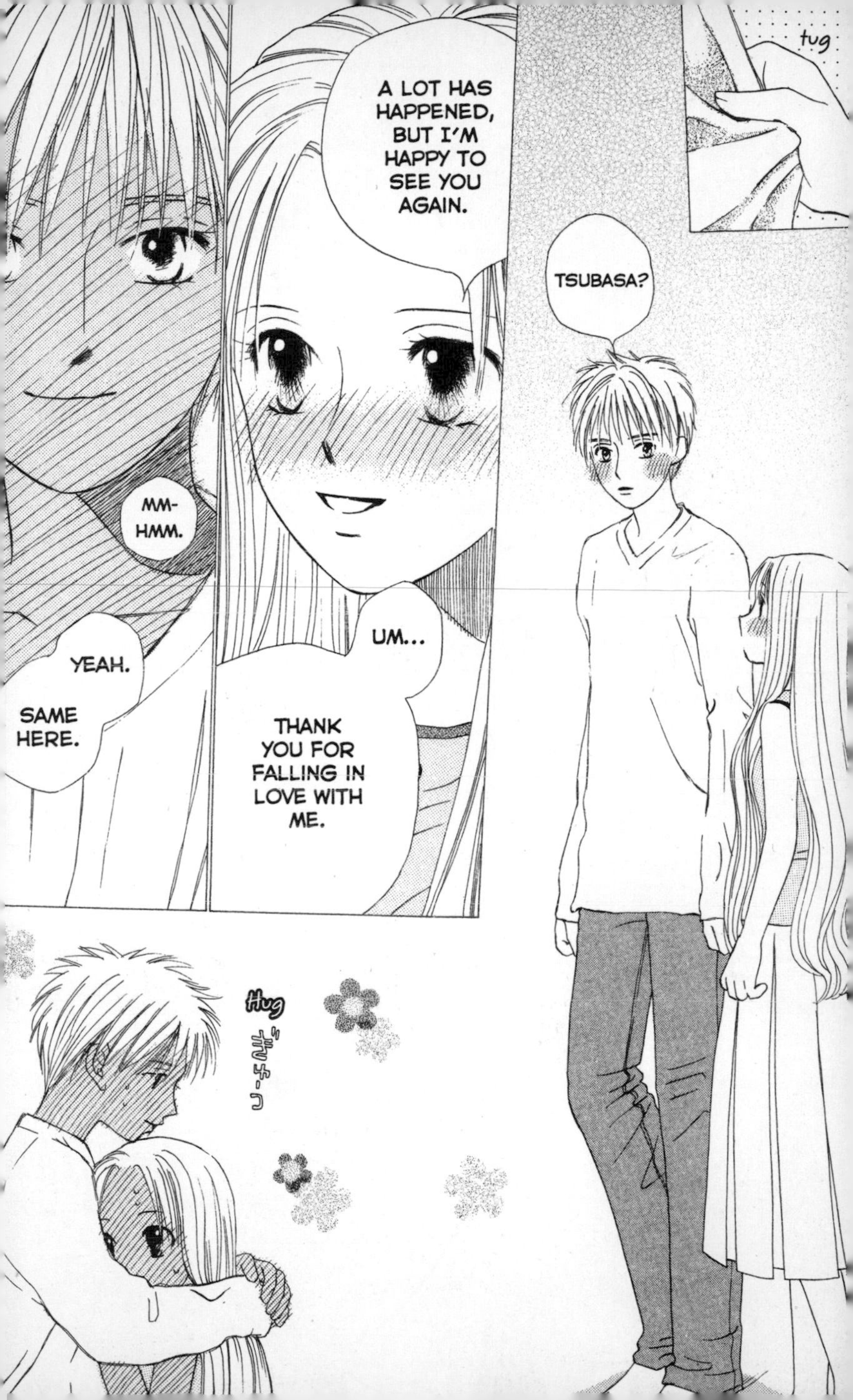

tug
TSUBASA?
A LOT HAS HAPPENED, BUT I'M HAPPY TO SEE YOU AGAIN.
MM-HMM.
UM...
THANK YOU FOR FALLING IN LOVE WITH ME.
YEAH.
SAME HERE.
Hug

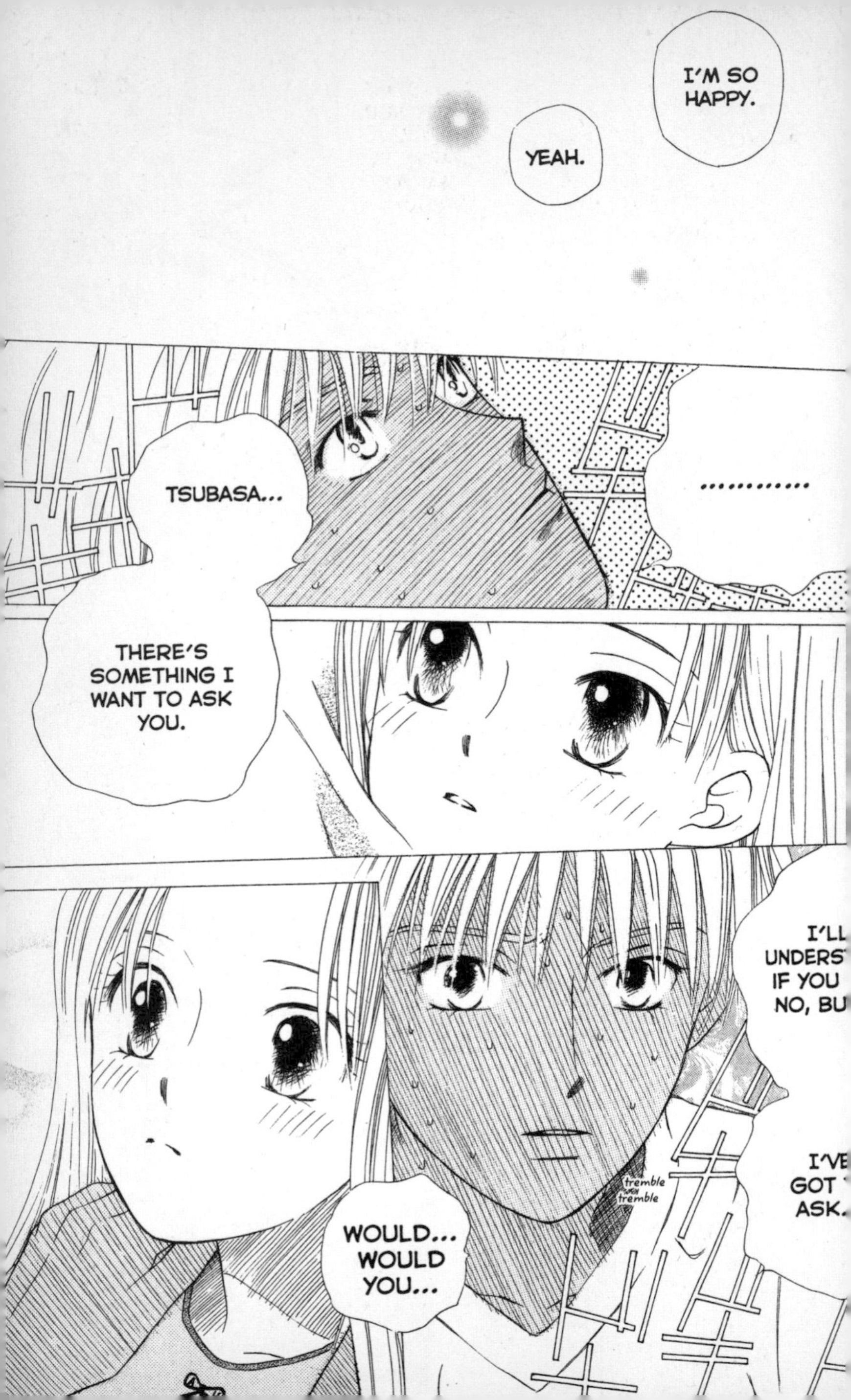
I'M SO HAPPY.
YEAH.
....
TSUBASA...
THERE'S SOMETHING I WANT TO ASK YOU.
I'LL UNDERST IF YOU NO, BU
I'VE GOT ASK.
tremble tremble
WOULD... WOULD YOU...

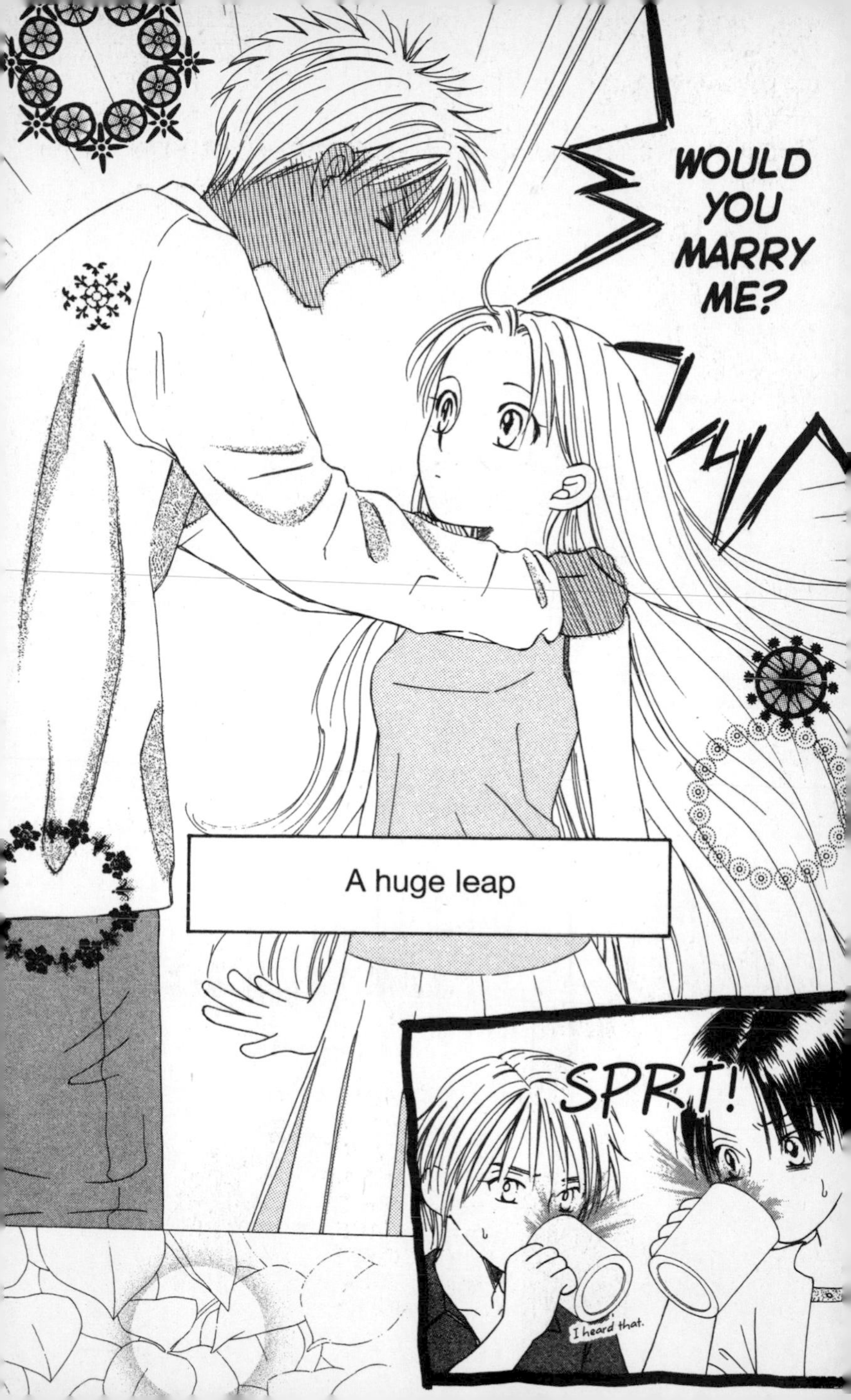
WOULD YOU MARRY ME?
A huge leap
SPRT!
I heard that.

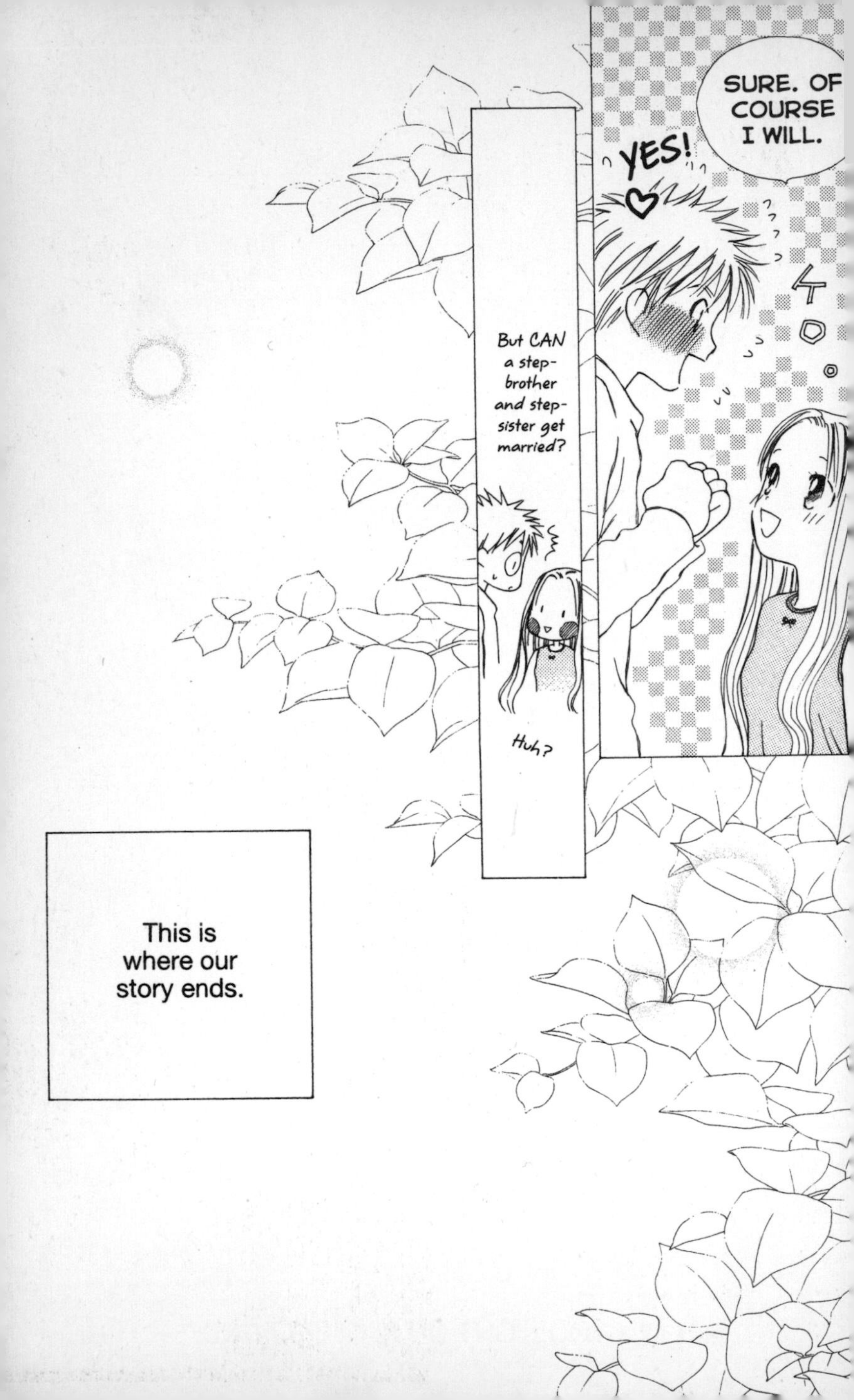
SURE. OF COURSE I WILL.
YES!
But CAN a step-brother and step-sister get married?
Huh?
This is where our story ends.

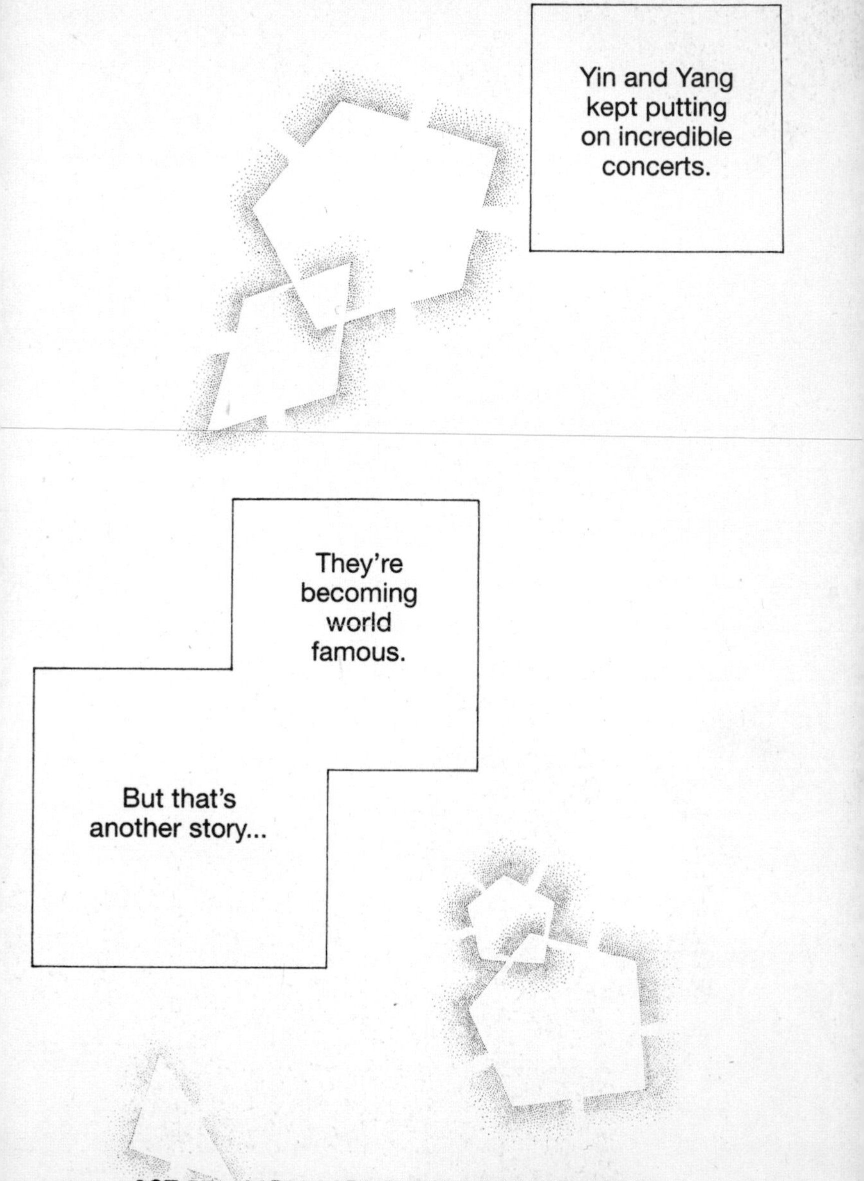
Yin and Yang kept putting on incredible concerts.
They're becoming world famous.
But that's another story...

ACT 57 ★ YOU LIGHT UP MY LIFE / END

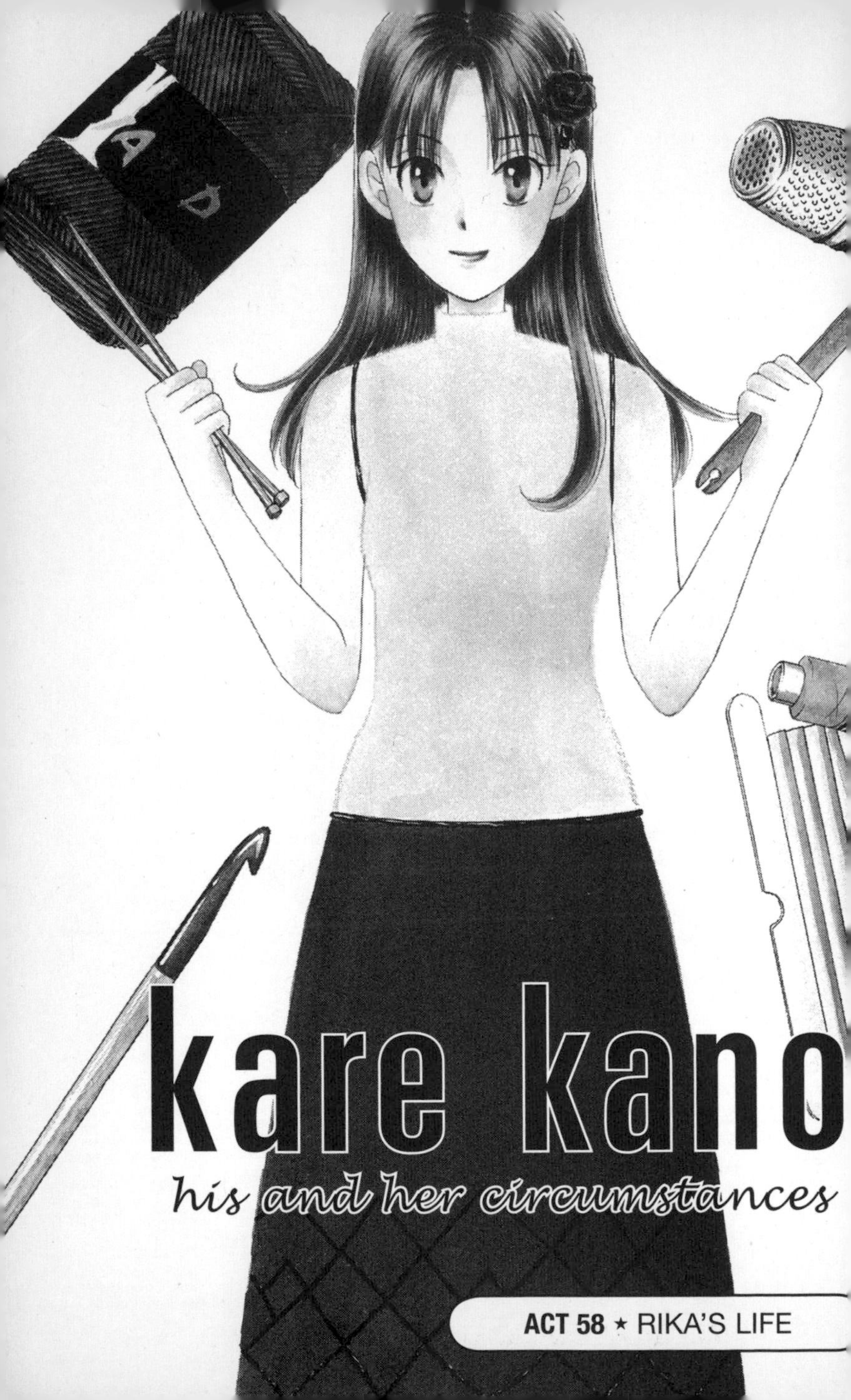
kare kano
his and her circumstances
ACT 58 ★ RIKA'S LIFE

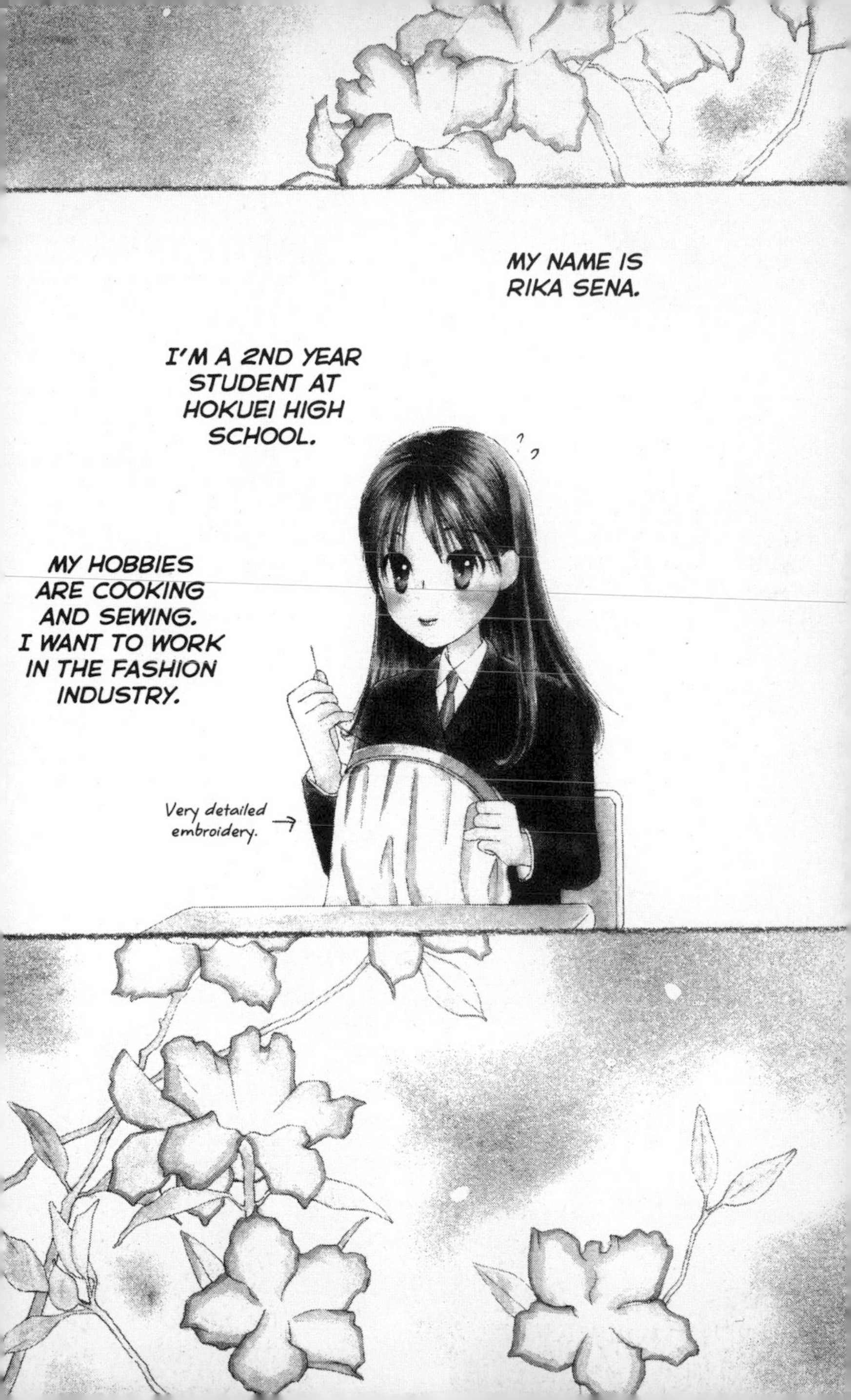
MY NAME IS RIKA SENA.
I'M A 2ND YEAR STUDENT AT HOKUEI HIGH SCHOOL.
MY HOBBIES ARE COOKING AND SEWING. I WANT TO WORK IN THE FASHION INDUSTRY.
Very detailed embroidery.

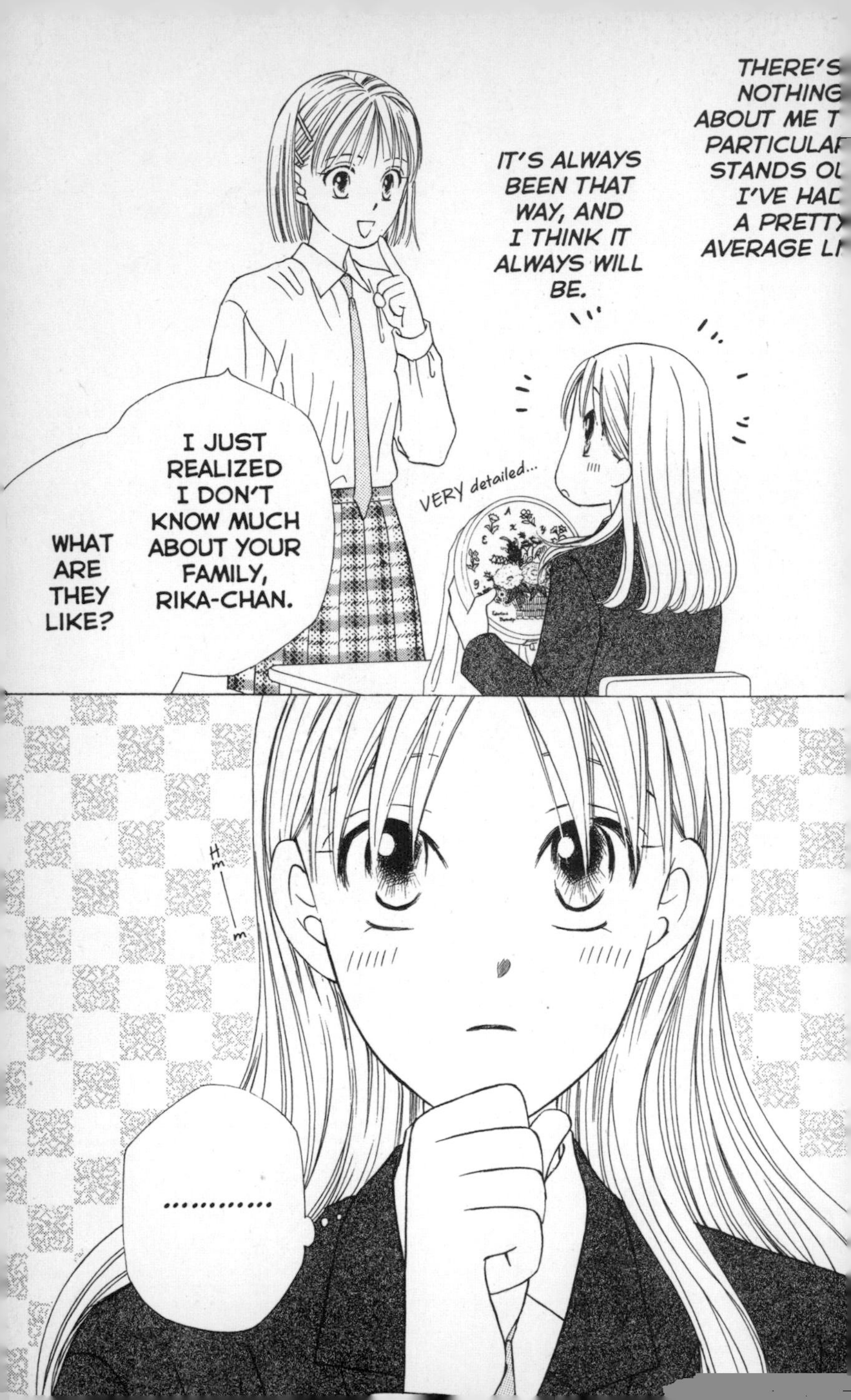
THERE'S NOTHING ABOUT ME T PARTICULA STANDS O I'VE HA A PRETT AVERAGE L
IT'S ALWAYS BEEN THAT WAY, AND I THINK IT ALWAYS WILL BE.
VERY detailed...
I JUST REALIZED I DON'T KNOW MUCH ABOUT YOUR FAMILY, RIKA-CHAN.
WHAT ARE THEY LIKE?
Hm—m
....

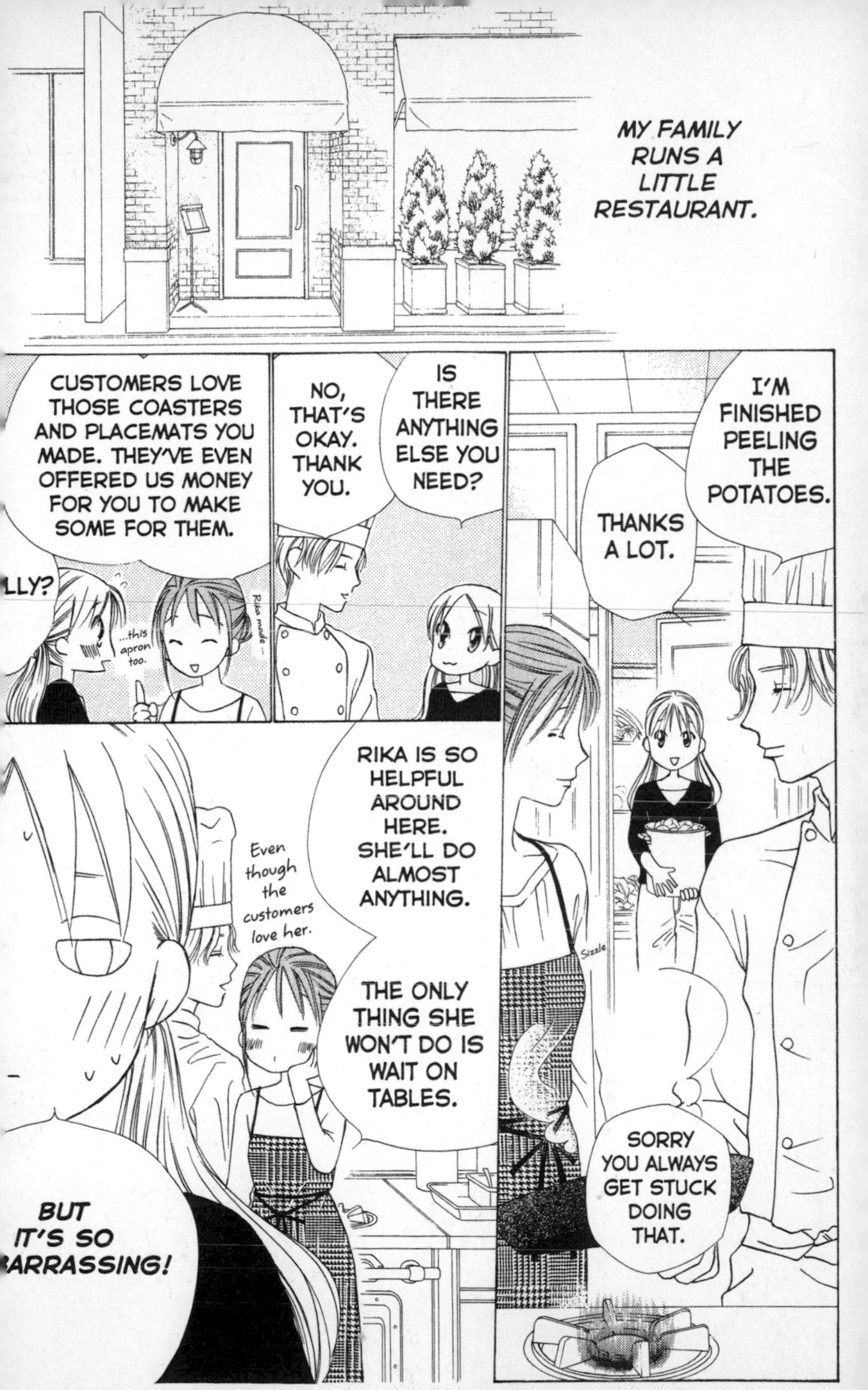
MY FAMILY RUNS A LITTLE RESTAURANT.
I'M FINISHED PEELING THE POTATOES.
THANKS A LOT.
Sizzle
SORRY YOU ALWAYS GET STUCK DOING THAT.
IS THERE ANYTHING ELSE YOU NEED?
NO, THAT'S OKAY. THANK YOU.
CUSTOMERS LOVE THOSE COASTERS AND PLACEMATS YOU MADE. THEY'VE EVEN OFFERED US MONEY FOR YOU TO MAKE SOME FOR THEM.
LLY?
Rika made ...
...this apron too.
RIKA IS SO HELPFUL AROUND HERE. SHE'LL DO ALMOST ANYTHING.
THE ONLY THING SHE WON'T DO IS WAIT ON TABLES.
Even though the customers love her.
BUT IT'S SO
ARRASSING!

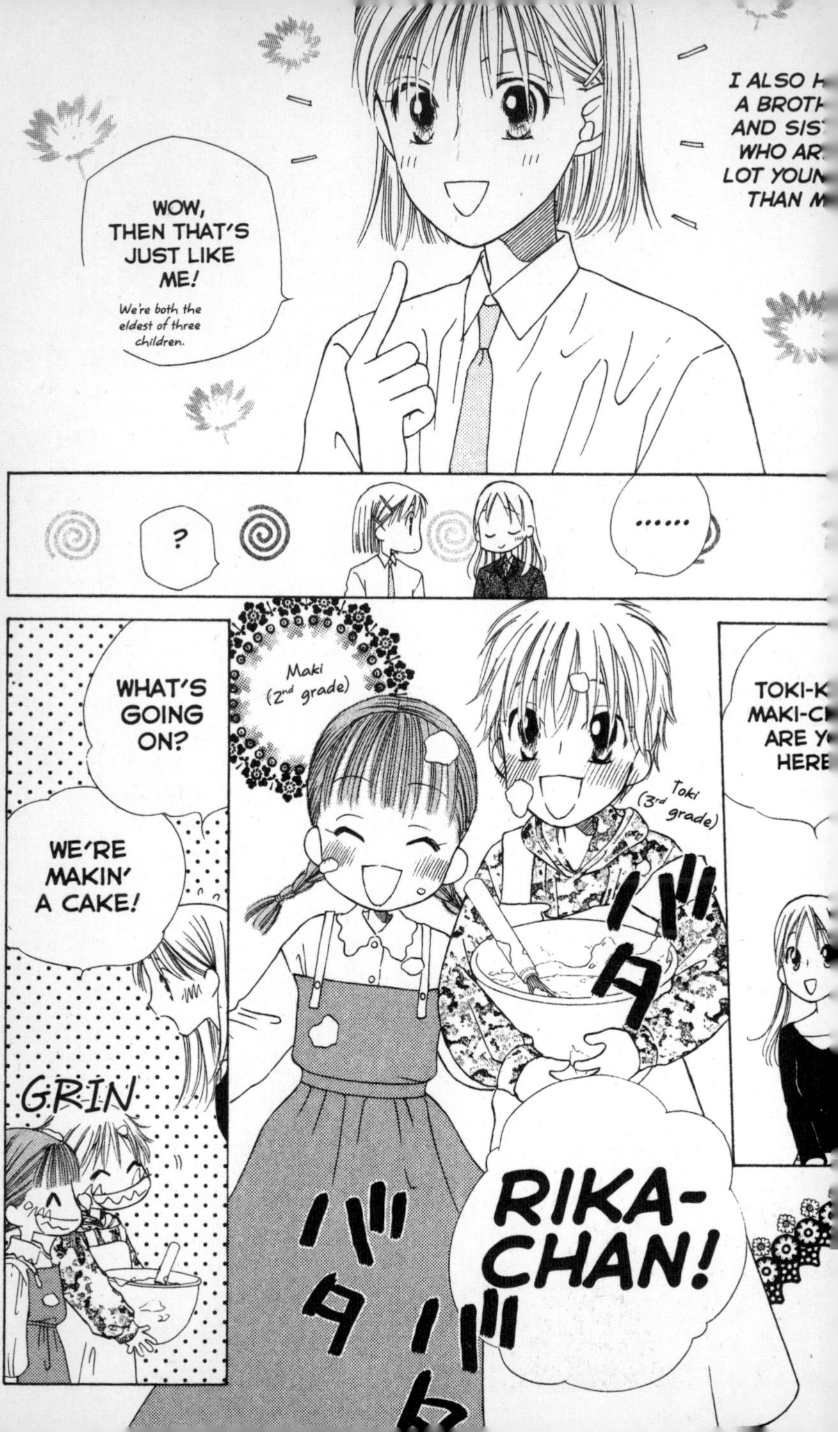
I ALSO H
A BROTH
AND SIS
WHO AR
LOT YOUN
THAN M
WOW, THEN THAT'S JUST LIKE ME!
We're both the eldest of three children.
......
?
TOKI-K
MAKI-C
ARE Y
HERE
RIKA-CHAN!
Toki (3rd grade)
Maki (2nd grade)
WHAT'S GOING ON?
WE'RE MAKIN' A CAKE!
GRIN

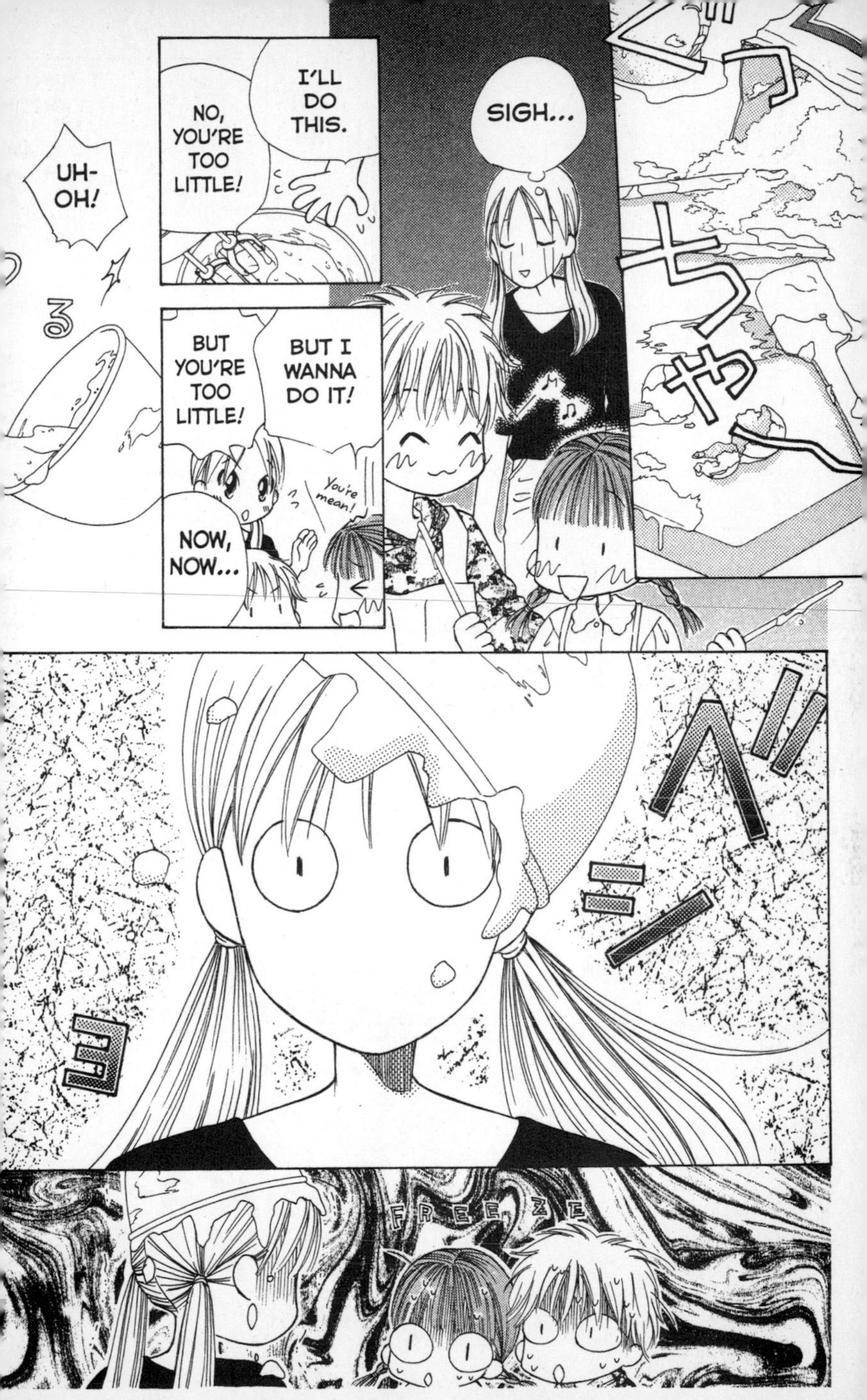
SIGH...
I'LL DO THIS.
NO, YOU'RE TOO LITTLE!
UH-OH!
BUT I WANNA DO IT!
BUT YOU'RE TOO LITTLE!
You're mean!
NOW, NOW...
FREEZE

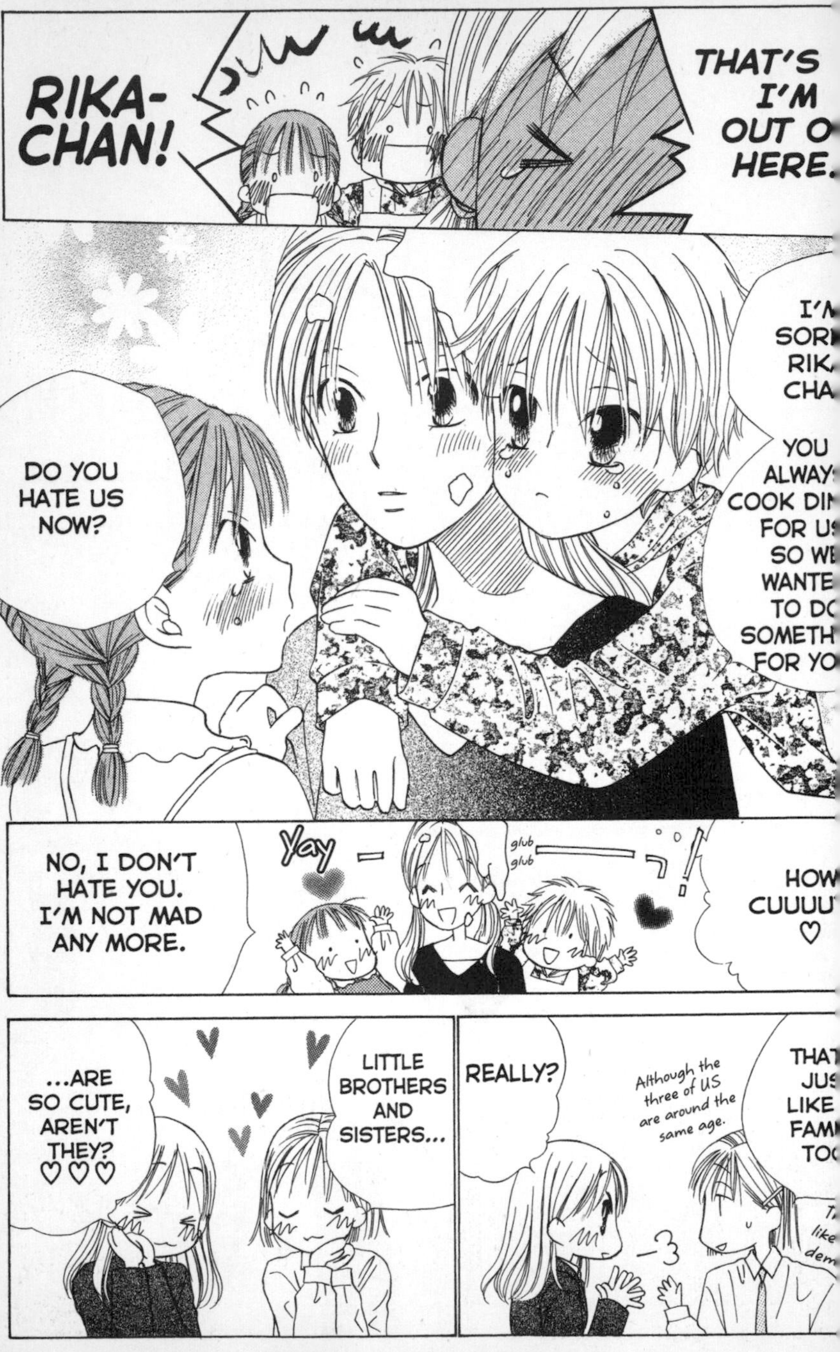
THAT'S I'M OUT O HERE.
RIKA-CHAN!
I'M SORR RIKA CHA
YOU ALWAY COOK DIN FOR US SO WE WANTE TO DO SOMETH FOR YO
DO YOU HATE US NOW?
HOW CUUUU ♡
glub glub
Yay
NO, I DON'T HATE YOU. I'M NOT MAD ANY MORE.
THAT JUS LIKE FAM TOO
Although the three of US are around the same age.
REALLY?
LITTLE BROTHERS AND SISTERS...
...ARE SO CUTE, AREN'T THEY? ♡♡♡

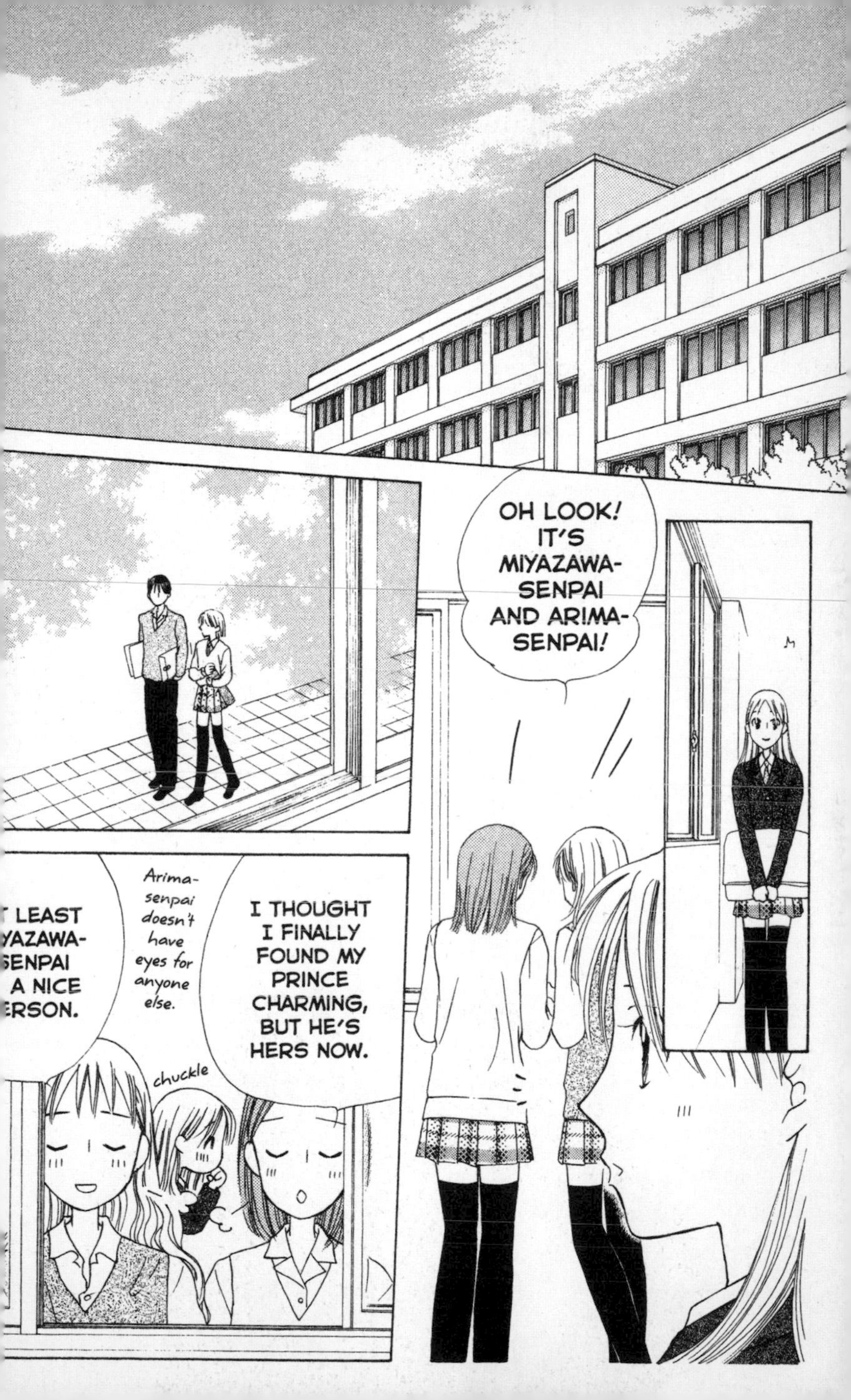

OH LOOK! IT'S MIYAZAWA-SENPAI AND ARIMA-SENPAI!
I THOUGHT I FINALLY FOUND MY PRINCE CHARMING, BUT HE'S HERS NOW.
Arima-senpai doesn't have eyes for anyone else.
T LEAST YAZAWA-SENPAI A NICE ERSON.
chuckle

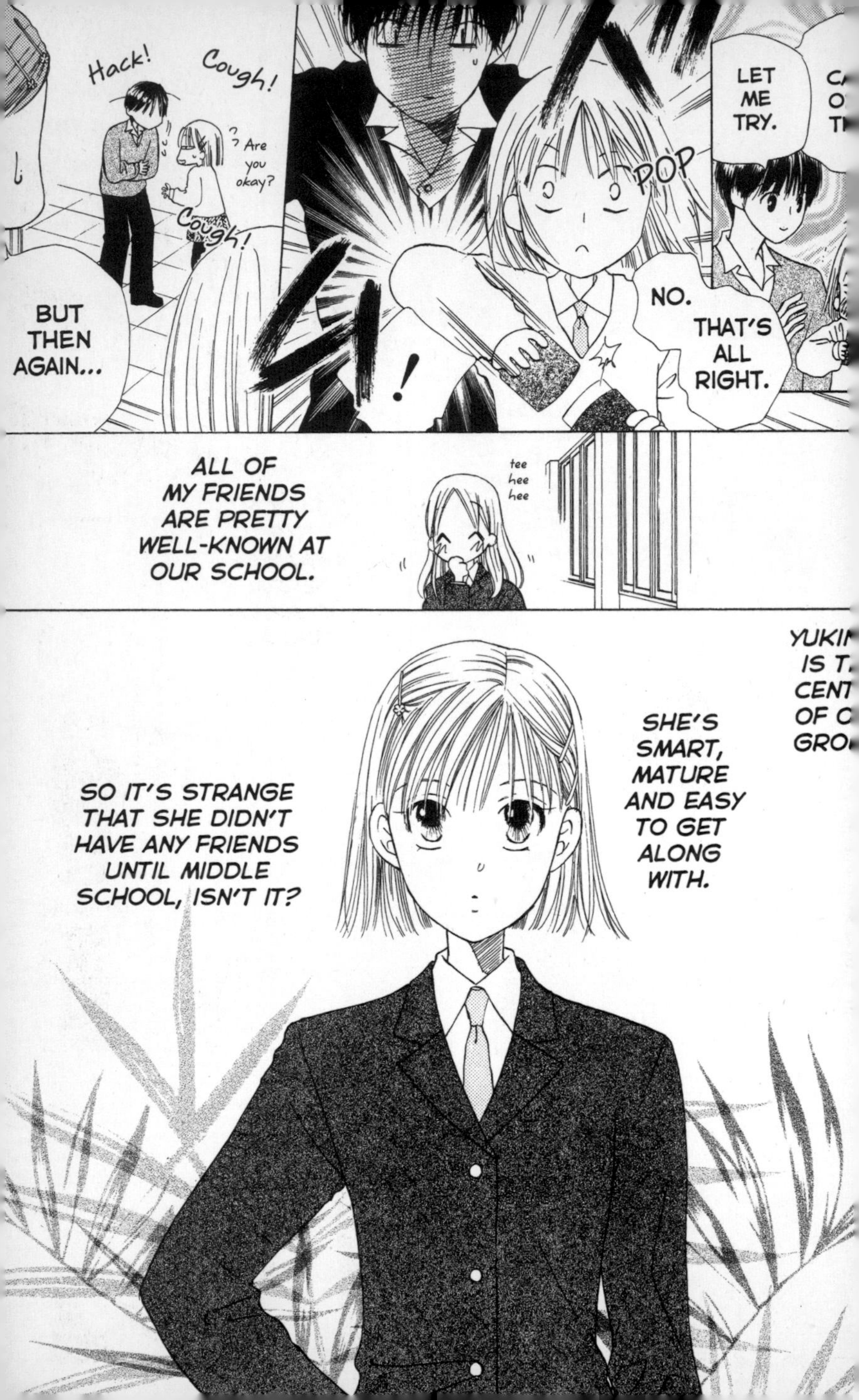
LET ME TRY.
NO. THAT'S ALL RIGHT.
POP
!
Hack!
Cough!
Are you okay?
Cough!
BUT THEN AGAIN...
ALL OF MY FRIENDS ARE PRETTY WELL-KNOWN AT OUR SCHOOL.
tee hee hee
SHE'S SMART, MATURE AND EASY TO GET ALONG WITH.
SO IT'S STRANGE THAT SHE DIDN'T HAVE ANY FRIENDS UNTIL MIDDLE SCHOOL, ISN'T IT?

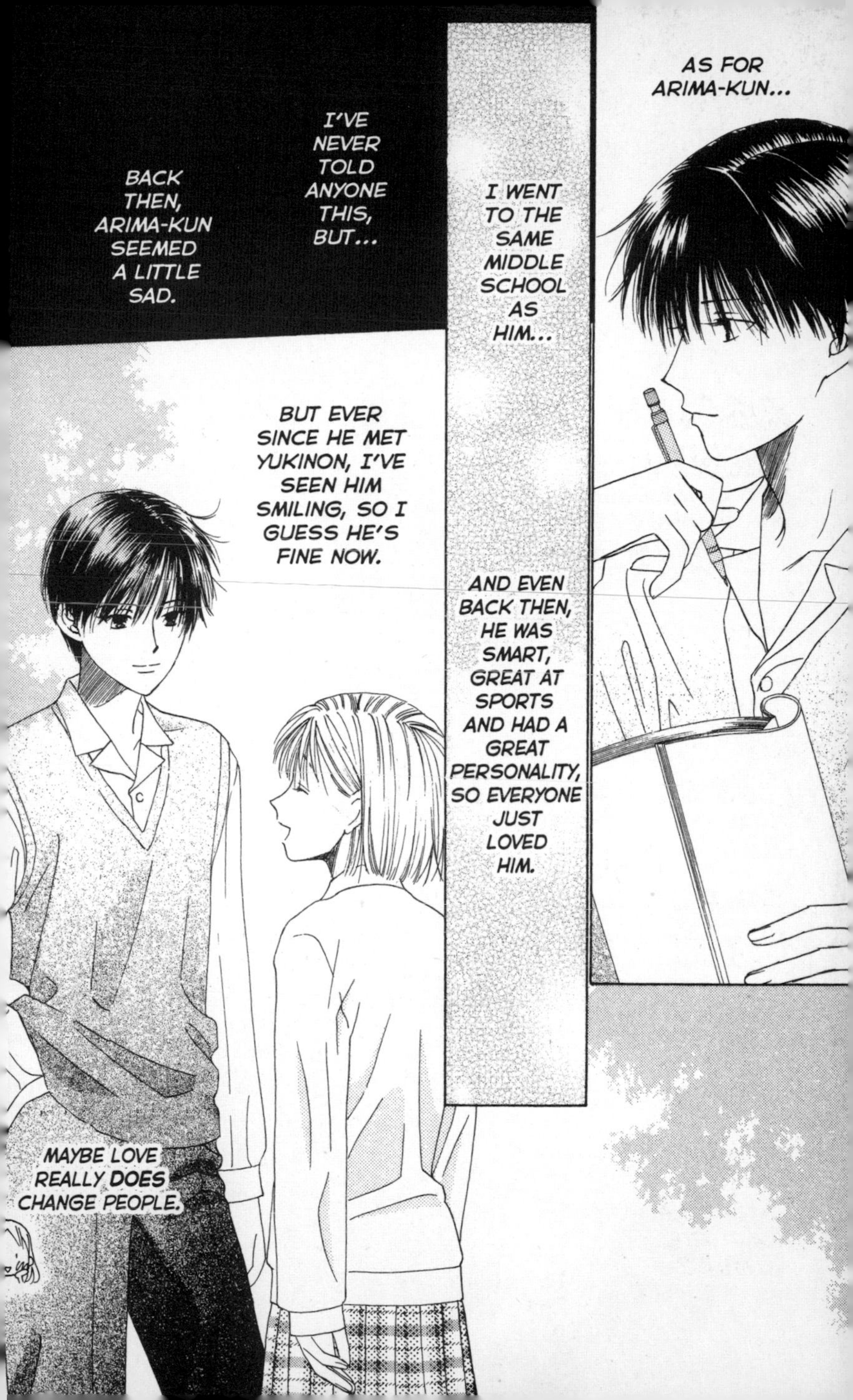
AS FOR ARIMA-KUN...
I WENT TO THE SAME MIDDLE SCHOOL AS HIM...
AND EVEN BACK THEN, HE WAS SMART, GREAT AT SPORTS AND HAD A GREAT PERSONALITY, SO EVERYONE JUST LOVED HIM.
I'VE NEVER TOLD ANYONE THIS, BUT...
BACK THEN, ARIMA-KUN SEEMED A LITTLE SAD.
BUT EVER SINCE HE MET YUKINON, I'VE SEEN HIM SMILING, SO I GUESS HE'S FINE NOW.
MAYBE LOVE REALLY DOES CHANGE PEOPLE.

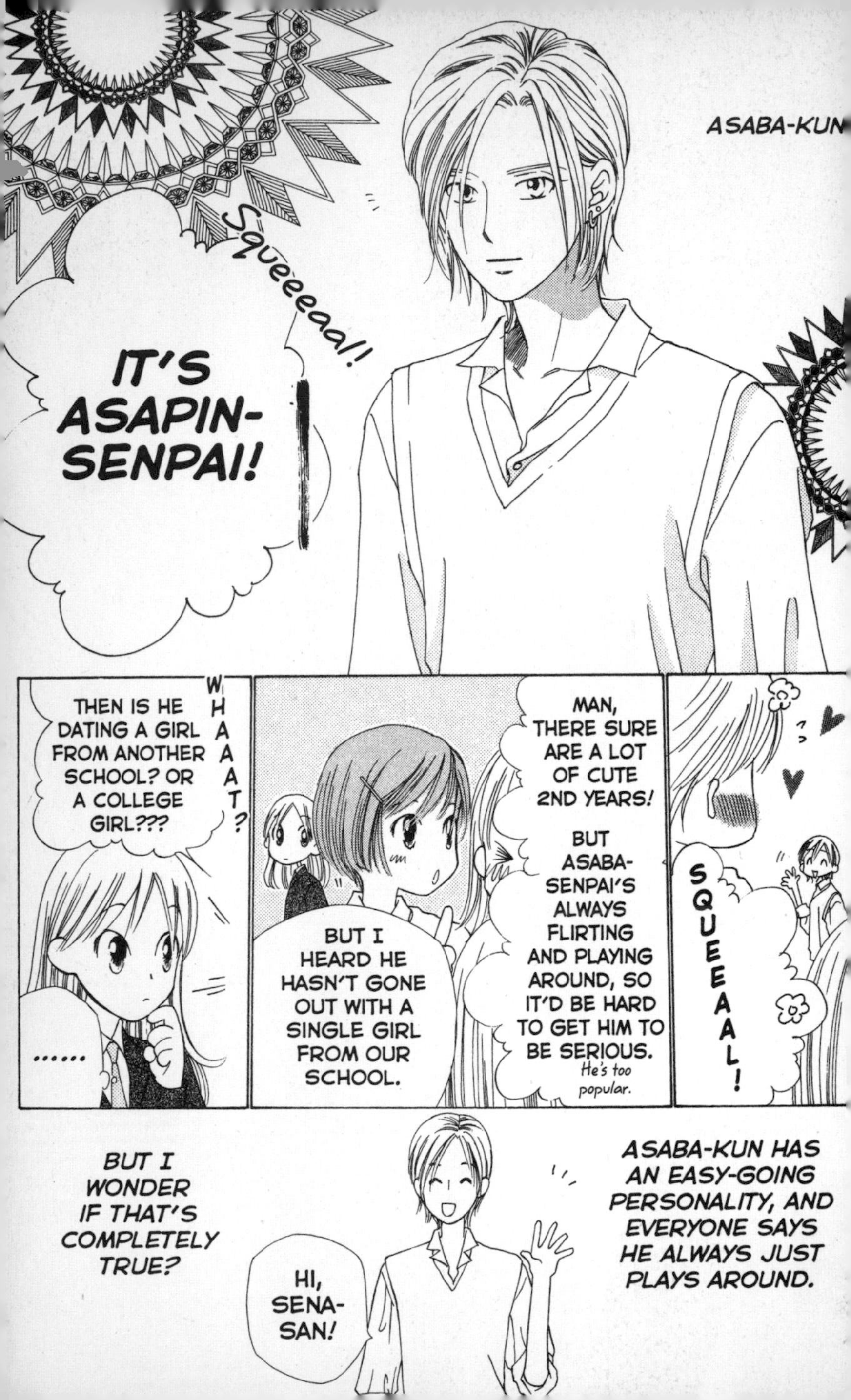
ASABA-KUN
Squeeeaal!
IT'S ASAPIN-SENPAI!
SQUEEAAL!
MAN, THERE SURE ARE A LOT OF CUTE 2ND YEARS!
BUT ASABA-SENPAI'S ALWAYS FLIRTING AND PLAYING AROUND, SO IT'D BE HARD TO GET HIM TO BE SERIOUS.
He's too popular.
BUT I HEARD HE HASN'T GONE OUT WITH A SINGLE GIRL FROM OUR SCHOOL.
WHAAAT?
THEN IS HE DATING A GIRL FROM ANOTHER SCHOOL? OR A COLLEGE GIRL???
......
ASABA-KUN HAS AN EASY-GOING PERSONALITY, AND EVERYONE SAYS HE ALWAYS JUST PLAYS AROUND.
HI, SENA-SAN!
BUT I WONDER IF THAT'S COMPLETELY TRUE?

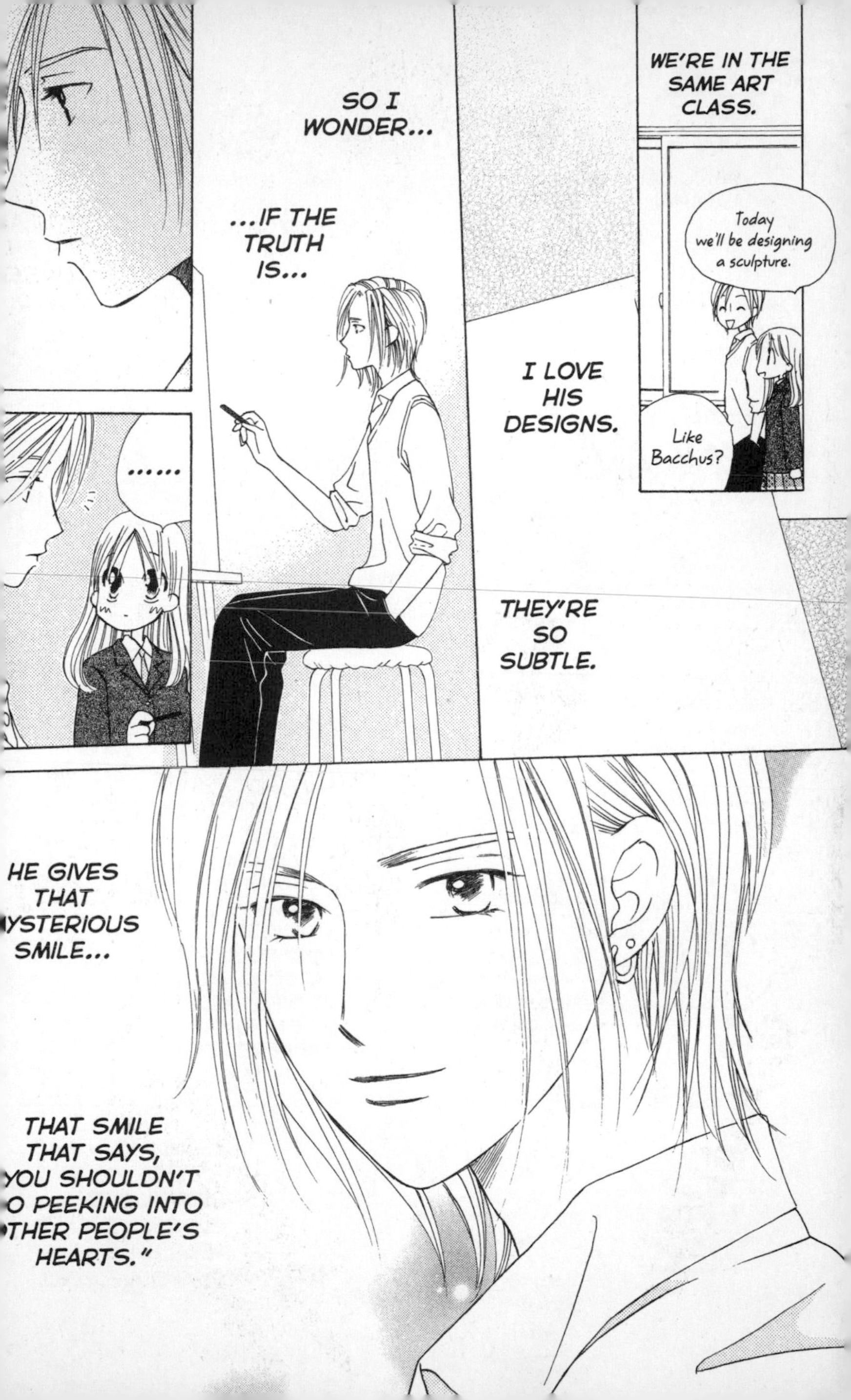
WE'RE IN THE SAME ART CLASS.
Today we'll be designing a sculpture.
Like Bacchus?
I LOVE HIS DESIGNS.
THEY'RE SO SUBTLE.
SO I WONDER...
...IF THE TRUTH IS...
......
HE GIVES THAT YSTERIOUS SMILE...
THAT SMILE THAT SAYS, YOU SHOULDN'T O PEEKING INTO THER PEOPLE'S HEARTS."

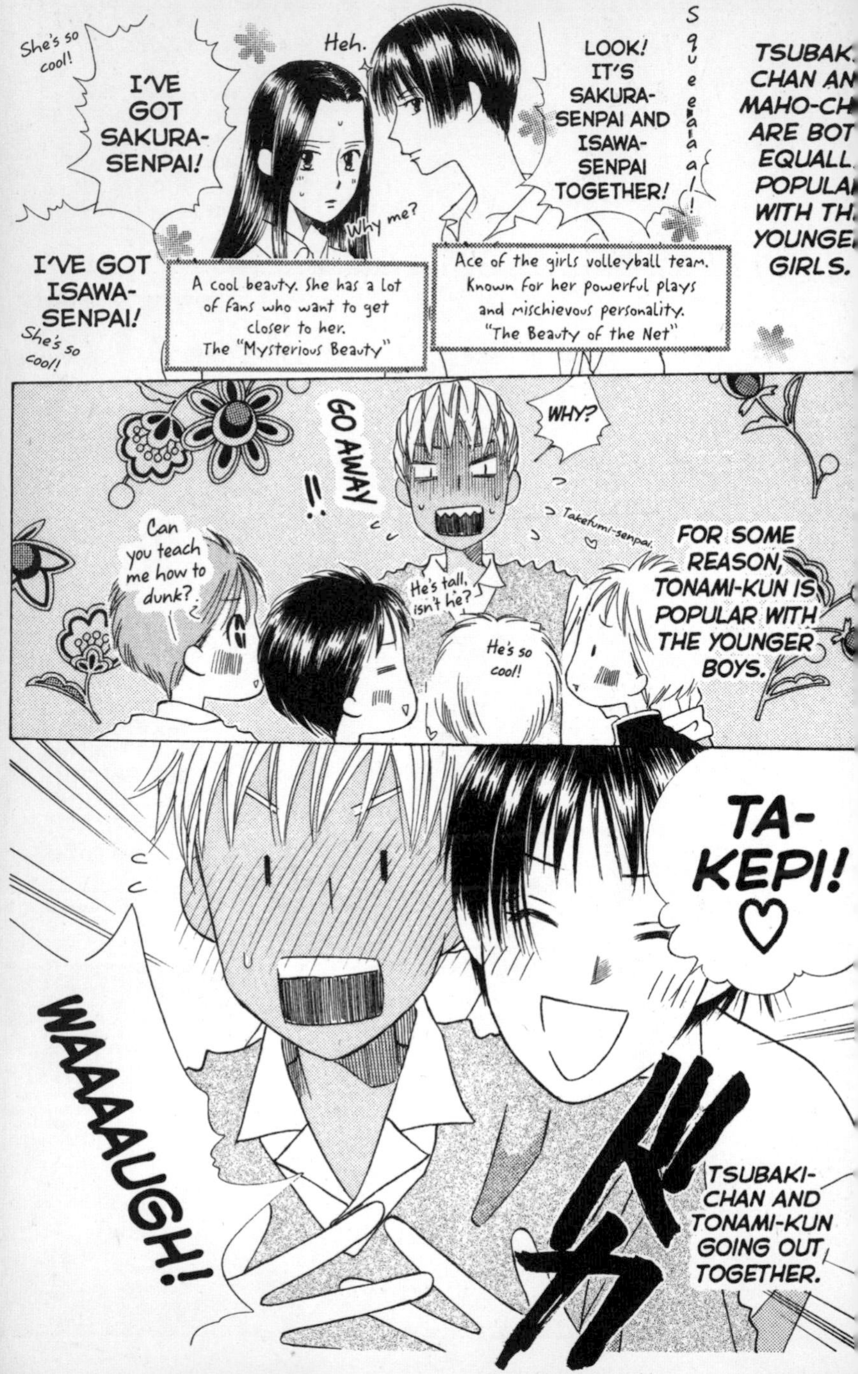
TSUBAK
CHAN AN
MAHO-CH
ARE BOT
EQUALL
POPULA
WITH TH
YOUNGE
GIRLS.
Squeeaaal!
LOOK! IT'S SAKURA-SENPAI AND ISAWA-SENPAI TOGETHER!
Heh.
Ace of the girls volleyball team. Known for her powerful plays and mischievous personality. "The Beauty of the Net"
Why me?
A cool beauty. She has a lot of fans who want to get closer to her. The "Mysterious Beauty"
I'VE GOT SAKURA-SENPAI!
She's so cool!
I'VE GOT ISAWA-SENPAI!
She's so cool!
FOR SOME REASON, TONAMI-KUN IS POPULAR WITH THE YOUNGER BOYS.
Takefumi-senpai.
WHY?
GO AWAY!!
He's so cool!
He's tall, isn't he?
Can you teach me how to dunk?
TSUBAKI-CHAN AND TONAMI-KUN GOING OUT TOGETHER.
TA-KEPI! ♡
WAAAAUGH!

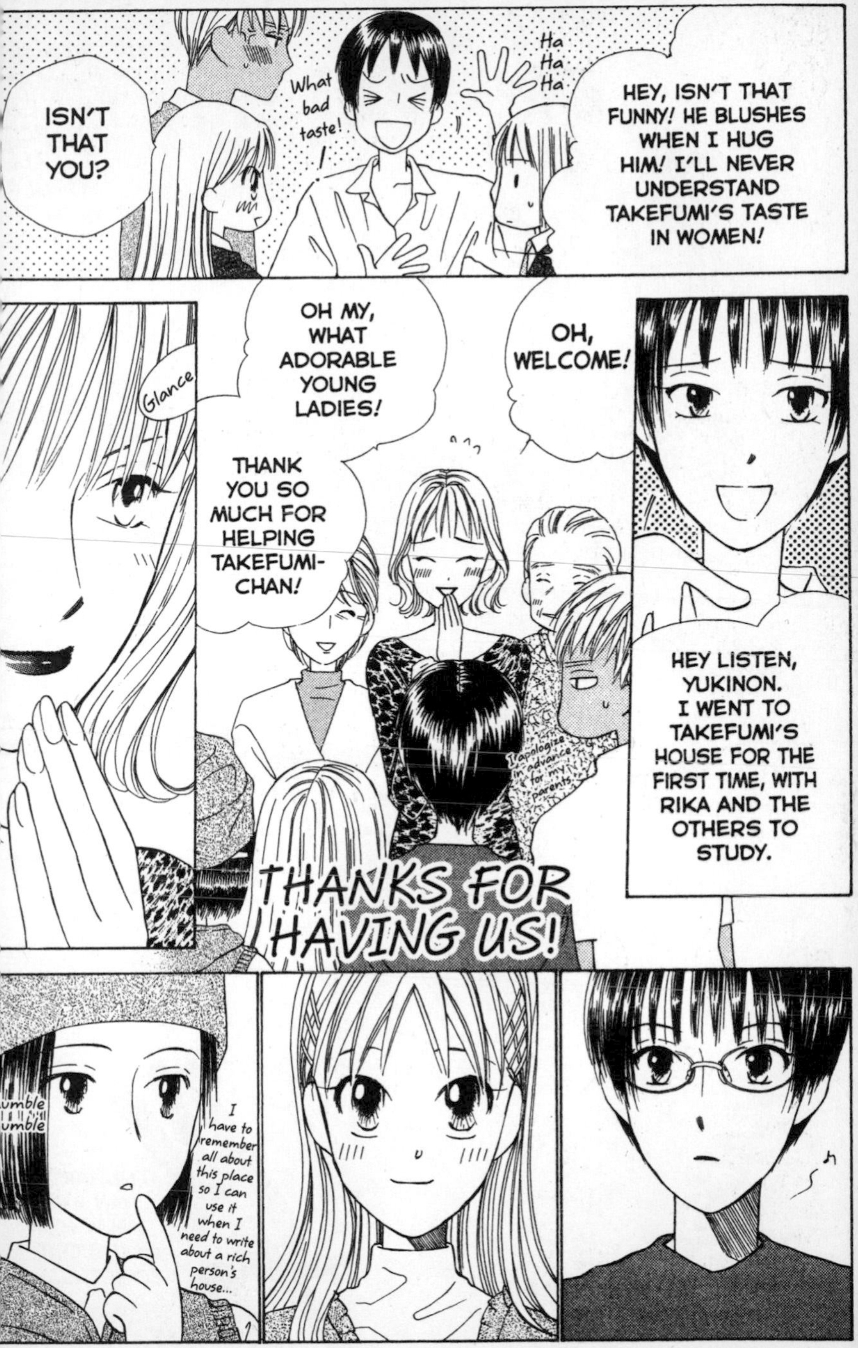

HEY, ISN'T THAT FUNNY! HE BLUSHES WHEN I HUG HIM! I'LL NEVER UNDERSTAND TAKEFUMI'S TASTE IN WOMEN!
Ha Ha Ha
What bad taste!
ISN'T THAT YOU?
HEY LISTEN, YUKINON. I WENT TO TAKEFUMI'S HOUSE FOR THE FIRST TIME, WITH RIKA AND THE OTHERS TO STUDY.
OH, WELCOME!
OH MY, WHAT ADORABLE YOUNG LADIES!
THANK YOU SO MUCH FOR HELPING TAKEFUMI-CHAN!
I apologize in advance for my parents.
THANKS FOR HAVING US!
Glance
I have to remember all about this place so I can use it when I need to write about a rich person's house...

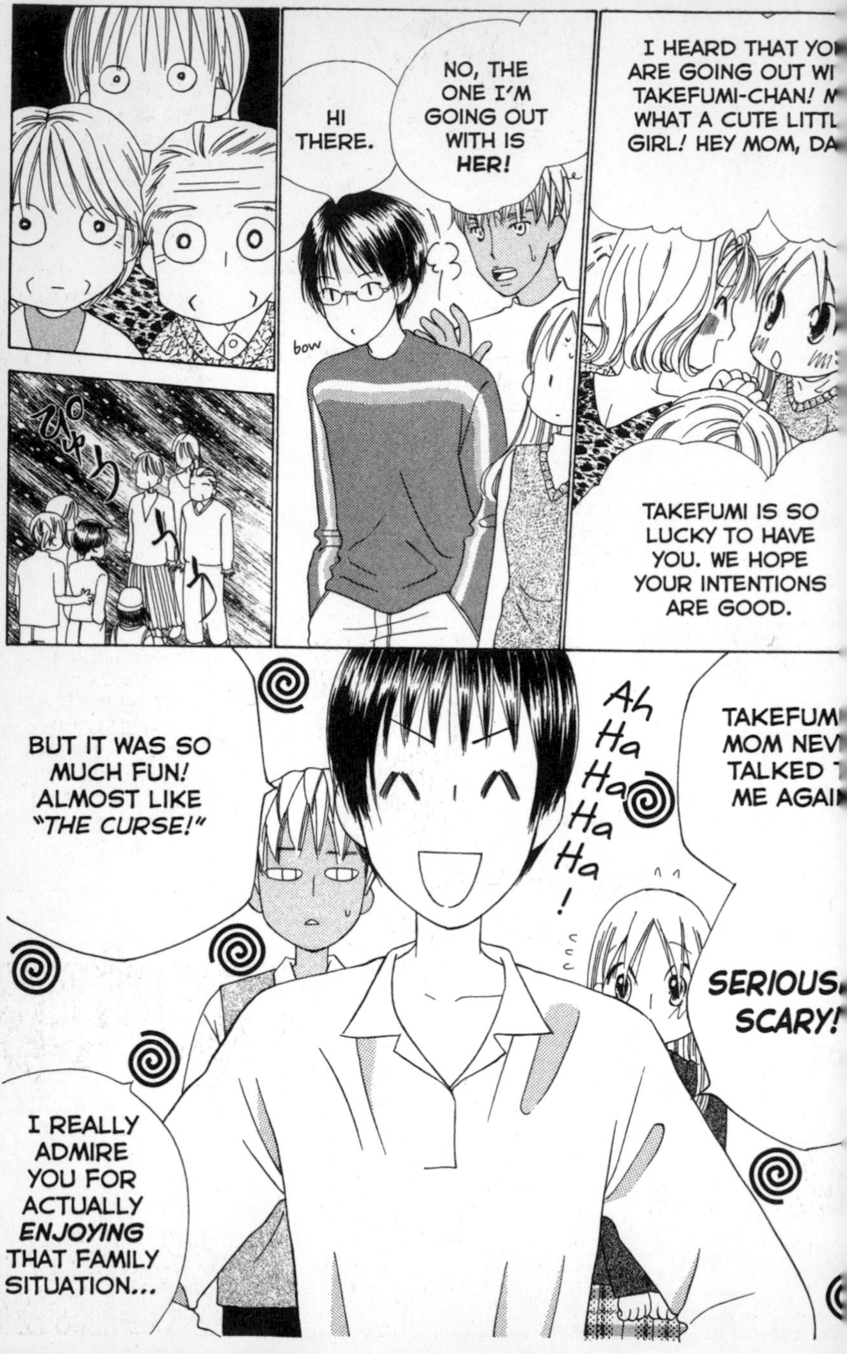
I HEARD THAT YO ARE GOING OUT WI TAKEFUMI-CHAN! M WHAT A CUTE LITTL GIRL! HEY MOM, DA
TAKEFUMI IS SO LUCKY TO HAVE YOU. WE HOPE YOUR INTENTIONS ARE GOOD.
NO, THE ONE I'M GOING OUT WITH IS HER!
HI THERE.
bow
TAKEFUM MOM NEV TALKED T ME AGAI
SERIOUS SCARY!
Ah Ha Ha Ha Ha!
BUT IT WAS SO MUCH FUN! ALMOST LIKE "THE CURSE!"
I REALLY ADMIRE YOU FOR ACTUALLY ENJOYING THAT FAMILY SITUATION...

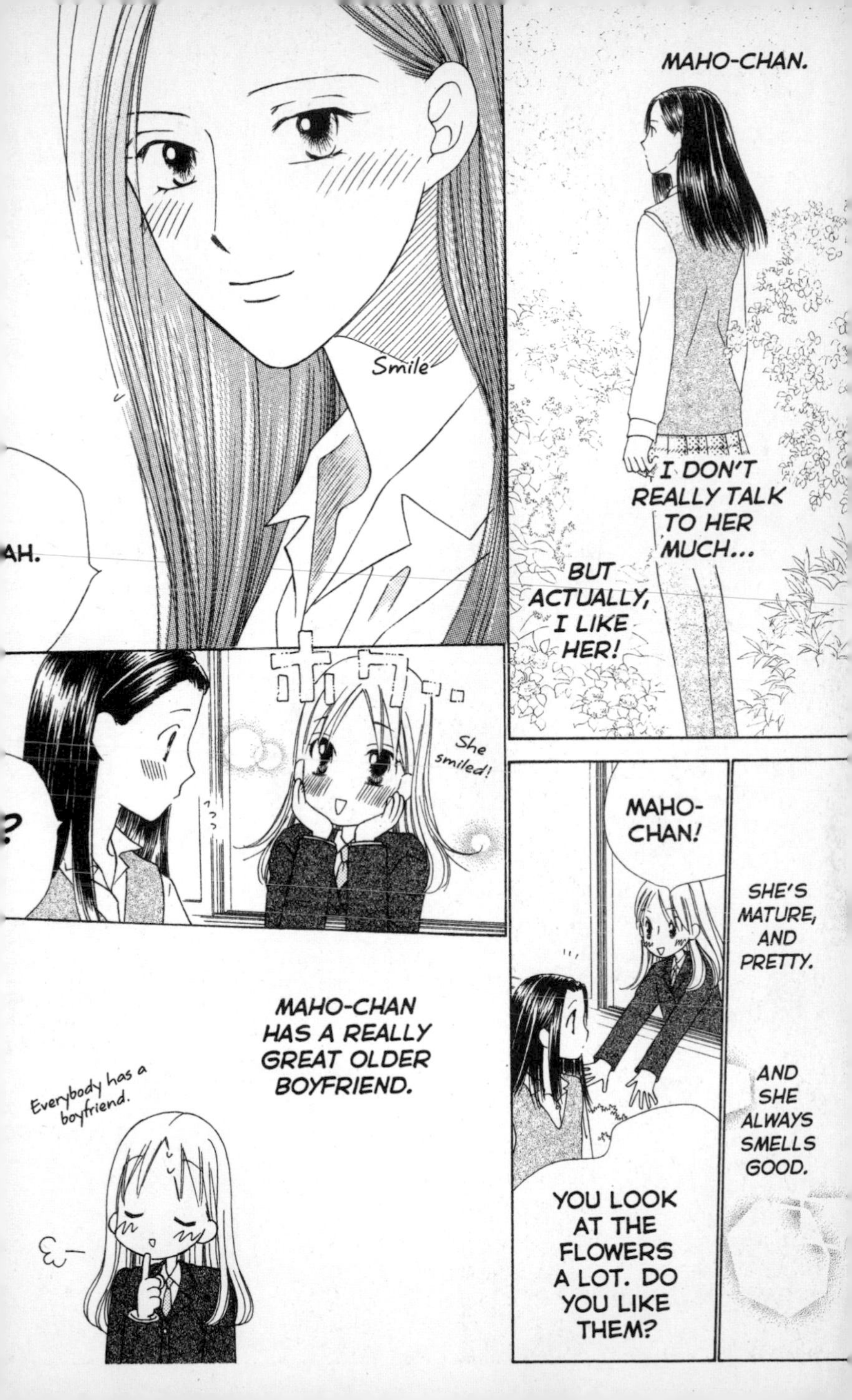
MAHO-CHAN.
I DON'T REALLY TALK TO HER MUCH...
BUT ACTUALLY, I LIKE HER!
MAHO-CHAN!
SHE'S MATURE, AND PRETTY.
AND SHE ALWAYS SMELLS GOOD.
YOU LOOK AT THE FLOWERS A LOT. DO YOU LIKE THEM?
Smile
AH.
?
She smiled!
MAHO-CHAN HAS A REALLY GREAT OLDER BOYFRIEND.
Everybody has a boyfriend.

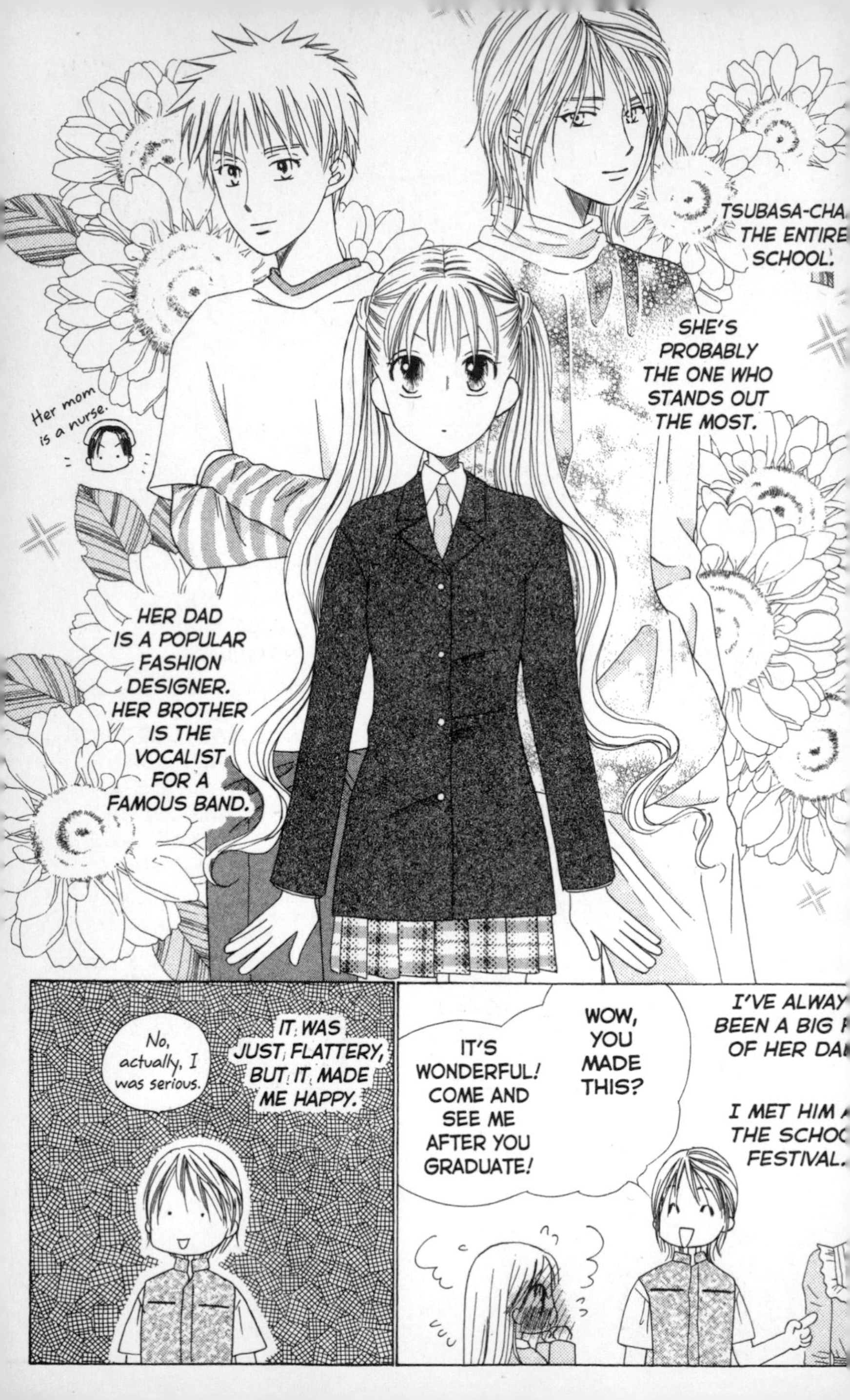
TSUBASA-CHA THE ENTIRE SCHOOL.
SHE'S PROBABLY THE ONE WHO STANDS OUT THE MOST.
HER DAD IS A POPULAR FASHION DESIGNER. HER BROTHER IS THE VOCALIST FOR A FAMOUS BAND.
Her mom is a nurse.
I'VE ALWAY BEEN A BIG OF HER DA
I MET HIM THE SCHO FESTIVAL.
WOW, YOU MADE THIS?
IT'S WONDERFUL! COME AND SEE ME AFTER YOU GRADUATE!
IT WAS JUST FLATTERY, BUT IT MADE ME HAPPY.
No, actually, I was serious.

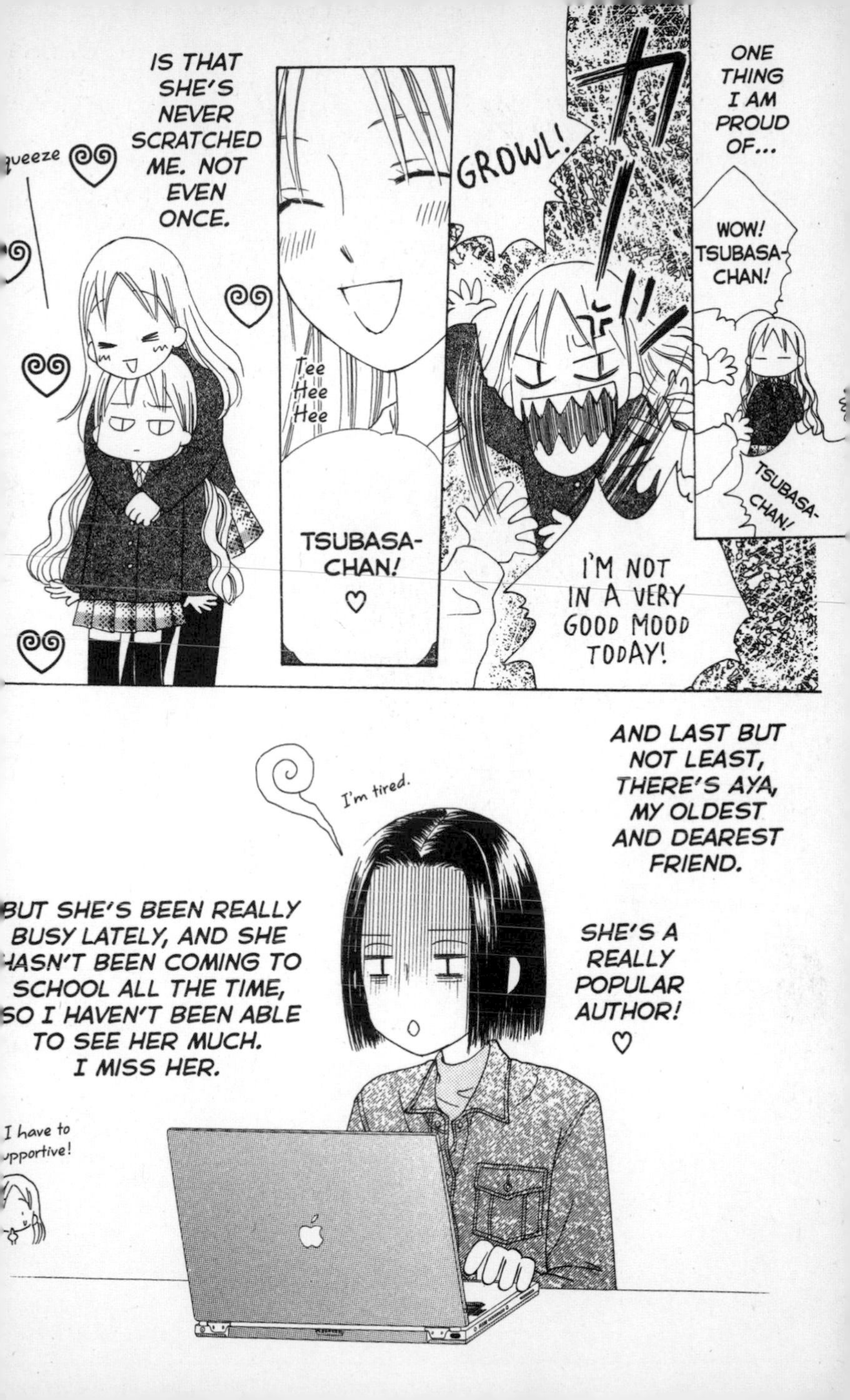

ONE THING I AM PROUD OF...
WOW! TSUBASA-CHAN!
TSUBASA-CHAN!
GROWL!
I'M NOT IN A VERY GOOD MOOD TODAY!
Tee Hee Hee
TSUBASA-CHAN! ♡
IS THAT SHE'S NEVER SCRATCHED ME. NOT EVEN ONCE.
AND LAST BUT NOT LEAST, THERE'S AYA, MY OLDEST AND DEAREST FRIEND.
SHE'S A REALLY POPULAR AUTHOR! ♡
I'm tired.
BUT SHE'S BEEN REALLY BUSY LATELY, AND SHE HASN'T BEEN COMING TO SCHOOL ALL THE TIME, SO I HAVEN'T BEEN ABLE TO SEE HER MUCH. I MISS HER.

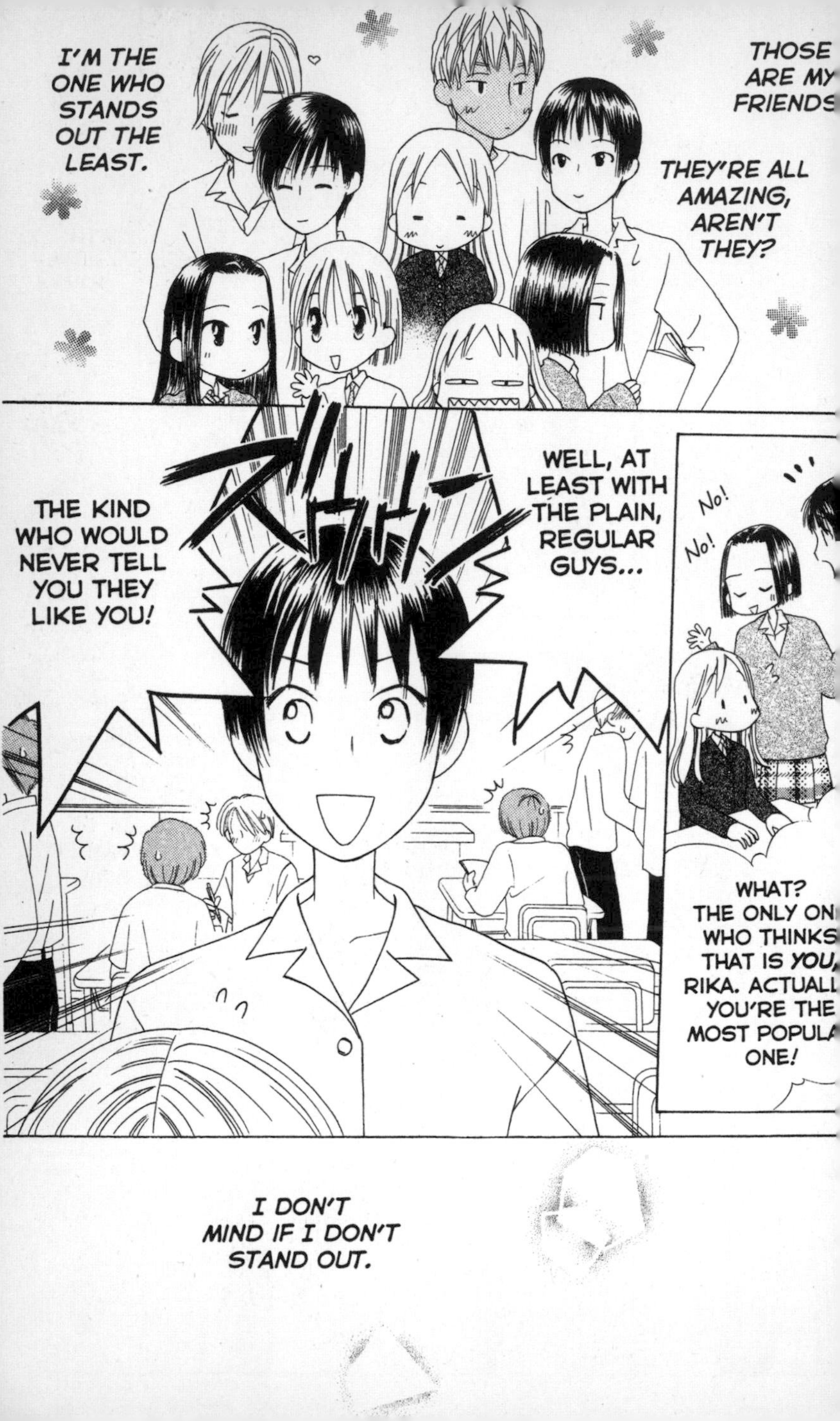
THOSE ARE MY FRIENDS
THEY'RE ALL AMAZING, AREN'T THEY?
I'M THE ONE WHO STANDS OUT THE LEAST.
No! No!
WHAT? THE ONLY ON WHO THINKS THAT IS YOU, RIKA. ACTUALL YOU'RE THE MOST POPULA ONE!
WELL, AT LEAST WITH THE PLAIN, REGULAR GUYS...
THE KIND WHO WOULD NEVER TELL YOU THEY LIKE YOU!
I DON'T MIND IF I DON'T STAND OUT.

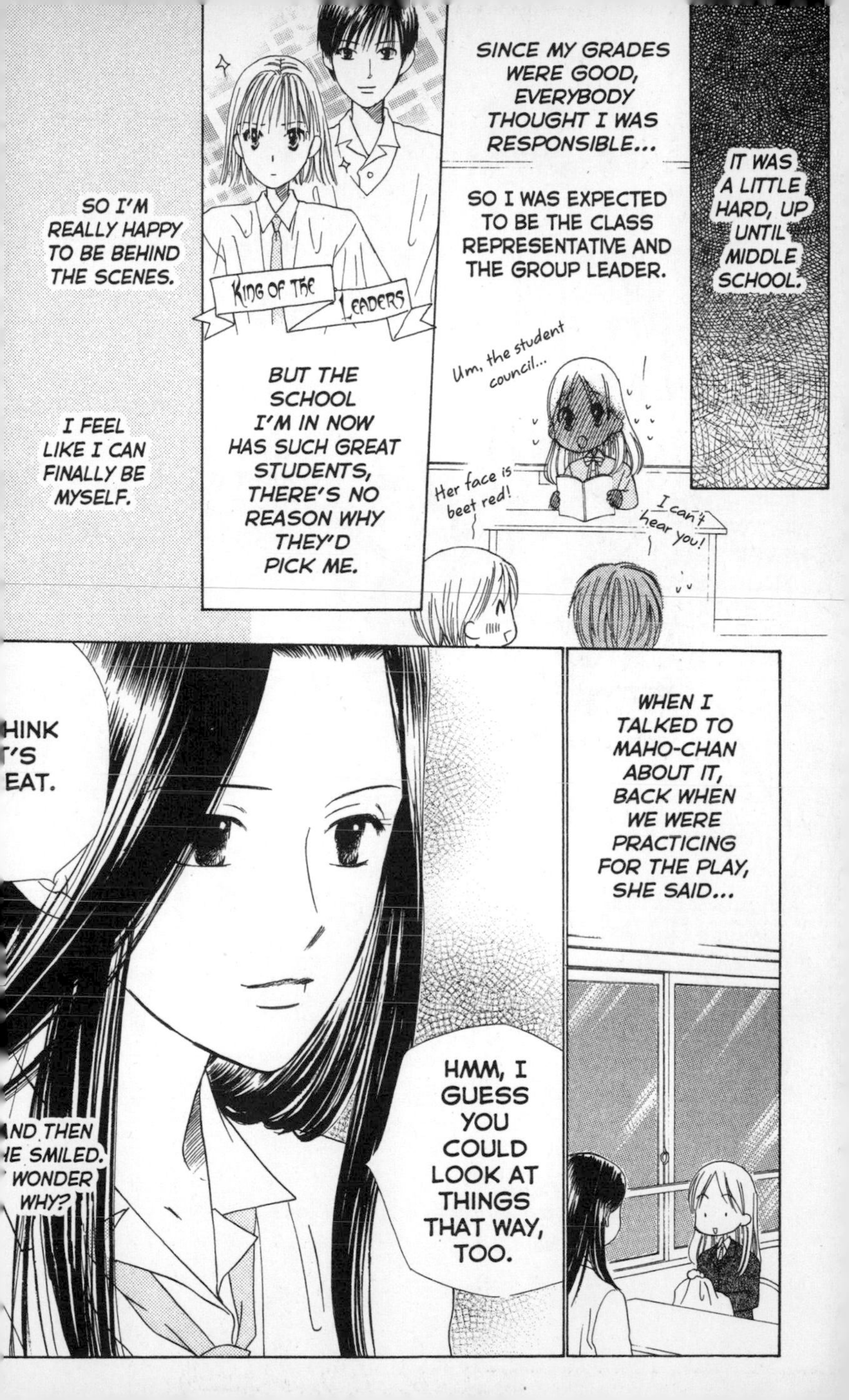
IT WAS A LITTLE HARD, UP UNTIL MIDDLE SCHOOL.
SINCE MY GRADES WERE GOOD, EVERYBODY THOUGHT I WAS RESPONSIBLE...
SO I WAS EXPECTED TO BE THE CLASS REPRESENTATIVE AND THE GROUP LEADER.
Um, the student council...
Her face is beet red!
I can't hear you!
KING OF THE LEADERS
BUT THE SCHOOL I'M IN NOW HAS SUCH GREAT STUDENTS, THERE'S NO REASON WHY THEY'D PICK ME.
SO I'M REALLY HAPPY TO BE BEHIND THE SCENES.
I FEEL LIKE I CAN FINALLY BE MYSELF.
WHEN I TALKED TO MAHO-CHAN ABOUT IT, BACK WHEN WE WERE PRACTICING FOR THE PLAY, SHE SAID...
HMM, I GUESS YOU COULD LOOK AT THINGS THAT WAY, TOO.
HINK 'S EAT.
ND THEN HE SMILED. WONDER WHY?

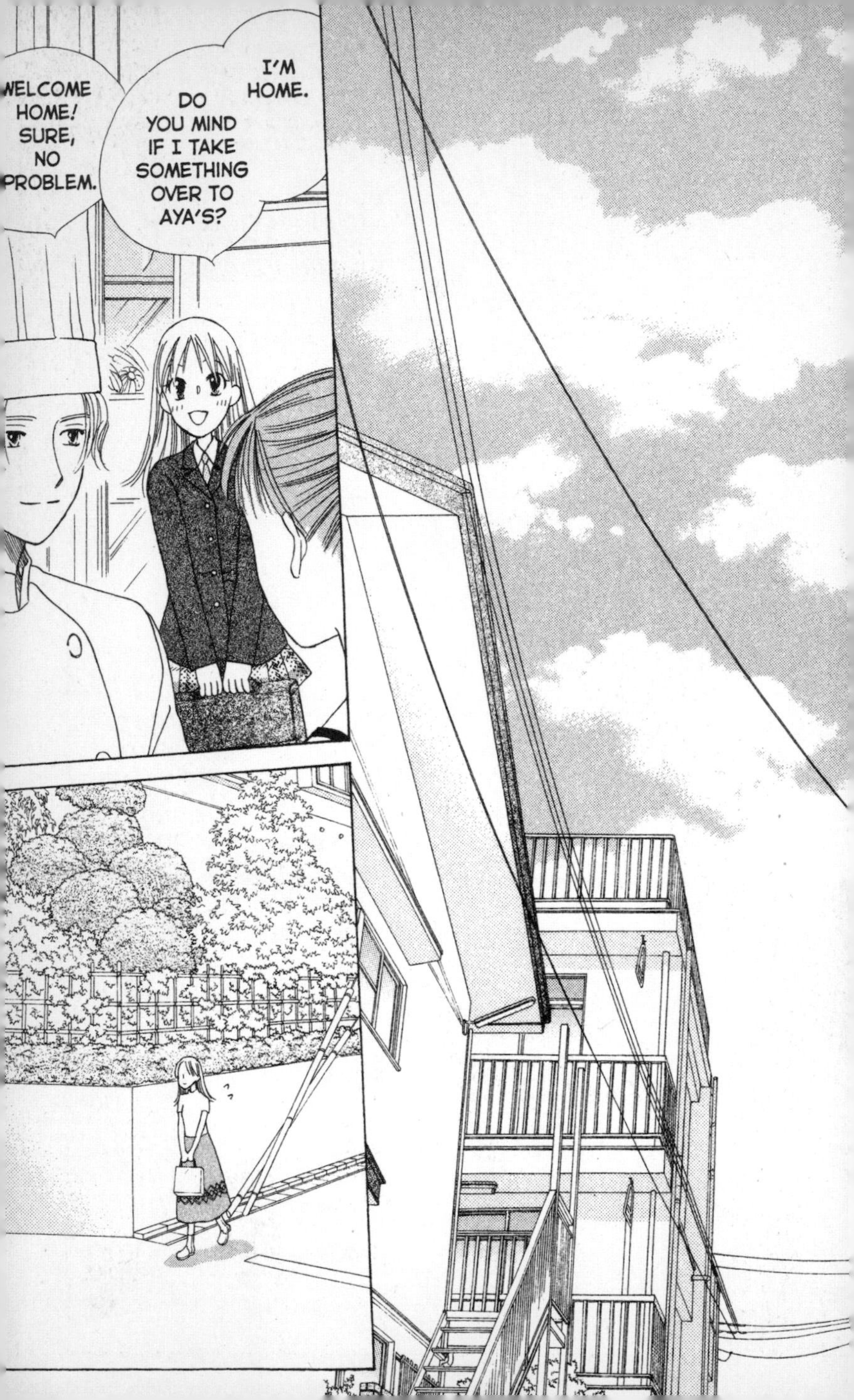
I'M HOME.
DO YOU MIND IF I TAKE SOMETHING OVER TO AYA'S?
WELCOME HOME! SURE, NO PROBLEM.

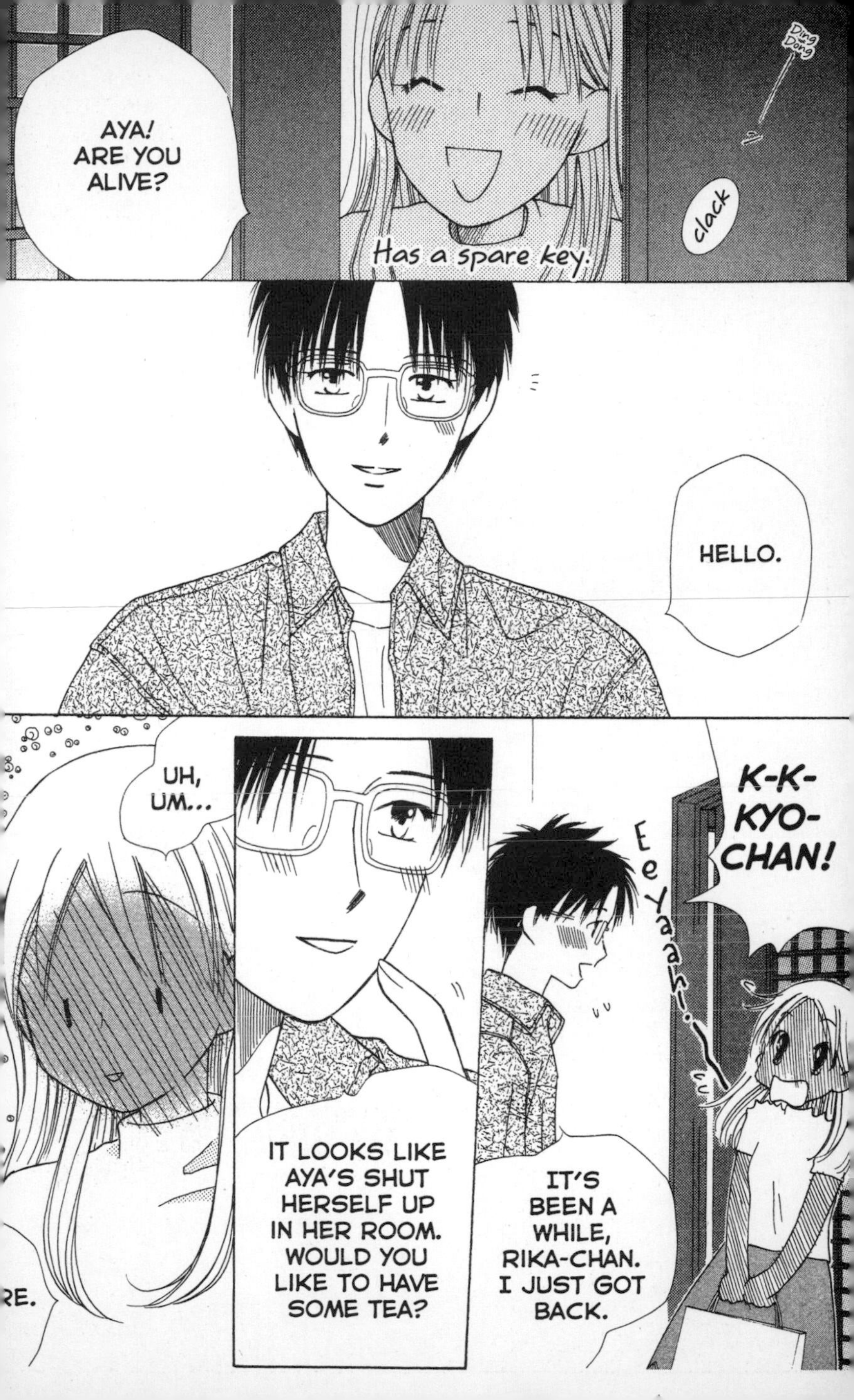
Ding Dong
clack
Has a spare key.
AYA! ARE YOU ALIVE?
HELLO.
K-K-KYO-CHAN!
IT'S BEEN A WHILE, RIKA-CHAN. I JUST GOT BACK.
IT LOOKS LIKE AYA'S SHUT HERSELF UP IN HER ROOM. WOULD YOU LIKE TO HAVE SOME TEA?
UH, UM...

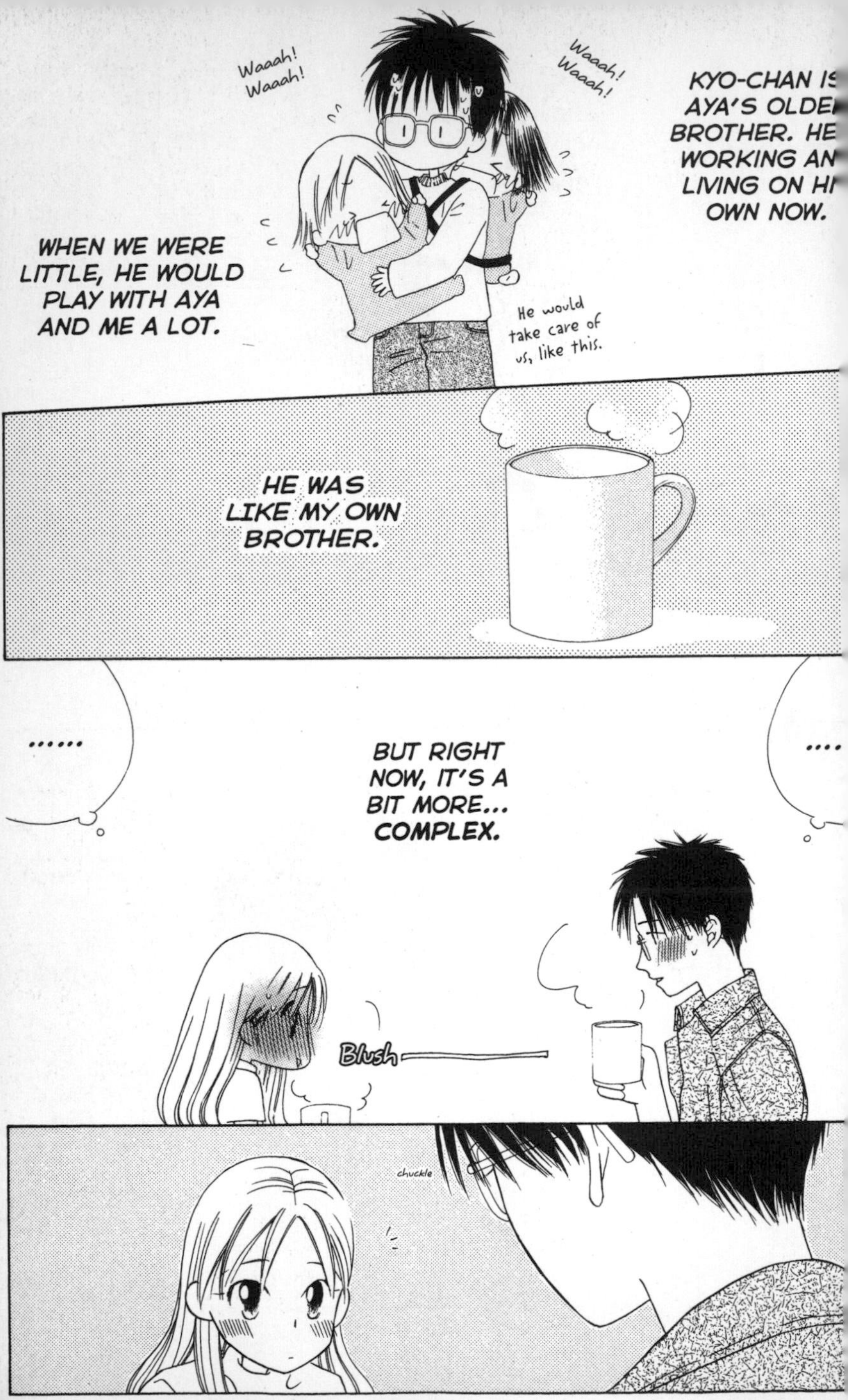
Waaah! Waaah!
KYO-CHAN IS AYA'S OLDE BROTHER. HE WORKING AN LIVING ON HI OWN NOW.
Waaah! Waaah!
WHEN WE WERE LITTLE, HE WOULD PLAY WITH AYA AND ME A LOT.
He would take care of us, like this.
HE WAS LIKE MY OWN BROTHER.
....
BUT RIGHT NOW, IT'S A BIT MORE... COMPLEX.
......
Blush
chuckle

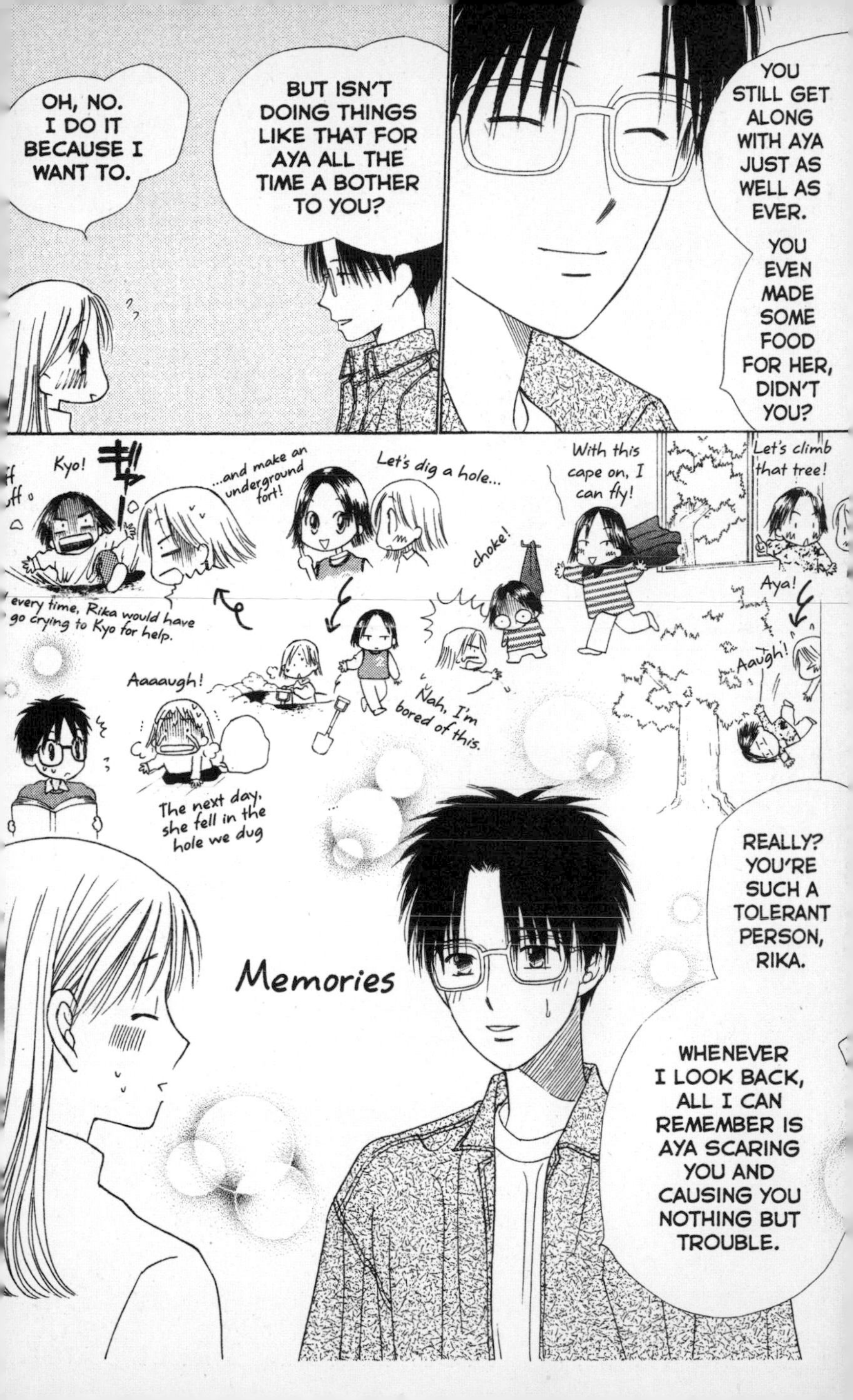
YOU STILL GET ALONG WITH AYA JUST AS WELL AS EVER.
YOU EVEN MADE SOME FOOD FOR HER, DIDN'T YOU?
BUT ISN'T DOING THINGS LIKE THAT FOR AYA ALL THE TIME A BOTHER TO YOU?
OH, NO. I DO IT BECAUSE I WANT TO.
Let's climb that tree!
Aya!
Aaugh!
With this cape on, I can fly!
choke!
Let's dig a hole...
...and make an underground fort!
Nah, I'm bored of this.
Kyo!
every time, Rika would have go crying to Kyo for help.
Aaaaugh!
The next day, she fell in the hole we dug
REALLY? YOU'RE SUCH A TOLERANT PERSON, RIKA.
Memories
WHENEVER I LOOK BACK, ALL I CAN REMEMBER IS AYA SCARING YOU AND CAUSING YOU NOTHING BUT TROUBLE.

5

Well then, Tsubasa and Kazuma's story comes safely to a close. And I know it's been a loooong time, but next we'll be going back to Yukino and Arima's story.

Yukino Arima

I've drawn some things here and there to use for the Arima Arc, and kept them nice and neat in a file. Some of it might get used for ads or something... Well anyway, this is what I want to draw most right now, so I'll do my best.

Masami Tsuda

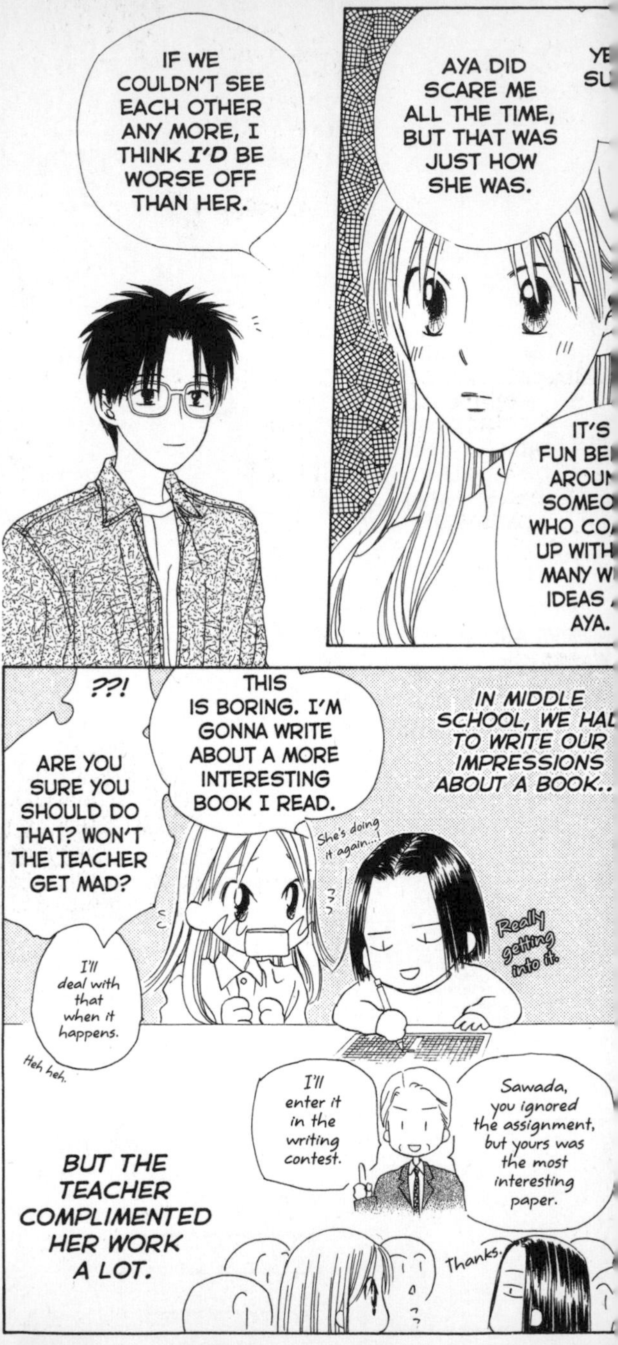
AYA DID SCARE ME ALL THE TIME, BUT THAT WAS JUST HOW SHE WAS.
IT'S FUN BE AROUN SOMEO WHO CO UP WITH MANY W IDEAS AYA.
IF WE COULDN'T SEE EACH OTHER ANY MORE, I THINK I'D BE WORSE OFF THAN HER.
IN MIDDLE SCHOOL, WE HA TO WRITE OUR IMPRESSIONS ABOUT A BOOK..
THIS IS BORING. I'M GONNA WRITE ABOUT A MORE INTERESTING BOOK I READ.
??!
ARE YOU SURE YOU SHOULD DO THAT? WON'T THE TEACHER GET MAD?
She's doing it again...!
Really getting into it.
I'll deal with that when it happens.
Heh heh.
Sawada, you ignored the assignment, but yours was the most interesting paper.
I'll enter it in the writing contest.
BUT THE TEACHER COMPLIMENTED HER WORK A LOT.
Thanks.

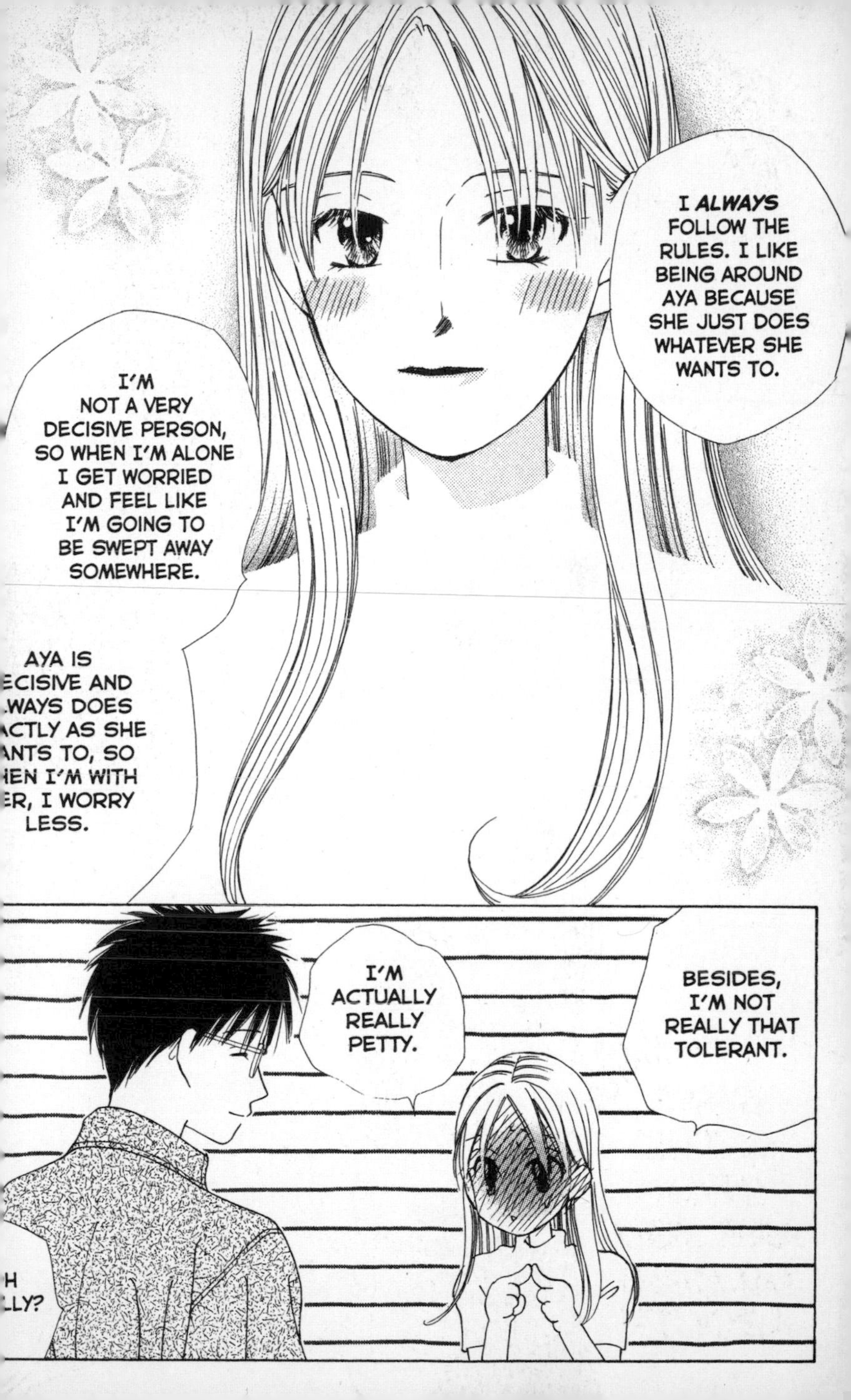
I *ALWAYS* FOLLOW THE RULES. I LIKE BEING AROUND AYA BECAUSE SHE JUST DOES WHATEVER SHE WANTS TO.
I'M NOT A VERY DECISIVE PERSON, SO WHEN I'M ALONE I GET WORRIED AND FEEL LIKE I'M GOING TO BE SWEPT AWAY SOMEWHERE.
AYA IS ECISIVE AND WAYS DOES CTLY AS SHE ANTS TO, SO HEN I'M WITH ER, I WORRY LESS.
BESIDES, I'M NOT REALLY THAT TOLERANT.
I'M ACTUALLY REALLY PETTY.
H LLY?

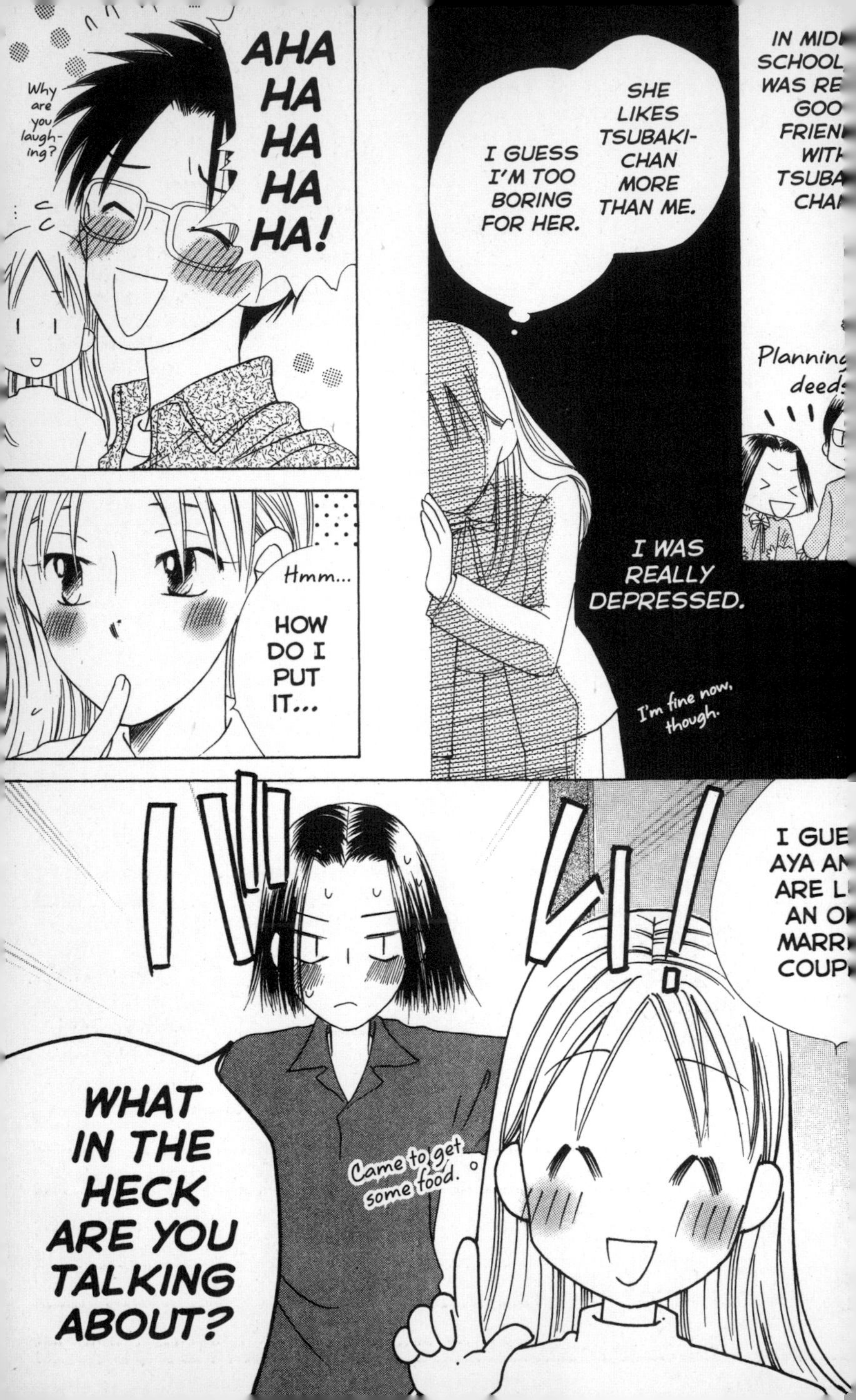

IN MID SCHOOL WAS RE GOO FRIEN WITH TSUBA CHA
Planning deeds
SHE LIKES TSUBAKI-CHAN MORE THAN ME.
I GUESS I'M TOO BORING FOR HER.
I WAS REALLY DEPRESSED.
I'm fine now, though.
AHA HA HA HA HA!
Why are you laughing?
Hmm...
HOW DO I PUT IT...
I GUE AYA AN ARE L AN O MARR COUP
WHAT IN THE HECK ARE YOU TALKING ABOUT?
Came to get some food.

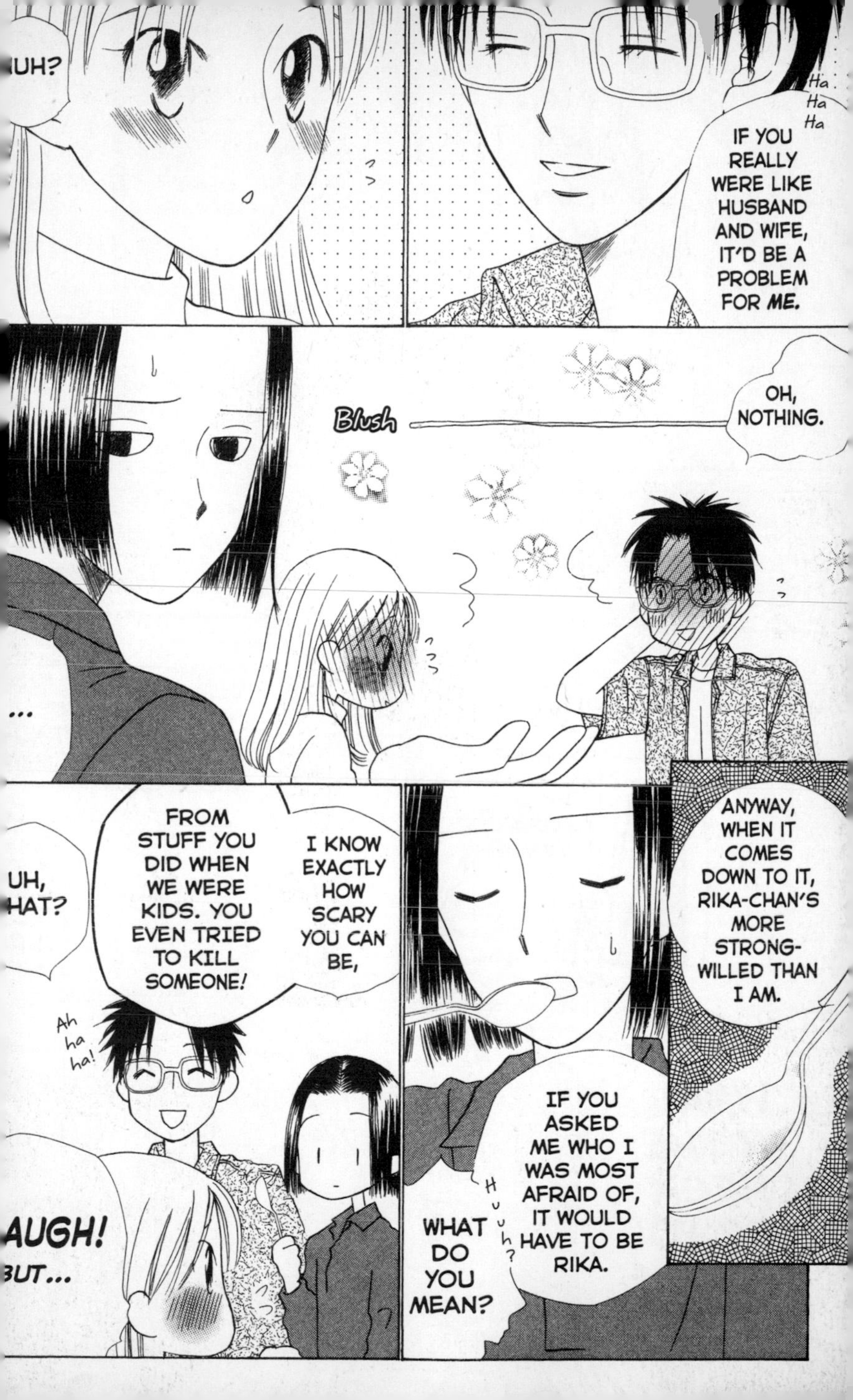
Ha Ha Ha
IF YOU REALLY WERE LIKE HUSBAND AND WIFE, IT'D BE A PROBLEM FOR ME.
UH?
OH, NOTHING.
Blush
...
ANYWAY, WHEN IT COMES DOWN TO IT, RIKA-CHAN'S MORE STRONG-WILLED THAN I AM.
IF YOU ASKED ME WHO I WAS MOST AFRAID OF, IT WOULD HAVE TO BE RIKA.
Huuh?
WHAT DO YOU MEAN?
I KNOW EXACTLY HOW SCARY YOU CAN BE,
FROM STUFF YOU DID WHEN WE WERE KIDS. YOU EVEN TRIED TO KILL SOMEONE!
Ah ha ha!
UH,
HAT?
AUGH!
BUT...

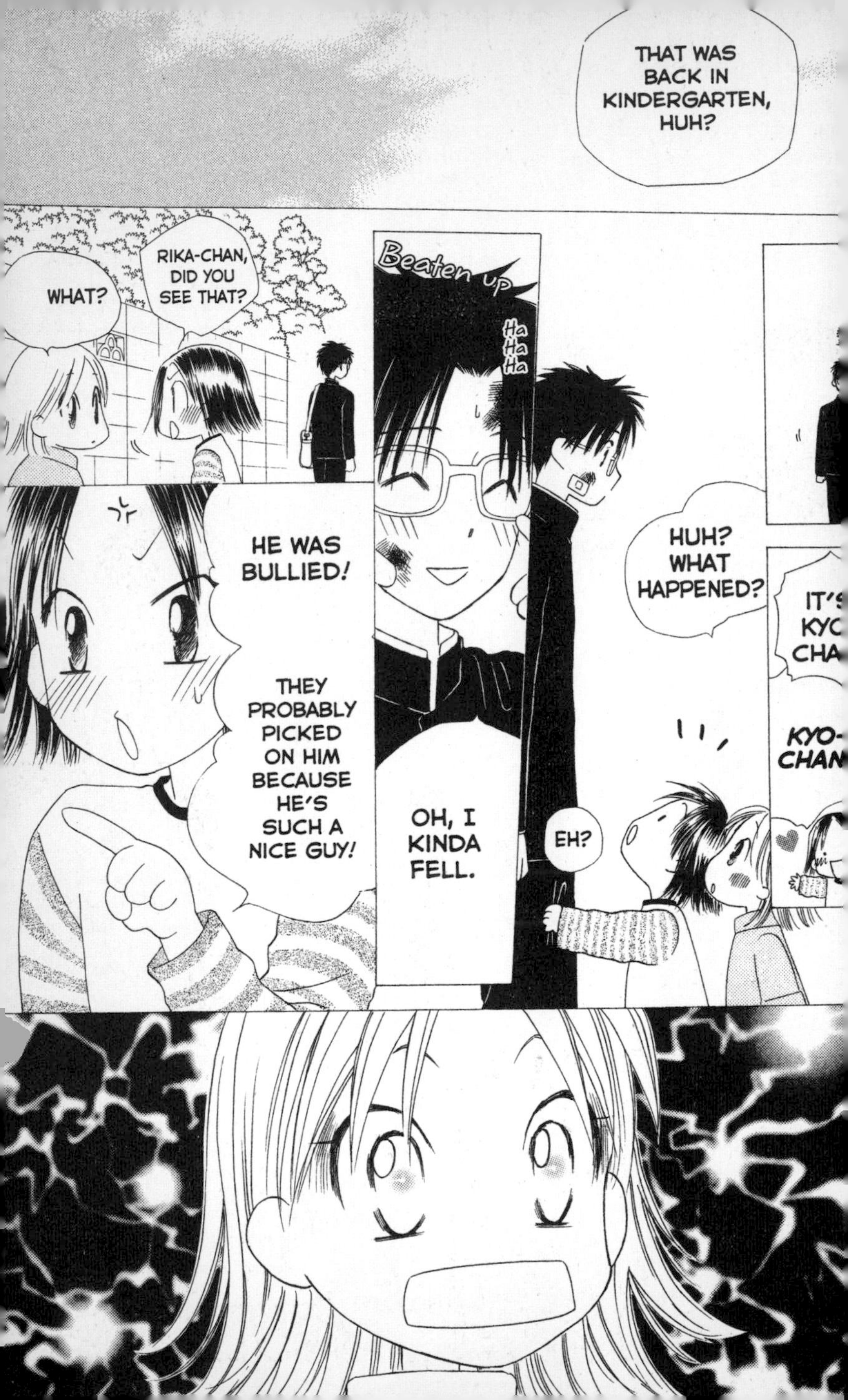
THAT WAS BACK IN KINDERGARTEN, HUH?
Beaten up
Ha Ha Ha
RIKA-CHAN, DID YOU SEE THAT?
WHAT?
HUH? WHAT HAPPENED?
EH?
OH, I KINDA FELL.
HE WAS BULLIED!
THEY PROBABLY PICKED ON HIM BECAUSE HE'S SUCH A NICE GUY!

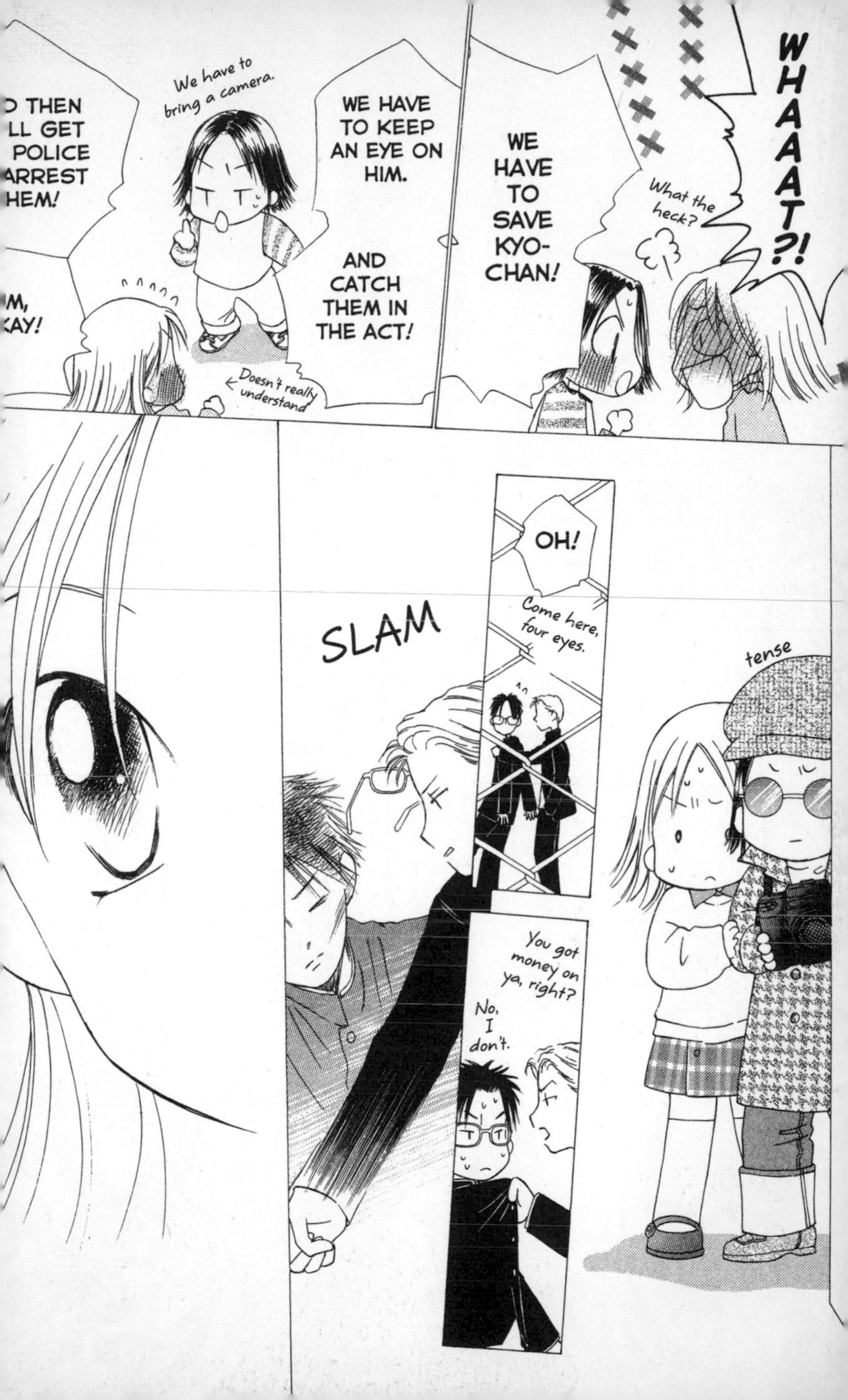
WHAAAT?!
What the heck?
WE HAVE TO SAVE KYO-CHAN!
WE HAVE TO KEEP AN EYE ON HIM.
AND CATCH THEM IN THE ACT!
We have to bring a camera.
Doesn't really understand
THEN LL GET POLICE ARREST HEM!
M, KAY!
tense
OH!
Come here, four eyes.
You got money on ya, right?
No, I don't.
SLAM

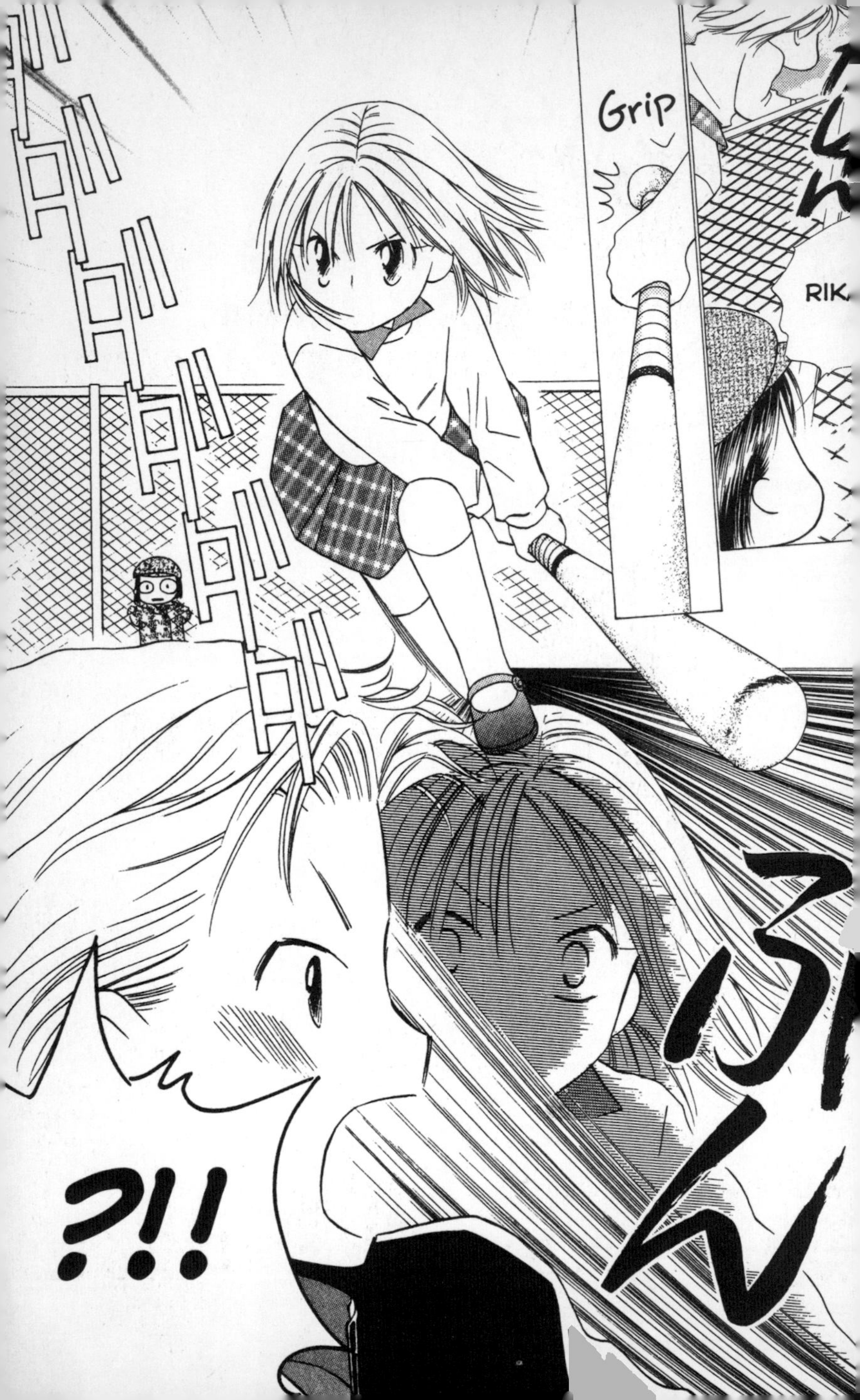

Grip
RIKA
?!!

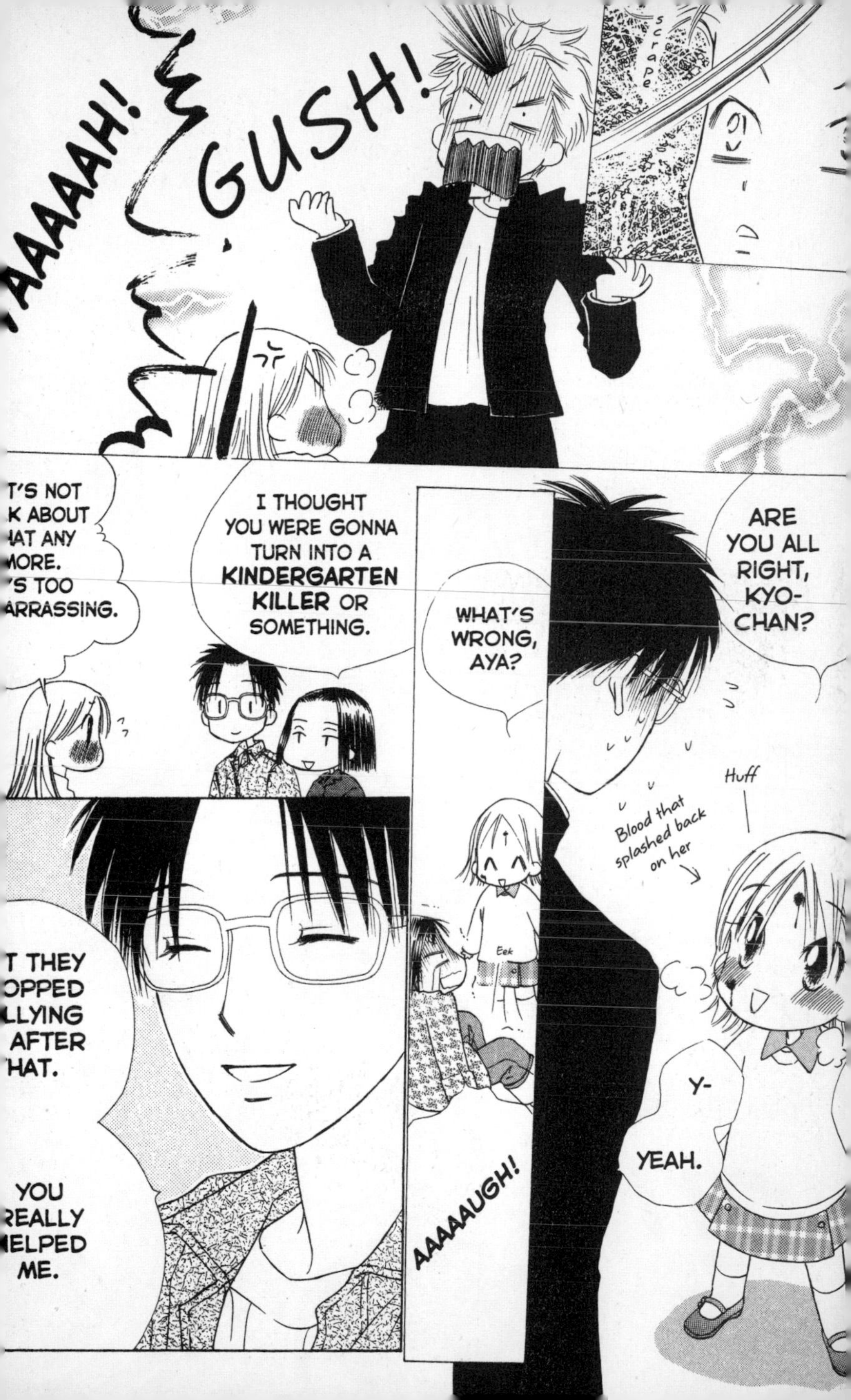
scrape
GUSH!
AAAAAH!
ARE YOU ALL RIGHT, KYO-CHAN?
WHAT'S WRONG, AYA?
I THOUGHT YOU WERE GONNA TURN INTO A KINDERGARTEN KILLER OR SOMETHING.
T'S NOT K ABOUT IAT ANY MORE. 'S TOO ARRASSING.
Huff
Blood that splashed back on her
Y-
YEAH.
Eek
AAAAAUGH!
T THEY OPPED LLYING AFTER HAT.
YOU EALLY ELPED ME.

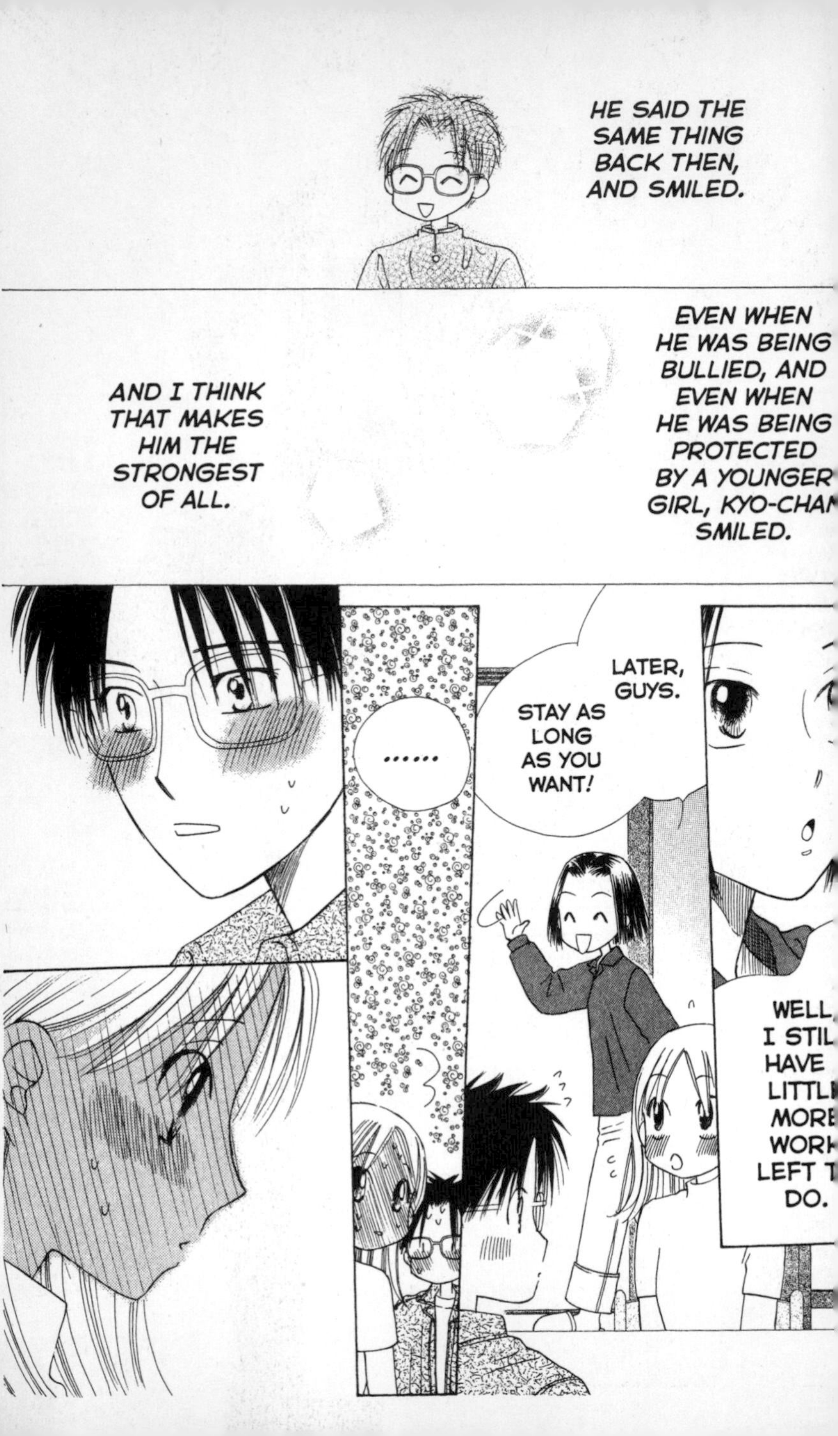

HE SAID THE SAME THING BACK THEN, AND SMILED.
EVEN WHEN HE WAS BEING BULLIED, AND EVEN WHEN HE WAS BEING PROTECTED BY A YOUNGER GIRL, KYO-CHA SMILED.
AND I THINK THAT MAKES HIM THE STRONGEST OF ALL.
WELL, I STIL HAVE LITTL MORE WOR LEFT T DO.
LATER, GUYS.
STAY AS LONG AS YOU WANT!
......

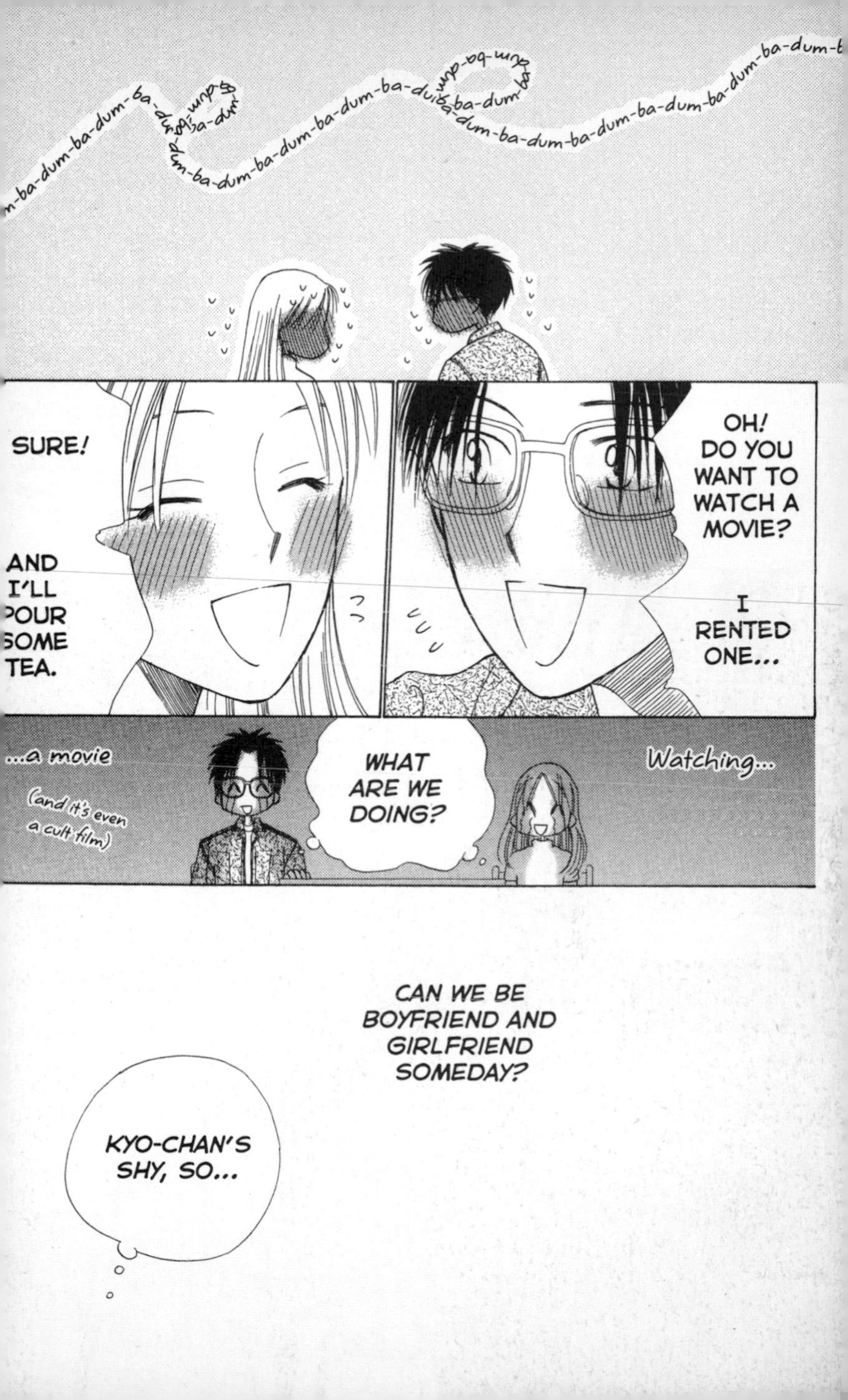
ba-dum-ba-dum-ba-dum-ba-dum-ba-dum
OH! DO YOU WANT TO WATCH A MOVIE?
I RENTED ONE...
SURE!
AND I'LL POUR SOME TEA.
Watching...
WHAT ARE WE DOING?
...a movie
(and it's even a cult film)
CAN WE BE BOYFRIEND AND GIRLFRIEND SOMEDAY?
KYO-CHAN'S SHY, SO...

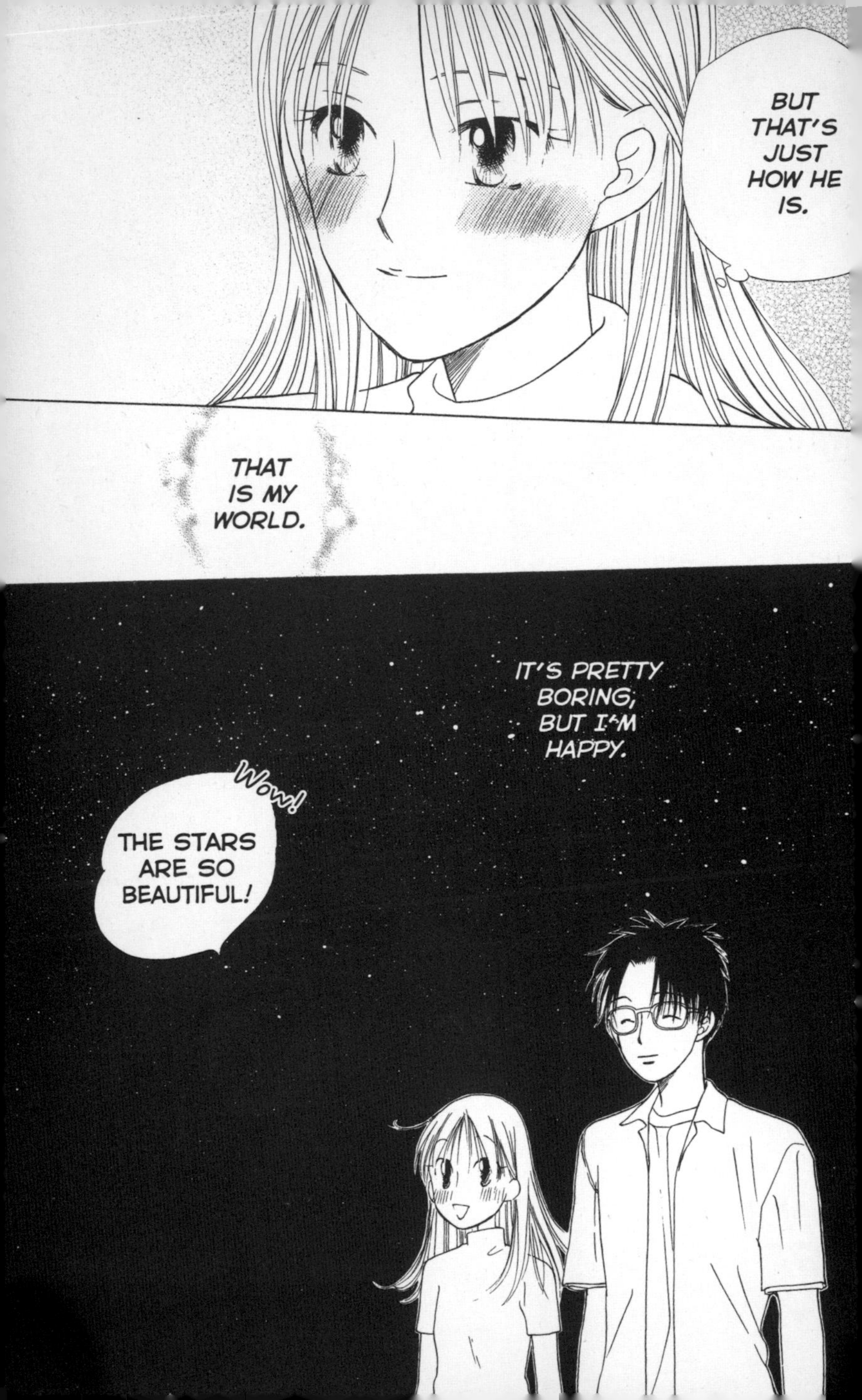
BUT THAT'S JUST HOW HE IS.
THAT IS MY WORLD.
IT'S PRETTY BORING, BUT I'M HAPPY.
Wow!
THE STARS ARE SO BEAUTIFUL!

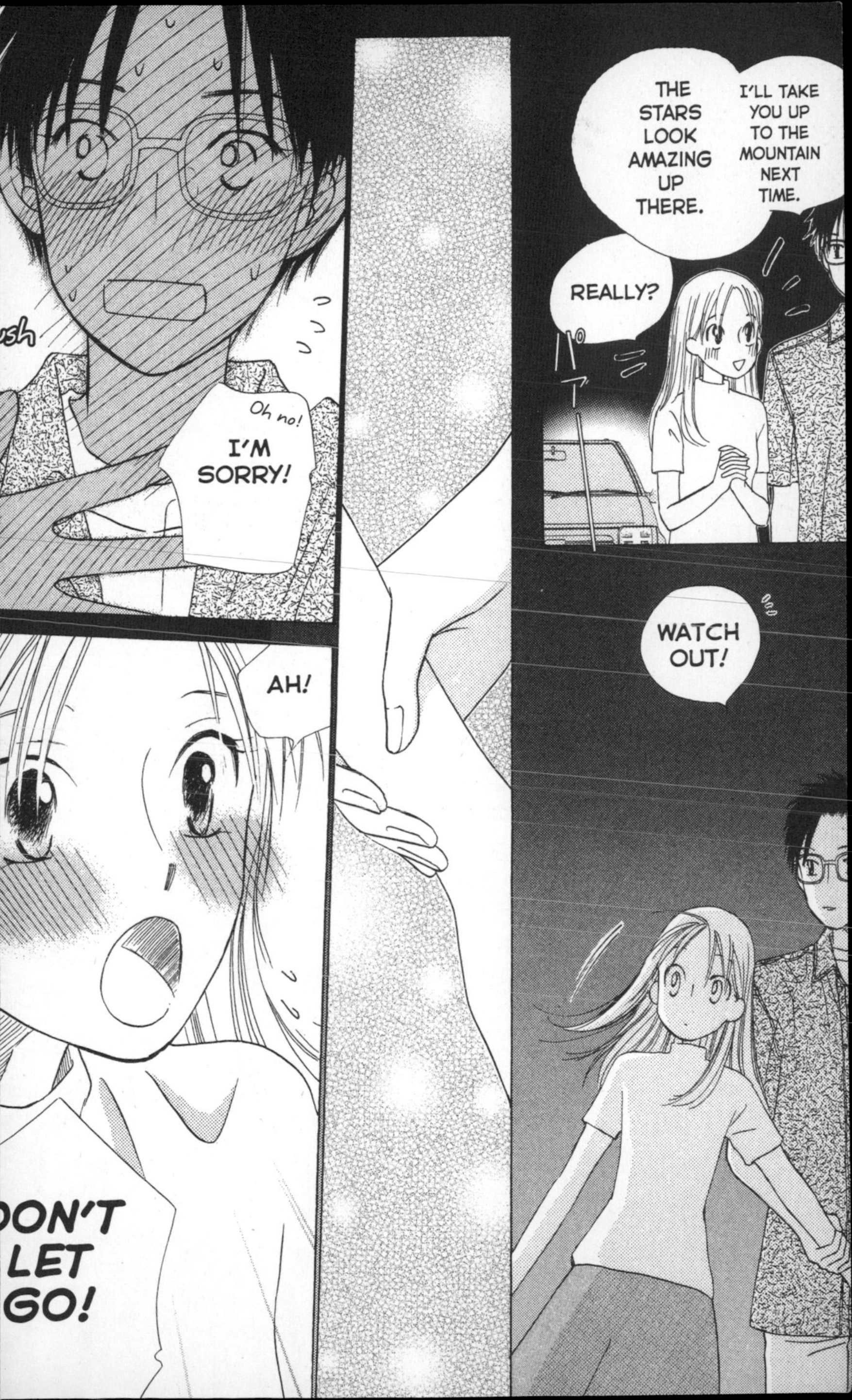
I'LL TAKE YOU UP TO THE MOUNTAIN NEXT TIME.
THE STARS LOOK AMAZING UP THERE.
REALLY?
WATCH OUT!
Oh no!
I'M SORRY!
AH!
DON'T LET GO!

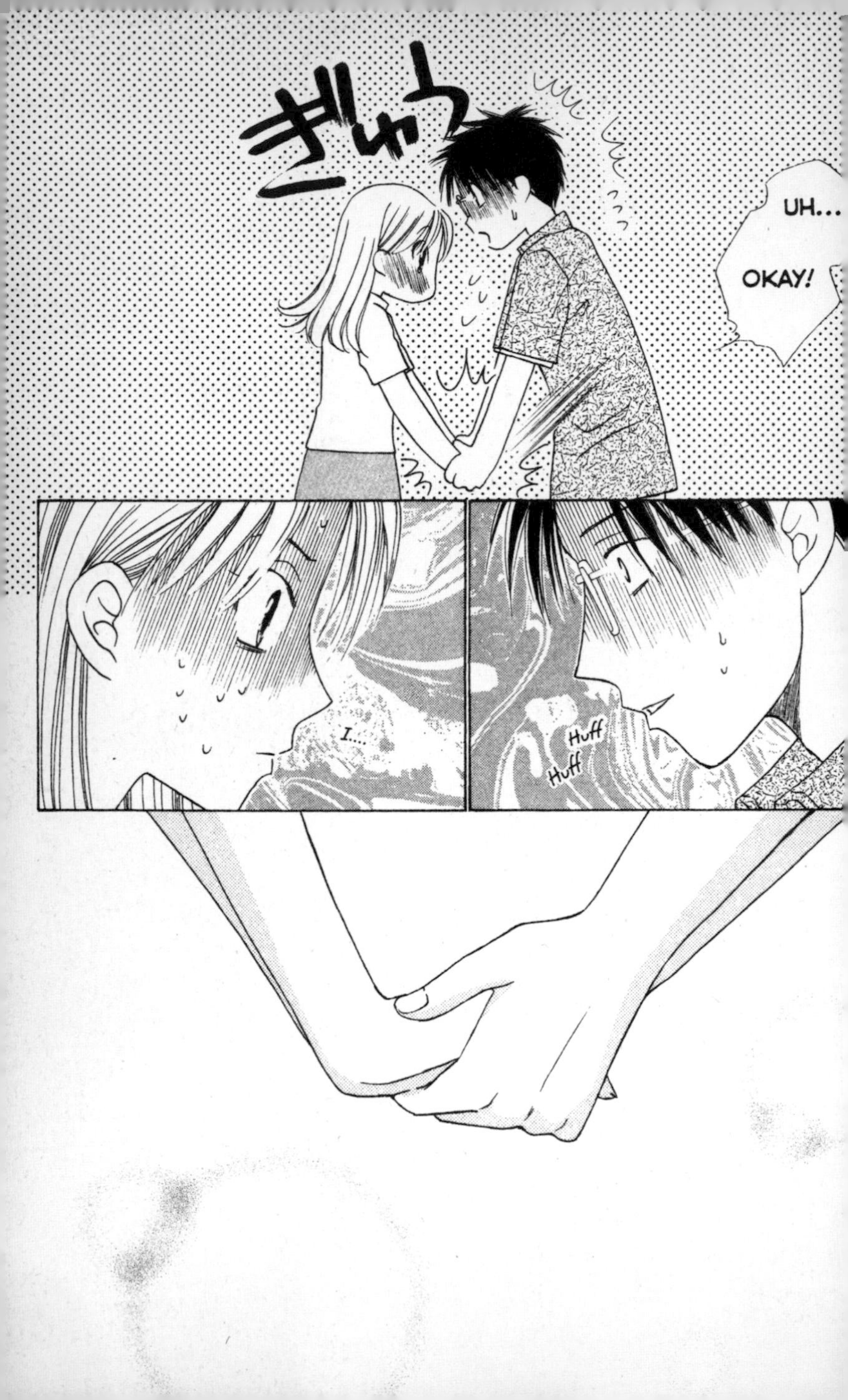
UH... OKAY!
ぎゅう
Huff
Huff
I...

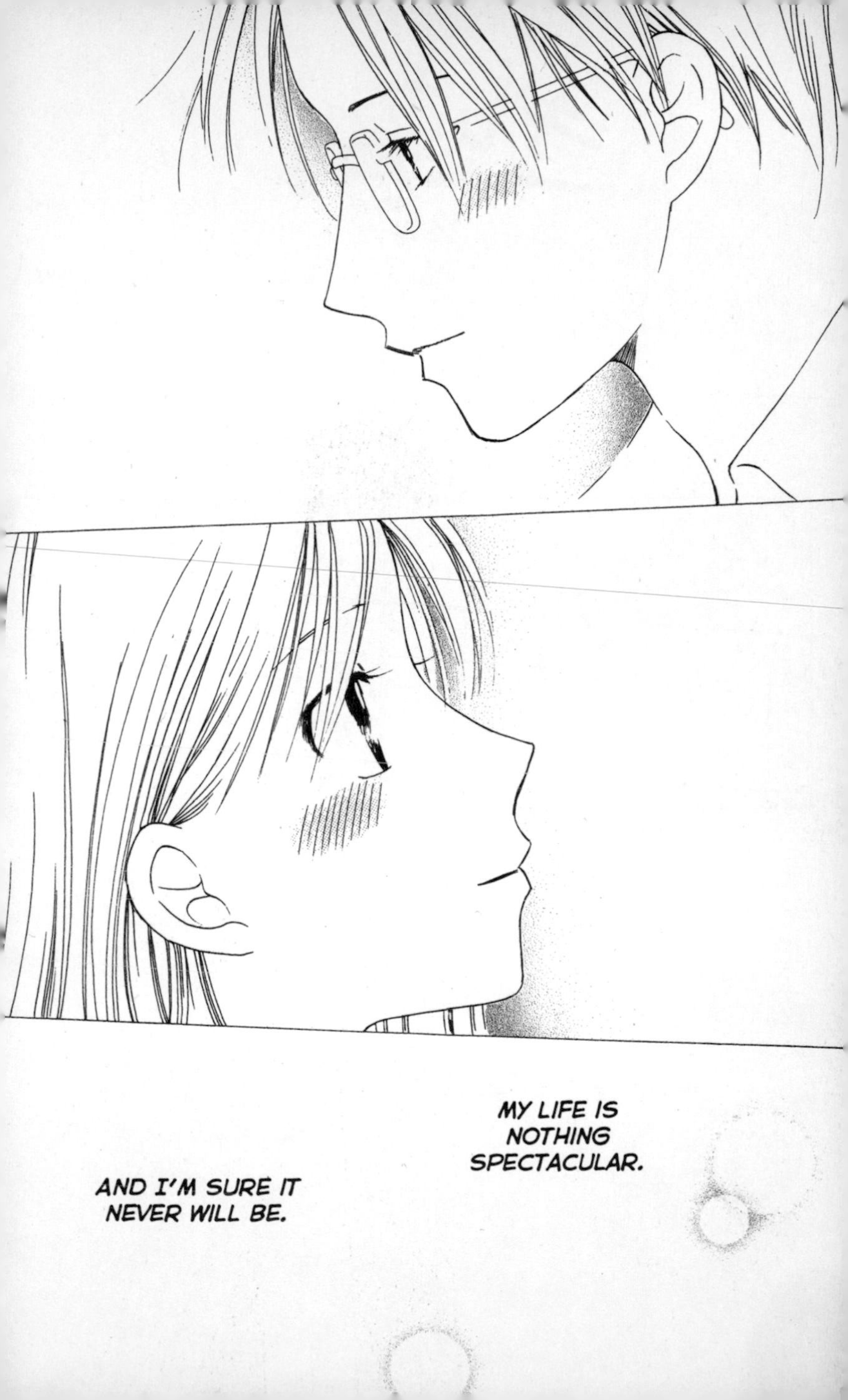
MY LIFE IS NOTHING SPECTACULAR.
AND I'M SURE IT NEVER WILL BE.

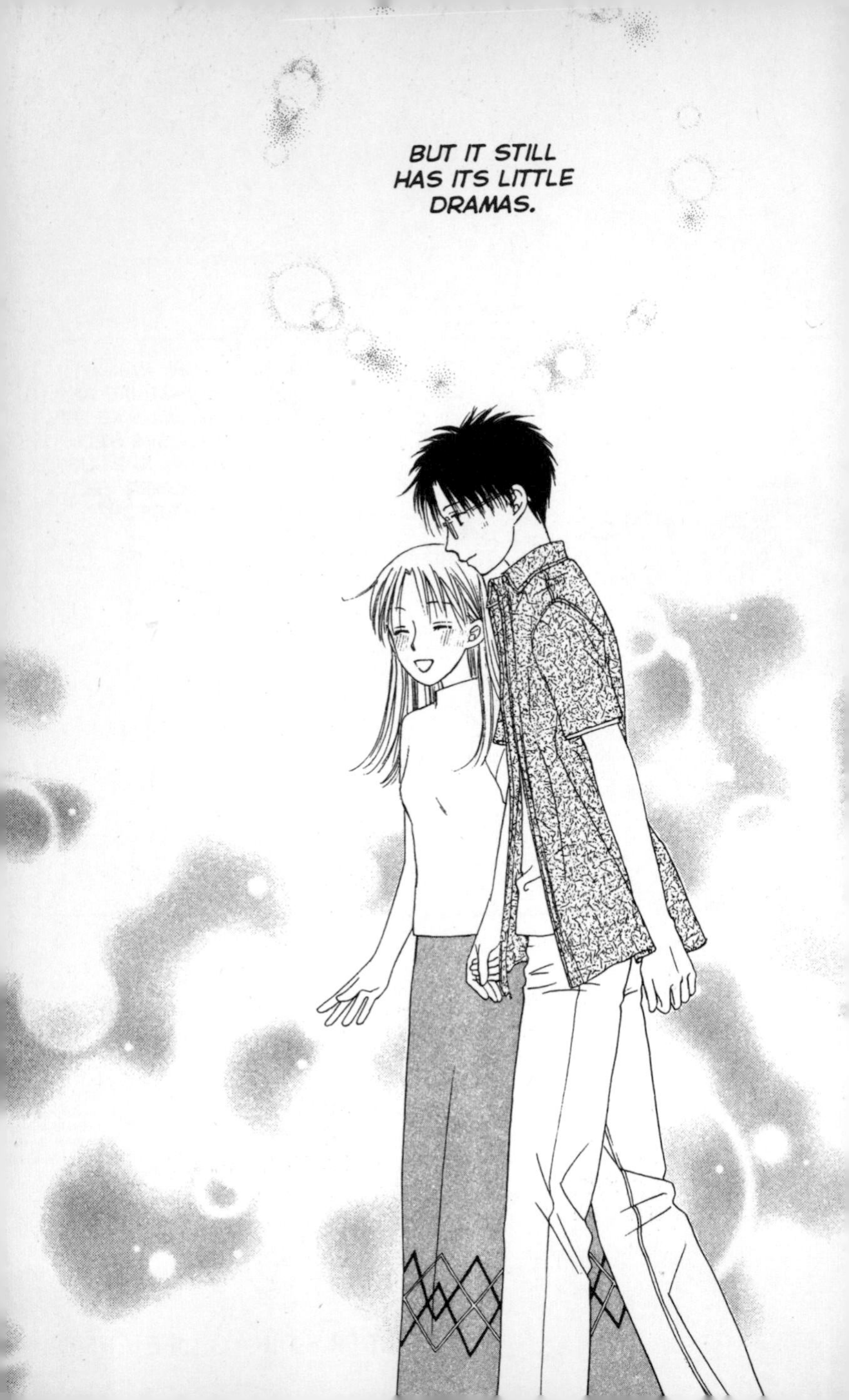
BUT IT STILL HAS ITS LITTLE DRAMAS.

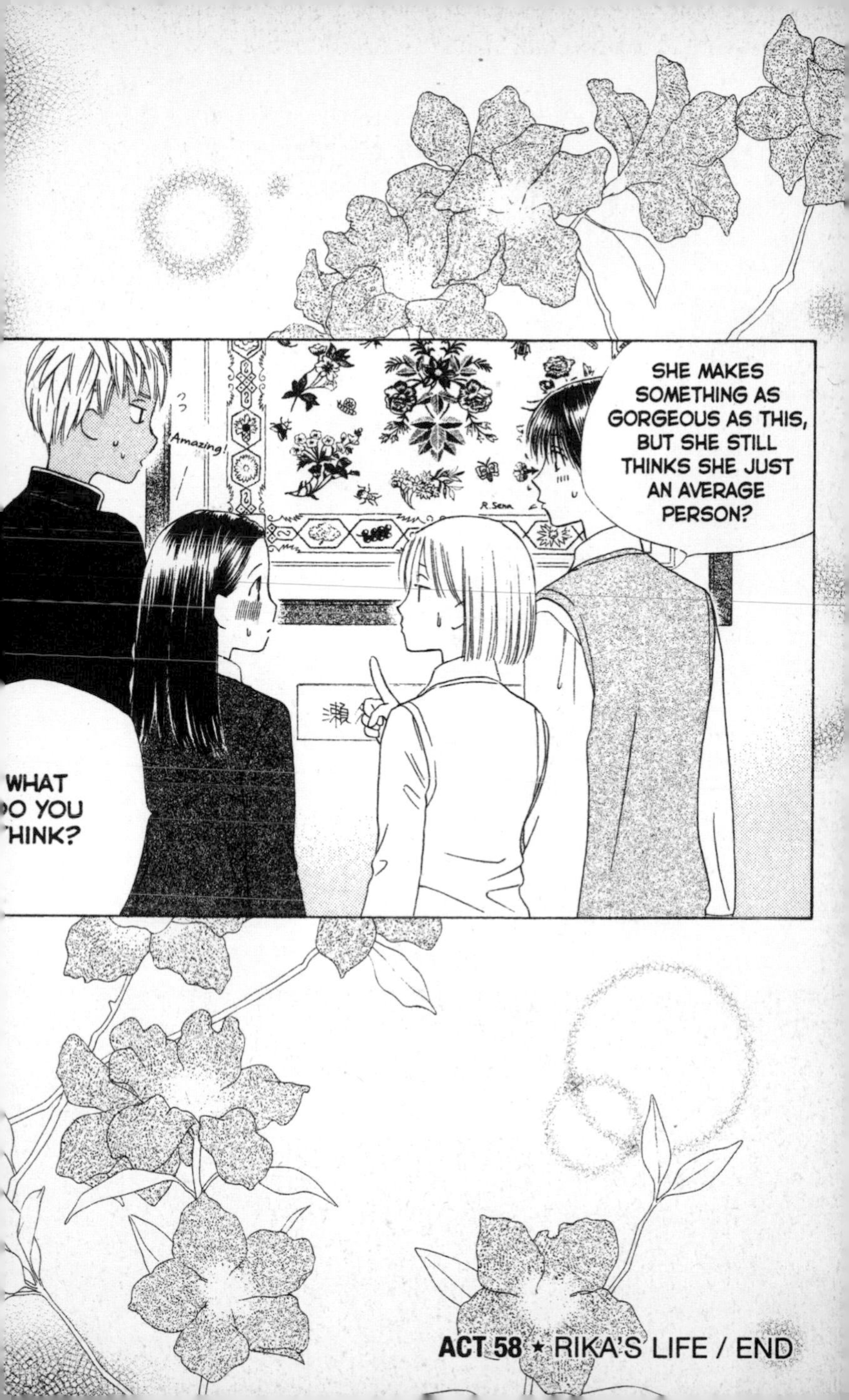
SHE MAKES SOMETHING AS GORGEOUS AS THIS, BUT SHE STILL THINKS SHE JUST AN AVERAGE PERSON?
R. Sena
瀬
Amazing!
WHAT O YOU HINK?
ACT 58 ★ RIKA'S LIFE / END

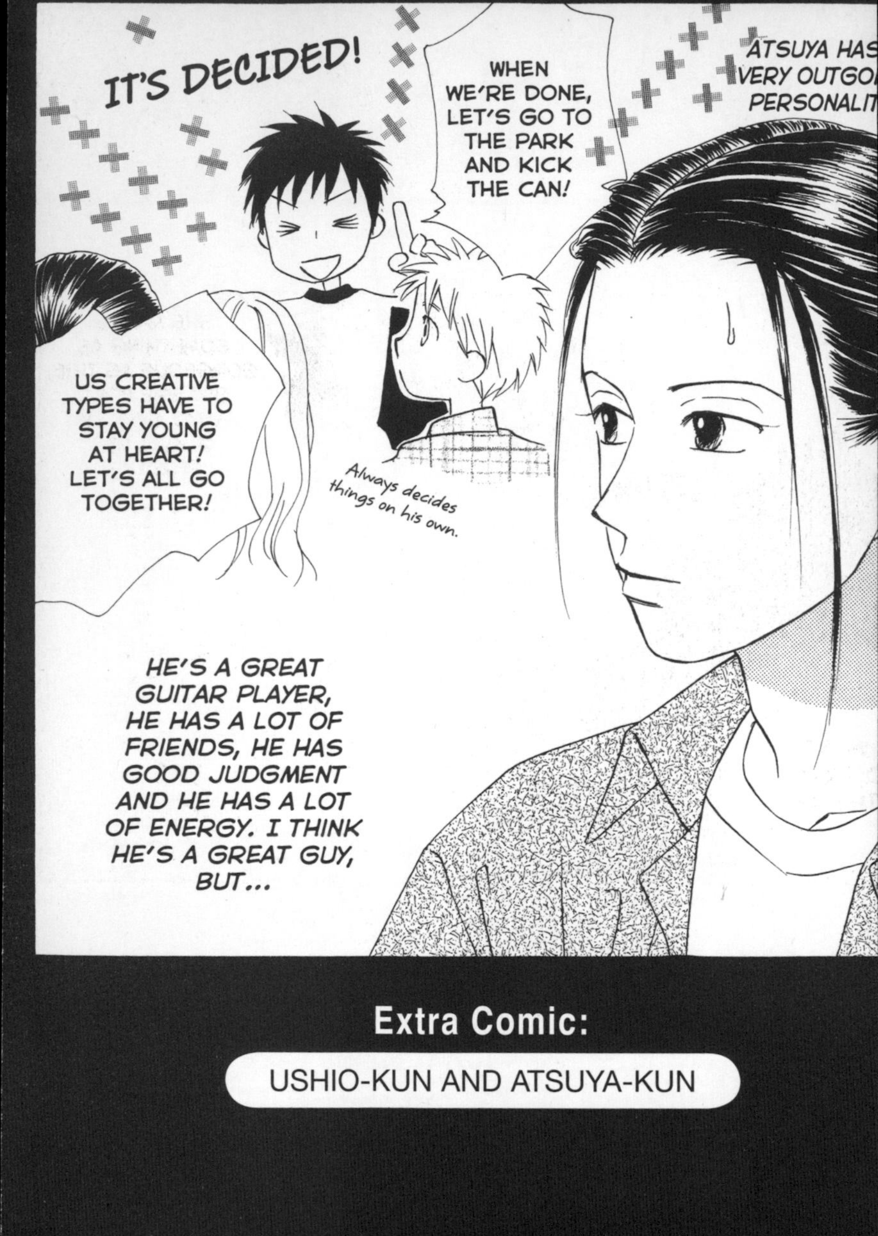
ATSUYA HAS VERY OUTGO PERSONALIT
WHEN WE'RE DONE, LET'S GO TO THE PARK AND KICK THE CAN!
IT'S DECIDED!
US CREATIVE TYPES HAVE TO STAY YOUNG AT HEART! LET'S ALL GO TOGETHER!
Always decides things on his own.
HE'S A GREAT GUITAR PLAYER, HE HAS A LOT OF FRIENDS, HE HAS GOOD JUDGMENT AND HE HAS A LOT OF ENERGY. I THINK HE'S A GREAT GUY, BUT...

Extra Comic:

USHIO-KUN AND ATSUYA-KUN

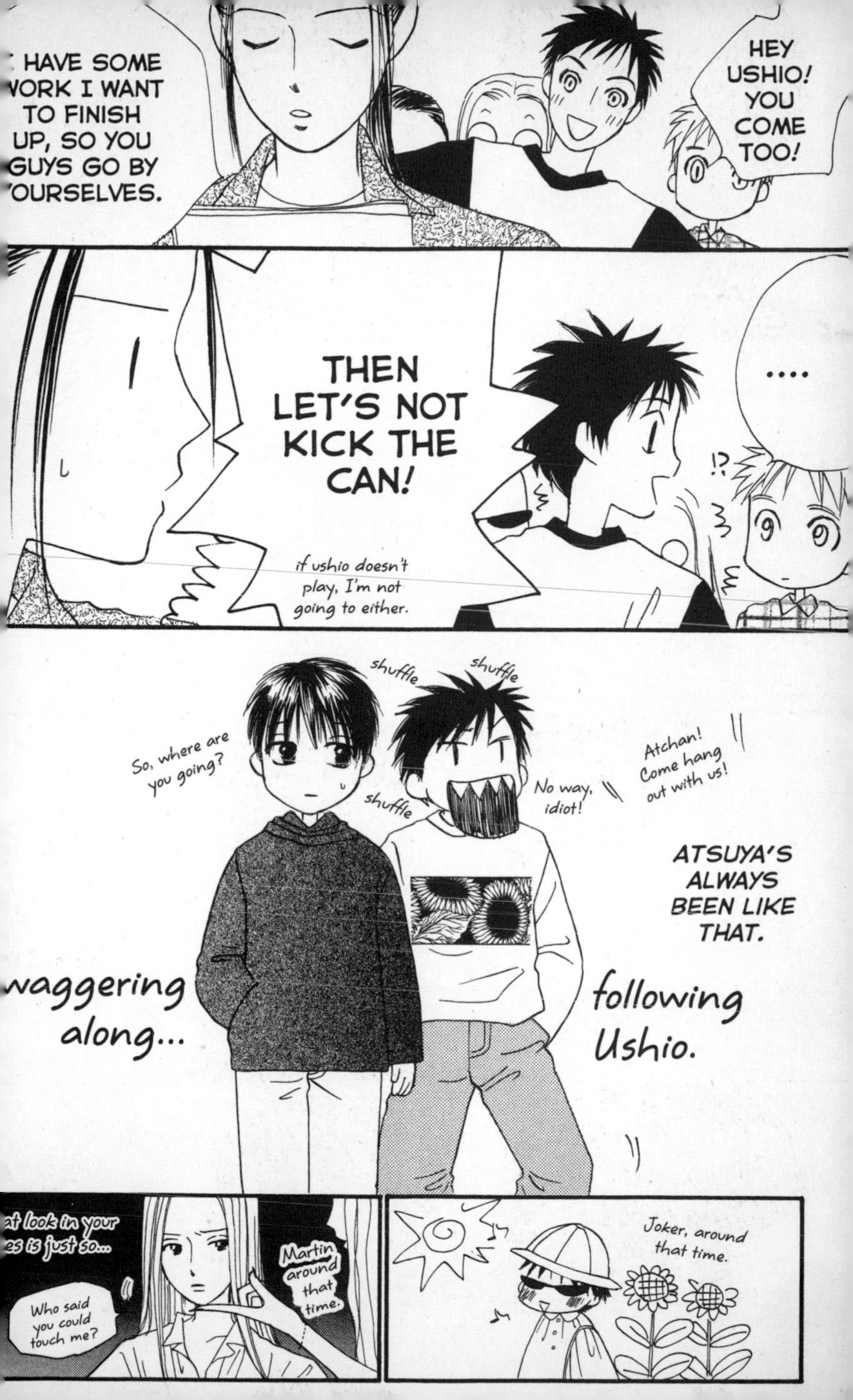
HEY USHIO! YOU COME TOO!
HAVE SOME VORK I WANT TO FINISH UP, SO YOU GUYS GO BY OURSELVES.
....
!?
THEN LET'S NOT KICK THE CAN!
if ushio doesn't play, I'm not going to either.
Atchan! Come hang out with us!
No way, idiot!
shuffle
shuffle
shuffle
So, where are you going?
ATSUYA'S ALWAYS BEEN LIKE THAT.
following Ushio.
waggering along...
Joker, around that time.
Martin around that time.
at look in your es is just so...
Who said you could touch me?

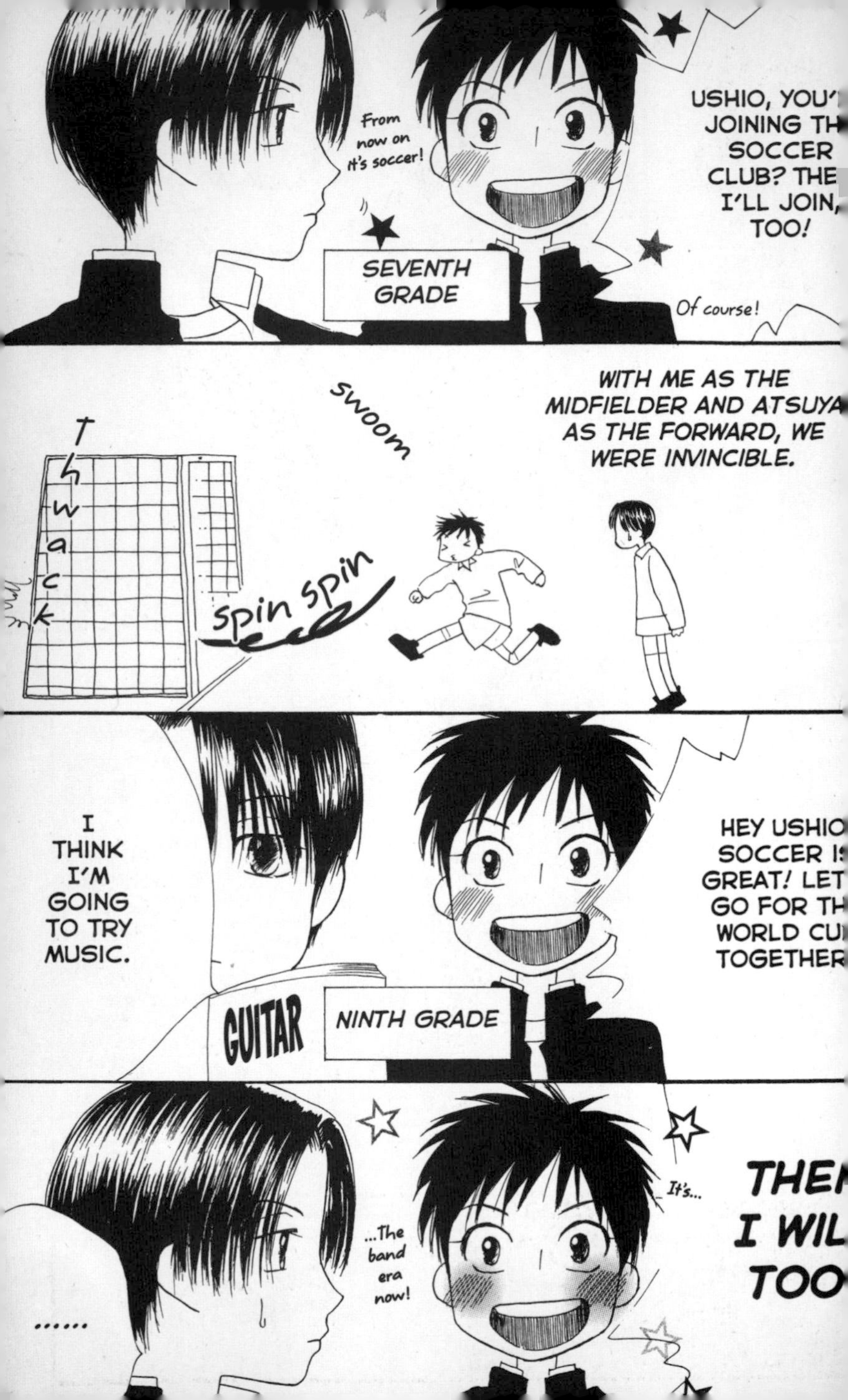

USHIO, YOU' JOINING TH SOCCER CLUB? THE I'LL JOIN, TOO!
Of course!
From now on it's soccer!
SEVENTH GRADE
WITH ME AS THE MIDFIELDER AND ATSUYA AS THE FORWARD, WE WERE INVINCIBLE.
swoom
spin spin
thwack
HEY USHIO SOCCER I GREAT! LET GO FOR TH WORLD CU TOGETHER
NINTH GRADE
GUITAR
I THINK I'M GOING TO TRY MUSIC.
THE I WIL TOO
It's...
...The band era now!
......

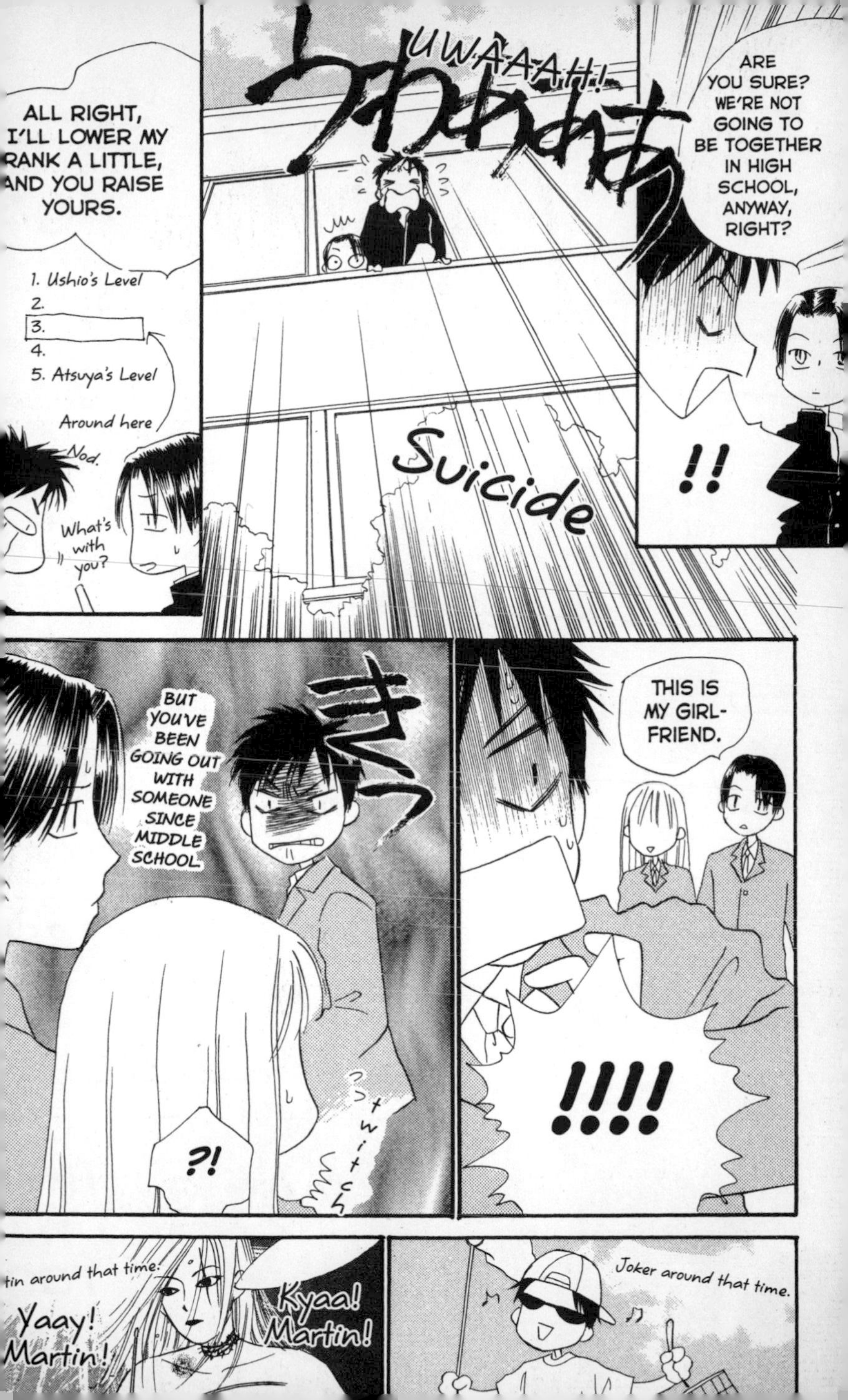
ARE YOU SURE? WE'RE NOT GOING TO BE TOGETHER IN HIGH SCHOOL, ANYWAY, RIGHT?
!!
UWAAAH!
Suicide
ALL RIGHT, I'LL LOWER MY RANK A LITTLE, AND YOU RAISE YOURS.
1. Ushio's Level
2.
3.
4.
5. Atsuya's Level
Around here
Nod.
What's with you?
THIS IS MY GIRL-FRIEND.
!!!!
BUT YOU'VE BEEN GOING OUT WITH SOMEONE SINCE MIDDLE SCHOOL.
?!
twitch
Joker around that time.
tin around that time.
Kyaa! Martin!
Yaay! Martin!

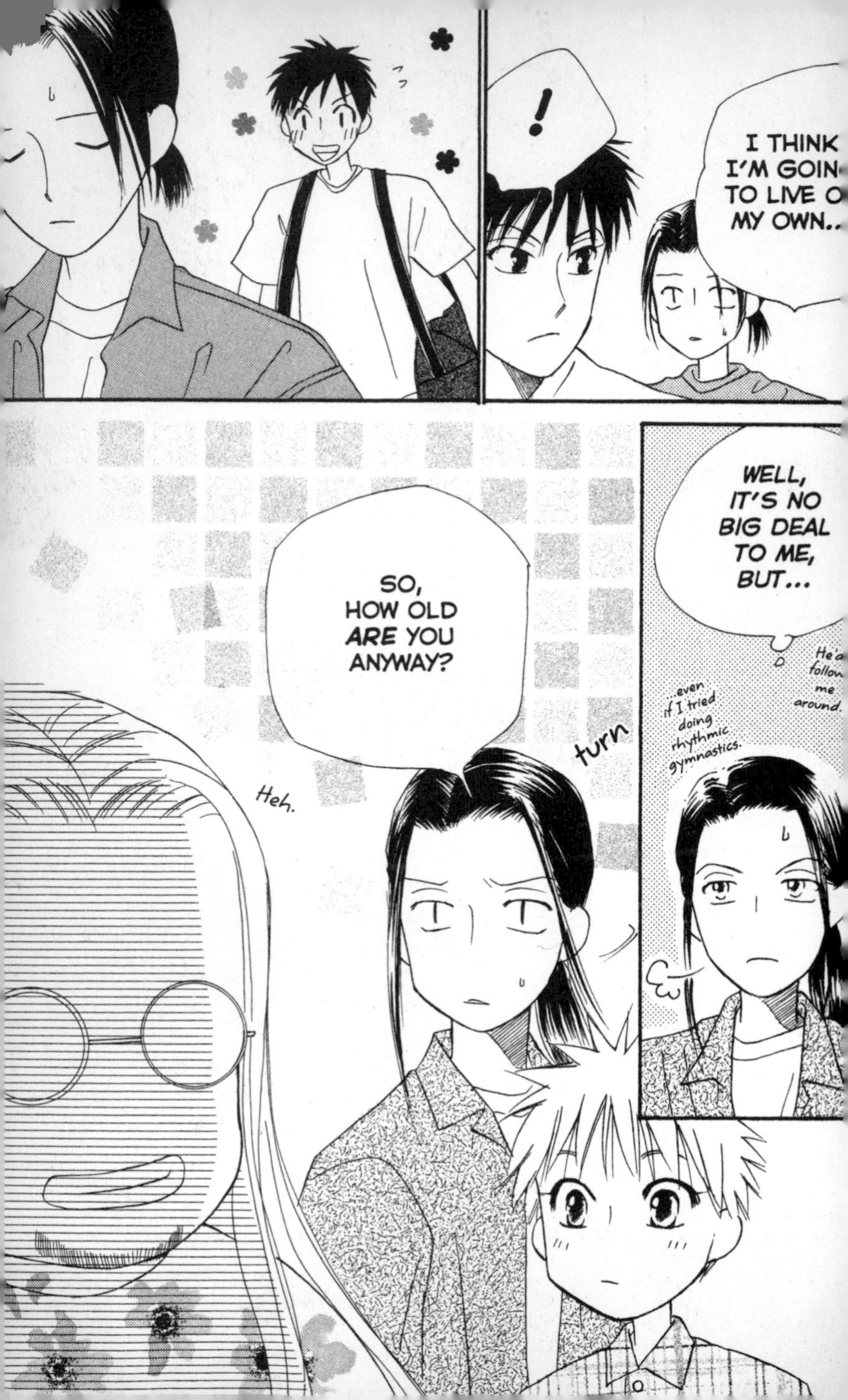
I THINK I'M GOIN TO LIVE O MY OWN..
WELL, IT'S NO BIG DEAL TO ME, BUT...
...even if I tried doing rhythmic gymnastics.
SO, HOW OLD ARE YOU ANYWAY?
turn
Heh.

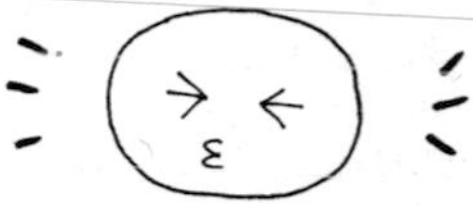

Thanks to the following people:

Editor S. Taneoka

Staff N. Shimizu
R. Ogawa
Y. Etō
R. Takahashi

AND K. U.

coming soon

kare kano
his and her circumstances

volume thirteen

It's the end of high school, and everyone is looking toward the future--especially Soichiro Arima. He's got it going on: good grades, great body, and all the popularity! However, there is much more to Soichiro than meets the eye. This model student is plagued by inner demons, which force him to look at Yukino in a whole new light. Will he end his relationship with his one true love?

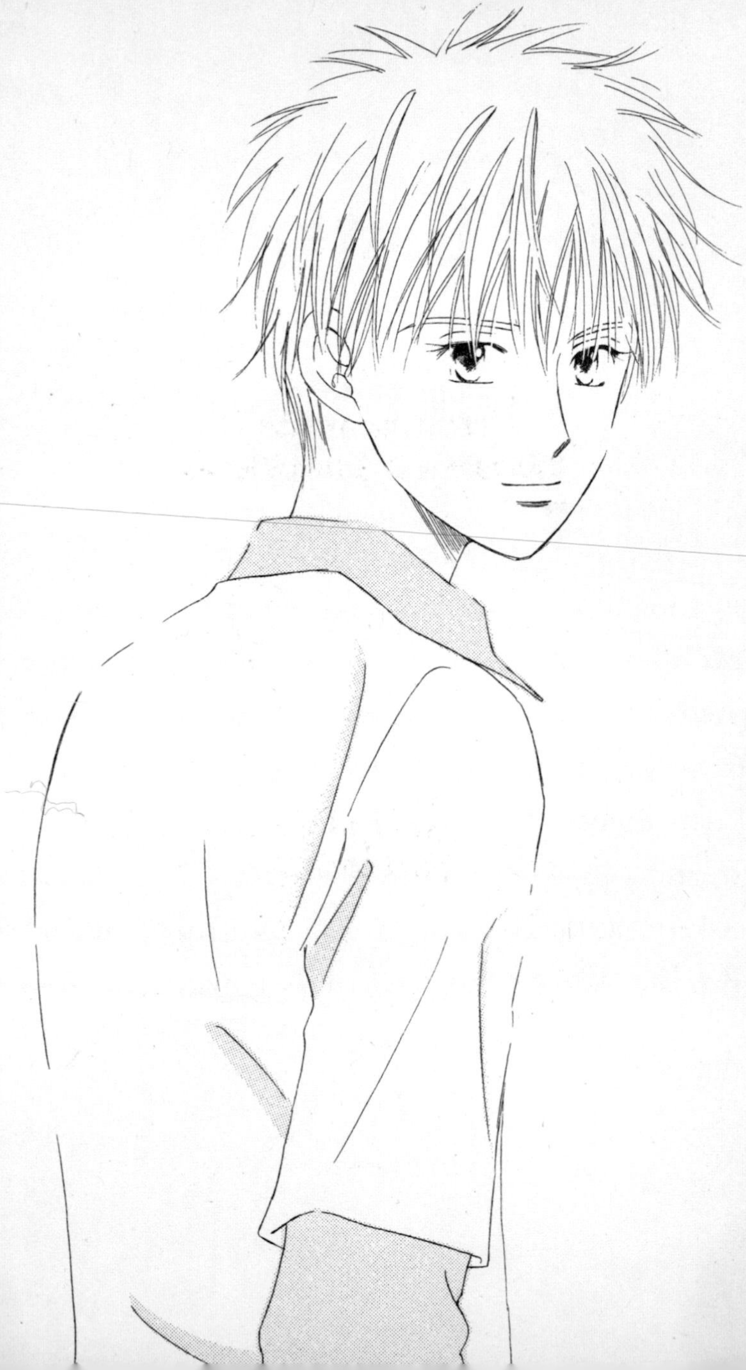

Masami Tsuda
Interview & Short Works

PEROPERO THE DOG

Part 2 of a 2
part series

...out Kare Kano

...e thing that people love about Kare Kano is the unique "pauses." I would say that ...y give the work a mysterious atmosphere and tempo. What are your thoughts on ...s?

...l myself, "I want to give off a certain atmosphere," but in reality, it isn't that simple. ...arding the pauses you mention, I think it's like music—I'm trying to set a laid back tempo ...t sets a certain mood.

..."are Kano" is in the second half of its run. When it was decided that it would be a ...g-term serialization, was it also decided how long the story would go until? At that ...nt in time, had you already decided on the ending?

...ause I could see that the story was going in a certain direction, the general path the ...y would take was decided in one fell swoop. Little by little I've gotten down the scenes ...t I've really wanted to draw. At this point, I've drawn ... of those scenes but I'm definitely looking forward ...he years when I can draw everything else I've got ...nned.

...ce it's been decided that "Kare Kano" will go ...g-term serialization, there's been an increase of ...aracters. But at the start, who was the very first ...aracter you created?

...ba-kun. But, when I think about it, right now I don't ...e a single memory of how he was first conceptualized. ...t's because I kept practically no record of it.

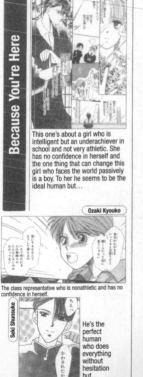

Because You're Here

This one's about a girl who is intelligent but an underachiever in school and not very athletic. She has no confidence in herself and the one thing that can change this girl who faces the world passively is a boy. To her he seems to be the ideal human but...

Ozaki Kyouko

The class representative who is nonathletic and has no confidence in herself.

Seki Shunsuke

He's the perfect human who does everything without hesitation but...

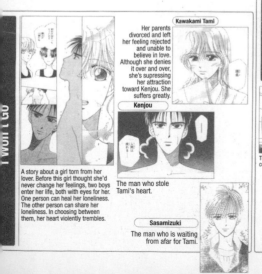

I Won't Go

A story about a girl torn from her lover. Before this girl thought she'd never change her feelings, two boys enter her life, both with eyes for her. One person can heal her loneliness. The other person can share her loneliness. In choosing between them, her heart violently trembles.

Kawakami Tami

Her parents divorced and left her feeling rejected and unable to believe in love. Although she denies it over and over, she's supressing her attraction toward Kenjou. She suffers greatly.

Kenjou

The man who stole Tami's heart.

Sasamizuki

The man who is waiting from afar for Tami.

When Kazuma appeared, Tsubasa Shibahime was rescued. On the other hand, the m Arima Souichiro falls in love with Miyazawa Yukino the more insecure he becomes. What exactly is the difference between these two?

The depth of their darkness. Tsubasa-san's existence was blessed from the start but Arima kun is quite the opposite.

As "Kare Kano" goes on, many different characters have appeared. But for you, Tsud sensei, what kind of people do you admire?

Professionals. I have a weakness for working people...firefighters, policemen, nurses... (It's little messy when it comes to doctors because there are some that really irk me...) Chefs a also good. Lawyers. Construction workers are also pretty hot... (♡) I also fall head over he for working women. I like people who have pride and always inspire!

Of the various characters you've spotlighted, I feel that only Asaba Hideaki has yet t be fully explored. Is there a possibility that his situation (his past, present condition and thoughts) will be written about?

That's coming up actually. He's one guy I really want to write about. Heh heh heh heh.

Why was the first song written for Tsubasa Shibahime the kind of song it was?

She's the type of person who still has the heart of a child; perhaps for her entire life!

Why does Maho Isawa want to become a brain surge

The idea just sorta popped into my head: "A female doctor!" Of course this author may have been inserting my own pipe-dreams: "I want to solve the riddles of the brain, and if I were smarter, I want to do brain research." like the grotesque combination of a beautiful woman in a doctor's coat.

The Room That An Angel Inhabits

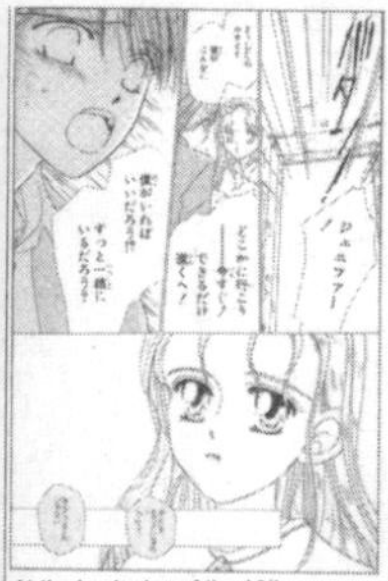

At the beginning of the 19th century in some corner of England, a young boy and girl live quietly together. It's just like playing house, but with serious love. But an encounter between the boy and a gentleman sets the wheels of fate turning into confusion… A work that portrays the two extremes of money and love.

Jennifer

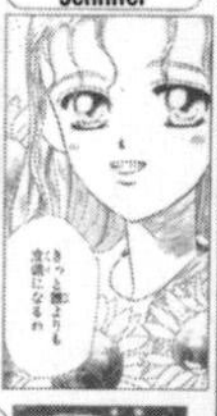

The orphan that Louie picked up.

Louie

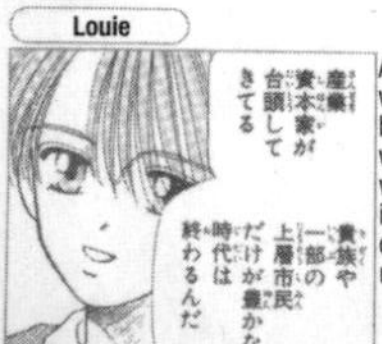

A wise boy who works in the coal mine.

Bertram S. Ashby

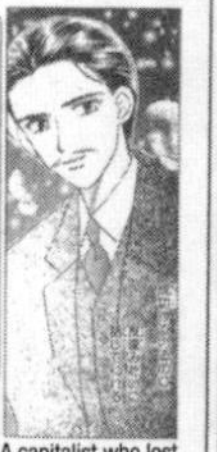

A capitalist who lost his daughter.

Awkward Relationship

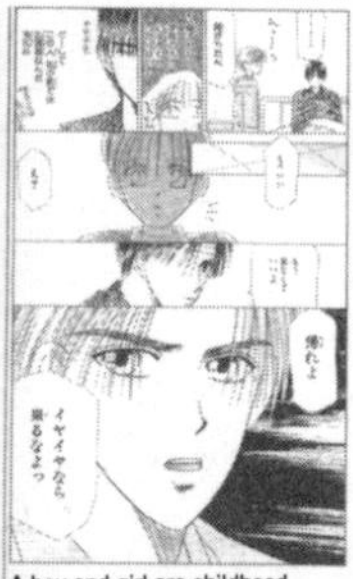

A boy and girl are childhood friends. But that doesn't necessarily mean they'll stay friends for life. While growing up, their personalities began to change and before they knew it, the two couldn't stand even being next to each other. An insightful work on the theme of "childhood friendship", the boy and girl lose their bearings and true love blossoms.

Oohara Chisato

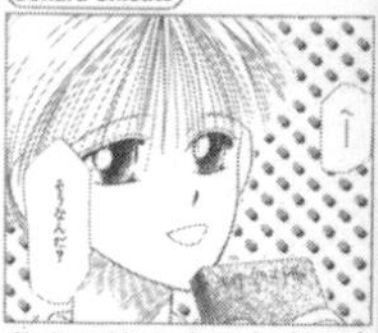

She's a girl who loves books and will risk her life for the sake of reading. She hates gaudy things and so she has a hard time relating to the Takashi of today.

Isozaki Takashi

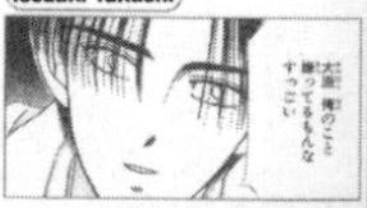

Chisato's materialistic childhood friend.

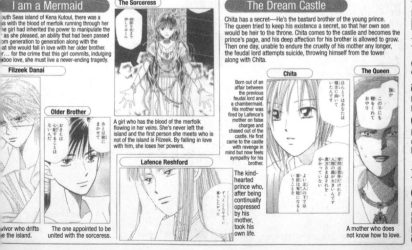

ɹed) ·

been established that Tsubasa Shibahime, who's said that she has no special l whatsoever, is actually a superb chef, but...if I'm not mistaken, there are other racters who can cook. (Having already shown their skills, Asaba and Tonami are eptions.)

after Arima-kun's girlfriend starts prodding into his life, he conspicuously improves his s…at least enough to make Miyazawa-san easy to handle.

:e her childhood, Maho-san was educated on all the basics of cooking from her mother.

sently, Tsubaki-san can harvest and eat edible plants, and catch fish to sell and eat but she ld very well grow capable of even strangling her own fowl and beasts to sell and eat. She's ınter in chef's clothing!

-san has no interest in gastronomy. So Rika-chan makes Aya-san eat in accordance with d nutrition.

at kind of clothes does Tsubasa Shibahime's father design?

ple and stylish Lolita taste. With a romantic city air. He also does boys' and adult fashions.

here any chance that Yukino Miyazawa's father's favorite t-shirt (Daughter Love) is nemade?

n't know so well myself but I'm sure they're not sold in stores.

hapter 24, the sight of Soichiro Arima wearing a necklace was very unexpected. Are na's accessories some kind of personal hobby? Or, was it that he was influenced by eaki Asaba or Yukino Miyazawa?

t would probably be Asaba-san's gift of love. But Arima himself is indifferent to Asaba's ntions.

I am a Mermaid

outh Seas island of Kena Kutoul, there was a s with the blood of merfolk running through her ne girl had inherited the power to manipulate the as she pleased, an ability that had been passed om generation to generation along with the at she would fall in love with her older brother. r… for the crime that this girl commits, indulging aboo love, she must live a never-ending tragedy.

Filzeek Danai

vivor who drifts e the island.

Older Brother

あとは僕に まかせて
おまえは 心配することは ないんだ

The one appointed to be united with the sorceress.

The Sorceress

A girl who has the blood of the merfolk flowing in her veins. She's never left the island and the first person she meets who is not of the island is Filzeek. By falling in love with him, she loses her powers.

Lafence Reshford

ずっとこんなふうに 暮らしたかった

The kind-hearted prince who, after being continually oppressed by his mother, took his own life.

The Dream Castle

Chita has a secret—He's the bastard brother of the young prince. The queen tried to keep his existence a secret, so that her own son would be heir to the throne. Chita comes to the castle and becomes the prince's page, and his deep affection for his brother is allowed to grow. Then one day, unable to endure the cruelty of his mother any longer, the feudal lord attempts suicide, throwing himself from the tower along with Chita.

Chita

Born out of an affair between the previous feudal lord and a chambermaid. His mother was fired by Lafence's mother on false charges and chased out of the castle. He first came to the castle with revenge in mind but now feels sympathy for his brother.

ほんとうはあなたは 領主に向いて いたんです
学問は苦手だけれど 人間の器が大きいんです 奥方さまはそれを 分かっていない
よい主人の下では 家臣は有能になると いうことを

The Queen

誰か この子にも 罰をくれて おやり

A mother who does not know how to love.

I thought to myself, "Arima-kun sure has a simple attire." and for some reason or other just nailed him with them. Year by year, I've come to enjoy men wearing accessories...Ev though I don't always have girls wear them, you know?

All the characters of "Kare Kano" are very fashionable; there must have been magazines and brands that were referenced for the clothing, no?

They're not that fashionable...(weep weep). For my own characters, no matter what I ma them wear, it never fits them well, you know? Only Takashi-san was exceptionally flashy and fun. Recently, I've been able to catch hold of a little bit of a knack for such things...I' trying hard.

The truth is I enjoy drawing them in things like traditional clothing...

Arima is based on a dumbfounded Kanagawa dog but (laugh), why did that becom such a surprising development?

Believe it or not, on the radio, they said that there's such thing as a Nagoya dog so I thought, "If there's a Nagoya dog then there's no reason why there couldn't be a Kanaga dog?"

Pero-pero has a puppy, but who is the other parent?

That must be the same beautiful Kanagawa dog we were just talking about, eh?

Shocking the readers the same way the Kanagawa dog did, the establishment that "Martin used to be in a Visual Kei band!" was also planned from the start, wasn't i

The reason was since the first time I drew him, I quite spontaneously thought, "Hmm...le make him visual kei." There was no doubt about it whatsoever.

The Dream Castle - Magic-User Series

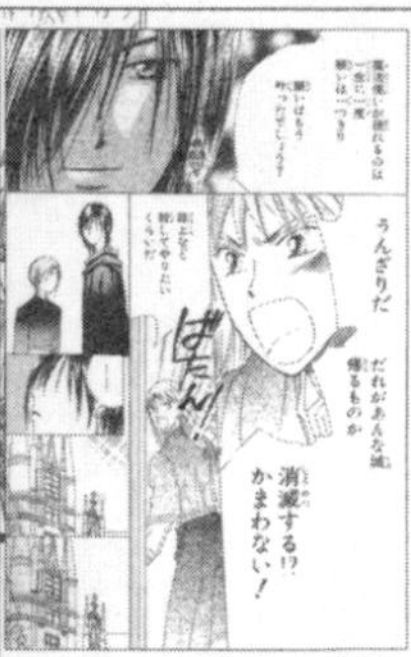
うんざりだ
だれがあんな城に帰るものか
ばん
消滅する!?
かまわない!

The Dream Castle

A three-part fantasy story in which a magic user that can grant any wish appears. Each work has its own take on the world and can be enjoyed on its own. The magic-user is fascinating in his ability to explain the unexplainable and solve all mysteries.

The Magic-User

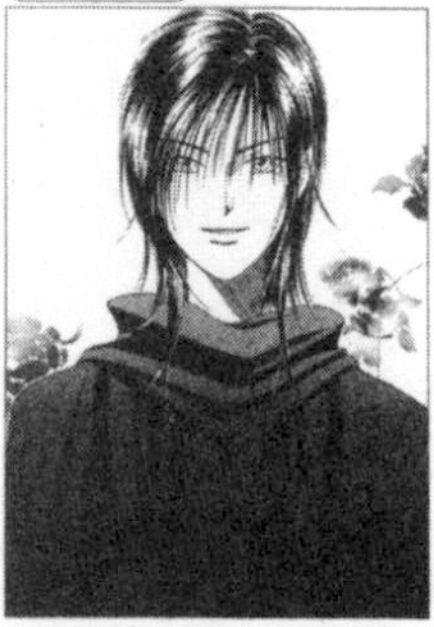

"I will grant you only one wish. Be it of sinister design, or an act of mercy; a blessing or a curse; do as you please..." He will only tell this to a person he chooses himself and is a mysterious entity who will lend his power free of compensation. Throughout the stories, it is never revealed what he is thinking. He is truly a neutral figure and does not judge the worth of a life as measured by the values of good and evil.

In the Forest

A story about a girl who has lived in the forest sin she was a child. Communicating with the animals and accepting nature's blessings, it is a quiet and comfortable life. However, one day her tranquility abruptly brought to an end. She is chosen to be th King's concubine. Now she must struggle with he new Court life and her feelings toward the King...

Sana Fal Khan

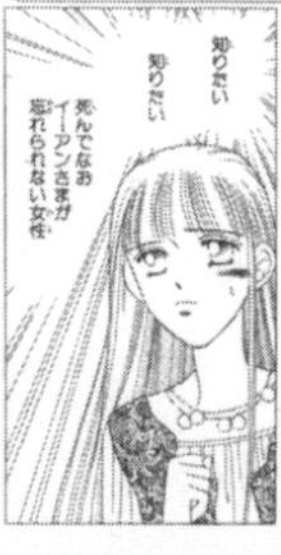
知りたい
知りたい
死んでなお
イーアンさまが
忘れられない女性

A girl who lived in the fore and made it her job to tak care of injured animals. W the passing away of the Q and other aristocratic rela the King makes her his concubine. She suffers fro jealousy of the Queen.

King Ian

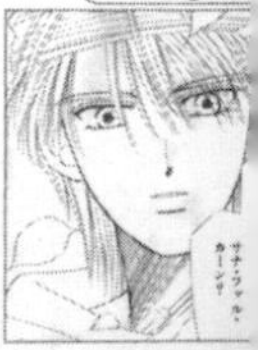

A grieving King who has lost his beloved wife.

ctually, the members of Yin and Yang have notable age differences but please nlighten us as to the conditions that led to them creating the band.

artin was emperor of the Visual Kei world.

ker was a jazz piano wiz.

e two felt dissatisfied and wanted to live a more interesting and amusing life and with ose feelings, came across Ushio and Atsuya while on the search for companions and hit it f quite well with them.

ith their heavy drinking and love for fighting, compatibility was a sure thing.

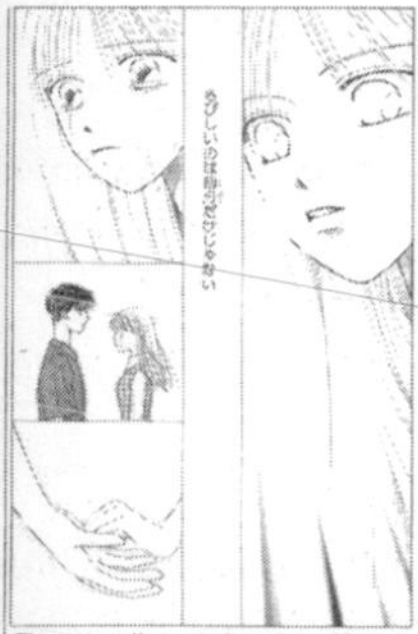

Three omnibus stories about bitter love.

There's a story about a girl who always only sees people for their complexions until she liberates her own heart; one about a theatre girl who suffers from jealousy as she falls in love with an exceptionally talented actor. Each story deals just a smidgen with the concept of heartache.

Over The Rainbow

Kijishima

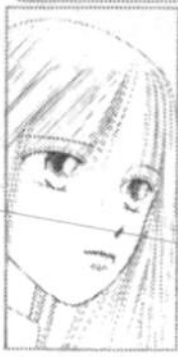

Conforms to everyone's values.

Ryuuj Sakashta

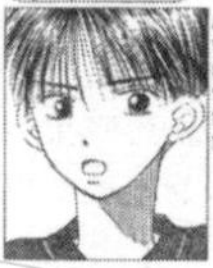

A boy who says what he thinks frankly.

Beautiful Dream

Tsukiho

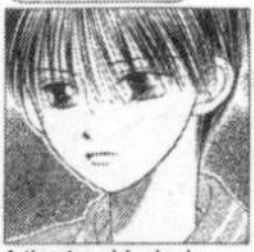

A theatre girl who is jealous of the skill of the one she loves.

Ikegami Natsuki

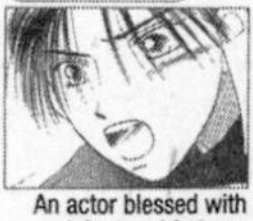

An actor blessed with talent and fortune.

The End Of The World

Kaya

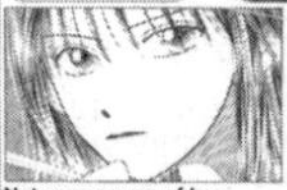

Not even aware of her own heart, she's a lonely princess.

Ryou

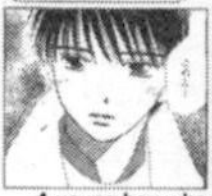

A young boy who notices Kaya's loneliness.

Shitou Youko

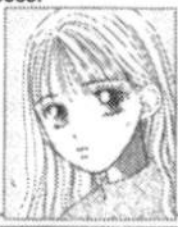

With an eye for seeing the truth, she's an adult woman.

Let's Forget

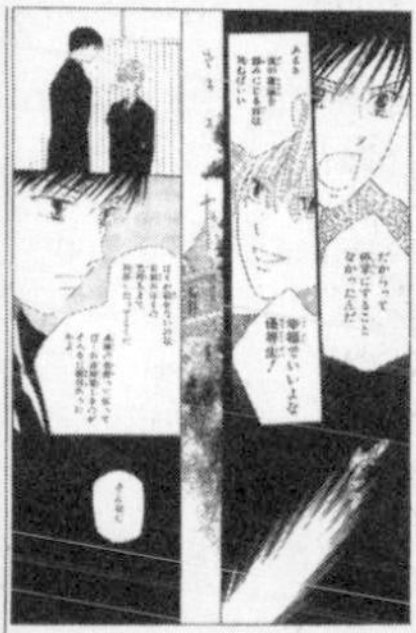

Due to an illness, Harua's body stopped growing. Since childhood he's had his eye on Tomoya, who tends to close off his heart from his surroundings. Tomoya, who harbors a secret love for his friend, feels constant heartache... This is a work that deals with the difficulty in sympathizing with people.

Minami Tomoya

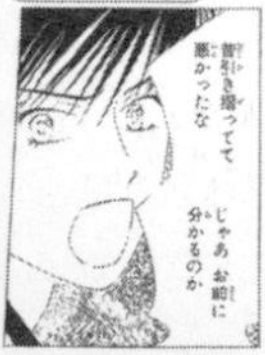

A boy whose love for Harua causes him longing agony.

Narukami Harua

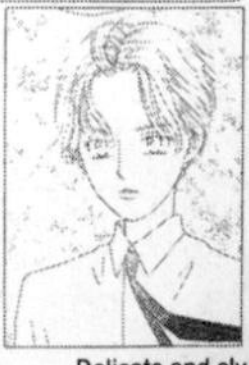

Delicate and sly ageless boy.

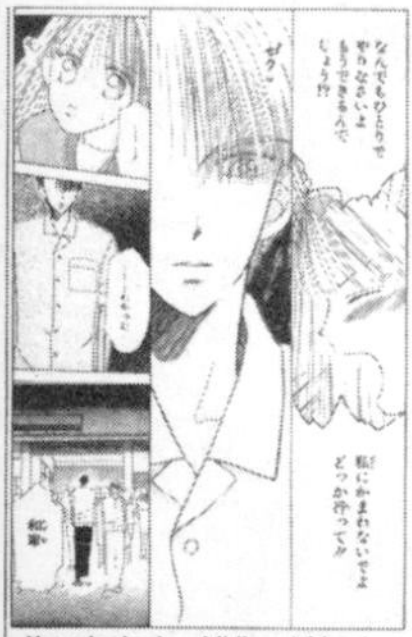

Kamoko had a childhood friend with the kindness of an angel. However, when they became high schoolers, he became a delinquent who made bullying his life. In a chance encounter with their childhood days, they realize their feelings haven't become love. Will the two change?

Sakuraya Kamoko

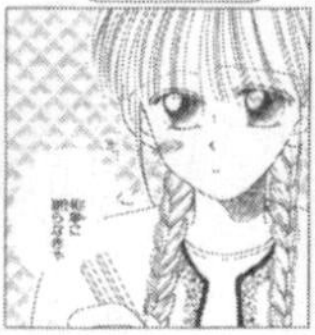

A little clumsy, she increasingly depends on Kazune. However, while she's frightened by Kazune's bullying ways, she has vowed not to give up on him.

Moriwaka

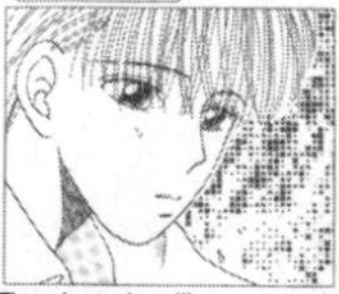

The prince who will protect Kamoko?!

Wakui Kazune

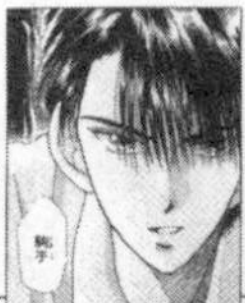

The violent delinquent attached to Kamoko.

After Kazuma joined, the other members quickly adopted the role of older brother, putting aside some of their less-than-role-model-worthy past.

You've written that Yin and Yang's routine was based on your surroundings; can you tell us some specific things that gave you flair and (unconsciously) supplied joke material for your stories or became models for your characters?

My mother and little brother are number one in this respect. Because just like the stereotype of women in a hair salon, when she hears something interesting she gossips away.

Friends, my manager, and my assistants were also inspirations.

Because I like watching people, even when I'm strolling down the road, there are plenty of interesting things for me.

In the act "Steel Snow," there were countless scenes that had stage productions accompanied by BGM. Have you considered adding additional episodes with music like this one? If there was such a thing, would you tell us a few of them?

There's one more song I'd like to use. It'll be out soon.

Any last messages for the fans?

I'm forever indebted to you all. With only kindness in my heart, there are days and days in which I will happily go on trying to draw. The climax of "Kare Kano" is coming up and I plan to work my fingers to the bone and let loose all the fun I've kept pent up.

'Til we meet again soon!

The Tiger & The Chameleon - A Promise For One Week

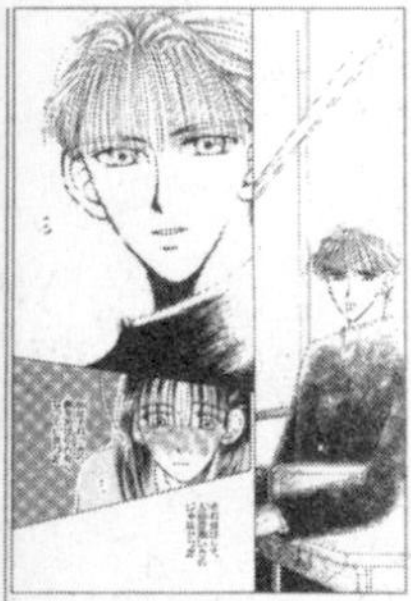

A romance story about a girl who, while in middle school, was told by someone she liked that she was "ugly." Now she can never show her face in public. She's a girl who has a deep complex over her physical appearance but through an interaction with a boy, regains confidence in herself.

Sakajou Toshiro

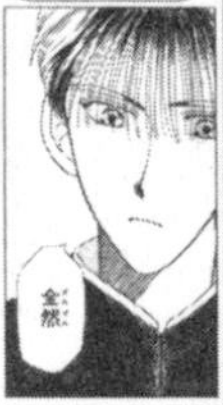
全然

Has a bad rep, but is actually a nice guy.

Koharu Mizumoto

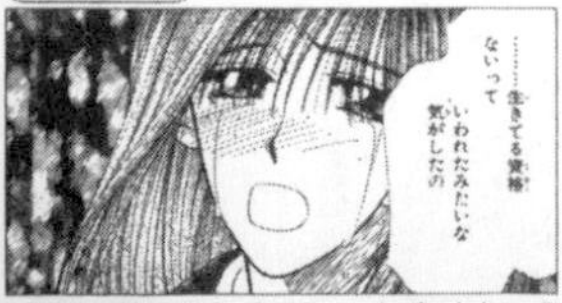
……生きてる資格
ないって
いわれたみたいな
気がしたの

Hasn't been able to lift her face to people after being called "ugly" years ago.

Tomorrow Let's Meet in the Forest Again, Shall We?

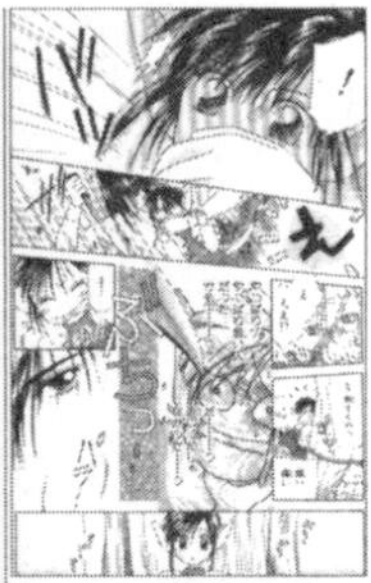

Four thousand light years from Earth is the planet of Kanpaset. There, like something out of a fairy-tale, lives a race of rabbit people who loathes aliens. Should any outsider penetrate this closely-knit society, he must be rejected, or else... A SF/fantasy story with a complex theme.

Idi Fan

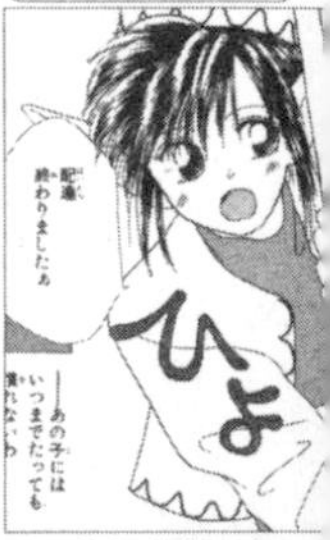
配達 終わりましたぁ
ひょ
—あの子には いつまでたっても 慣れないわ

A boy who has had to endure torment for his mixed breeding.

Ryuuj Sakashta

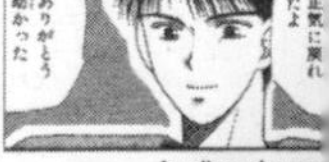
正気に戻れたよ
ありがとう 助かった

An alien who ma[...] emergency lar[...]

SUKI™
A like story...
by CLAMP
TOKYOPOP®
T TEEN AGE 13+
99 CLAMP. ©2004 TOKYOPOP Inc. All Rights Reserved.
www.TOKYOPOP.com

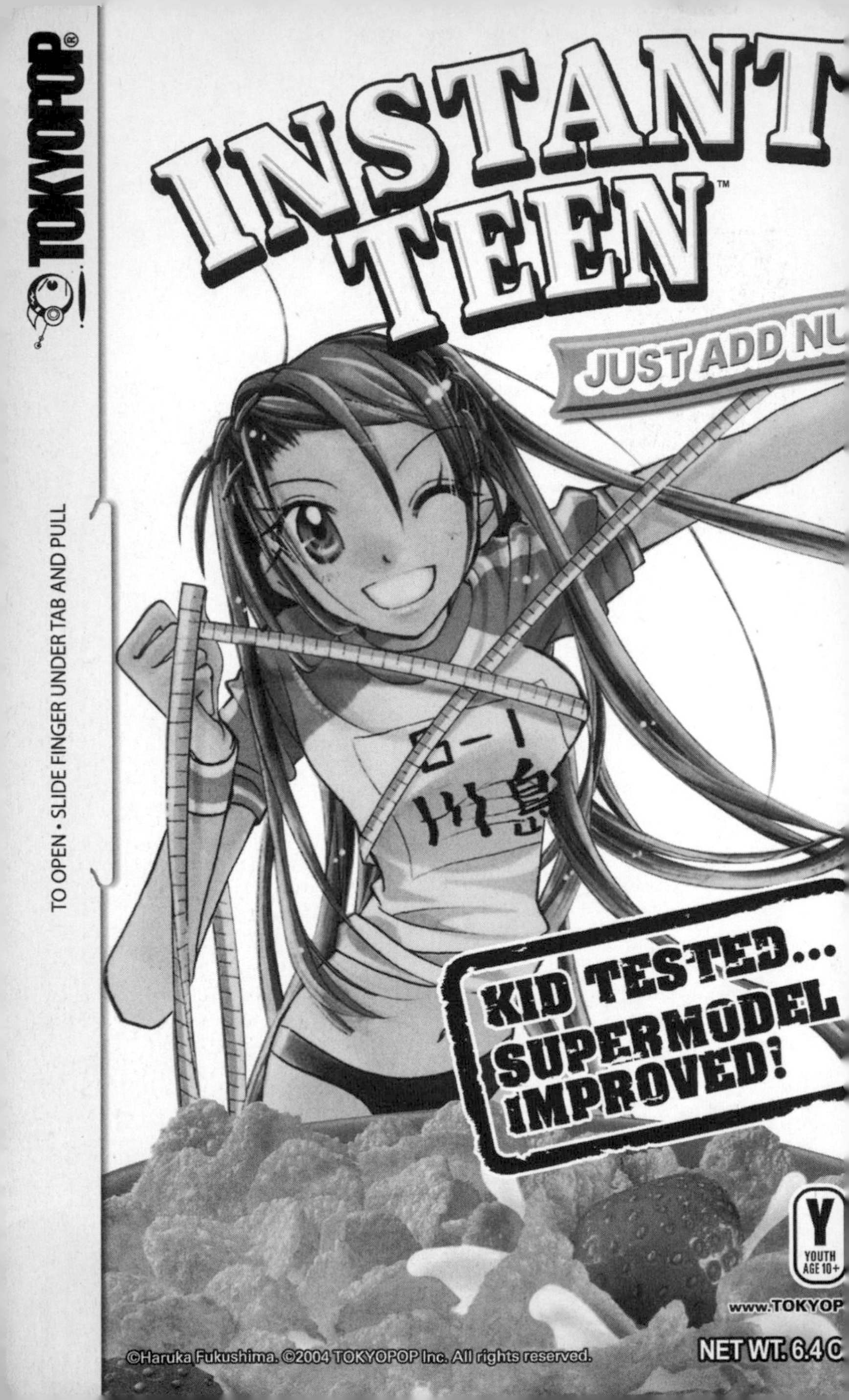
TOKYOPOP®
INSTANT TEEN™
JUST ADD NU
TO OPEN • SLIDE FINGER UNDER TAB AND PULL
KID TESTED... SUPERMODEL IMPROVED!
Y
YOUTH AGE 10+
www.TOKYOP
NET WT. 6.4 O
©Haruka Fukushima. ©2004 TOKYOPOP Inc. All rights reserved.

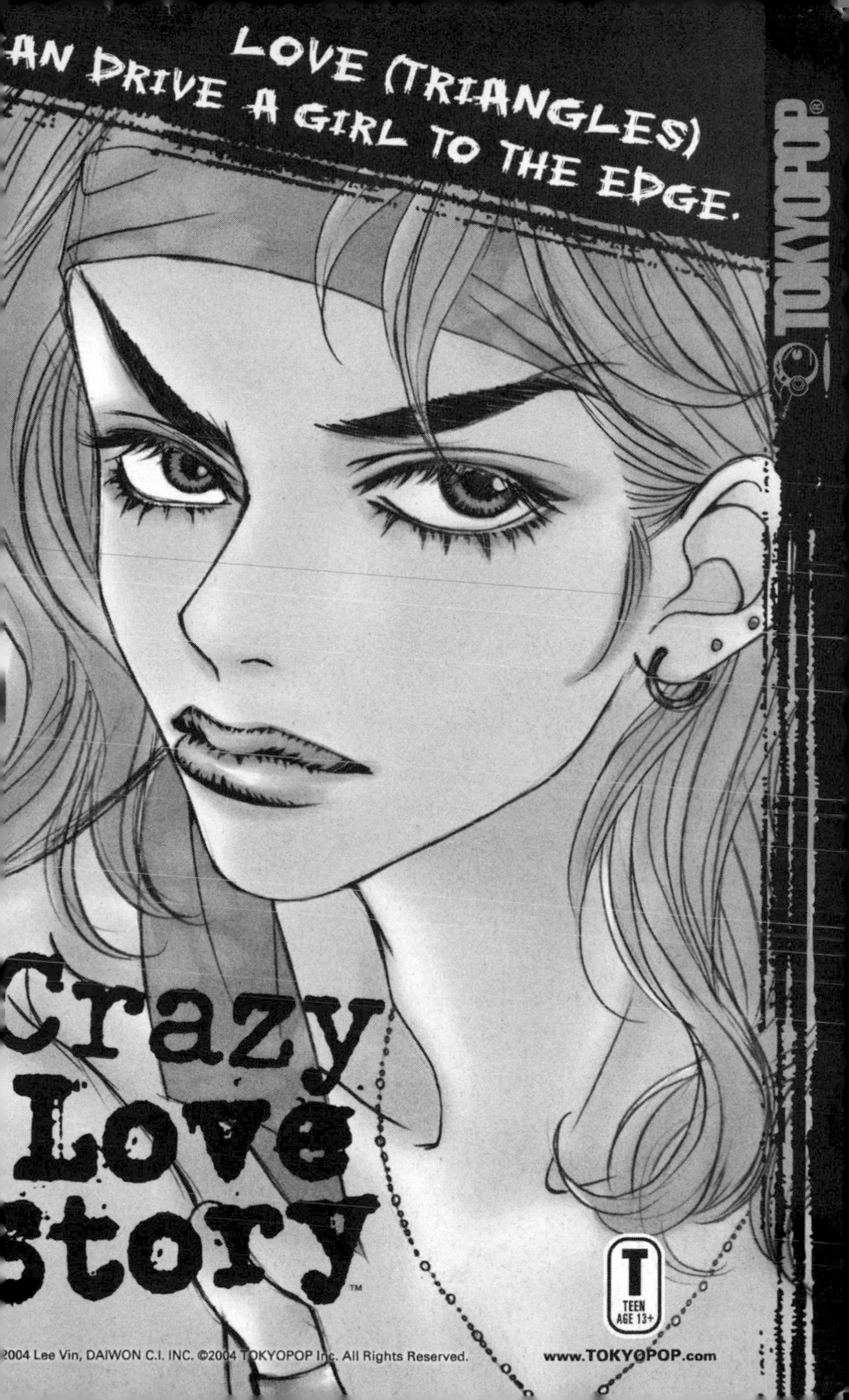
LOVE (TRIANGLES)
AN DRIVE A GIRL TO THE EDGE.
TOKYOPOP®
Crazy Love Story™
T TEEN AGE 13+
2004 Lee Vin, DAIWON C.I. INC. ©2004 TOKYOPOP Inc. All Rights Reserved.
www.TOKYOPOP.com

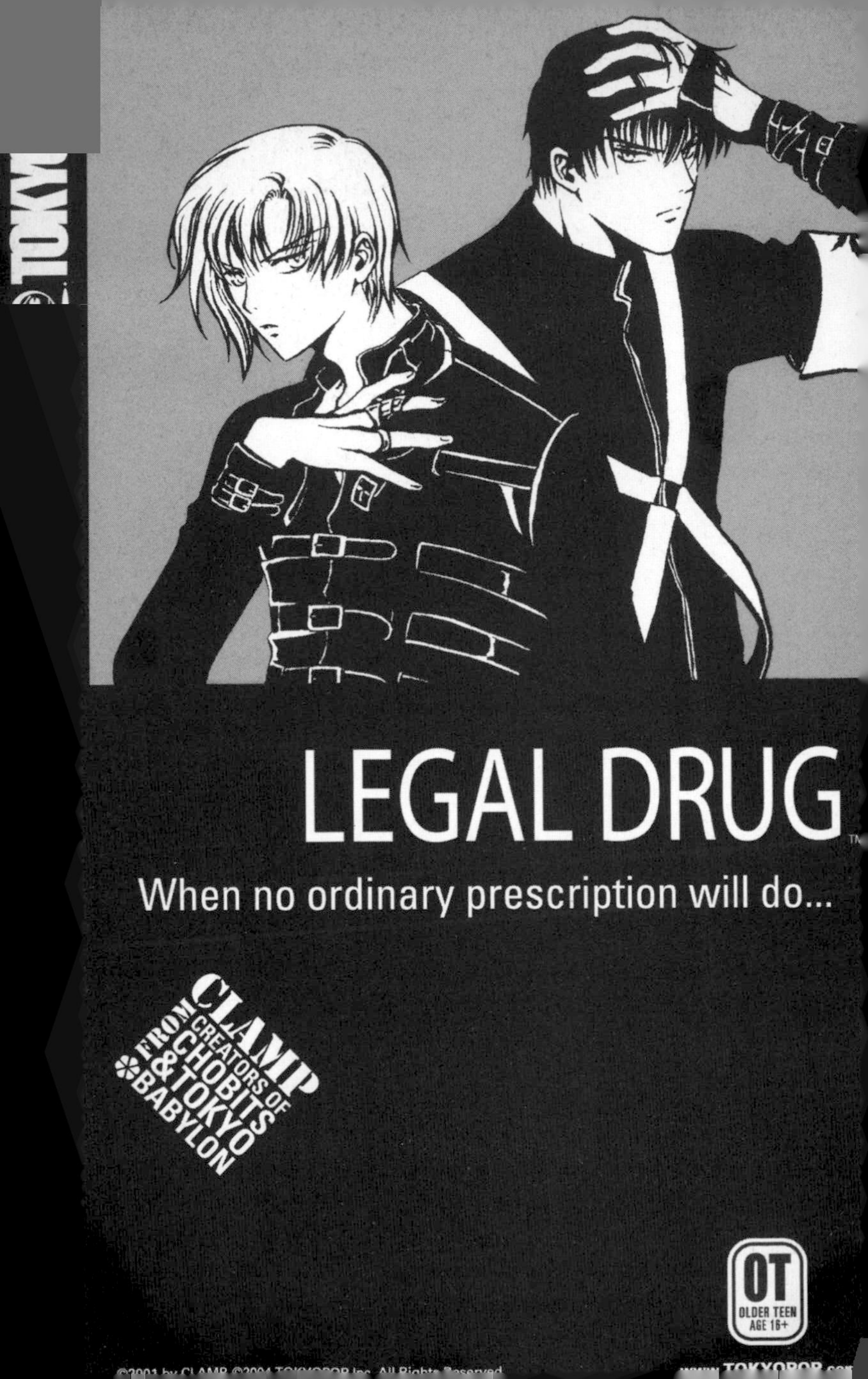

LEGAL DRUG™
When no ordinary prescription will do...
FROM CLAMP CREATORS OF CHOBITS & TOKYO BABYLON
OT
OLDER TEEN AGE 16+

You want it? We got it!
A full range of TOKYOPOP
products are available **now** at:
www.TOKYOPOP.com/shop

07.15.04T

ALSO AVAILABLE FROM  TOKYOPOP®

MANGA

.HACK//LEGEND OF THE TWILIGHT
@LARGE
ABENOBASHI: MAGICAL SHOPPING ARCADE
A.I. LOVE YOU
AI YORI AOSHI
ANGELIC LAYER
ARM OF KANNON
BABY BIRTH
BATTLE ROYALE
BATTLE VIXENS
BOYS BE...
BRAIN POWERED
BRIGADOON
B'TX
CANDIDATE FOR GODDESS, THE
CARDCAPTOR SAKURA
CARDCAPTOR SAKURA - MASTER OF THE CLOW
CHOBITS
CHRONICLES OF THE CURSED SWORD
CLAMP SCHOOL DETECTIVES
CLOVER
COMIC PARTY
CONFIDENTIAL CONFESSIONS
CORRECTOR YUI
COWBOY BEBOP
COWBOY BEBOP: SHOOTING STAR
CRAZY LOVE STORY
CRESCENT MOON
CROSS
CULDCEPT
CYBORG 009
D•N•ANGEL
DEMON DIARY
DEMON ORORON, THE
DEUS VITAE
DIABOLO
DIGIMON
DIGIMON TAMERS
DIGIMON ZERO TWO
DOLL
DRAGON HUNTER
DRAGON KNIGHTS
DRAGON VOICE
DREAM SAGA
DUKLYON: CLAMP SCHOOL DEFENDERS
EERIE QUEERIE!
ERICA SAKURAZAWA: COLLECTED WORKS
ET CETERA
ETERNITY
EVIL'S RETURN
FAERIES' LANDING
FAKE
FLCL
FLOWER OF THE DEEP SLEEP, THE
FORBIDDEN DANCE
FRUITS BASKET

G GUNDAM
GATEKEEPERS
GETBACKERS
GIRL GOT GAME
GRAVITATION
GTO
GUNDAM SEED ASTRAY
GUNDAM WING
GUNDAM WING: BATTLEFIELD OF PACIFISTS
GUNDAM WING: ENDLESS WALTZ
GUNDAM WING: THE LAST OUTPOST (G-UNIT)
HANDS OFF!
HAPPY MANIA
HARLEM BEAT
HYPER RUNE
I.N.V.U.
IMMORTAL RAIN
INITIAL D
INSTANT TEEN: JUST ADD NUTS
ISLAND
JING: KING OF BANDITS
JING: KING OF BANDITS - TWILIGHT TALES
JULINE
KARE KANO
KILL ME, KISS ME
KINDAICHI CASE FILES, THE
KING OF HELL
KODOCHA: SANA'S STAGE
LAMENT OF THE LAMB
LEGAL DRUG
LEGEND OF CHUN HYANG, THE
LES BIJOUX
LOVE HINA
LOVE OR MONEY
LUPIN III
LUPIN III: WORLD'S MOST WANTED
MAGIC KNIGHT RAYEARTH I
MAGIC KNIGHT RAYEARTH II
MAHOROMATIC: AUTOMATIC MAIDEN
MAN OF MANY FACES
MARMALADE BOY
MARS
MARS: HORSE WITH NO NAME
MINK
MIRACLE GIRLS
MIYUKI-CHAN IN WONDERLAND
MODEL
MOURYOU KIDEN: LEGEND OF THE NYMPHS
NECK AND NECK
ONE
ONE I LOVE, THE
PARADISE KISS
PARASYTE
PASSION FRUIT
PEACH GIRL
PEACH GIRL: CHANGE OF HEART
PET SHOP OF HORRORS
PITA-TEN

07.15.04T

STOP!

This is the back of the book.
ou wouldn't want to spoil a great ending!

s book is printed "manga-style," in the authentic Japanese right-to-left
nat. Since none of the artwork has been flipped or altered, readers
to experience the story just as the creator intended. You've been
ing for it, so TOKYOPOP® delivered: authentic, hot-off-the-press,
far more fun!

DIRECTIONS

1
2
3
4
5
6
7
9
0

If this is your first time reading manga-style, here's a quick guide to help you understand how it works.

It's easy... just start in the top right panel and follow the numbers. Have fun, and look for more 100% authentic manga from TOKYOPOP®!